IT'S ABOUT THE PEOPLE!

!

IT'S ABOUT THE PEOPLE!

UNLOCKING THE SOCIAL ART OF ARCHITECTURE

WRITTEN AND EDITED BY

Benjamin Clavan

Architect; Coordinator, The Berkeley Prize

FOREWORD BY RAYMOND LIFCHEZ

Architect and Professor; Founder, The Berkeley Prize

ORO EDITIONS

ORO Editions
Publishers of Architecture, Art, and Design
Gordon Goff: Publisher

www.oroeditions.com
info@oroeditions.com

Published by ORO Editions

Editor: Benjamin Clavan
Project Manager: Jake Anderson
Copy Editor: Julia Van den Hout

Book Design: Pablo Mandel, Micaela Carraro / CircularStudio
Typeset in TT Norms, DIN, and Academy Sans Stencil

10 9 8 7 6 5 4 3 2 1 First Edition

ISBN: 978-1-961856-67-7

Prepress and Print work by ORO Editions Inc.
Printed in China

ORO Editions makes a continuous effort to minimize the overall carbon footprint of its publications. As part of this goal, ORO, in association with Global ReLeaf, arranges to plant trees to replace those used in the manufacturing of the paper produced for its books. Global ReLeaf is an international campaign run by American Forests, one of the world's oldest nonprofit conservation organizations. Global ReLeaf is American Forests' education and action program that helps individuals, organizations, agencies, and corporations improve the local and global environment by planting and caring for trees.

COVER ILLUSTRATION

Peaceful crowds gather each afternoon at 2:00 P.M. from March 1-19 to celebrate and participate in Valencia, Spain's Mascletàs de las Fallas, a series of rhythmic pyrotechnic explosions and fireworks celebrating the yearly, centuries-old, social and religious Fallas festival that formally takes place from March 15–19. The pyrotechnics themselves last only between 5 and 7 minutes, but draws crowds in the thousands, some of whom stake out the best vantage point several hours ahead of the event.

This scene is a full block away from the city's historic center, the Plaza del Ayuntamiento, the base of activities for Fallas and the heart of the city and metropolitan area. Celebrations for Fallas, however, are spread throughout the community and are a prime example of the built environment helping to demonstrate the power and benefits of the social art of architecture on a massive civic scale. (Photo: Benjamin Clavan, 2022)

The International Berkeley Undergraduate Prize For Architectural Design Excellence

25 Years

3785 Students

88 Countries

188 Awards

225 Individual Winners

Remarkable Mentors

Remarkable Students

Remarkable Ideas

U.C. Berkeley

Throughout this book there are multiple references to University of California Berkeley's College of Environmental Design (CED) and its support for and links to the international Berkeley Undergraduate Prize for Architectural Design Excellence.

Although the Department of Architecture within the CED has publicly and whole-heartedly endorsed the Prize since almost its start, the University and the CED have played no role whatsoever in the funding, administration, and/or editorial content of the prize.

The Berkeley Prize has been a personal and philanthropic effort funded and administered by Professor Raymond Lifchez with academic support from colleagues around the world, including many from U.C. Berkeley.

DEDICATION

To William Wurster and Catherine Bauer

Leaders in the founding of the University of California, Berkeley College of Environmental Design, without whose arguments for the power and necessity of integrating the teachings and methodologies of the social science disciplines into the study of architecture...

The Berkeley Prize might never even have been imagined.

What Follows

4 THE STUDENTS

Foreword

The Berkeley Prize: Personal Reflections by Raymond Lifchez

Founder, Chair, and Benefactor

A quarter century has passed since my late wife Judith Stronach and I launched the Berkeley Prize—formally, the international Berkeley Undergraduate Prize for Architectural Design Excellence. The prize started with a competition that was held one weekend at University of California Berkeley's College of Environmental Design in collaboration with Oakland's California College of the Arts. But in a personal sense, the roots of the Berkeley Prize were planted in the 1930s in Columbia, South Carolina, and were nurtured by significant encounters with others across a long career. This career combined teaching with practice, a trajectory that gave meaning to my life and to the works I produced. A fuller history of the Berkeley Prize is contained in the following pages; my intention here, however, is to describe a journey in which the prize is a significant part—not so much a culmination as a vehicle to keep certain values alive.

The Berkeley Prize – Personal Roots

As a young child, I was taken on walks by an African American member of our household, whom—typical of the time—I knew only as Lulu. She was a woman I loved dearly. Lulu was the first to help me experience another culture, often impoverished and oppressed but also vibrant, distinct yet no less valuable. This early valuation of "others" became formative, and it began a trajectory in which many mentors expanded opportunities and ideas.

After graduating from the University of Florida's Bachelor of Architecture program, I was offered a scholarship to the School of Architecture at Columbia University where I received a Master of Science in Architecture (1957). During this period of intense fertility and support, I took a serious interest in architectural history, and the school encouragingly awarded me the Margaret Thompson Biddle scholarship (1956) for study and travel in Europe, part of which was as a student at the Ecoles d'Art Américaines de Fontainebleau in France. Upon graduation from Columbia, I received a William Kinne Fellows Traveling Prize.

With architectural historian Rudolf Wittkower's encouragement, I spent two years abroad, first at the American School of Classical Studies in Athens, Greece, and then as a draftsman for the Byzantine Institute in Istanbul, Turkey. There I assisted Paul Underwood with his work documenting the fourteenth-century Church of Our Savior in Chora. This opportunity introduced me to Istanbul's dervish halls and stimulated my interest in preserving subcultures and traditions at risk of extinction. All of this led me to return to complete a Master of Arts in Art History at Columbia and focusing on becoming an historian rather than an architect.

Two giants in the field of Urban Studies changed my mind. First, Professor Percival Goodman, best known as co-author of the landmark *Communitas: Means of Livelihood and Ways of Life,* a study which championed green spaces in urban design, and called for creating human-scale living communities where humans dwell and work; second, architectural and art historian Sybil Moholy-Nagy, under whom I began to teach architectural history at Pratt Institute (1961). Moholy-Nagy's *Matrix of Man*: *An Illustrated History of Urban Environment* was one of the first books in the new field of urban ecology, and considered history a crucial part of understanding the importance of what is *there* by tracing the social significance of a building.

I also spent three years working for the office of twentieth-century American icon architect, Eero Saarinen, but eventually I returned to Columbia where I taught design and history in the School of Architecture. The student takeover at Columbia, in May 1968, altered my future dramatically. I was not particularly politically adept. I found myself on the opposite side of some former teachers and colleagues, and my efforts to heal these breaches failed.

The outcome? In 1970, I fled to the University of California Berkeley to pursue a Master of City Planning. What I found at the College of Environmental Design (CED) was what I had been gravitating toward all along: a core faculty applying the "human arts and sciences" to their teaching and research. It was exactly what I thought architecture should be about. The college would be my new home.

The CED was established 1959 by a remarkable couple, Catherine Bauer and William Wurster. Their idea was to integrate pedagogy by bringing the fields of architecture, design, landscape architecture, and city and regional planning together under one roof. What Bauer and Wurster envisioned was a college under the aegis of a pre-eminent public university. The CED would become a model for integrating fields and disciplines that traditionally tended to silo. The motive was public service. Individually and collectively, the various fields of environmental design would gain human-centeredness while keeping the rigor inherent in each of the separated yet related fields that support their work.

The Berkeley Prize derives directly from both the ethos of the CED and the haven it provided me to teach, research, and push my understanding of architecture and city planning in new direction—into what I called the "social arts." I benefited greatly from outside collaborators such as Peter Pragnell, Aldo van Eyck, and Irving Zola; and CED colleagues Christopher Alexander, Clare Cooper-Marcus, Russell Ellis, Roslyn Lindheim, Lars Lerup, and Richard Bender.

The Berkeley Prize – Origins and Philosophy

As the prize's founders and endowers, Judith Stronach and I shared an interest in misperceived and often excluded populations or oppressed within broader society: disabled people, those lacking shelter, people of color, the LGBTQ+ community, and anyone whose beliefs, backgrounds, age, or states of health place them outside the mainstream. Traditionally, these groups have been labelled as "other."

My professional work with these supposed "other" people began when I was an architect in New York, charged with improving the open spaces of a public hospital. I met and befriended a cohort of differently abled people who were effectively marooned there. I found a similar population in Berkeley that received individual, direct public support which allowed them to live independently. The contrast was eye-opening—something I never forgot.

In the 1970s and 1980s, a new approach to designing for people with disabilities gained traction and eventually become known as *Universal Design*. While originally focused on physical disabilities, the underlying philosophy recognizes humanity's full diversity and pushes for people's rights of mobility and access, whether this is understood in physical, social, psychological, legal, or creative terms. It is a philosophy of liberation.

The Berkeley Prize supports the idea of that architecture and planning aim for this universality of built space. In many senses, we are all the "other." The aim of the prize is to situate architecture and planning within what might be called "the human arts and sciences." The professions of architecture and planning are social in their basis and purpose, existing to address humanity's relationships with the world we inhabit. From the outset, those engaged in these professions take up this responsibility implicitly.

Traditionally, the finest architecture has been seen as a delicate balance of functionality, technology, and aesthetics. Architecture in its current adolescence of fully digitized design often focuses primarily on aesthetics through geometric wizardry that, at the very least, skews the needed harmony among the three attributes. Planning, similarly supported now by "Big Data" analysis that build policies from statistics, reduces issues like urban density into targets and broad-brush legislation that omits or ignores urbanity. To counter these abstract distortions, the Berkeley Prize is rooted in observation and exploration of existing environments. This process relates, in turn, to two essential qualities that architects and planners should bring to their work: empathy and intentionality.

In his famous 1980 book, *The Way of Being*, the humanist psychologist Carl Rogers defined empathy as a way of being with other people, temporarily living in their lives without making judgements. More than just interacting with these others, empathy actively values them. Empathy seeks to understand how others give meaning to their world by inviting them to reveal it. Intentionality, on the other hand, encompasses two aspects of human experience. First, it brackets so that the parts come forward in relation to the whole—a way to simplify what would otherwise be overwhelmingly complex. But intentionality does not lose sight of the people who figure in the environment—it understands how actions reflect intentions.

Empathy and intentionality speak to the goal implicit in architecture and planning: to provide a suitable context for human activity—not perfect fits, but rather a *mise en scène*. I believe it was Peter Pragnell, one of the leading modernist proponents of the integration of social factors in design, who points out that Le Corbusier's sketches convey scenarios of human interaction. We see through them that a building or dwelling is really a setting for others to inhabit and mark with their particular imprint.

Drawing by hand—unlike what architects do in computer design—helps planners understand the form and character of what they see or imagine, including—as Le Corbusier's sketches show—how people will use them. The Dutch architect, Aldo van Eyck, an early member of the *Congrès Internationaux d'Architecture Moderne* (CIAM) and then a co-founder of its even more "radical" and influential offshoot, Team 10, notes how designers lose touch with reality if they ignore the people who will live in their buildings. In his short essay, *Place and Occasion*, Van Eyck writes, "a house is a tiny city, a city a huge house ... for each person and all people." He urges architects to "get closer to the shifting center of human reality" and provide that space. How to emulate and translate that quality to digital drawing is the task for a new generation of both teachers and students.

Ray Lifchez (center right) leading the precedent-setting, undergraduate Architecture 101 studio on "Designing for People with Disabilities" that he started at the U.C. Berkeley College of Environmental Design five decades ago.

(Photo provided by Raymond Lifchez, ca. 1984)

The intent of the Berkeley Prize's inaugural competition was first to combine research with observation of existing environments, then to propose solutions using both hand drawings and written descriptions. The focus topic considered everyday settings used by the elderly in nursing homes and the staff who cared for them. We quickly realized that undertaking an international *design* competition was much too ambitious. What we could better accomplish would be to ask students from around the world to go out into their communities to observe and question completed projects that reflect everyday ideas about human activity, and then, most importantly, to write about them.

The underlying methods came directly from my teaching Architecture 101, a hands-on studio required of all would-be architects at the CED. Using large models that were deliberately built to be taken apart and reassembled, students created appropriate settings for people in different situations. The studio also brought in real people as "clients" to work directly with the students. We invited disabled people, older people, even convicts—the *others*. The friendships that formed over many working sessions fuelled the students' empathy and helped them grasp the intentions of others toward the places and settings they designed and analysed together.

The Berkeley Prize — Meaning and Future

Over the years, Berkeley Prize requirements evolved to encourage collaboration, especially across fields. From the outset, the prize aimed to draw competitors from anywhere architecture and planning are studied and practiced. It has achieved this goal beyond what even I had hoped.

Ideally, such prizes will be open to all comers, that is to anyone for which the prize's goals and meanings resonate enough to enter, even if it means a candidate stepping out of his or her cultural comfort zone. That the Berkeley Prize has resonated with a truly global cohort gives a meaning beyond anything I envisioned for it initially. My own hope is that the cosmopolitan spirit of the Berkeley Prize will continue to expand.

After twenty-five years, the Berkeley Prize has achieved a degree of fame and importance, but its real value to me is that it established a precedent—a model, not an institution. I never intended that it would exist frozen in perpetuity but that it would inspire emulation and proliferation. I would expect others to create prizes of their own that more closely reflect their regions and cultures always keeping in mind the social art of architecture.

The Berkeley Prize targets young practitioner-scholars at a formative time in their lives. The topics and essays invite the free exercise of their powers of observation and synthesis. Winners' reflections on how the experience influenced their work and thinking amply shows the value the Berkeley Prize has to the participants and, ultimately, the profession. Those who entered found themselves taken seriously by the readers and sometimes singled-out by the final jury, and all came away with a larger sense of themselves as eminently qualified to build upon a long, vitally important, and worthy tradition. It was my conviction that I had a clear responsibility to foster this growth. I am honored by the privilege of having done so.

Raymond Lifchez—architect, professor, social activist, philanthropist, and friend—died from natural causes on the brink of his ninety-first birthday in the Fall of 2023. He had been actively involved in the prize and in following the progress of this book almost until the end. Part of his life's work lives on in these pages.

1

Toward A Social Art Of Architecture

The Why and How

Modern Architectural Theory

Investigating a Transformational Approach

Working to (Re-)Integrate the "New" Perspective

Into Architectural Education

Confronting the Academic Stagnation of the Last Quarter Century

At the core of the prize is the conviction that a better architecture only happens as a result of closer interaction, dialogue, and research with the people who live, work, and interact with the buildings that architects design.

The Why and How

People-centered Architecture. Inclusive Design. Human-centric/Human-centered Design. Universal Design. Design for All. Whatever you call it, good architecture—and a better architecture—starts with a deep understanding of the people who will use a building or a place. If you fail to capture the living patterns of the family for whom you are designing a residence, your house design will merely be and remain a barren shell, regardless of how elaborate its geometry. If you do not have an idea about how seniors actually lead their lives or want to lead their lives, your design for a nursing home will fail, however handsome the structure. If you do not have an idea about how a town, a city, or a region can integrate the lessons of environmental sustainability and public health into its urban design and building programs, your master plans will fail, however dramatic or visually astounding. Addressing these demands and responding to their imperatives is the framework of the social art of architecture.

There is now nearly seventy-five years of revealing studies investigating the frontiers of this enlightened approach to architecture. It is clear, however, that this energy has not resulted in any widespread, radically different physical environments. The actual *how* (not to mention the ever-present *why*) of applying the findings and lessons of the social sciences to the learning and teaching of architecture remains largely unanswered. There are signs, including the founding of the Berkeley Prize, that it is beginning to be addressed in a more systematic way. Whatever the results of these efforts, the overriding objective must be to discover ways to discharge the false dualism between social concerns and creative design, and between people-driven design and object-driven design that remains entrenched in architecture.

Part of the problem has been that, however committed to the goals of social justice, architects and architecture schools do not know what to do with the ever-expanding theoretical, experimental, and practical social and behavioral information bubbling up, or more succinctly lying fallow, around them. Accepting the tenets of what is now called "evidence-based design" is one thing; qualifying that evidence and applying it to architectural design is another.

At the same time, the idea that one can *teach* another person anything is a conceit. Education is, at its best, a goal: a structured pursuit to encourage and enable students to *learn*. At the same time, learning can mean many different things.

Helping students how to think critically for themselves is one level of success. At an even higher level, learning is a free-flowing awakening of the brain's neurons in ways yet unclear to us that allows the individual to make untold mental connections, both old and new, that result in a deep understanding of the world around them and a glimpse of the world that could be.

Advances in the professions, including architecture, rely on exactly this kind of learning. As the world's population explodes exponentially, the number of minds looking at one subject also increases at unfathomable rates. To this bubbling ferment of exploration, you must also add the super reality of exploding sources of information. In such a hotbed of potential learning, even small portions of creativity suddenly can become something really important—to us as individuals, to those around us as part of our community, and to the world at large which will thrive on just such knowledge or backslide without it.

Knowledge in architecture has always been highly suspect. Knowledge means that one thing is right and its opposite is wrong; one thing is good and its opposite is bad. Placing a stint in an artery and watching a damaged heart begin pumping blood once again is generally considered non-controversial proof that what was done was right and good. Setting aside issues of building technologies, most people do not believe that architecture ever has, can, or should behave or be evaluated in this scientific manner.

One major source of this conflict is the tripartite nature of architecture as famously identified by the Roman scholar Vitruvius, now commonly thought of as *commodity, firmness,* and *delight*. Depending on the times, depending on the practitioner, depending on the wider real-world context, the product of architecture bends one way or the other against the head winds of these seemingly often conflicting demands. The ultimate prize? An architecture which succeeds brilliantly when examined from the lofty heights of all three pillars of wisdom.

This ideal amalgam is seen so infrequently and is so difficult to duplicate that it becomes a seemingly unobtainable and excessive goal. The result, particularly now in a world of eight billion people clamoring for shelter and other structures for daily life, is a vast majority of indifferently conceived and haphazardly executed buildings. Whole populations are often poorly served not only in their housing, but in the commercial and public facilities on which they depend. This extends to civic planning as a whole. Very few structures, let alone urban designs, are based on values—on good and bad; right or wrong; or even, more acceptable or less acceptable.

And here, we must look back at a little history.

A depiction of Vitruvius presenting *De Architectura* to Augustus by Sebastian Le Clerc, 1684.

(Photo: Wikimedia Commons, public domain)

Modern Architectural Theory

Since its establishment in the last quarter of the seventeenth century, the École Nationale Supérieure des Beaux-Arts de Paris was regarded as the leading institution for the education of architects and artists in the Western world and parts beyond. From the nineteenth century forward, architectural schools throughout much of the world employed Beaux-Arts principles as the basis for the development of their individual curricula.

These methodologies included establishing a hermetic learning environment in which there was a strict hierarchy of teachers and students attempting to keep alive an aesthetic of romantic design based on classical precedents. All of it happens in the studio. Here, the public can be restricted or altogether prohibited. The product of architecture becomes solely a discussion between peers. Our built environment is no longer a community and/or social effort. The result? Architecture loses its connection to the everyday lives of the people it serves and becomes an esoteric academic discipline.

The proponents of modern architecture, as it developed at the close of the nineteenth century and well through the first half of the twentieth century, saw something much different; they saw need. Need for basic housing for vast portions of their populations as a result of mushrooming populations and migration patterns. Need for altogether new and hugely expanded architectural components of public services. Need for reorganization of the urban landscape to facilitate the enormous growth in cities. Need for individuals to experience and express pleasure in their built environment.

Thus started a vast experiment in re-making architecture. Architects began to harness science and technology to aid the building process. They stripped buildings bare of centuries of accumulated and "useless" ornament and debris. They began to talk in complex and often esoteric ways about form and function that only the fully educated could pretend to understand. In the process, architecture all but lost whatever artisan roots it still had. Although this transformation was part of a wider scheme of professionalism fostered by the academies during the nineteenth century, the addition of complex academic research and methodologies meant that architects were even further distanced from the population whom they had served for centuries as master builders.

In a positive view, this modernization was a well-intentioned mash-up of dozens of new intellectual currents swirling in the *fin-de-siècle* of one stage of human social development and at the beginning of another. People suffered less in the newer built world, at least viscerally. On the negative side, it was simply an excuse to exercise creativity in the name of a new style. A number of scholars go

Nineteenth century: What was. The cloistered academy. École nationale supérieure des Beaux-Arts, Paris, France by architect François Debret. Completed in 1829, it was home to generations of architecture students from France and abroad.

(Photo: Selbymay, 2012: sourced on Wikimedia Commons-Creative Commons Attribution-Share Alike 3.0 Unported license)

21st Century: The changing landscape. Inviting the people to participate. A•lava Summer Stage, Helsinki, Finland. Designed and constructed by students of the Aalto University Department of Architecture, Helsinki *Wood Program* in 2017, the A•lava pavilion provides a sheltered stage for the Annantalo Arts Centre in Helsinki. The project accommodates a variety of events from concerts and theater to exhibitions and banquets.

The studio Instructors for the program were Pekka Heikkinen, Philip Tidwell, and Willem van Bolderen. Philip Tidwell is the BP2003 First Place Essay Prize winner; a BP Committee Member, and now Assistant Professor at U.C. Berkeley's College of Environmental Design.

(Photo: Marc Goodwin)

further and posit that it was through this transformation that people further lost their heretofore synergetic connection to their habitats and their larger environments. Architecture became even more of a commodity provided by a complex, mainly fiduciary infrastructure.

Fast-forward to the social upheaval of the 1960s. A combination of a rising tide of prosperity, more thoughtful education leading to new levels of social investigation and awareness, profound breakthroughs in science and technology, and the overall expansion of the human population (more minds looking at more questions producing more answers), resulted in a process whereby every intellectual discipline was re-examined for its relevancy, productivity, and contribution to the human good. Many were found lacking. Re-organization, re-thinking, re-creating was the task of the day and of the time. Experiments in living were matched with experiments in building; architecture was pressed to search for its social roots.

This time around, things would be different. Architectural theorists scrambled to apply the lessons and findings of sociologists, psychologists, anthropologists, and even the religious (notably the Buddhists and their special awareness of the power of the *thoughtful mind*) to the production of building. Evidence-based design was the goal. We should learn not only from the lessons of the past, but from the burgeoning data fields being created by armies of social investigators going out into the world, asking questions, recording answers and, yes, stirring up the pot. *Architecture for people* seemed to be not only an actual possibility but became a mantra for a new generation of students and faculty.

Teaching and Investigating a New Theory

Much has changed in the study of architecture in the United States in the last seventy-five years. A series of curricula changes at the country's top schools of architecture are direct evidence of this change, starting with Harvard's Graduate School of Design (GSD) in Boston, Massachusetts. Founded in 1936, their new academic *umbrella* brought together for the first significant time students from architecture, planning, and landscape architecture into one school to provide a broad, unified approach to design for people.

In 1945, Catherine Bauer, who was later to play an integral role in the creation of Berkeley's College of Environmental Design, was the first woman appointed to the faculty at the GSD. In the 1930s, American scholars such as Bauer had begun to study and advocate public or social housing in the United States based on already successful European examples. Bauer eventually served and advised three presidents on housing and urban planning strategies and, among other achievements, she penned the U.S. Housing Act of 1937.

In the late 1930s, a collective of San Francisco planners, landscape architects, and architects formed one of the first social advocacy-in-design groups, Telesis. In 1939, Telesis mounted a pivotal exhibition at the San Francisco Museum of Art titled, "Space for Living," in which the idea of environmental design and environmental analysis was at the forefront. One architect—Vernon DeMars—became one of Telesis's leading proponents. He contributed extensively to the 1939 exhibit with his studies of "Living as is" and "Living as it should be." He would later become a pivotal member of the CED faculty.

In 1945, William Wurster, a noted San Francisco Bay Area architect, was appointed dean of the School of Architecture at Massachusetts Institute of Technology (MIT) in Cambridge, Massachusetts, across the river from Boston. He combined two departments—architecture and city and regional planning—into the combined School of Architecture and Planning at MIT. Similarly, at the University of Pennsylvania in Philadelphia, starting in 1950, the schools of architecture, city planning, landscape architecture, and the fine arts were gradually pulled together under one roof and under the guiding principle of the social basis of architecture. The result was the Graduate School of Fine Arts, which was inaugurated in 1958.

In 1950, Wurster left MIT to become dean of the College of Architecture at Berkeley. There, he was joined by the transformative figure of Catherine Bauer, whom he had married ten years earlier. She entered the planning department as the first woman to represent the department. As at Harvard's GSD, her presence at the CED—and Veron DeMars who Wurster persuaded to join the faculty—was indicative of the role social architecture was beginning to have nationwide.

Unlike the private higher education strongholds of Harvard and MIT, institutional change at the public University of California, Berkeley took more time. It was not until 1959 that the four separate schools and departments of architecture, planning, landscape architecture, and graphic design all became departments with their own chairpersons under the aegis of Wurster, who was named dean of the newly formed College of Environmental Design. The seemingly slow transformation in the 1950s also incorporated, however, a dramatic shift in priorities, linking design with research and placing both on an equal footing.

It was Wurster, in fact, who is credited with popularizing the phrase, "architecture is a social art." The derivation of the term, an idea reflected even in the ancient writings of Vitruvius, can be traced in modern times to the early 19th century. Victor Hugo explored social art of architecture themes in *Hunchback of Notre Dame* (1831), perhaps taking cues from earlier work by German philosopher Georg Wilhelm Friedrich Hegel. John Ruskin, working in the following decades and whose art and architecture criticism were to transform the way people looked at art, insisted that art and architecture are the direct expression of the social conditions in which they are produced. The International Congress of Modern Architecture (CIAM) founded in 1928 and the most influential advocate of a new architecture into the early 1950s, vigorously promoted the cause of "architecture as a social art."

To help solidify all this bubbling academic awakening, Wurster promoted the design and construction of a new building to house the new College. He helped select DeMars, Joseph Esherick and Donald Olsen to design the structure. Esherick is famous as a leader of the San Francisco Bay Area Architecture style, a modern rethinking of the traditional wood and timber Bay tradition, while Olsen was a major proponent of the International style. The building, which soon after was named Wurster Hall in honor of William and Catherine Bauer Wurster, was completed in 1964. Wurster had resigned as Dean of the College in 1963, but Bauer was appointed Associate Dean. She was never able to fully engage in the position because of her death in a hiking accident the next year. The building was finally renamed the *Bauer Wurster* Hall in 2020.

Despite its Brutalist and unwelcoming facade and interiors, its daunting and circulation-numbing ten-story tower, and an equally stoic and meandering three-story base, the building has a number of socially conscious elements, particularly in its program and layout. Not all the massing decisions were the architects' fault. It is reported that the University demanded a tall structure to physically signify the northern-most boundary of the immense Berkeley campus. A prime example of people-conscious architecture clashing with institutional prerogatives.

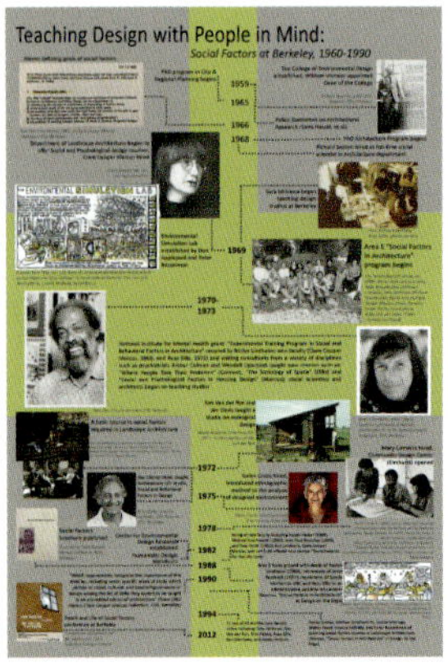

Poster prepared by U.C. Berkeley's Environmental Design Archives to accompany the exhibit, "Teaching Design with People in Mind: Social Factors at the College of Environmental Design,1960-1990," mounted at the school in the Spring of 2018. Raymond Lifchez was one of the three curators for the exhibition and his face accompanies the entry for 1972.

Russ Ellis, Faculty portraits, CED Records,

Marcus, 1969, and Russ Ellis, 1970) and visiting consultar such as psychiatrists Arthur Colman and Wendell Lipscon "Where People Take Their Problems" (Colman), "The S "Social and Psychological Factors in Housing Design" (architects began co-teaching studios

Sim Van der Ryn and Jim Davis taught a studio on ecological design

Wood structure, Inverness, CA, 1972. Photo courtesy of Sim van der Ryn

A basic course in social factors required in Landscape Architecture

Left: Students discuss plaza evaluations in downtown San Francisco, 1991. Photo courtesy of Clare Cooper Marcus. Below: Clare Cooper Marcus and students in discussion. Photo courtesy of Clare Cooper Marcus.

1972

Ray Lifchez hired, taught Architecture 101 studio, Social and Behavioral Factors in Design

Ray Lifchez, Faculty portraits, CED Records, EDA, Berkeley

1975

Galen Cr introduced eth method to th of designed en

Galen Cranz, pl from ced

1978

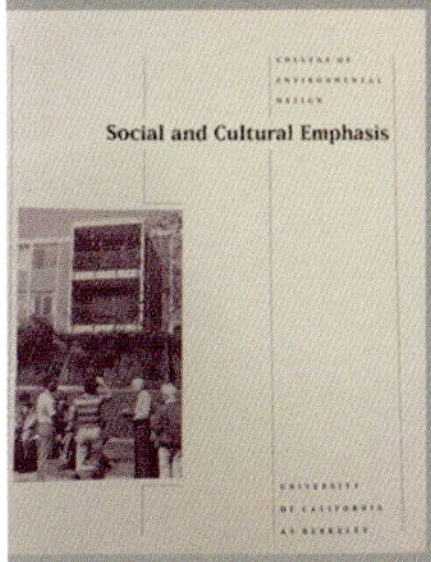

Social Factors brochure published

Courtesy of Clare Cooper Marcus Collection, EDA, Berkeley

Center for Environmental Design Research established

Humanistic Design Manifesto

1982

hiring of new fac Michael Southw and Paul Groth (Marcus, and Len for the Life Cycle

1988

Ar

"NAAB requirements recognize the importance of this field by...including seven specific areas of study which pertain to social, cultural, and psychological issues in design among the list of skills they expect to be taught in an accredited school of architecture" (from 1992 memo, Clare Cooper Marcus collection, EDA, Berkeley)

1990

(M

1994

11 out of 40 Archite retire including: Sar Van der Ryn, Dick Pe Ken Simmons, and S

Death and Life of Social Factors conference at Berkeley

Conference poster and call for papers, ca. 2012. Courtesy Georgia Lindsay.

2012

Wurster Hall, University of California, Berkeley, home to the College of Environmental Design; Architects: Vernon DeMars, Joseph Esherick, and Donald Olsen,1964.

(Photo: Benjamin Clavan, circa 1975)

The field of Environmental Design in the United States became institutionalized in 1969 when the Environmental Design Research Association (EDRA) was formed. Working on a base of then-recent government-funded sociological research in architecture, EDRA effectively introduced and legitimized the study of the interfaces between people and architecture. As noted in EDRA's mission statement, during the ensuing years, their members and followers have helped create and continue to promote EDRA's legacy. This includes "environment and behavior studies, evidence-based design, facility evaluation methods, sustainability, active living, participation, community planning, universal design, diversity in design, workplace design and informatics, design education, and digital technologies."

In Europe, EDRA's counterpart, the International Association for Person-Environment Studies (IAPS) was officially formed in 1981, although its origins go back to a series of successful conferences in several European countries from

1969 onwards. IAPS advertises that its members are engaged in both theoretical and applied research, as well as practice and have links to policy making. These institutional efforts continue to generate a storehouse of research and information on people-environment relationships.

Even more globally and more recently, the International Union of Architects (UNESCO/UIA) Charter for Architectural Education—initially approved in 1996, revised in 2004–2005, and revised yet again between 2008 and 2011—was finally approved by the UIA General Assembly in 2011. Its preamble reads, "We, the architects, concerned for the future qualitative development of the built environment..." Section 3 of the document outlines that architectural education should include the following fundamental objectives:

- Understanding of the relationship between people and buildings, and between buildings and their environment, and of the need to relate buildings and the spaces between them to human needs and scale.
- Understanding of the profession of architecture and the role of the architect in society, in particular by preparing briefs that take account of social factors.
- Understanding of the methods of investigation and preparation of the brief for a design project....Training in research techniques as an inherent part of architectural learning, for both students and teachers.

In essence, the charter calls for architecture education to give the student the "ability to act with knowledge of historical and cultural precedents in local and world architecture." What better way to describe the social art of architecture?

In the United States, the American Institute of Architects (AIA), the voluntary professional organization of architects that was founded nearly 170 years ago, has developed a Framework for Design Excellence to "inspire sustainable, resilient, and inclusive design" among its members and throughout the profession. This framework, "challenges architects with a vision of what the profession strives to achieve," a toolkit that provides practical resources to help all architects achieve the vision. Included in the framework are nine goals:

**Design for integration; Design for equitable communities;
Design for ecosystems; Design for water; Design for economy;
Design for well-being; Design for resources; Design for change;
and Design for discovery.**

To summarize: *Design for people.*

Working to Integrate the New Perspective into Architectural Education

Today's architectural education is at the very least *informed* by the work of these noted socially conscious individuals, leading academic institutions, and national and international organizations. There is, however, continued resistance to interdisciplinary learning, let alone in-the-field-learning and application. Design styles might have changed over time, but the basic hierarchical education has not. And in the majority of schools, it has little to do with an attempt to understand the people for whom architects design.

The outline of a new discipline of architectural studies was clear enough. Some teachers of architecture began to show signs of shifting focus from "what does the building look like," to "how does or can architecture actually make people matter?" Students began studying and graduating in joint degree programs with other disciplines, particularly the social sciences: architecture and sociology, architecture and anthropology, architecture and psychology. Architects began to actively interact with consultants from outside the traditional engineering disciplines.

The CED hired sociologists such as Galen Cranz and William (Russ) Ellis; additional scholars in social housing architecture such as Claire Cooper Marcus and Jean-Paul Bourdier; theorists and design methodologists such Christopher Alexander, Jean-Pierre Protzen, and Horst Rittel; environmentalists such as Sim van der Ryn and Donlyn Lyndon. Included in this wide-ranging recruitment was Raymond Lifchez.

Professor Lifchez introduced the groundbreaking Architecture 101 course "Social and Behavioral Factors in Design." Its aim was to formally bring and apply social factors into the design studio. The course used large-scale, three-dimensional models of proposed environments using mounted photographs of actual people in a variety of situations as a tool to help beginning design students think about people first. This was coupled with programmatic "clients" like the disabled and elderly—the *others* who were ourselves. Lifchez would go on to become one of the nation's leading architectural advocates for accessible design.

From the late 1960s and through the early 1980s, the CED was one of the leading voices in architectural education for environmental design and the social art of architecture in the United States, if not the world. In fact, as a result of this emphasis, by the mid-1970s the discipline of drawing had become so reduced in the CED curriculum that proactive measures were taken to re-introduce the historic basics of the architecture profession back into the degree coursework. Students were once again required to take architectural drawing classes.

At the same time, the new students might have been more prescient than their teachers: the experience of many of the CED graduates of this era was that although they might not be hirable in the typical architectural shop, within a few years they would be principals of their own firms or leaders in other firms, and they would themselves be hiring architecture graduates from other colleges to help them produce the drawings necessary for a new generation of building projects. In reality, the new students were not at Berkeley to learn how to draw; they were there to learn how to design a new era of socially significant buildings. Architecture, as they saw it, was undergoing a revolution.

One of the more than 200 projects built by Rural Studio, an off-campus design-build program, sponsored by the School of Architecture, Planning and Landscape Architecture of Auburn University, Auburn, Alabama, U.S.A. Founded in 1993 by architecture faculty Samuel Mockbee and D.K. Ruth, Rural Studio was "created to teach architecture students how to not just be good designers, but how to engage with community members, address difficult problems and find design solutions with limited resources."

The studio, which started by working one-on-one with poverty-stricken clients who had no reasonable housing options, has now broadened its scope of services to larger-scale community projects where little or no funding is available. It has become the model for similar university endeavors throughout the United States.

(Photo: Alpha Stock, 2010, sourced on Alamy)

Confronting the Academic Stagnation of the Last Twenty-five Years

Today in architecture schools, it is generally accepted that there is something else out there that needs to be addressed. The idea of actively engaging the users has become a new construct. In fact, the very definition of "users" has been widely extended from those entering for the specific purpose for which the building was designed, to including those who maintain and service it, those who are impacted simply by its presence such as the building's neighbors; and those who are affected by the building on a larger urban scale.

Architecture needs to be considered for its potential impact on the community at large—both positive and negative—and as a major consumer of natural resources from construction through decades of operation. This new approach has, in effect, opened an entirely new way of looking at and evaluating the product of the architecture, with intellectual movements as *Design Thinking* applied to the process, and the public often becoming an active part of the design and planning.

There is no lack of an attempt to keep the CED current and to continue to cover all of the social bases, while simultaneously preparing its graduates for a more traditional professional life. There are four departments in the CED: Architecture; City + Regional Planning; Landscape Architecture + Environmental Planning; and Real Estate Development + Design. In addition, minor programs include Environmental Design and Urbanism in Developing Countries; History of the Built Environment; Social and Cultural Factors in Environmental Design; Geospatial Information Science and Technology; and Sustainable Design. Within the college, a Master of Urban Design program is also offered.

Outside the doors of Bauer Wurster Hall, but still on the U.C. Berkeley campus, can be found such undergraduate minors as Disability Studies; International and Area Studies (including societal studies); Energy; and Global Poverty and Practice. Concurrent graduate programs with other schools and colleges on the campus include International and Area Studies; Law; New Media; and Public Health.

There is also a growing list of colleges and universities that sponsor one-off, socially conscious projects outside the campus. These include housing for the poor, experiments in sustainable design, and attempts at positing radical changes in traditional building types. These enterprises are matched in the profession by a small, but growing number of those who, as in the titles of the most widely received recent books on the subject, provide their architectural services *pro bono*, and design as if they *give a damn*.

This trend is furthered by a few socially conscious architecture firms that have grabbed the public's interest. One example is the non-profit architectural firm MASS (Model of Architecture Serving Society), which was named the Architecture Innovator of the Year by the *Wall Street Journal* in 2020. The firm was showcased on the perennial weekly American television news show, *60 Minutes* in 2021, under the title, "The MASS Model of Community-Focused Architecture."

Almost simultaneously, one of the world's current foremost starchitects, Jacques Herzog of Basel-based Herzog & de Meuron, was highlighted on the present state of architecture in a long interview by Rowan Moore that appeared in *The Guardian* on 31 October 2021. Herzog is quoted as saying, "Architecture is the art of facts. You do a building or you don't, and if you do a building, do it right. *We shouldn't have a moralistic standpoint* [editor's emphasis]. But make things so that they work, they are sustainable and they are beautiful." Clearly, this only skims the edges of the social art of architecture—if at all.

Lobby, Copenhagen Opera House (Operaen på Holmen), Copenhagen, Denmark; Architect: Henning Larsen, 2005. Does a wonderful building like this get designed and built without placing the users - the people who visit, those who perform, and the community in general - first and foremost in the architect's mind?

(Photo: Benjamin Clavan, 2017)

The actual *how*, not to mention the questionable *why* of applying the findings and lessons of the social sciences to architecture remain unanswered. What are architecture faculty and students expected to do with the exploding and often seemingly extraneous theoretical, experimental, and practical social information now becoming more and more available to them? This is a dilemma that is exacerbated by the very state of academic studies.

If anything, not only the social sciences but science itself has become somewhat suspect in recent years. From the roots of 1960s counterculture claims that scientists created a world gone amuck, we have entered a new age where the very definition of the truths—or *untruths*—of science are debated. The idea that architecture as a methodology is open to the application of theory and testing is also suspect in many quarters. This makes the practice of architecture, as well as the learning and teaching of architecture, that much more complex.

Many schools of architecture are still reluctant to deal directly with the day-to-day human realities of the worlds of their clients in which their students must ultimately work once they leave the academy. Among the possible reasons?

- For teachers of architecture not particularly experienced with dealing in the social sciences—or frankly, messy people in general—exploring the relationship between architecture and society is easily subsumed by the technical aspects of the discipline.
- For students of architecture, social factors are seen as an altogether different academic subject and program. They want to learn how to make buildings, not how to study (*messy?*) people and their interactions.
- For both teachers of architecture and students of architecture, the visual subsumes the textual. On-site research, documentation and analysis is a foreign discipline often difficult to learn, accept its importance, and to integrate into the typical course structure.

All of these issues are further complicated by the introduction of computer-aided design, which has transformed the profession over the last few decades. Today, it seems the only conversation one needs to have to design a building is with programs on the computer screen. The introduction of artificial intelligence into architectural design programs portends even more withdrawal from actual interaction with the users of buildings and places.

Clearly, despite decades of attempts to widen the discussion, there is still a gap between the professional discipline of architecture and the social act of building. Such was the professional and academic environment we found ourselves facing twenty-five years ago in attempting to foster a new renaissance in the study of the social art of architecture.

"I have made a decision to create a fairy tale for old people wanting them to experience (one more time) the gratuitous joy and innocence only a child could feel. A location for the fairy tale would be where all fairy tales take place- in a land far, far away, outside the framework of reality...Since Televizorke, the apartment block, is two long buildings... the buildings themselves have to disappear, so the fairy tale could happen on their roofs."

(Image: Milica Stojanovic, University of Belgrade, Serbia, one of BP2014 Teaching Fellow Ruzica Bozovic-Stamenovic's students.)

2

The Berkeley Prize Begins

A Starting Point

Making the Berkeley Prize Happen: The Mechanics

Assessing the Results

Focusing on People-centered Architecture

Fostering a change to the seemingly inexorable disconnect between *people-centered* and *object-centered* architecture is at the very heart of the Berkeley Prize.

A Starting Point

In 1998, a few faculty and alumni of University of California Berkeley's College of Environmental Design (CED) gathered to think about how to re-energize interest in the still nascent social art of architecture. The discussion was convened and led by the late Raymond Lifchez, who taught at the CED for fifty years and eventually retired as Professor Emeritus of Architecture & Urban Planning.

The question then and now is how to interest young architecture students to explore for themselves the range of issues, investigations, and built examples outside of the lingering form-focused architectural curriculum and the faculty who teach it. Ray had a very straightforward proposal: He presented the idea of a prize program to address these avenues of inquiry. The ultimate goal? Provide an incentive for participation in the investigation and implementation of this social perspective in design by undergraduate students of architecture.

Focusing on undergraduate students was an almost *a priori* decision. The need to impress on students at an early point in their education that social factors are not an additional or esoteric part of design, but an integral part of the design process is the very basis of making people the focus of architecture. Architecture is more than physical design. It is about the place of people in design. This is the focus of the social art of architecture. Given the perceived reluctance to introduce such basics in the architectural curriculum gave increased importance to making the Berkeley Prize's center of attention the start of the architectural education process, not simply advanced study down the road.

Architectural design competitions have now actually become ubiquitous. Beginning in 1720, the École des Beaux-Arts in Paris awarded students the Prix de Rome, offered by the French government for the winner to study (classical) architecture in Rome for several years. From the first award in 1720 to its last in 1967, the work of the students of the École was focused on winning the prestigious prize. If fact, the School and the Prize codified the Beaux Arts style and made it the preeminent architectural trope well into the first quarter of the twentieth century.

Fortunately, today there is also a thrust by the profession to acknowledge and award the wider discussion about the role of architecture. The American Institute of Architects (AIA) Committee on the Environment (COTE), for example, sponsors an annual Top Ten Award for excellence in sustainability and design. Awards are based on their previously noted, socially conscious, Framework for Design Excellence.

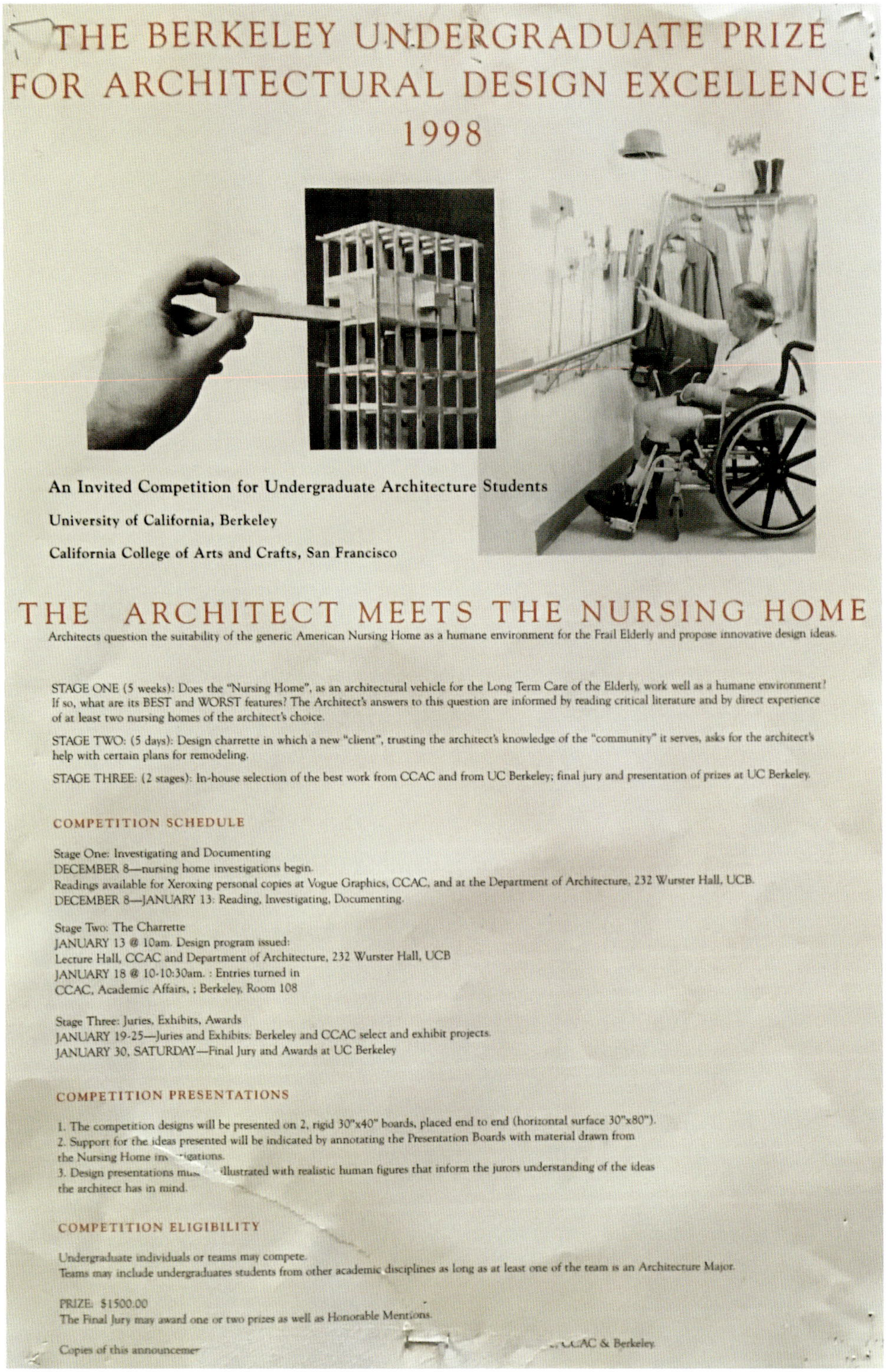

THE BERKELEY UNDERGRADUATE PRIZE FOR ARCHITECTURAL DESIGN EXCELLENCE
1998

An Invited Competition for Undergraduate Architecture Students
University of California, Berkeley
California College of Arts and Crafts, San Francisco

THE ARCHITECT MEETS THE NURSING HOME
Architects question the suitability of the generic American Nursing Home as a humane environment for the Frail Elderly and propose innovative design ideas.

STAGE ONE (5 weeks): Does the "Nursing Home", as an architectural vehicle for the Long Term Care of the Elderly, work well as a humane environment? If so, what are its BEST and WORST features? The Architect's answers to this question are informed by reading critical literature and by direct experience of at least two nursing homes of the architect's choice.

STAGE TWO: (5 days): Design charrette in which a new "client", trusting the architect's knowledge of the "community" it serves, asks for the architect's help with certain plans for remodeling.

STAGE THREE: (2 stages): In-house selection of the best work from CCAC and from UC Berkeley; final jury and presentation of prizes at UC Berkeley.

COMPETITION SCHEDULE

Stage One: Investigating and Documenting
DECEMBER 8—nursing home investigations begin.
Readings available for Xeroxing personal copies at Vogue Graphics, CCAC, and at the Department of Architecture, 232 Wurster Hall, UCB.
DECEMBER 8—JANUARY 13: Reading, Investigating, Documenting.

Stage Two: The Charrette
JANUARY 13 @ 10am. Design program issued:
Lecture Hall, CCAC and Department of Architecture, 232 Wurster Hall, UCB
JANUARY 18 @ 10-10:30am. : Entries turned in
CCAC, Academic Affairs, ; Berkeley, Room 108

Stage Three: Juries, Exhibits, Awards
JANUARY 19-25—Juries and Exhibits: Berkeley and CCAC select and exhibit projects.
JANUARY 30, SATURDAY—Final Jury and Awards at UC Berkeley

COMPETITION PRESENTATIONS

1. The competition designs will be presented on 2, rigid 30"x40" boards, placed end to end (horizontal surface 30"x80").
2. Support for the ideas presented will be indicated by annotating the Presentation Boards with material drawn from the Nursing Home inv[illegible]igations.
3. Design presentations mus[illegible] illustrated with realistic human figures that inform the jurors understanding of the ideas the architect has in mind.

COMPETITION ELIGIBILITY

Undergraduate individuals or teams may compete.
Teams may include undergraduates students from other academic disciplines as long as at least one of the team is an Architecture Major.

PRIZE: $1500.00
The Final Jury may award one or two prizes as well as Honorable Mentions.

Copies of this announceme[illegible] CCAC & Berkeley.

This first BP announcement poster was circulated to two architecture schools in 1998 to raise interest in the competition.

Similarly, the Royal Institute of British Architects (RIBA) has a number of design prize programs including its International Awards that are presented every two years to buildings outside the United Kingdom that "demonstrate design excellence and meaningful social impact." The RIBA International Prize 2021 winner was the Friendship Hospital, Satkhira, an eighty-bed community hospital situated in a remote rural area of southwest Bangladesh, designed by Bangladeshi architect Kashef Chowdhury/URBANA. RIBA also acknowledges architectural research through its RIBA President's Awards for Research. These are awarded in four categories: Cities and Communities, History and Theory, Design and Technical; and the annual theme, Education.

As the statistics indicate, architectural writing competitions, both historic and contemporary, are much less common. The European Association for Architectural Education (EAAE) sponsored a bi-annual writing competition from 1991 to 2012. Their prize was limited to member schools of architecture and the individual EAAE members themselves. More recently, CEPT University in India and India's Council of Architecture Training and Research Centre (COA-TRC) sponsored individual essay competitions. Online architecture blogs like Archiol.com, and Bee Breeders, a competition-mounting service, have similarly introduced one-off writing competitions.

The first year of the Berkeley Prize (1998–1999) was, in fact, both a research, writing and design competition limited to undergraduate architecture students in two venerable San Francisco Bay Area, California, U.S.A. colleges: the CED in Berkeley and the Architecture Division of the California College of Art and Crafts (now the California College of the Arts or CCA) in San Francisco. Professor Lifchez believed that, as a first step in reinvigorating the study of the social art of architecture, it would be valuable to foster a sister relationship with another school of architecture that would allow for the interchange of students and faculty, and for a greatly needed interchange of ideas. The competition topic was *The Architect Meets the Nursing Home*.

In 2000, the CED closed for renovations, making it difficult to host an on-site design competition. Scot Thrane Refsland and Alonzo C. Addison, two CED researchers in the study and application of computer technology to architecture, approached Ray and said that they were interested in testing if an online competition could substitute for the in-person charrette. They asked, "Why don't you take the Berkeley Prize digital and make it a written competition?" It was an interesting proposal for several reasons:

- It was by now clear that the wholesale adoption of the computer into the studio had transformed the teaching of architectural design. Could the worldwide web also be used to transform architectural education in other

ways, introducing people-environment studies to students who might not otherwise be exposed to these ideas?
- At the same time, writing about architecture and about the world of ideas in architecture seemed to be on an ever-increasing decline with more books being published, but less new thoughts being explored.
- On a practical level, architects in everyday practice are increasingly asked to write about their projects, if only to submit planning applications or to archive their ideas to client and neighborhood groups.
- The opportunity to make the discussion of the social art of architecture much more universal was also very inviting.

Bottom line: While accepting the necessity of training the new generation of students in computer-aided drawing, why not at the same time also encourage them to hone their skills at thinking and writing about the architecture project. To make it all that more enticing, it seemed appropriate to offer a financial incentive to do so.

The second Berkeley Prize, BP2000, launched its first online essay competition as an early experiment. This first attempt was open to eight schools of architecture throughout the United States. The prize asked students to respond to the question, *What role can architecture play as a socially responsive endeavor in the future?* The responses were encouraging, both in number and content. Each year thereafter, a new topic was announced, and a new question posed. Within just a few years, the prize had officially become an international essay competition. Various fellowship competitions were to follow.

Making the Berkeley Prize Happen: The Mechanics

The format was straightforward. Each year the Berkeley Prize Committee selected a topic integral to the social art of architecture and then posed a question or a prompt to which undergraduate architecture students responded. From the first essay topic, *The Architect Meets the Nursing Home,* to the most recent, *Architecture Designed for Aging*, young architects were encouraged to go out into their communities and explore the world in which they live and then to write about their findings. A cash award was given for the best essays and for the Fellowship awards.

It is the topics and questions themselves that those associated with the prize hope will continue to point to a new avenue for both learning and teaching architecture. The topics certainly reflect subject matter that still is rarely dealt with in the design studio, let alone in any other subject-specific coursework. The questions range from the achingly straightforward yet exceedingly difficult to answer in any easy way, to the exceedingly difficult ones that are much easier to answer with the specific and relevant on-site data.

The Berkeley Prize Topics Through the Years

2023: Architecture Designed for Aging
2022: Design Guided by Clients' Needs: Applying Social Factors Research to Architecture
2021: Architects in Service to the Community
2020: Designing Civic Buildings: The Architect Works With a Team
2019: Architecture and Climate Resilience
2018: Applying the Social Art of Architecture
2017: Architecture Reveals Communities
2016: Sheltering Those In Need: Architects Confront Homelessness
2015: Architects Confront Poverty
2014: The Architect and the Healthful Environment
2013: The Architect and the Accessible City
2012: Architecture for the Public Good
2011: Valuing the Sacred
2010: Historic Preservation/Heritage Conservation
2009: Sustainable Architecture/Traditional Wisdom
2008: Competing To Serve
2007: Making Social Architecture
2006: Children and the City
2005: Memorable Public Spaces
2004: The Architect Reports On Refugees, The Homeless and The Urban Poor
2003: Buildings That Achieve World-Class Status
2002: The Role of the Street In Fostering Social Life
2001: The Street Mediates Between Public and Private Lives
2000: Architecture as a Social Art
1999: The Architect Meets The Nursing Home

All of the topics have started with the basic premise: *Go out into your community*. How else could there be a social art of architecture without looking, listening, and hearing the people who use the buildings and places we design? This is more than an ethnographic approach to design. The ethnographer questions, examines, and records. The work that architects do—or should be doing—is both questioning and doing. In the end, it is about making things that serve people. The very point of the social art of architecture is to make *better* buildings.

Each year, the topic has been introduced by essays or articles specifically solicited from or published by well-known figures in the study of the selected topic. Some of these contributions are included in the chapters that follow. Students have been given a further incentive to compete: each year the selected twenty-five or more semifinalists were given the opportunity to participate in a series of Fellowship opportunities.

Full-time students enrolled in any undergraduate architecture degree program, Diploma in Architecture program, or majoring as an undergraduate in architecture throughout the world have been invited to submit a 500-word essay proposal responding to the question. From each year's pool of essays, approximately twenty-five to twenty-eight have been selected by the prize committee as particularly promising. These semifinalists have then been asked to submit a 2,500-word essay expanding on their proposals. The Berkeley Prize Committee members, acting as readers, select approximately eight of the best essays and send these finalists on to an annual, topic-specific jury of international academics.

As the essay prize increased its reach, three fellowship opportunities have been offered to all semifinalists and an additional fellowship open only to architecture faculty:

Travel Fellowship (2004–2019; 2023). This award has recognized the vital role that exposure to other cultures and environments plays in helping to demonstrate the reality and importance of the social art of architecture. All semifinalists for the essay competition have been eligible to submit proposals demonstrating how they would use the opportunity to travel to an architecturally significant destination or event, preferably to participate in a hands-on, service-oriented situation related to the yearly topic. The winning student(s) have been provided with airfare, living expenses, and program fees. During the thirteen years of the fellowship fifty-two students have been awarded travel stipends. (In 2020, the Travel Fellowship was suspended due to the Covid-19 pandemic. In lieu of this potential travel opportunity, all semifinalists were given a cash award toward a future journey.)

Community Service Fellowship (2021–2022). Started in response to the worldwide pandemic, this new fellowship replaced the Travel Fellowship. It asked students to develop or join a project or program that fosters the role of architecture in strengthening the lives of their local community.

Architectural Design Fellowship (2008–2011). This award offered students the opportunity to organize their own local design competition for other undergraduate architecture students based on further development of the yearly topic. All semifinalists for the essay competition were invited to submit proposals for this or another fellowship award. The Berkeley Prize provided the selected students an honorarium and allocated additional money to fund prizes for the winners of the regional competition.

Teaching Fellowship (2013–2014). The Berkeley Prize Committee broadened the scope of the activities of the Prize by offering faculty who teach undergraduate architectural design an academic-year Teaching Fellowship. The primary goal for the Berkeley Prize Teaching Fellowship was to explore methodologies for the teaching of the social art of architecture. During the two-year experiment, the Teaching Fellowship was based on the prize topic and supplemented on-going courses taught by the faculty member.

As a result, the Berkeley Prize has developed into one of the world's leading academic showcases for the study of the social art of architecture. In recognition of these efforts, the American Institute of Architects (AIA) awarded the prize a 2009 AIA Collaborative Achievement Honor Award, and a 2002 AIA Education Honor Award. In partial recognition of the prize's international outreach through digital technology, the 2003 Berkeley Prize Competition was named a Special Event of "World Heritage in the Digital Age," a Virtual Congress helping to commemorate the thirtieth anniversary of the UNESCO World Heritage Convention.

This has been an ambitious project with many moving parts. It required prize-specific development; extensive committee, student, and juror outreach; and website creation and review by several people working on a part-time basis. The prize was only made possible by the work of our Berkeley Prize Committee, averaging over sixty architects, allied professionals, social scientists, and generally interesting and informed people who, along with our year- and topic-specific jurors, have read and reviewed the multiple student submittals. (See *NOT* THE BACK MATTER for a top-line profile of the prize administration and the list of prize committee members.)

As of 2023, its twenty-fifth prize cycle year, the Berkeley Prize has had 3,785 undergraduate architecture students participate from eighty-eight countries and the prize presented 188 awards to 225 individual students, some working in teams of two.

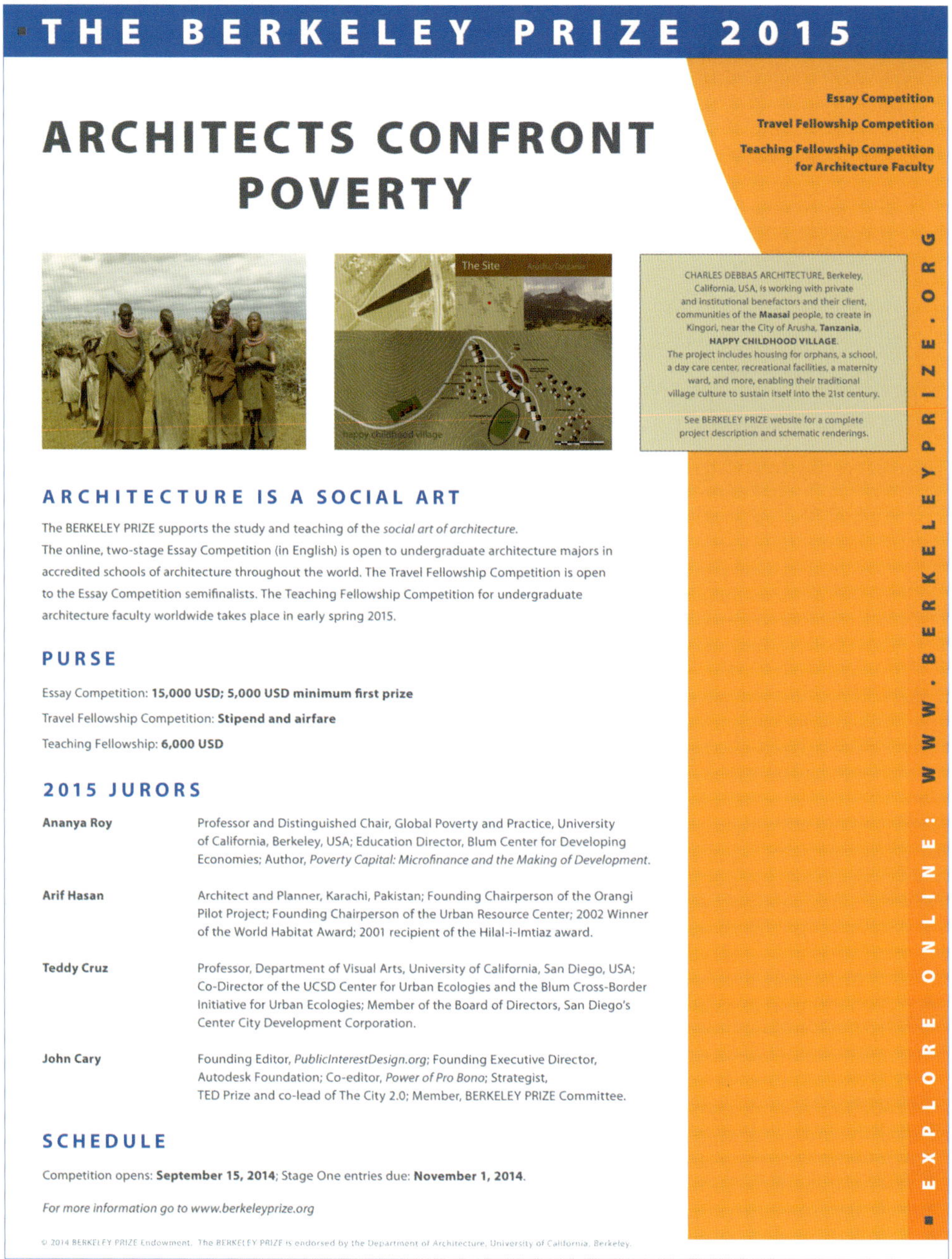

THE BERKELEY PRIZE 2015

Essay Competition

Travel Fellowship Competition

Teaching Fellowship Competition for Architecture Faculty

ARCHITECTS CONFRONT POVERTY

The Site

CHARLES DEBBAS ARCHITECTURE, Berkeley, California, USA, is working with private and institutional benefactors and their client, communities of the **Maasai** people, to create in Kingori, near the City of Arusha, **Tanzania**, **HAPPY CHILDHOOD VILLAGE**. The project includes housing for orphans, a school, a day care center, recreational facilities, a maternity ward, and more, enabling their traditional village culture to sustain itself into the 21st century.

See BERKELEY PRIZE website for a complete project description and schematic renderings.

ARCHITECTURE IS A SOCIAL ART

The BERKELEY PRIZE supports the study and teaching of the *social art of architecture*.
The online, two-stage Essay Competition (in English) is open to undergraduate architecture majors in accredited schools of architecture throughout the world. The Travel Fellowship Competition is open to the Essay Competition semifinalists. The Teaching Fellowship Competition for undergraduate architecture faculty worldwide takes place in early spring 2015.

PURSE

Essay Competition: **15,000 USD; 5,000 USD minimum first prize**

Travel Fellowship Competition: **Stipend and airfare**

Teaching Fellowship: **6,000 USD**

2015 JURORS

Ananya Roy — Professor and Distinguished Chair, Global Poverty and Practice, University of California, Berkeley, USA; Education Director, Blum Center for Developing Economies; Author, *Poverty Capital: Microfinance and the Making of Development*.

Arif Hasan — Architect and Planner, Karachi, Pakistan; Founding Chairperson of the Orangi Pilot Project; Founding Chairperson of the Urban Resource Center; 2002 Winner of the World Habitat Award; 2001 recipient of the Hilal-i-Imtiaz award.

Teddy Cruz — Professor, Department of Visual Arts, University of California, San Diego, USA; Co-Director of the UCSD Center for Urban Ecologies and the Blum Cross-Border Initiative for Urban Ecologies; Member of the Board of Directors, San Diego's Center City Development Corporation.

John Cary — Founding Editor, *PublicInterestDesign.org*; Founding Executive Director, Autodesk Foundation; Co-editor, *Power of Pro Bono*; Strategist, TED Prize and co-lead of The City 2.0; Member, BERKELEY PRIZE Committee.

SCHEDULE

Competition opens: **September 15, 2014**; Stage One entries due: **November 1, 2014**.

For more information go to www.berkeleyprize.org

EXPLORE ONLINE: WWW.BERKELEYPRIZE.ORG

Right, the BP2015 poster distributed throughout the world.

Opposite page, from the 2015 Berkeley Prize introduction: Debbas Architecture, Berkeley, California, U.S.A., led by Charles Debbas who is a member of the Berkeley Prize committee, is working with private and institutional benefactors and their client—communities of the Maasai people—to create Happy Childhood Village.

This is an on-going project incorporated in 2014 in Kisongo, near the city of Arusha, Tanzania. The project includes housing for orphans, a school, a day care center, recreational facilities, a maternity ward, and more, enabling their traditional village culture "to sustain itself into the 21st century."

(Photos: Debbas Architecture's Introduction and Concept Document for the Happy Childhood Village and his firm's website: https://www.debbasarchitecture.com/)

Existing village structure.

New structures,"designed and built in a modular way."

Assessing the Results

Rather than only dealing with metrics and three-dimensional form, the Berkeley Prize asked questions about everyday life and its interaction with the buildings we use and inhabit: How is a place best designed to accommodate the everyday moments of human life? How can buildings be further designed to accommodate people of all ages, people with different physical or mental capacities, people with different—even radically different—perspectives on life? More importantly, how can architecture contribute to the creation of communities for all people?

These sorts of questions require a completely different approach to learning architecture, to teaching architecture, and to the public face of architecture. The answers to these questions also point to new ways for students to study and implement the design process, and for the public to begin to read buildings differently. This book provides examples of the resulting initial work toward creating a road map to do exactly this.

The selected introductions by invited scholars on the yearly competition topic provide not only a current overview of the issue at hand, but also a set of ideas about how to pursue in-depth research on the subject. As the prize matured, we also added bibliographic resources for the students to pursue. We asked that the students refer to this material in their proposals and essays. This yearly syllabus is in itself an almost complete course that can be used by architecture faculty to aid in developing courses in the social art of architecture.

To celebrate our twentieth anniversary in the 2018 prize cycle, we asked of our top-winning students to tell us about how the prize had affected their professional lives. We were curious about whether our goals of creating more socially responsive architects was essentially "paying off." We were somewhat surprised at the responses. Now practicing architects, they see architecture in an entirely different light than that promulgated by most academic architecture programs today. Moreover, those who decided to pursue alternate career paths applied the lessons learned from the Berkeley Prize in a variety of different ways. Although perhaps a narrow control group, there is an important message for those now teaching and learning architecture around the world. At the very least, the prize has shown that discovering the social art of architecture through onsite research, writing, and criticism has a variety of positive outcomes.

The Berkeley Prize Teaching Fellowship has also produced some incisive results and questions. The Teaching Fellowship presented a unique opportunity for the faculty to investigate and evaluate teaching the social art of architecture and to speculate why it is overwhelmingly not taught more rigorously. The first Teaching Fellowship coincided with the 2013 topic of *The Architect and the Accessible City*;

the second with the 2014 topic, *The Architect and the Healthful Environment*. All of the selected fellows agree that inclusive architecture does not develop as a result of special, code-related responses for one client group or another, but that it grows from developing an approach to designing the built environment in which everyone is treated equally.

This is, at heart, a definition for people-centered design. Within this community of agreement is a great range of perspectives, all of which are informed by the special context in which the courses are taught. By supporting such investigations in a range of diverse settings and situations, the prize both augmented student efforts, but also opened new avenues of study.

Another way to gauge the success of the Berkeley Prize is to follow the Travel Fellowship winners as they crisscross the globe in search of hands-on research and building opportunities toward a better understanding of the social art of architecture. The reports of the student Travel Fellows that appear throughout the text provide a glimpse into what can be learned from immersing oneself in a different culture. They also demonstrate what can be done hands-on even at an early stage of architectural education in remaking building as part of a community's tradition. The summary and excerpts from the Travel Fellows' reports essentially demonstrate in real life terms why architectural education cannot and should not continue to be limited to the studio.

Most importantly, the selection of winning essays of the student scholars that are highlighted in this book provide a unique baseline for *It's About the People!* They are a storehouse of thought and information regarding the social art of architecture from student architects in diverse cultures around the world. Notable is the number of dual-authored essays. Throughout the history of the prize, students have been encouraged to submit joint essays with one other student from allied professional and, more recently, social science programs. Such collaborations are exactly the kind of on-the-ground teamwork that is required to teach, learn, and create a truly people-centered architecture.

(l.) From the Introduction to the 2016 Berkeley Prize: Architects Confront Homelessness: An ordinary scene In the center of São Paulo, Brazil

(Photo: Benjamin Clavan, 2014)

(r.) One of 2016 essay juror Kyohei Sakaguchi's "Zero Yen Projects" to house the homeless, this iteration complete with solar-powered energy.

(Photo: 2001, Sourced on Wikimedia Commons-Creative Commons Attribution-Share Alike 3.0)

The street entry to the Ed Roberts campus, Berkeley, California, U.S.A., Leddy Maytum Stacy Architects (LMSa), San Francisco, California, 2011. A 82,500 sq. ft. center for ten organizations serving people with disabilities. This includes the Center for Independent Living: Access for All (CIL).

(Photo: Patrick Civello, February 2019, sourced on Alamy)

Ed Roberts Campus, Berkeley entry foyer, a grand gathering space. The orange panel-clad ramp is wide enough for two wheelchairs to move abreast.

In 2018, Ray Lifchez, founder of the Berkeley Prize, was named a recipient of the Ed Roberts Award from the renowned organization. The award honors pioneering individuals who have made major contributions to the independent living/disability rights movement in the United States and internationally.

(Photo: Kristin Cato, March 2020, sourced on Alamy)

Focusing on People-centered Architecture

Nearing the quarter-century mark of the twenty-first century, the social art of architecture is still an outlier in terms of both student interest and student learning. Architecture starts with people. Architecture serves people. By pinpointing specific user groups or specific social problems each year the Berkeley Prize has provided both a focus for investigation and a potential to make people's lives better. This is the kind of focus that future architects will need to excel and maintain personal excitement in the crowded and often confusing worlds of design. This is the kind of focus for which all education should strive.

Without having examined the specific moments in time in which people live, work, and otherwise enjoy themselves, architecture will truly only ever be about form and geometry and its generators. If the universally accepted measure of value in architecture remains the outward appearance of buildings and places, we are inevitably left with the following questions:

- Where is the discussion about the people who use the buildings we design?
- Where is the discussion about the impact of architecture on the community?
- Where is the discussion about *ourselves* in the design of our environment?

The Berkeley Prize set out to change this dynamic by providing students—and hopefully, some of their faculty—the view of another way to examine the study of architecture, design methodology, and the resulting architectural product. If nothing else, the prize presents the opportunity to explore subject matter that students and faculty probably still do not normally find in their typical program. The hope, of course, has been that the Berkeley Prize would generate a level of interest that would eventually lead to significant and permanent changes to today's architecture curriculum and perhaps, architecture itself.

What is especially interesting is the introspective nature of all the following chapters. The focus is not just the student work and the student achievement. It is about how the lives of the students, faculty, and the people who are at the heart of these studies change when challenged with having to talk about architecture in non-traditional ways.

Good architecture and a better architecture reflect and promote both physical and mental health, and as a prerequisite and a consequence, social health. Good architecture and design are reiterative processes that must start and end with the input and acceptance of user/experts—the people who actually inhabit and use the spaces and things we design. Good architecture starts with students who are made aware of and are hopefully particularly sensitive to the complexity of people-centered issues that should drive the design process and results.

All these realizations open the door to the systematic investigation of the question of value, of what works and what does not, of what is good and bad. Inside the academy, it questions the accepted dogma of subjectivity and neutrality in traditional teaching, particularly as it applies to subjects of taste and perception in architecture. Outside the academy, it requires a willingness to engage with the community in ways much different from traditional observation and recordation. The result is a much different and much more sensitive relationship between the teacher and the student, and between the student and their peers, and yes, between teachers and their peers. It requires a seminal change in the way we look at the production of architecture as a whole.

These are not new ideas. They are, perhaps, newer ideas to this generation of faculty and students. What was hinted at the turn of the twentieth century, demanded in the 1960s, and now re-awakened in the twenty-first century is an architecture based on theory, tested and proven in the field, with rules and ways of doing things that can be shared and constantly re-tested to obtain the best possible outcome.

Nothing is lost: not beauty, not individuality, not academic freedom, nor the necessity and willingness to experiment. The wonder of it all is that there is everything to gain.

3

The Scholars and Practitioners

An International Platform for People With Ideas

Selected Competition Introductions

An International Platform for People With Ideas

Each year, the Berkeley Prize has invited leaders in the study of the social art of architecture to provide statements to introduce the current competition topic. Many of these scholars—faculty at architecture schools or practicing architects from around the world; social scientists; professionals in allied fields—provided overviews of the topic and suggested prompts for the students' essays. At the same time, these introductions became a resource in themselves—an outline for the teaching and study of architecture from this engaging perspective.

What is particularly interesting about the yearly Berkeley Prize introductions by learned academics and experienced practitioners is that they talk about architecture in ways that also provide clues for emerging architects on ways they can bridge the gap between the world of building and the building of people studies.

The overall idea of the Berkeley Prize is that all of us—students, teachers, practitioners, and the general public—can learn from looking: Looking at how those around us live their everyday lives. Looking at what can and has been done toward improving the built environment to serve people better. Looking for answers, not just data.

The overall idea of the Berkeley Prize is that we learn from listening: Listening to those for whom we design: their issues and aspirations, their specific problems and dreams, and their gaps in thinking about what they want and what they actually need. Listening for clues, not just responses.

The overall idea of the Berkeley Prize is that we learn from researching: Researching what has been done; what went right, what went wrong, and what was unable to be addressed. Researching the analytical studies, but also looking for what academic studies do not always reveal, particularly those responses that are subjective, even visceral, rather than quantifiable.

The issue is even more complex when the neophyte student's mindset is considered. Few undergraduate students know what architecture is, let alone know how to create architecture. The students know *building*. They are excited about the appearance and about the experience of being in these wonderful places.

They are intrigued by how to create places to live, work, and learn. Some see this as a calling, a vocation; others, as a particularly wonderful way to make art. All need to be guided to think about the architecture's impact, good and bad, on the people who will use their buildings.

In teaching architecture to architecture students, the game plan is clearly different than explaining architecture to the lay person or studying it from within a different discipline. While understanding the client's needs theoretically comes first, the built object is the student's goal. Studying historic structures, learning about current trends in building, imagining things to come, all are at the forefront of the architecture student's mind. The product, not the process is at the forefront.

Through these introductory essays, scholars attempted to explain to the participants that looking, listening, and researching any architectural project must be done within the context of everyday lives of the people for whom the students will one day design. Much more needs to be done in this arena. The thoughts and ideas outlined in the following pages demonstrate a significant step in this direction.

Selected Competition Introductions

BP2021
Vishaan Chakrabarti

THE TOPIC
Architects in Service to the Community

THE QUESTION
As a future architect, what is the best way you can serve the needs of your local community?

For decades, if not more, many architects have bemoaned their place in society. Concerned about low pay and disrespect from clients, many have suffered from low self-esteem, have argued that we should seize the means of production by embracing real estate development skills, or have moved away from the field altogether.

Yet all of that feels like ancient history.

Beset by a global pandemic, climate change, righteous calls for social and racial justice, and increasing scrutiny about the inequities both in and perpetuated by the field, architecture is clearly at a turning point. Some may continue to embrace the celebrity model of the profession that has dominated the field's academic and media establishments, but this would seem to be an unlikely focus for the upcoming generation, particularly at a place like Berkeley's College of Environmental Design (CED), a place that historically has eschewed the architectural establishment. But protest and rejection are not enough.

President Obama asked us to define ourselves by what we are, not by what we are not. If the pursuit of architecture is not centered on the goals of stardom and outsized commissions aimed to garner spectacular media spreads, or just as a simple means to make a living, upon what should it center? How is the profession relevant to the challenges of today—challenges like public health and climate change and racial equity—that in some cases will likely demand a century or more to address?

Your essay could be a starting point to confront this question, a manifesto for why architecture is relevant to today's world. Among the more unique aspects of the CED are the origin stories of our students, many of whom hail from historically marginalized communities. How could both an architectural education and the profession serve the kinds of communities from which many of our students come? If in those communities there are populations in need—communities of color that have suffered disproportionately from this pandemic, elderly or young populations with insufficient access to social infrastructure, high numbers of individuals with physical or mental impairments, or a general lack of economic and educational opportunity fueled by racism and classism that has led to intergenerational poverty—what can architecture do?

A rich territory to investigate would be to ask where most architects begin, which is the site analysis process itself. Diana Agrest said that to "write" in a place with architecture one must first "read" it. What are the processes for reading a

(NOTE: All biographical references date from the year when the Introductions first appeared.)

place? Would you begin with community conversations? Historical research? Understanding of physical climate and context? And in so doing, what personal baggage, what unconscious bias, might you bring with you in your work? How, if we are to be relevant, can we take action while having this consciousness?

Recently CED faculty member and renowned landscape architect Walter Hood has publicly criticized the term "placemaking," arguing that the terminology, the pedagogy, and the practice of "making places" needs to be interrogated given the role such actions may have in the gentrification and displacement of communities who go unacknowledged in such a process. Ironically and historically, Berkeley was an epicenter of this terminology of place-making, itself a revolution against the emphasis on neutral space (as opposed to place) that was once espoused by orthodox modernists and is still in vogue among some practitioners. So, if Berkeley was once a place that mounted a challenge against the mainstream architectural practices of their day, could it do so again, and could it do so by mounting a challenge to its own revolution from decades ago?

Perhaps one starting point could be the re-emergence among a variety of practitioners and thinkers about the early roots of places like Berkeley and MIT, namely the work of the so-called "humane" modernists such as the members of Team 10, Alvar Aalto, Kevin Lynch, and others who centered themselves on ideas of "structuralism" as put forth by thinkers like John Habraken. An advocate for a modernism of self-determination, Habraken argued for architectural processes that included communities as makers of form and creators of inhabitation and use. Aldo van Eyck, famed architect of this movement, famously argued for the importance of place and occasion over Sigfried Gideon's emphasis on space and time, thus leading to the ideas of placemaking that came to dominate CED, ideas that clearly need to be re-examined in light of race, gender, colonial history, and economic disenfranchisement.

With bridge figures from the Team 10 period like Pritzker laureate Balkrishna Doshi still forging ahead in the areas of low-income housing and community driven architecture, a new group of practitioners have emerged such as Tatiana Bilbao, Lacaton and Vassal, and Pritzker laureate Alejandro Aravena as thought leaders in a new structuralist movement intent on community self-determination with laser like focus on the marginalized, but without the dogmatic aspects of placemaking. Aravena's now famous "half a house" project has emerged from the decades old "sites and services" paradigm in which community members are provided with core infrastructure upon which they are able to build and customize to suit their evolving needs.

Markedly different from both celebrity architecture and the more romantic contextual concerns of placemaking, could a third way be emergent among a new group of architects who, while looking to the history of structuralism, are forging a new trail for not just architecture, but for the relevance of the architecture profession itself?

Your essay could criticize this assertion, or investigate the work of such architects much further, or unearth yet the next generation of young practitioners who are taking this nascent movement and pushing it to a new level of relevance. Regardless of what aspect you might take on, perhaps the most important question for you to answer for yourself is what makes this field relevant for you as a student and as a future practitioner or scholar? What position do you hold for the field in light of the tremendous challenges society faces? Do you see the most effective methods for bringing change to be formal, sociological, technological, political, environmental, or through an entirely different lens?

Perhaps the question of relevance, of effectiveness, of impact in the world, may itself be problematic. Perhaps you view the study of architecture as a path to a different type of awareness regardless of capacity for societal impact. But then what, in your view, is specific to the discipline and instrumentality of architecture to bring much-needed change to our troubled world, as opposed to the more general needs you might envision for political, social or economic transformation regardless of architecture?

In short, why architecture?

Vishaan Chakrabarti, 2020–2022 William W. Wurster Dean, College of Environmental Design, University of California, Berkeley

BP2019
Donlyn Lyndon

THE TOPIC
Architecture and Climate Resilience

THE QUESTION
What have architects done in the past and what can they do in the future to help reduce the negative effects of climate and climate change?

Whenever we are indoors, buildings are part of the climate we experience. Through openings in their walls and roofs they structure our experience of the sun and the light of day. Those same or filtered openings channel the way air moves through spaces. Walls and roofs condition the heat that enters living spaces. Transparent materials quickly transmit the heat of the sun and convey more slowly the temperature outside. When walls are thick and obscure, they absorb and delay the transmission of solar energy and ambient temperatures, slowly yielding warmth to the inside and releasing some of it back into the atmosphere as the day cools. Roofs offer shelter from all that comes from the sky: sun, moisture, rain, gusts of wind and falling debris.

When outdoors, trees and vegetation often offer similar but less radical modifications to the climate, but not always, depending on the climate zone. Deciduous trees are especially benign, offering shade in the warm parts of the year and then shedding their leaves to let sun through their branches. We all know these things; though they are modified by the climate conditions in the places where we live. But do we absorb that knowledge into our creative thinking and make it a part of design for the places where we live, work, play, and join with others in community?

Condominium One on the hills overlooking the Pacific Ocean at Sea Ranch, a 5000-acre planned community located in Sonoma County, California, U.S.A., 1966. Design team: Architect and planner Al Boeke; architects Joseph Esherick, Donlyn Lyndon, Charles Moore, and Richard Whitaker (MTLW); landscape architect Lawrence Halprin.

Condominium One was the first project in the development which started in the early 1960s. The structure contains 10 condominium units and was designed with ecological imperatives at the forefront to serve both people and to respect the environment. The building has received numerous awards, including being placed on the U.S. National Register of Historic Places.

(Photo: Alpha Stock, 2013, Sourced on Alamy)

We've often been prone to consider climate a stable matter, a set of rhythms and seasonal changes in sun location, temperatures, rainfall, and winds, which we learn to expect through the years and to accommodate. If we are observant, have our wits about us, and work closely to traditions and conventional wisdoms, we assume that our well-being will be served. Or, that failing, we undertake to suppress the effects of the climate by technical means, creating power sources and distribution systems to fabricate internal climates.

Those assumptions no longer serve. The climate is becoming increasingly unpredictable. It is changing over time—sometimes with ferocity, always with unanticipated costs. Also, the sources of energy we can afford to use, and their distribution are changing. These include diminishing carbon-based resources and the environmental cost of offsetting the release of carbon dioxide and chemical emissions into the atmospheric blanket that envelops our globe, creating havoc beyond what the imagination can immediately grasp; but which nevertheless the frequent news of forest fires, hurricanes and floods presents to us frequently and vividly.

How can we, as architects, landscape architects, and planners learn to design with the climate and make it an ally in forming places that equitably allow inhabitants to live safely, freely, productively, and with joy in the places that are built? How, further, can we translate those insights into complexes of buildings and their surrounding landscapes or cityscapes, so that whole settlements can be adaptive and resilient for future changes?

Your essay should address the need for ongoing inquiry through observation, measurement, and imagination. Study known sources, connect their insights to the life of buildings that you can experience. Imagine in what way conditions might change. Then marshal all your resources into a call for action. Scout out a way that others may follow. Speak truths.

To get there be sure to observe your two selected buildings as if you were living there and seeking comfort, then watch how those who inhabit or work there spend their days and note what they enjoy. Return on differing days and times. Ask questions and carefully note answers so that they can be analyzed and assembled. Pose tough questions for yourself that challenge your preconceptions about what will be, what can be, and where answers might lie.

Be especially aware of the surroundings; the landscape and buildings around the examples you study. They are essential. Remember that no building can go it alone. We always are affected by and experience buildings within a larger context, especially with respect to the climatic impacts. The effects of sun and wind are tempered or disturbed by buildings and vegetation that affect the local microclimate; shadows that move during the day, heat that is absorbed in the ground around or in adjoining walls, light reflected off building surfaces and winds and water that are deflected by nearby structures or channeled between them.

The construction of buildings has importance, not only through their shapes and the effect of the materials, but through how and by whom they are made and what resources were used. What sizes will you imagine? Are there new materials to be expected that will offer possibilities and challenges? What provisions for workers and for the transportation of materials will have been made, how might those become important in future building projects and how might that change over time and with alterations in climate? How was the site for the building transformed during construction, how has drainage been altered and accommodated, have the levels of water collection proven to be effective and how might they be expected to perform in periods of extreme rainfall and violent storms? Is the infrastructure that others have installed to service the site been adequate now and for the future, and if not, what might be done?

To address the question before us, it is necessary to consider many things, but especially to be aware of how people interact with their surroundings, what changes the climate and societal conditions may bring about and what measures are already being taken by governments and community organizations to address changing needs. Hence the questions you should think about and ask will have many dimensions and require astute, informed imagination.

Above all, imagine how the places that you and your world embody might be very different as climates change and sea levels rise. How will that affect the lives of the inhabitants and their community? What resources will be available to them? Propose priorities and develop commitments. Write in ways that will rally responses, open ways to think about what might lie ahead, what paths can lead to a resilient future, and how you, your readers, friends, and colleagues can make a difference.

Donlyn Lyndon is Eva Li Professor Emeritus of Architecture and Urban Design, Berkeley's College of Environmental Design. He was one of four contributors to the landmark book, *Design with Climate: Bioclimatic Approach to Architectural Regionalism* (Princeton University Press, 2015).

BP2013
Elaine Ostroff, Honorary AIA

Berkeley Prize 2013 is dedicated to the United Nations Convention on the Rights of Persons with Disabilities and the World Health Organization which is helping to promote and implement the Convention.

The Power of Inclusion

Remarkable as it might sound, within your lifetime, the understanding and definition of those who were formerly seen as "handicapped" has dramatically changed. The millennia-old *medical* emphasis, which focused on the limitations of our physically disabled relatives, friends, and neighbors and in the process often denied their rights, has been transformed. Today, *accessible design* and *inclusive (or universal) design* are the key phrases that point to an acceptance of the almost startling idea that "they" are "us."

Accessible design says that every facet of the built environment should be able to be easily used by all of us. This is true whether we have full use of our bodies and minds or have some illness or accident that makes us temporarily dependent on crutches, or require, for instance, the long-term use of a walker or a wheelchair. Inclusive design takes the notion of accessibility one step further by giving it a new social dimension. As architects, we should not think of ourselves as designing special solutions for a particular sub-group of people, but for all of us. *We are them.*

One of the most visible indications of this shift in thinking is the adoption in 2006 of the United Nations Convention on the Rights of Persons with Disabilities. The Convention, which has now been signed by 153 countries, incorporates the World Health Organization's (WHO) official redefinition of disability. WHO asserts that disability is not only a set of characteristics within the person; disability is increased or overcome by environmental conditions.

These are not abstract problems. Two statistics shine a spotlight on the problem: First, last year's landmark *World Report on Disability*, produced jointly by WHO and the World Bank, estimates that more than a billion people in the world today experience disability. Second, this number is certain to increase even more dramatically in coming years. The world's population of people over the age of sixty will double by 2050. These older persons experience functional disabilities at upwards of triple the rate of younger people.

This is a powerful international call for action and opportunity for architects to rethink their role in society and to more fully appreciate the power of design. As the creators of the physical environment, this is an extraordinary time for architects to work to create human-centered design that makes it possible for people of all abilities to participate fully in community life. Architects have the power to

THE TOPIC
The Architect and the Accessible City

THE QUESTION
What have architects done in the past and what can they do in the future to help reduce the negative effects of climate and climate change?

Provide us with an overview of what is being done in your city to make it accessible to people who have physical disabilities. In your opinion as an architect, What more can be done?

help create an inclusive city that improves all of our lives. You have the power to enable or to disable, to include or to exclude.

The American architectural journalist and current head of the American Institute of Architects, Robert Ivy, says it in a way that reaches out to all of us:

Have you ever broken your arm and tried to open a door? Been late for a plane and had to negotiate a crowded airport?...Struggled to understand direction signage in the streets of an unfamiliar city? Felt left out at a neighborhood meeting because you couldn't see or hear the speaker? Reached to settle your belongings on a high self that lies just beyond your reach? If so, you have faced the consequences of design, an activity that has the power to affect our daily lives, for good or ill.

(From the Foreword, *Universal Design Handbook* by Wolfgang F. E. Preiser and Elaine Ostroff, McGraw Hill Professional, 2001)

Inclusive design is an approach to making buildings and places that honors human diversity. It addresses the right for everyone from childhood into their older years to use all spaces, products and information in an independent and equal way. This is not simply compliance with regulations for accessibility, but re-imagining how accessibility could work.

The 2013 Berkeley Prize asks what has been done and what more could be done in your community to create an inclusive city that welcomes and ennobles every person. As you look about your city using the eyes of a disabled person, what do you see? If you required a wheelchair to be mobile for either a day, a month, or your lifetime how would you get from Point "A" or Point "B"? Tell us about the journey. If you were blind, how would shop for your food, get to work, meet friends for entertainment and participate fully with them? Tell us about how your community has made these daily functions more accessible for all us.

Finally, tell us how all of these design interventions could be made even more inclusive and how.

Elaine Ostroff, co-founded Boston-based Adaptive Environments in 1978. In 1989 she developed the Universal Design Education Project (UDEP) at Adaptive Environments. She coined the now universally-used term "user/expert" in 1995 to identify the individuals whose personal experiences give them unique critical capacity to evaluate environments. In 1998, she convened the Global Universal Design Education Network and its Online Newsletter. She now works as a consultant with the Institute for Human Centered Design/Adaptive Environment where she directs the Access to Design Professions Project, with funding from the National Endowment for the Arts.

BP2022
Dorit Fromm

(One of the four introductions by the year's jury members.)

THE TOPIC
Design Guided By Clients' Needs: Applying Social Factors Research To Architecture

THE QUESTION
You have been asked to design a housing project for the disadvantaged in your local community. What do you need to know to ensure that your design will both reflect the lives and aspirations of those for whom you design and for the project to be a proud, long-term addition to the fabric of your community?

In the face of global catastrophes, inequities, divisions, and isolation, take this year's question as an invitation toward more collaborative and experimental living. Housing that improves residents' daily life. Housing that encourages residents to take an active role in saving resources and creating community. Housing that connects households to each other and the larger neighborhood: visually, casually, through space and over time. All require willing residents as well as good design.

What if the social connections of the residents came before architectural program and built form? Households that share ideas and hopes of how they imagine their day-to-day life together, and make some agreements on their intentions, are more likely to follow through once moved in.

The *Fondazione Housing Sociale*, in Italy, has a course for would-be residents to decide together on the design and use of a common space in their about-to-be-built housing projects. For the first year, a part-time facilitator helps residents in coordinating activities in the space.

In designing the Swiss "Mehr als Wohnen" (More Than Housing) cooperative, a group of nonprofits listened to potential residents about their needs. The development team included professionals versed in facilitating and interpreting user preferences, resulting in a wide mix of affordable and innovative housing types, participation of residents in their housing community, and neighborhood-shared amenities.

A group of people can self-organize, pool their resources, then decide on their development team. Site layouts can encourage social interactions: pedestrian-oriented, with private units that have a view and orientation to the commons. Resident connections and ample common facilities encourage task-sharing.

Tell us about resident choice, flexibility of space, need for household privacy, management participation and ways to solve conflicts—these help to form a strong housing community. How will your success be measured in this social art? Over time, evaluations of the housing and resident satisfaction inform future efforts, demonstrating where words and ideas have *separated from reality*.

In short, your task is to be a resident-connecting designer and a writer about that design. What if your reader's connection to your writing came first?

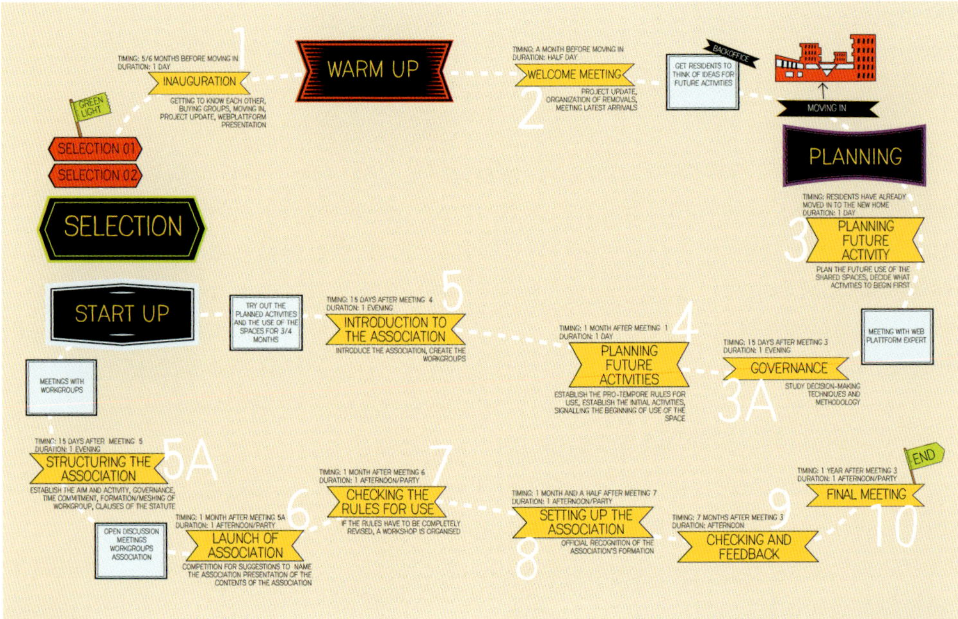

The Community Start Up "Path" developed by Fondazione Housing Sociale, Milan, Italy. From their manual, "Starting Up Communities, A Design Kit for Collaborative Housing," 2016.

(Photo: Fondazione Housing Sociale)

A meeting of the Community Start Up Path of the social housing project, *Cenni di Cambiamento* (Hints of Change), Milan, Italy. Winner of the European Collective Housing Award, 2017.

(Photo: Fondazione Housing Sociale)

Dorit Fromm is a design researcher, writer and architect. She has also worked in communications for the design industry. As part of these endeavors, she has studied a variety of community and housing designs, conducted post-occupancy evaluations of multi-unit housing, and presented on new forms of housing internationally. Her book, *Cluster Cohousing Revisited (Social + Design, 2021)*, co-authored with social housing researcher Els de Jong, is a deep look into the first Dutch cohousing project, from the perspective of design and social relationships. She is a BP Committee Member.

BP2016

(Edited excerpts from four distinguished practitioners.)

Christopher Herring

Millions of people in cities across the globe dwell without a roof, and millions more without a home. Despite the halving of global poverty in the past twenty years, more of the world's urban population exists without an abode than at any other point in human history. While homelessness takes on different meanings in different national contexts—from refugees in camps, to nomadic groups in caravans, families in sub-standard dwellings, and the poor who reside on the pavement, it is an issue to which cities, regions, and countries, rich and poor alike, are having to increasingly respond.

The causes of homelessness are just as varied—from housing shortages to rural displacement, armed conflicts, environmental disasters, and economic crises. In more developed countries, mental illness and substance abuse account for a disproportionately large number of those without shelter. Family conflicts create more homeless. In one study of 4,000 homeless teenagers in New York City, 40% identified themselves as homosexual: their families had disowned them and thrown them out onto the streets. Physical and sexual abuse of children in their home creates more runaways who typically have nowhere to go. No matter what its form or causes, the problem of sheltering those in need invokes a built response. A built response has by its very nature an architectural component.

THE TOPIC

SHELTERING THOSE IN NEED: Architects Confront Homelessness

THE QUESTION

(This year, in two parts)

Who is doing what in your community to confront the issue of the men, women, young people, and children without any shelter?

As both an individual and as a professional, how do you see yourself assisting in providing shelter to those in need?

EXPLORE!

Read the complete introductions by all four contributors here.

Side street, Dignity Village, Portland, Oregon. Dignity Village partnered with architecture students at Portland State University, Portland, Oregon, U.S.A., to transform their illegal tent-city into a legalized eco-village comprised of personalized tiny homes and public open spaces for the community.

(Photo: David Hull, 2007, Sourced on Wikimedia Commons-"Released without limitation")

This year's Berkeley Prize competition asks students to investigate the sheltering of those in need within their own communities by approaching architecture as a social art: designing for the needs, desires, and interests of the marginalized while considering the architect's role in the wider social, economic, and political relations of the city.

As you approach this year's essay, ask yourself how the work or space you examine is situated within the broader socio-political structure and how it conditions the limits and possibilities of the architecture of shelter.

- How are or how might architects in your community work in solidarity with grassroots organizations and those in need?
- In what ways does the work being done in your community mitigate the suffering of those without housing?
- How does it politicize the issue?
- And how might architecture assist in providing ameliorative relief for those experiencing homelessness while also working to abolish the conditions of economic deprivation, racism, and oppression that undergird it?

These lines of inquiry render architecture much more than a technical practice, but as a social vocation that can help solve, rather than merely react to, the problem of sheltering those in need today.

Christopher Herring is a Doctoral candidate of Sociology at the University of California, Berkeley. He is currently a Fellow at Harvard University's Inequality in America Initiative. In 2022, he will join the Sociology Department of the University of California Los Angeles (UCLA) as an Assistant Professor.

The Architecture of Recovery: A Specific Building Type

It is important to think about homelessness as a continuum rather than a binary situation, even for the chronic homeless. Homelessness equates with shelter living. The important question to ask is, what kinds of housing makes sense for people not currently housed to help them move to a safe, livable place where they can stay in definitely? Most chronically homeless need special assistance with housing. What is the "match" to meet their housing needs? Sober housing is one variation of that answer.

In (our) above illustration, the Clean and Sober Transitional Living (CSTL) recovery housing project, as many as one-third of the residents are coming from detox facilities or jail after a period being homeless or living sporadically on the streets. The most important part of the project is how to get the plan to reflect the

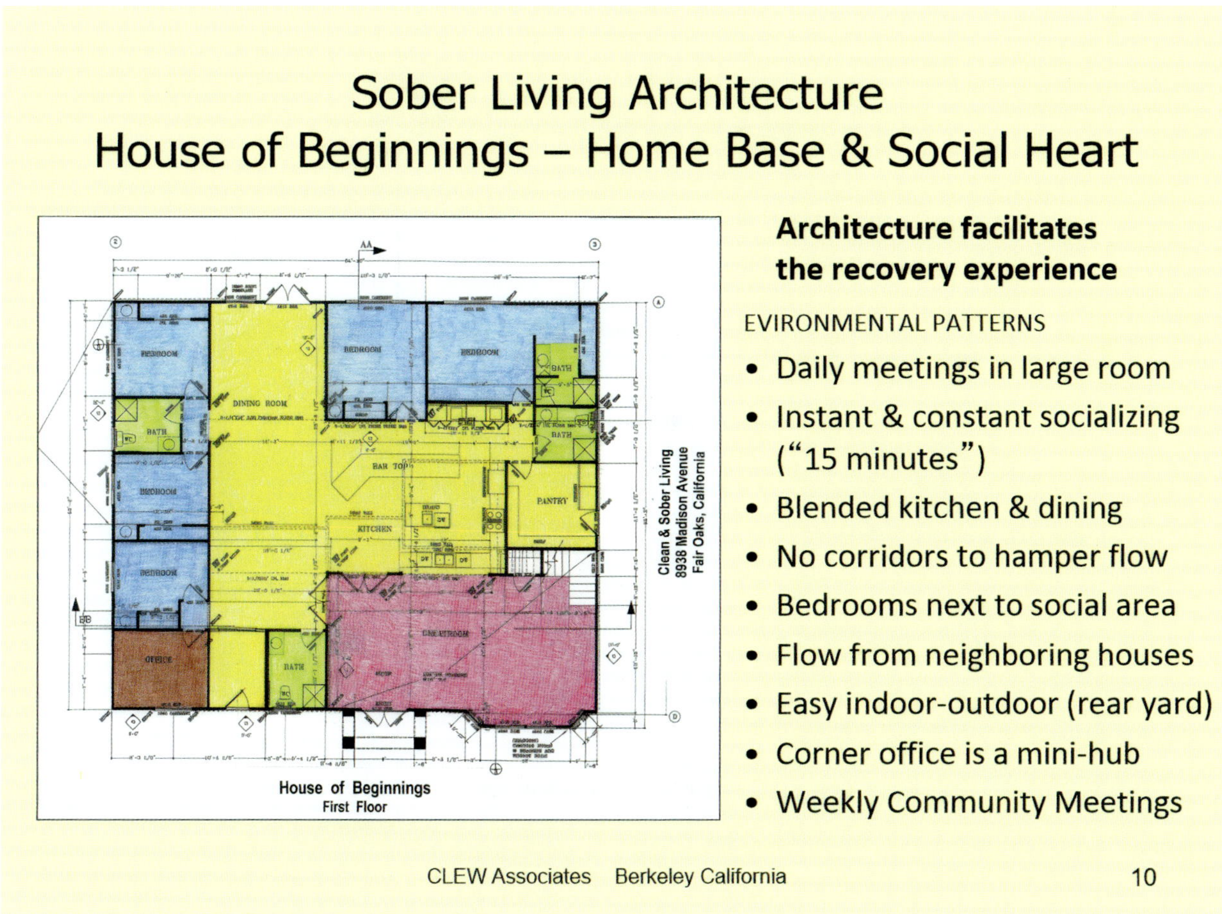

program; the architecture, serviceable or more exciting, must be seen as an outgrowth of the specific needs of this specific group of clients.

It is a difficult, sometimes very difficult effort. Two presentations that I have authored discuss some of the parts of this effort: *A Case Study in Architecture for Sober Living Households.* This is a PowerPoint presentation exploring the complexities of providing housing for a challenging population**.** *The Setting is the Service: How the Architecture of Sober Living Residences Supports Community-based Recovery.* An in-depth article analyzing the architecture of a community-based residential recovery service.

(These presentations can be sourced online at the Berkeley Prize website.)

Friedner D. Wittman has forty years of experience in community planning for health and social services, environmental design, and architectural programming. Much of this experience involves development of housing to serve homeless people with alcohol and other drug (AOD) problems. He founded and directed the Community Prevention Planning Program at the Institute for the Study of Social Change, U.C. Berkeley from 1988 through 2011. Currently he is president of CLEW Associates, a consulting firm he founded in 1988 that specializes in architectural programming and environmental design to support delivery of community health, safety, and social services.

Kyohei Sakaguchi

Zero Yen House

Fascinated by informal living structures, and inspired by birds building their nests, Sakaguchi began his field research on how Japan's "homeless" populations create shelter. Since 2008, he has devoted his time to photographing, designing, and writing about homes that can be built at no cost (0 yen).

"I first met Kyohei Sakaguchi in the fall of 2001. He had recently completed the Graduate Program in the Department of Architecture at Waseda University, Japan and he showed me his inspired and amazing book Tokyo House, which was his graduate thesis. Already dog-eared and tattered from use, this hand-made, 200-page book consisted of photographs, sketches and technical drawings of houses built by people in Tokyo who are generally referred to as 'homeless.' Sakaguchi became fascinated with this type of architecture when he stumbled on a carefully constructed dwelling built by a 'homeless' man on the side of the Tama

Kyohei Sakaguchi, "Solar zero yen house drawing 2," August 23, 2001. NOTE: Text is in Japanese.

(Photo: Sourced on Wikimedia Commons-Creative CommonsAttribution-Share Alike 3.0.)

River. With this encounter, Sakaguchi became aware of the great human potential for self-built dwellings. This discovery, along with Sakaguchi's other field research, is the point of departure for Zero Yen House."

(Makiko Hara, Curator for the Zero Yen House exhibition, *Vancouver Art Gallery, Vancouver, Canada, September 23, 2006–January 1, 2007)*

Sam Davis, FAIA

The writing and design work of Sam Davis

Take a look at the work of architect and BP Jur5r Sam Davis, U.C. Berkeley Emeritus Professor of Architecture, who has a depth of experience designing for the homeless. In his book, *Designing for the Homeless: Architecture that Works* (University of California Press, 2004), Davis presents a variety of design responses for providing shelter for those in need. From his book and the firm's website (http://www.sdavisarchitecture.com/homeless.html):

Transitional Shelter, Warehouse Renovation, Concord, California, U.S.A.: Sam Davis Architecture, Berkeley, California, U.S.A.

(Photo: Sam Davis Architecture)

"For the past several years I have been working with non-profit emergency housing and service providers designing shelters and facilities for the homeless. Through my clients I have come to appreciate how much a modest amount of design can do. Often it is merely figuring out the logistics of getting the requisite number of beds in a space. Increasingly, however, design is seen as a means of establishing trust between the provider and the homeless, and a way to create a sense of belonging for those with little or no social connection.

"It is within this difficult and often tragic arena that architecture serves its highest purpose. A visit to a museum can be a powerful and moving experience. Public buildings are a reflection of our culture. But if we believe that architecture serves a society as well as reflects its values, then we must provide for those with the most need and the fewest options."

In addition to *Designing for the Homeless*, Sam Davis is author of two other books on housing, *The Form of Housing;* and *The Architecture of Affordable Housing*. He is a principal at Sam Davis Architecture, a Berkeley, California, U.S.A. firm with four decades of housing experience. He taught at U.C. Berkeley from 1971 until 2009. Among his several administrative positions in academia, he also has served as the Interim Dean of the School of Social Welfare on the Berkeley campus from 2011–12.

BP2015
Anthony W. Schuman

Toward an Architecture of Solidarity

THE TOPIC
Architects Confront Poverty

THE QUESTION
Which architects, individuals, or institutions have made an effort to improve the living, working, education, and recreation places for the poor and underserved in your community?

In the fall of 1968, together with a dozen classmates from Columbia University's School of Architecture (New York, U.S.A.), I went off to New York's East Harlem neighborhood to spend a semester with the Real Great Society (RGS) Urban Planning Studio. RGS was a grass-roots organization working to hold together a distressed neighborhood by challenging urban renewal plans and offering innovative approaches to housing and community services. For many of us it was a transformative experience. We realized that architecture was, on its own, incapable of transforming life in low-income communities; that poverty was more powerful than architecture. The underlying issue was not the built manifestation of poverty but the residents' lack of access to political and economic power.

Notwithstanding this sobering experience, or perhaps because of it, many of us sought to use our professional training as architects to confront poverty. Mossik Hacobian served for twenty years as the executive director of a leading community development corporation in Boston. Bruce Dale was vice-president of a non-profit bank that financed the rehabilitation of moderate-income housing in the Bronx and Harlem. I have devoted my career in education to probing architecture's social dimension, an orientation introduced to us during our first year in school by critics Peter Prangnell and Ray Lifchez, founder of the Berkeley Prize. The 60s generation of activists gave rise to advocacy organizations like Architecture 2001 in Pittsburgh, the Pratt Center in Brooklyn, Urban Field Service at Harvard, and Urban Deadline in New York.

I cite this personal history because the notion of using architecture to confront poverty does not immediately leap to mind as a winning proposition. Why would someone take on this intractable problem? If the underlying issue lies beyond the power of architecture to transform, why do we keep at it? In part we persevere because architecture is, after all, an inherently optimistic profession. But mostly it is because we understand architecture to be a social art, a contingent practice whose work is embedded in and implicated by its social, political and economic context.

Recent years have seen a welcome rise in attention to what might be called architecture's social vocation. Starting with Architecture for Humanity, founded by Cameron Sinclair and Kate Stohr in 1999, a number of organizations have marshalled resources to improve communities through design. These efforts intensified and multiplied in response to a series of natural disasters, notably the Indian Ocean tsunami in 2004 and Hurricane Katrina in 2005. Many architects enlisted their talents in humanitarian rebuilding projects. Schools devoted design-build studios to reconstruction efforts. Professionals launched initiatives like the Gulf Coast Community Design studio in Biloxi, Mississippi. A more general call to service was issued by Public Architecture's 1% pro bono program, started in San Francisco in 2005.

For the most part these humanitarian efforts are ameliorative; that is, they alleviate immediate crises and provide beneficial amenities for communities in need. At the same time, they are generally short-term interventions that do not attack the underlying structures of poverty that render these hard-hit communities so vulnerable to begin with. No less a personage than Frank Lloyd Wright, whose Usonian house was an effort to extend the benefits of good design (in this case, his own) to a broader segment of the community, acknowledged the limitations of ameliorative efforts. "Beneficial though some of the attention is," he wrote, "'housing'" by our government can only practice putting off, by mitigation of a daily horror, the day of actual regeneration for the poor." (Wright, p. 161)

So how can architecture contend with the strictures of poverty beyond humanitarian and ameliorative relief? One starting point is programmatic. Because poverty equates most directly with the inability to earn a living wage, architecture that facilitates revenue-producing activity is particularly relevant. For example, the first large social housing complex in England, the Boundary Street Estate opened by the London County Council in 1899, provided workshops behind the flats to assist residents in providing for themselves. Located in the East End garment district, the workshops were occupied initially by upholsterers and furniture makers. In France, architect Lucien Kroll included detached workshops as part of his renovation of the housing estate of Perseigne near Alençon, completed in the 1970s.

Two California architects, Pyatok Architects and Estudio Teddy Cruz, have developed innovative residential designs that include work space for revenue-generating activity as well as social services. Pyatok has designed houses that anticipate the transformation of ground floor space to accommodate workshops or retail

Boundary Street Estate Workshops, London County Council, 1899.

(Photo: provided by Anthony Schuman)

Workshops, Perseigne Housing Estate, Alençon, France, Lucien Kroll, Architect, 1979

(Photo: provided by Anthony Schuman)

activity, and larger housing projects that include space for street vendors and indoor vendor halls. Cruz's housing and neighborhood plans for Casa Familiar, slowly unfolding in San Ysidro, a suburb of San Diego on the Mexican border, incorporate workplace, educational and social services in an incremental open weave that supports informal economies and social organization.

Historically, in addition to providing workplaces, social housing developments have often comprised educational and social service facilities to offer a setting for constant education, cultural development, and collective action. The great modern housing estates of the 1920s in the Netherlands, Germany and Vienna typically included kindergartens, libraries, senior centers, and allotment gardens along with public meeting rooms. In the United States, starting with the Amalgamated Dwellings in New York in the 1927, a series of limited-equity, cooperative housing developments built by a union-sponsored non-profit offered many such amenities. The limited-equity ownership form, moreover, offered the possibility of homeownership for working class families.

Harlem River Houses, built in the 1930s among the first public housing projects in the United States, opened a two-room library on site in 1955. The smallest of New York City's branch libraries, it remains in operation. In the 1990s, David Burney, then director of the Design and Capital Improvement Division of the New York City Housing Authority, oversaw an ambitious program that engaged talented young architects to design or renovate over a hundred youth and senior facilities in public housing projects.

Architecture is often described as a collaborative effort, starting with the project team within the office and a network of professional consultants and extending to include the client, funder, builder, and public officials. When it comes to confronting poverty, however, there is no commissioning client and often no building at all. Here, the necessary collaboration is more likely to be with grass-roots initiatives, linking architects with on the-ground knowledge, experience, and determination. A recent exhibition: *Cities*, mounted by the Cooper-Hewitt Design Museum in 2012, presented sixty projects from forty countries that combine grass-roots input with professional support. *(See "Noted Articles" below.)*

The projects include street vendor carts in South Africa, mobile phone apps (for health education and wire funds transfer) in Uganda and Kenya, floating life-boats (schools, libraries and clinics) in Bangladesh, new social space constructed along with hard infrastructure in Caracas, grassroots mapping in Lima and Nairobi and micro-lending and savings schemes fostered by Slum Dwellers International in several Indian cities.

A recent volume entitled *The Architecture of Change: Building a Better World* is explicit in linking design efforts with grass-roots activism aimed at challenging the status quo in defense of working class communities. A compendium of articles from *Designer/Builder* magazine, the chapters document street furniture and grocery vans in West Oakland, a hip-hop high school in St. Paul, a children's playground in Thailand, housing construction in Afghanistan, and design/build in Mexico. The heroes of these stories are not the architects, planners and landscape architects who figure in many of them, but the larger community efforts of which they are part. Yes, part of the goal is always to improve communities through better design, but the ultimate goal is to improve them through better lives. As French philosopher Michel Foucault observed, "(Architecture) can and does produce positive effects when the liberating intentions of the architects coincide with the real practice of people in the exercise of their freedom." (1)

So as you approach your essay research this year, ask yourself how the work you examine represents a form of solidarity between the architect and communities in need. How is the work linked to a broader effort that aims at helping people rise out of poverty and challenges the way in which poverty is etched into the physical landscape in terms of race and class? What is the architect's understanding of her or his agency in the process of social change? The scope of the intervention may be modest, in both physical and social terms, but the catalytic potential may be vast!

REFERENCES

(1) Foucault, Michel. "Space, Knowledge and Power, in Paul Rabinow, ed. The Foucault Reader (New York: Pantheon Books, 1985), 245-56.

NOTED BOOKS

Hammett, Jerilou & Maggie Wrigley, eds. The Architecture of Change: Building a Better World (Albuquerque: University of New Mexico Press, 2013).

Smith, Cynthia E. et al. Design with the Other 90%: Cities (New York: Cooper Hewitt National Design Museum, Smithsonian Institution, 2011).

Wright, Frank Lloyd. *The Living City* (New York: New American Library, 1958).

NOTED ARTICLES

Schuman, Tony. Review of "The Architecture of Change: Building a Better World", Jerilou Hammett & Maggie Wrigley, eds., in *Progressive Planning* magazine, No. 198, Winter 2014.

Schuman, Anthony. Review of "Design with the Other 90%: Cities" exhibit at Cooper-Hewitt National Design Museum, in *Journal of Architectural Historians* 72, no. 1(March 2013), 98-104.

Anthony W. (Tony) Schuman is Associate Professor of Architecture at the New Jersey Institute of Technology, in Newark, New Jersey, U.S.A., where he is active in preservation and neighborhood development efforts. He is a past President of the Association of Collegiate Schools of Architecture and the New York City chapter of Architects / Designers / Planners for Social Responsibility (ADPSR) and was a founding member of several advocacy and activist organizations in architecture. Schuman's writing on architecture's social vocation appears in fifteen books and a number of academic and professional journals.

BP2014
Daniel Iacofano and Benjamin Clavan

THE TOPIC
The Architect and the Healthful Environment

THE QUESTION
HOW DO YOU DESIGN A HEALTHFUL ENVIRONMENT?

In your city, find a building or a public place that helps create a healthful environment. Describe the features of the healthful environment that you admire and why. Tell us what you believe the architect did specifically to make the healthful environment work as it does.

Then find a building or a public place that offers an unhealthful environment. Describe the features of the unhealthful environment that you do not admire and why. As an architect, describe specifically what you would have done differently, including working with what governmental and civic resources to Improve the situation.

Tell us what you have learned by this comparative analysis.

Either / Or?

This year the Berkeley Prize invites you to address this seemingly simple, but actually very complex question: *How can architecture—and architects—help create a more healthful environment?* Fortunately, there is very little grey area in creating healthful environments. There are two choices:

(I)

At their best, environments inspire, empower, and encourage. They stimulate the awareness of the movement of our bodies, engender sociability, and enable access to fresh foods, all of which support population health and prevent disease. The architecture of settlements, landscapes, buildings, and interiors is also sensual, influencing our physical, social and emotional health—be it for good or ill.

(II)

At their worst, environments depress, restrict, isolate, subjugate, demoralize, create stress, and discriminate, all of which increase levels of disease-causing hormones due to environmental pressure and anxiety (or what traditional practitioners call bad *Feng Shui*). They also increase contagion and contaminate the body with toxins as we breathe, drink and eat—all of which undermine health on individual and societal levels.

These two opening alternatives are found front and center in literature from the EDRA 44 conference, *Healthy + Healing Places* that took place in late May 2013 in Providence, Rhode Island, U.S.A. EDRA, the international Environmental Design Research Association, to which this year's Berkeley Prize is dedicated, is an interdisciplinary organization founded in 1968 by design professionals, social scientists, students, educators, and facility managers. Celebrating more than 40 years of research-based innovations, EDRA exists to advance and disseminate environmental design research. The organization's wide-ranging activities, bring focus to social issues—like health policy—in environmental design. This research improves our understanding of the inter-relationships of people with their built and natural surroundings toward creation and documentation of environments responsive to human needs.

At the same time, EDRA's goals are fully based on historical precedent. The connections between environment and human health have long been understood.

For instance, Vitruvius, the famous architect and city planner during Roman times, wrote about the need for cities to provide its inhabitants with fresh air, sunlight, clean water, and good sanitation. The result was features and attributes which placed many Roman towns and settlements well ahead of their times. You can also trace growing public health efforts at the urban scale from the Middle Ages through the Renaissance, and then during the 18th and 19th century's Industrial Revolution and into modern times.

Fortunately, after a long period of seeming separation from its public health roots and because of organizations like EDRA, modern city planning and building is now re-establishing and becoming more visible in its concerns with creating healthy environments. Likewise, the design of offices is becoming more domestic in an attempt to replicate the comfort of home. And, at home, the best houses of today reflect the attempt to understand and respond to specific environmental behavior on a much more personal level.

Conclusion? Human health thus becomes a lens for examining all aspects of the built environment and how architectural and urban design can support human development.

What does the human organism require in order to be healthy? The answer is multi-faceted:

- We require healthy and nutritious food, and safe and secure places to live, work and play.
- We need an environment free of toxins with clean land, air, and water.
- We want economic opportunity and quality wage jobs to provide for ourselves and our families.
- We crave the healing power of plants and trees and other living things to enrich our lives.
- We celebrate life and creative expression through art, music, and culture.
- We search for meaning in our very existence and for the chance to make meaningful contributions to the world we inhabit.

Healing requires above all environments that do no harm. While we typically think of a "caregiver" in terms of a healthcare provider, it is also the architect's responsibility to provide "care" and help restore health and promote recuperation. Buildings can go a long way to prevent disease by averting the spread of infections or accidents. In therapeutic terms, environments can support caregivers' activities at every step of the process, greatly expanding their power to heal. The physical environment can comfort patients, strengthen their physical and emotional condition, provide hope, and alleviate fear.

Healthful design is not limited to helping to prevent disease or to helping cure illness. Access to nature that is integrated with the buildings and places we design is one of the easiest and most visible ways to promote healthfulness. On a regional scale, towns and cities that are separated by a green prove to be more healthful with regard to public health issues. The British garden cities of the early 1900s showed this. Today, those lessons are emulated, in part, by communities designed according to the principles of the New Urbanism.

But on the intimate scale, designing the perfect window seat—a captivating view, just the right amount of light and without glare, an environment not too hot nor too cold, a comfortable chair or cushion to settle into, a surface to conveniently set a drink, a place overall that beckons you to sit without being disturbed for a while—is also the design of a healthful environment.

As you are researching this year's question, try to do two things:

- Imagine, on the one hand, a public place or an office building or home designed to foster both healthy everyday interactions and vigorous, but friendly debate; familial interchange and private contemplation—places where the architecture, based on the skillful resolution of situations and settings, promotes rather than discourages health.
- Imagine, on the other hand, the self-conscious architecture of confrontation where the driving motivation is the sculptural appearance and the intent is to challenge rather than resolve—places no less creative than designing for health, but often creating barriers to individual and public health.

Is either/or really a choice?

Daniel Iacofano, Ph.D., FAICP, founding principal of MIG, Inc., Berkeley, California, U.S.A., has over 25 years of experience in urban planning and community design, specifically for downtowns, transit-oriented development, neighborhoods and urban centers. He is nationally recognized as an expert and innovator in the areas of community participation, consensus building, and facilitation.

Benjamin Clavan, Ph.D., AIA, the Berkeley Prize competition and website coordinator, is Principal of Benjamin Clavan, Architect, AIA, Los Angeles, California, U.S.A., a classic atelier design firm with over 30 years of on-the-ground and advanced research experience providing highly personalized services for a wide range of select residential, commercial, landscape, and interiors projects.

BP2012
John Cary

Reflections on Architecture, Community, & Writing

In the aftermath of Hurricanes Katrina and Rita, which devastated the US Gulf Coast in 2005, a woman named Martha Murphy managed to charge her cell phone in a car cigarette lighter and summon help. Her first call was to an unlikely destination: the New York firm of SHoP Architects. The town of Pass Christian, Mississippi, had been hit hard—effectively wiped off the map, with 100% of its business and eight out of every 10 homes destroyed. "The first thing I realized after the storm," Murphy explained, "is that a community is not its buildings; a community is something different and more." But, she continued, "Our world was down, and it seemed incredibly important to see something go up. To be a community, we needed a structure; we needed a place to gather."

Whether we're talking about the extraordinary community center that SHoP ultimately designed in Mississippi, the celebrated "Birds Nest" designed by Herzog & de Meuron for the Beijing Olympics, or a humble thatch-roofed hut in a far more remote corner of the world, architecture is, at its core, a place to gather. This simple function is rarely without its challenges as fostering a sense of inclusion almost inevitably excludes some populations, whether intentionally or not. The challenge of this year's Berkeley Prize essay competition is thus a matter of distinguishing architecture that excites alone, with architecture that inspires and serves. Architecture for the public good, after all, must do both.

Architecture can be a beacon of hope and symbol of renewed prosperity in thriving and struggling communities alike. As author and philosopher Alain de Botton, whose 2006 book *The Architecture of Happiness* received world-wide attention, has so eloquently explained, we are, "...for better or worse, different people in different places. Architecture's task is to render vivid to us who we might ideally be."

On a Rwandan hillside, overlooking a valley at once lush and bone dry, stands a building that in so many ways embodies what architecture can and should be. A dignifying place to gather and to heal, the Butaro Hospital was designed by Harvard University students who graduated just months ago to focus fulltime on MASS, shorthand for a Model for Architecture Serving Society. The hospital they designed for the people of Rwanda, through the nonprofit Partners in Health, opened earlier this year, bringing state-of-the-art healthcare to a district of nearly 400,000 people where little care had been available previously. Beyond its beautifully crafted stone walls and spacious patient wards, the hospital is at its core a community space.

THE TOPIC
Architecture for the Public Good

THE QUESTION
Find a building in your community that serves the public—or a special population—and that you believe is particularly well-designed. Who was the architect? What is the purpose of the building? Who does it serve? Why do you think it works so well? How have all of these factors contributed to its unique public significance?

Butaro Hospital, Butara, Burera District, Rwanda; Architects: MASS Design Group, Boston, U.S.A.,2011.

(Photo: Amakuru, 2012: originally posted to Flickr, uploaded to Wikimedia Commons-Creative Commons Attribution 2.0)

Elsewhere around the world are equally inspiring spaces that serve. In Cambodia, the Sra Pou Vocational School by Finnish architects Rudanko + Kankkunen is filled with children and bright accent colors between meticulously laid clay bricks. In South Africa, the Mapungubwe Interpretation Center, designed by architect Peter Rich and built by local craftspeople, while distinguished with extraordinary vaults designed by former Berkeley Prize Juror, MIT Professor, and MacArthur Fellow John Ochsendorf, is nearly one with the landscape.

It is easy to fall in love with these unlikely examples of architecture in even less likely places, while chastising high-budget buildings by the usual suspect starchitects of our time. Yet each building deserves a more nuanced view. Nowhere is this more apparent than in Philip Jodidio's book, *Public Architecture Now!*, showcasing projects by a who's who of architects. Jodidio takes us first to France, where we see Jean Nouvel's gleaming, snow white public pool complex, Les Bains des Docks, and then to Taiwan, to see Toyo Ito's 2009 World Games Stadium, among dozens of other projects. Each exemplifies good design—even high design—aimed at serving the public, though never without challenges.

In his landmark book published by Metropolitan Books in 2007, *Better: A Surgeon's Notes on Performance*, author and doctor Atul Gawande offers some advice to those in his chosen field of medicine, but also to professionals of any kind, including architecture and design: "The published word is a declaration of membership in a community and also of a willingness to contribute something meaningful to it." Whether your Berkeley Prize essay proposal constitutes the first 500 words you've ever written, or you are already a true believer in the power of the pen, it matters. Writing is a way of expressing yourself, your observations of your community, and your values—as architects and designers, as well as citizens of the world.

While architecture education worldwide routinely honors students that keep their nose to the grindstone, working day and night in studio, this year's Berkeley Prize is an invitation to look up, walk outside your school, across campus, and deep into your community. It sounds like a simple challenge, but it can be equally exhilarating and terrifying. Like writing, truly taking part in the world around us is a sorely understated and even discouraged aspect of architectural education and practice. This competition call very well may be the first time you do so. It's an opportunity to really see and listen to a place as well as the people occupying it. The more you look and listen, the more you will learn and understand about whatever space ultimately captures your interest. Nowhere in this essay or on this website will you receive marching orders for where to look or who to talk to; that's for you to figure out and share.

We learned the harrowing details of Martha Murphy's fateful call to SHoP Architects in those hours after the hurricane by asking her. We cannot help but be captivated by the story of the Butaro Hospital as we listen to the designers who lived and worked on the site for months on end recount their first impressions, how they were received, and who they met. Both are tales about the power of architecture and design; and they are tales comprised as much of words as of glass, steel, stone, and wood.

And therein lies the power of writing and the beauty of the Berkeley Prize essay competition. In that spirit, we invite you to contribute your voice and your observations of a space or place in your community that truly represents architecture for the public good—for you, and for others.

John Cary is editor of *PublicInterestDesign.org* and author of *The Power of Pro Bono: 40 Stories about Design for the Public Good by Architects and Their Clients* (Metropolis Books, 2010). John is an Emeritus Member of the Berkeley Prize Committee.

BP2011
Part I: Paul Broches

THE TOPIC
Valuing the Sacred

THE QUESTION
What is a sacred space? Historically, certain buildings have served as sacred places for meditation, to celebrate a religious ritual, or simply to take refuge from the pressures of everyday life. Select a place, location, or setting in your community or your local environment that you personally believe to be sacred, but that has as yet not been widely accepted as important in this way. Tell us why it is sacred. What community resources are needed to ensure its preservation? What, if any, architectural intervention do you believe is appropriate to memorialize its special nature?

Two Observations on Sacred Space

The images in this brief photo essay were among observations made during two trips to India in 2007 and 2008. In my travels through Rajasthan, Tamil Nadu, and Kerala, I saw remarkable, religious architecture, Hindu and Muslim, imbued with serene and sensual religious content. I did not expect the secular architecture and the urban and rural landscapes also to be deeply rooted in the sacred realm. I wanted to "deconstruct" these places to better understand to what extent it was religious tradition and to what extent it was the force of human commonality that made the space sacred.

As I traveled through Rajasthan and the southern states, I frequently encountered sacred space. It was not necessarily a physical place that I could explain, but when I entered it, I knew. I can only reason that it is a state of mind that informs us as it informs the builders, often unknown, who create them.

The sacred and the sublime do not know international borders, religions, cultures. Of course, it is all of these that create the context for sacred space. Once attuned to my understanding—my version—of sacred spaces, I discovered them in random places: at the water's edge, in the marketplace, village square, in the fields, under a tree. Where do we find sacred places in the unique worlds that each of us inhabit?

Paul Broches is Principal at Mitchell Giurgola Architects, New York, New York, U.S.A. Founded in Philadelphia, Pennsylvania, U.S.A. in 1958, the firm's work has been recognized nationally and internationally. Paul is a Fellow in the American Institute of Architects (AIA) and a member of the Board of the International Architects Designers and Planners for Social Responsibility. He is a member of the Berkeley Prize Committee.

EXPLORE!

See the full portfolio of Paul Broches photographs from India

"Sacred space is...where awe turns our spirit."

(Photo: Paul Broches)

Tongariki ceremonial center, Rapa Nui (Easter Island),1000-1600 CE.

(Photo: Daves Rossell, 2024)

Part II: Daves Rossell

Josef Olbrich hoped "to erect a temple of art which would offer the art-lover a quiet, elegant place of refuge." (1) So began the construction of an icon of early modern architecture, *ver sacrum*, the sacred spring, the Secession Exhibition Building of 1897–98 in Vienna, Austria. The ancient Greek poet Pindar called the Altar to the Twelve Gods erected in the Athenian Agora in 522 BCE, "the omphalos (navel) of the city, much trodden, fragrant with incense." (2) It was a simple enclosure of posts and panels among many grander structures, but it served as a place of asylum for refugees and the point from which all distances from Athens were measured.

UNESCO lists over 900 sites around the world as having outstanding cultural or natural importance to the common heritage of humanity, holding them sacred to world heritage. But whereas some sacredness can be universally acclaimed for all peoples and all times, other sacred places are more particular and unique and special to one or a few. It's likely that the place that is special to you—in which you can be calm, where you go in times of stress—is probably not on the World Heritage list but addresses similar fundamental needs.

The need for someplace sacred is so clear. There are so many irritations and plights in life. First comes the buzz of the fly, the rattle of the dryer, the distant *clink, clink, clink*, the dull hum. There are so many headlines in so many magazines. Papers pile up. We are subject to incessant interfacing, constant connectivity. Everyone is texting. What is it that makes us so anxious? Is it the heat? Is it the cold? Is it the draft? Is it the still? Are we dirty and need a place to wash our feet? Are we surrounded by too much cleanliness and need some honest dirt? Life can be so busy and hectic and yet we can be so restrained and ineffective. Life can be so exciting looking and yet so boring and redundant in actuality. We need something real. There is such a thick multi-layered range of events and actions and yet wherever we go we run into a wall. We need some relief. And life can have such sadness. We need to express our sorrow and pay our respects.[...]

Consider some possible solutions to salve our wounds: the overnight cabin on a hike, a floating dock on a lake, a lull in the storm, the café, the covered bench. The recovery place provides solace, community and guidance. The sanctuary is a place where guns are not allowed. The organic farm is a place where one cannot get poisoned. The safety-crossing is a place where one cannot get run over. The school room is a place where one cannot remain ignorant. We close the door to our room. We say these trees cannot be cut. And each of these is equally a point of celebration.

Sacred can certainly mean spiritually divine, but it might just mean quiet. The telephone booth used to be a place where one could go and sit and close a folding door and be in a separate space, private and alone. We didn't have to use the phone. But today we live in a wireless maelstrom inundating us with connection to everything everywhere. According to Matt Richtel, who has been writing a series of articles on technology and attention for the *New York Times*, "In 2008, people consumed three times as much information each day as they did in 1960. And they are constantly shifting their attention. Computer users at work change windows or check e-mail or other programs nearly 37 times an hour." Richtel quoted Adam Gazzaley, a neuroscientist at the University of California, San Francisco, saying, "the nonstop interactivity is one of the most significant shifts ever in the human environment." (3) Quiet is an aural peace, but also a positive sign of inactivity, and thus rest and respite, a time to recharge perhaps, or simply to be in a pure unadulterated way.

Sacred usually implies considerable investment of meaning, but it can also just be an undisturbed place. Some boundary separates the outside from the inside. The thick stone walls of a Cistercian monastery like the earthwork ring and ditch that began Stonehenge provided enclosure, reinforcement, edge.[...]

Of course, the essence of a place is the space itself, and a sacred place is divine. The physical structure is something, but it is always secondary to the spirit invoked. Sacred places are sacred in part because their use and meaning transcends the particularities of any architectural detailing present. And that is such a struggle to respect. It is the divine that separates the sacred from the profane. Lao Tzu, the reputed founder of Taoism would have none of it, saying,

"Those who would take over the earth
And shape it to their will
Never, I notice, succeed.
The earth is like a vessel so sacred
That at the mere approach of the profane
It is marred
And when they reach out their fingers it is gone." (5)

But most would agree that sacredness exists on many levels in many places, shaped by humans and not. Tadao Ando the modernist admitted as much when he explained how he has forever tried to design in a traditional Japanese manner, "I prefer to deal not in the actual forms themselves, but in their spirits and emotional contents."(6) What is the tradition you seek to preserve? How is the space appropriate? Is the actual architecture helping or hindering the expression?

NOTES

(1) Carl E. Schorske, Fin-de-Siècle Vienna: Politics and Culture (New York: Vintage Books, 1981), 217.

(2) R. E. Wycherley, The Stones of Athens (Princeton: Princeton University Press, 1978), 33.

(3) Matt Richtel, "Attached to Technology and Paying a Price," The New York Times 6 June 2010, available online at http://www.nytimes.com/2010/06/07/technology/07brain.html?ref=technology

(4) (This footnote and the quotation to which it applies appears in the full text.)

(5) Lao Tzu, The Way of Life According to Lao Tzu, translated by Witter Bynner (New York: Capricorn Books, 1962), 43.

(6) Tadao Ando, "From Self-Enclosed Modern Architecture Towards Universality," in Tadao Ando: Buildings, Projects and Writings, ed. Kenneth Frampton (New York: Rizzoli, 1984), 140.

E.G. Daves Rossell, Ph.D. is a Professor of architectural history at the Savannah College of Art and Design, Savannah, Georgia, U.S.A. where he has taught since 1997. His department hosted the 7th Savannah Symposium on *The Spirituality of Place* in 2011. Daves is a Director of the interdisciplinary, North-American Vernacular Architecture Forum (VAF). He is a member of the Berkeley Prize Committee.

EXPLORE!

Read the complete introduction here.

BP2009
Part I: Alonzo C. Addison

THE TOPIC
Sustainable Architecture / Traditional Wisdom

THE QUESTION
How could a lost social tradition in your culture, once elegantly expressed through sustainable architectural design or building practices, be revived and why should it be?

Learning from Tradition in a Disappearing World

We live in a disappearing world. Irreplaceable sources of life and inspiration, heritage—from the pyramids of Giza to Darwin's Galapagos, and the temples of Angkor to the migration of the Serengeti—is under siege today. While the "global village" has brought untold benefits, as we have sped down the superhighway of change, much has been left at the wayside. Our heritage—from intangible traditions to great monuments and pristine wilderness—is being challenged by the pace of progress. Long before "globalization" was a household term or the internet had linked us all, the nations of the world joined together to identify and try to safeguard the earth's most outstanding and extraordinary places.

Exactly one hundred years after the "setting apart" in 1872 of the world's first National Park at Yellowstone "for the enjoyment of all," ideas of preservation came together at UNESCO in a unique international legal instrument to protect and conserve heritage sites of "outstanding universal value." Ratified by 185 nations, the 1972 "World Heritage Convention" today protects 878 cultural and natural sites in 145 countries, and notably recognizes that they are part of a heritage of all mankind, that their protection is our shared responsibility, and that they are held in trust for this and future generations. As the world's only treaty encompassing both natural and cultural heritage, the convention represents a unique and powerful link between culture, monuments, archaeological sites, biological diversity, endangered and migratory species, wetlands, and climate change.

Despite international protection efforts, many of these great sites are sadly under threat today. As detailed in the book I authored, *Disappearing World: 101 of the Earth's Most Extraordinary and Endangered Places*, threats range from conflict, to theft, development, unsustainable tourism, pollution, disasters, constraints (limited resources), changing uses, invasive species, and climate change. In architecture especially, time-honored methods have in recent decades been abandoned for newer, lower cost but less sustainable building and planning paradigms.

Yet there is hope. By understanding how our actions affect our heritage, we can reduce our impact. For example, polluting farm runoff and cruise ship trash is damaging the Belize Barrier Reef Reserve System, while relief efforts after the 2004 Asian Tsunami have added to the stripping of the Tropical Rainforest Heritage of Sumatra. Unregulated and unthoughtful development, be it sprawl surrounding Memphis and its Necropolis—the Pyramid Fields from Giza to Dahshur outside Cairo, Egypt or plans for a concrete highway bridge across the widest point of the Dresden Elbe Valley, is something design and planning professionals can help reduce. In our global village, the actions of some can impact

Angkor, Cambodia: UNESCO World Heritage Site

(Above) Lone monk at the water's edge before the crowds arrive.

(Below) Teaching about restoration and conservation at Angkor.

(Photos: Alonzo C. Addison, 2017)

many: from Hemingway's now vanishing "snows" of Kilimanjaro National Park to the encroaching desert threatening the Ancient Ksour of Ouadane, Chinguetti, Tichitt, and Oualata, climate change is having a dramatic impact.

By identifying the intrinsic values of these places, we can help them live on. Often in the heritage of others are lessons for us all: Great monuments and cities may reveal long-forgotten techniques and practices that can efficiently address modern challenges. Abandoned during a government cleanup half a century ago, the several-thousand-year-old, naturally-cooled, rock-hewn cathedrals of The Sassi and the Park of the Rupestrian Churches of Matera are slowly recovering as residents move back and rediscover their efficiency and sustainability.

Although largely destroyed in a 2003 earthquake, Bam and its Cultural Landscape in Iran show the beauty and efficiency of earthen architecture in a hot climate. From the ingenious Aflaj Irrigation Systems of Oman to the 800-year-old communal housing of the Fujian Tulou in China or wondrous carved city and water works of hidden Petra in Jordan, or efficient hillside utilization of the Historic Quarter of the Seaport City of Valparaíso, Chile, our predecessors have much to teach us.

As you embark on this year's Berkeley Prize Competition, I encourage you to learn more about our collective World Heritage and to seek lessons from it. Hopefully you will find examples and inspiration to help you bring sustainable solutions to the challenges we all face in building a better planet. Together, we can save these great places so they live on to educate and enrich the lives of future generations.

Alonzo C. Addison currently serves as Special Advisor to the Director of the United Nations Educational Scientific and Cultural Organization World Heritage Centre, guiding technology deployment in the heritage arena. He founded the University of California at Berkeley's Center for Design Visualization and in the early 1990s helped create the first high-accuracy long-range 3D laser scanner as Vice President of Cyra Technologies (now Leica Geosystems). Addison was one of the two CED researchers who proposed and enabled the transformation of the early Berkeley Prize into an online essay competition (see *Part 1—A Starting Point* above).

Part II: Chuck Davis, FAIA

Commitment to Sustainable Design

Sustainable design practices are engrained in the philosophy of EHDD Architecture and date back to our founder, Joseph Esherick's, (long-time CED Professor and one of the three architects for the CED's Bauer Wurster Hall) careful day-lighting and solar analyses done for the firm's residential designs of the 1950s. This philosophy evolved in the 1960s with the detailed site studies of The Sea Ranch along California's Mendocino Coast—a second home community that came to epitomize the term living lightly on the land.

Joe also initiated the Building Sciences Program at the University of California, Berkeley, a leading center for the development of sustainable technology. As a firm, we continue to lead in the advancement of high-performance buildings by applying four promising sustainable design practices: energy efficiency, appropriate allocation of resources, indoor environmental quality, and storm-water management, along with research in alternative materials, Design for Deconstruction (DfD), and zero-carbon buildings.

We believe that sustainable buildings should simply be better buildings—more inviting and comfortable to live and work in, able to enhance our daily lives, and more innovative and inspiring in their design. We also believe that the sustainable design approach should clearly reflect the specific vision and mission of each client and project.

Our design for the Audubon Center at Debs Park in Los Angeles became the first LEED® Platinum-certified project in the United States. The Center embodies the Audubon Society's environmental ideals, modeling sustainable design to the surrounding community and serving as prototype for future Audubon centers. An American Institute of Architects Top Ten Green Building award-winner, the Department of Global Ecology for the Carnegie Institution for Science at Stanford University is a highly energy-efficient building that harvests sunlight, catches and reuses rainwater, uses radiant slab heating and cooling, and uses a number of other sustainable design strategies to express the department's core goals. At Chartwell School, also LEED Platinum-certified, we focused on using sustainable strategies that also created a superior learning environment and could be integrated into the curriculum as a teaching tool. These three project examples tell a powerful story about sustainability and the client's vision.

As we struggle to attain higher levels of environmental awareness in our daily lives, we challenge our clients to ensure that their projects meet their fullest potential by supporting a holistic environmental philosophy within their own organizations, beyond the design of the building. It is by empowering clients and users to truly embrace this vision that they will make the ultimate contribution and see the

EHDD is proud to be on the forefront of sustainable design, and we look to a time when more municipalities will write the legislation necessary to promote sustainable design through incentives and partnerships with building departments. We also look to a time when good design and sustainable design will be one and the same, an embodiment of our philosophy.

A Senior Principal at EHDD Architecture, headquartered in San Francisco, California, Chuck Davis has been a key contributor to the firm's remarkable social and environmental design philosophy, practice, and body of work. In 2003, in recognition of his outstanding achievement in architectural design, the American Institute of Architects' California Council awarded Chuck its highest honor, the Maybeck Award.

BP2003
Benjamin Clavan

"Pride of Place in Paris"

"I should passionately like Paris to have a cultural center which would at once be museum and center of creation *(centre de creation)*"
(President of the Republic, Georges Pompidou, 1969)

Between 1972 and 1996 Marc Peitjean photographed each step of the architectural and sociological shock waves accompanying the construction of the Centre Georges Pompidou and the new Horloge district surrounding it.
(From an advertisement for the book, *Metro Rambuteau*)

The success of the Georges Pompidou Centre was as unexpected as it was instantaneous: twenty-five thousand visitors per day.
(*Paris Architecture*, 1900–2000)

THE TOPIC
World Heritage

THE QUESTION
When architects strive to create lasting monuments, some become part of the significant cultural heritage of our age. These successes seem to embody the most socially important values of a city, region, country, or even the world. Other attempts are only the reflection of the vanity of the designer or client and pass into oblivion. Worse, they become a permanent blight on the environment. As an architect, specifically, how can your work simultaneously embody the social values of one place, a particular culture, and universal human concerns?

The images are as dramatic as the story of its development. A six-story, 90,000-square-meter megastructure, with open floors 50 m by 170 m in size. A rectangular metal and glass box draped externally on the "street" side by brightly colored vertical ducts, elevator shafts, and stairways; and on the "entry" side, by a glazed escalator tube traveling diagonally up the face of the building. The whole, sitting on one side of a massive new plaza carved out of the traditional tightly packed Paris *quartier* of the Marais. The *Centre National d'Art et de Culture Georges Pompidou*, or as it is familiarly known, the Pompidou, houses the largest collection of modern art in the world–The National Museum of Modern Art, one of the largest public information libraries in France, conference and major performance spaces, children's play areas, two restaurants, and a roof-top terrace overlooking Paris.

This focal point and gathering place is estimated to draw anywhere from 8–9 million visitors per year. The visitors are not all tourists. The library itself has a vast clientele and lines form to use the research facilities. Residents of the surrounding Beauborg district and beyond flock to Place Georges Pompidou and its perimeter cafes to become part of the urban scene. The square itself has become a focus of official Paris activity. It is the site of gatherings, concerts, and all the kinds of impromptu social events that make up the life of a great city.

Controversial at first due to the clash between the high-tech building and its classical 17th century neighborhood, the Pompidou, completed in 1978, quickly became an overwhelming popular success. Perhaps due in part to this success, the building program and the structure quickly became outdated. The building's

Centre Pompidou, Place Georges-Pompidou, Paris, France. Architects Renzo Piano and Richard Rogers, 1977.

(Photo: Benjamin Clavan, 2023)

galleries housing the Museum of Modern Art's permanent collection were remodeled as early as 1986. Just four years later, the Fodor's travel guide to Paris describes a building, like many modern buildings, far down on its luck:

"...it has begun to show its age in no uncertain terms. The much-vaunted, gaudily painted service pipes that snake up the exterior—painted the same colors that were used to identify them on the architects' plans—need continual repainting. The plastic tubing that enclosed the exterior escalators are (sic) cracked and grimy. The skeletal supports in the interior are peeling and dirty."

The entire building was completely retrofitted from 1992–2000. This massive new project re-distributed the interior spaces, provided new interior stairways and elevators, and renovated all of the exposed structure. The Centre Pompidou was ready for the new Millenium. (1)

The two young architects who designed the Pompidou, Italian architect Renzo Piano and English architect Richard Rogers, faced a variety of challenges in creating this special place, and in re-designing it. Explicitly and implicitly, there were a variety of goals:

- The creation of a new arts facility that would offer functions that would appeal to a variety of local and international patrons, including scholars, artists, and lay people seeking cultural events within a communal setting.
- The desire to create a public place that would in some ways complement the public life associated with the nearby centuries-old Les Halles food market, which was recently removed to the outskirts of the city.
- The need in the finished product to complement the cultural heritage of the unique public architecture of Paris.
- The need to situate the building in a way that would serve as a Paris landmark for both local and foreign visitors.
- The desire to identify the entire site as a public place and socially inviting, characteristic of the ubiquitous French *place* and public gardens of which there was numerous precedents in the rich architectural history of Paris.
- The attempt to structure and style the building in such a way as to be innovative, responding to the primacy of innovation that is a hallmark of French art.
- The reinforcement of the French spirit of the public's free access to culture in the building and its open spaces.

The museum type has long been a major cultural event signifying the importance among the French of the arts as cultural patrimony. The transformation of the Palais du Louvre into a public museum starting at the time of the French Revolution is but one example of this particular society placing culture among its top priorities. It is interesting to note that the Centre Pompidou and the Place Georges Pompidou were also a stunning success for then President of the French Republic, Georges Pompidou, who used the project to spur his vision of a grand, totally revitalized cultural landscape for Paris. During the reign of his successor, Francois Mitterand, this vision would result in La Grande Arche; the new Opera; the completion of the Le Grand Louvre with the addition of the Pyramid; the new public park, Science and Industry Museum, and Public Concert Hall (Le grand auditorium de la Cite de la musique) at La Villette; the Grande Galerie de l'Evolution at the National Museum of Natural History; and a variety of other public/private cultural landmarks. Culture is serious business in France. It is to the credit of the designers that the Pompidou was not conceived as merely a reflection of this deep regard for culture and pride of place by adopting some sort of *recherche* historic style or amalgam of styles for the design. Instead, the choice was made to

Waiting to explore...and become part of the story.

(Photo: Abaca Press, 2023, sourced on Alamy)

create something completely new and of the age. My own initial reaction to the Pompidou, which I first visited late in 1980 during a long sojourn in Paris, was at best, mixed. From my journals:

> I drifted yesterday afternoon to the Centre Pompidou, probably this decade's most controversial building. It is certainly as bad as everyone says it is and, perhaps unfortunately, as good. It is an event, as the architects had wished and designed for, and thus is a brilliant tour-de-force. It is also ugly and out-of-place and has destroyed, inexorably destroyed the very fabric of a Paris district. It is that curious mixture of life and death that seems so natural to this city. Pairs is special, a place of a myriad of oppositions, a play on life.

Ten days later, I wrote,

> I spent the afternoon doing research at the library at the Pompidou. The place was mobbed. Crowds waiting just to get on the escalators (the *escalators!*); I did not even bother looking for the elevators... Packs of people everywhere. The place easily sustains such scenes, more like a train station than a museum. Of course, this isn't a museum, is it? It is a Centre, an event, a happening. It works.

The Centre Pompidou as a place is an important example of a contemporary building respecting the cultural heritage of a particular people in a specific setting. It does this while simultaneously addressing the importance of the arts in all of the world's cultures. It is also maddingly confrontational as a work of architecture. Which is to say, it is a work of art that forces you to accept and process contradiction and chaos and make from it a new viable whole? And is this not the true definition of a social architecture?

NOTE

(1) The museum will close for yet another five years starting in 2025 while it undergoes another renovation. The architects, chosen through a competition are a French office founded by Nicolas Moreau and Hiroko Kusunoki, with Mexico City-based Frida Escobedo Studio as associate designer. The selected architects have indicated they plan to collaborate with Renzo Piano, who was also on the new competition jury. (Richard Rogers died in 2021.)

From the Centre Pompidou's website:

(THE PROJECT): "...This cultural project aims to reinvent the original utopia of the Centre Pompidou while responding to the cultural, societal and environmental challenges of the coming years." (THE TECHNICAL PROGRAMME): "...It will notably allow for the renovation and removal of asbestos from all facades, enhanced fire safety, improved accessibility for people with reduced mobility, and optimised energy efficiency for the whole building..."

THE TECHINCAL PROGRAMME: "It will notably allow for the renovation and removal of asbestos from all facades, enhanced fire safety, improved accessibility for people with reduced mobility, and optimised energy efficiency for the whole building."

(https://www.centrepompidou.fr/en/the-centre-pompidou-is-transforming-itself/renovation-programme#26231)

From the Centre's published statement by Moreau Kusunoki, "Lead architect, Principal designer":

"...This renovation offers an opportunity to reconnect with some of the project's founding principles. Four main axes form the basis of the conceptual approach, aimed at transforming this attractive space into one rich in experiences that can meet the expectations of all visitors and staff...: Physical and Visual Porosities...Clarity of Paths...Activation and Requalification of Space... Dialogue with the Existing..."

(https://www.centrepompidou.fr/en/the-centre-pompidou-is-transforming-itself/the-scheduled-reopening)

Benjmain Clavan, Ph.D., is the coordinator for the Berkeley Prize and works as principal for his architectural firm located in Los Angeles, California, U.S.A. and Valencia, Spain. See his full biography in (NOT) THE BACK MATTER.

4

The Students

Researching And Writing

Traveling

Directed Community Service

Initiating Local Competitions

In Practice

IT'S ABOUT THE STUDENTS!

The Essay Prize is at the core of the work of the Berkeley Prize. It has been the entry gate, so to speak, for undergraduate architecture students from around the world to explore subjects typically outside the syllabus of their architecture programs. The essay competition asks the students to investigate on-site and with the people directly involved and affected by the project or projects under consideration. These are often built responses to problematic situations that often not been adequately addressed by architects in the past.

The fact that the students are asked to write about these found projects and issues rather than designing a physical response is deliberate. The prize has wanted to afford students the opportunity to think and write about the problems, issues, and potentials addressed in each prize cycle without being overwhelmed by the myriad of requirements involved with designing a physical structure. Too often these requirements overshadow the actual needs—and desires—of the people who will use the eventually built structure or infrastructure.

There is also a second issue at play here. Since many of the helpful and thoughtful design ideas are based on the work with actual people that is accomplished in the social sciences, thinking and writing about such investigations is of paramount and primary purpose. Sociology, anthropology, psychology, and even archeology, economics, and political science play decisive roles in the creation of places for people. The actual physical manifestation of these studies—the architecture, the buildings—should be the result of these studies, not the precursor to them.

To pursue these aims, each year the Berkeley Prize Committee has selected a topic important to the understanding of the interaction of people and the built world that becomes the focus of that year's prize competitions. The question that is posed is meant to focus the students research related to the specific topic. Students are not asked or recruited to become social scientists. They are asked to begin thinking about how to integrate the findings of the social sciences into their eventual designs for actual physical homes, buildings, and places. Writing about their findings is one way to do this, particularly given the need to communicate with other people—and eventual clients—who are not schooled in three-dimensional thinking, not to mention pervasive and often counter-productive architectural rhetoric.

The quality of the resulting essays, winners or not, is uniformly high. They exhibit a wide diversity and often intriguing responses to the posed question. Even when the students are not able to express themselves in the most elegant English because it is not their native language, there is often great passion for the subject and excitement in the writing. (The Berkeley Prize website maintains a "Reserve" of the top 15 or more essays from each prize cycle that provides the opportunity to read even those that were not selected as winners.)

The essays have been reviewed by at least three and often four selected Berkeley Prize Committee members and a small number of essays, averaging eight or nine, are finally named as finalists. The efforts, as in any competition, are to select the "best-of-the-best" responses to the year's question. The top-scoring—and occasionally other "wild-card" or intriguing essays—are finally forwarded to the year's specially selected jury, chosen because of their unique association and/or first-hand experience with the subject of that year's competition. These jury members determine the overall winners of the competition, normally four in number.

This is an intensive review process involving a lot of organization and procedural safeguards. For instance, no reviewer from a school of architecture should be reading and reviewing an essay by a student in their school. The individual teams of readers should also be balanced as far as possible to include both architectural faculty, practitioners and those representing the social sciences. What started as a small inter-college competition quickly morphed into something much more complicated and rewarding.

The essay extracts included below and the subsequent writings and results from the other linked Berkeley Prize student competitions show, first and foremost, the willingness of students to investigate. They also show that there is an intense desire by the students to go out into the world and learn about the meaning of architecture for those who inhabit and use the structures that the students themselves will design or collaborate on in the future.

At the same time, architecture programs have traditionally not attempted in any formative way to bridge the gap between the academic studio and the ever-present and ever-changing world that people inhabit. A traditional academic design project in the second half of the 20th century would list the objectives and the drawing requirements. These would increase as the student progressed through the entire three-to-five-year program.

A formal visit to the site and, perhaps, to a similar facility or structure to inaugurate the semester's project was not unheard of, but not necessarily part of the program. Lacking any real time information about the potential users of the simulated project, the more curious students would often search the library and architectural publications for examples of previous designs for similar projects. After that, it was all about the student's creativity; the intended users could and, in actual built projects, would have to adjust accordingly.

The creation of Berkeley's College of Environmental Design was a major attempt to change this methodology. The very idea of a college of *environmental* design program was in itself a new approach to the study of architecture. As has been described, the CED brought in social and behavioral scientists to augment the student's curriculum and exposure to the world of people studies. The new curriculum was about asking questions, not looking for formal design approaches. Some of the potential answers were found in deep study of the *timeless way of building*; other answers, in applying the latest breakthroughs in computer-aided research and design.

The bottom line: get students to go out into the world, research on site, listen and ask questions. This is exactly the methodology the Berkeley Prize advocates to architecture schools around the world. The 25 years of the Prize has directly attempted to confront this issue in a variety of ways.

As the Prize matured, additional competitions open specifically to the Semifinalists, have been created to further this exploration. These include the opportunity to travel outside of the student's home country for the purpose of directly investigating the social art of architecture: the Travel Fellowships. Experiments in having students participate in direct, built world-related community service programs; and to mount local social art of architecture competitions were also mounted. In an effort to assess the long-term results of these efforts, the winning students are asked to describe their current professional lives. All of these efforts are described below.

So, yes, it is about the students.
More importantly, it is about the *people*, the users of the built world.

This has been the core of the work of the Berkeley Prize. How the students responded to this truism and apply it to their work is what follows.

NOTE: To reinforce the primary goal of researching, thinking, and writing about architecture, students have been asked to submit only a minimum number of illustrations describing their selected topic as a footnote to their essays. The photographs are a way of confirming the content of the student-selected themes and have not been part of the judging process.

The students have also been required to be submit the photographs at a low resolution. As a result, the images are often of lower quality than would be normally desired. In a number of instances, these images are not adequate for publication. Better quality images or other images of the topics have been sourced online and are added to the essays below to give a better sense of the places described.

Researching and Writing

The students respond to the topics, questions, and prompts.

Some of the Berkeley Prize competition winners.

(Photo: www.BerkeleyPrize.org, montage created by Jessie Canon)

Winning Essay #1

BP2012
First place

THE TOPIC
Architecture for the Public Good

THE QUESTION
Find a building in your community that serves the public or a special population that you believe is particularly well-designed. Who was the architect? What is the purpose of the building? Who does it serve? Why do you think it works so well? How have all these factors contributed to its unique public significance?

WINNER
Loh Kin Kit and Phoaw Yen Shan
(Second year architecture students at National University of Singapore, Singapore)

EXPLORE!

See the complete text on the Berkeley Prize website

The Greatest Public Good is Public Space

Before anything can be built upon reclaimed land, the land must lie fallow for a period of time. This process created a unique situation. For as long as we could remember, there sat a large stretch of reclaimed land that lay across a river from Singapore's city center. Every weekend, we could see from a nearby flyover a lively scene as people gathered there to fish and fly kites on that open field. Nothing could have been stranger than to see this almost rural scene laid out against the backdrop of silver towers gleaming in the distance, a feeling that was even more significant for having happened here in Singapore.

We live in a meticulously planned city. As Chua Beng Huat, a local scholar and author of *Political Legitimacy and Housing: Stakeholding in Singapore* (Routledge, 1997) writes, "Singapore is already a fully conquered island in the imaginary, in that every foot of space is already assigned to a particular use. No space has been left to chance, and even nature has to have the permission of the planning agencies to survive." Such scenes as we remember them begin to take on a rare and unexpected quality. It is heartening to see how a vacant field may find its use even if it has already taken on the life of a building in the projections of the city's planners.

It was only natural that in time, the temporary lease of life for the reclaimed land expired and was replaced instead by a frenzy of construction. As part of the Marina Bay Area, it was a part of a massive project to transform the city center into a waterfront financial hub. But as the construction work commenced, we felt as if something was being lost for good.

It was encouraging then to see the construction in 2008 of the Marina Barrage by Architects Team 3, a local firm with a long history in public buildings. Built as a dam and a "lifestyle hub," the Barrage is a curved concrete ramp that shelters under it the essential equipment for the dam, its *raison d'etre* that has allowed the reclamation of that original scene. Atop the ramp is a vast field looking out toward the sea, on which people from all walks of life may once again enjoy the activities that used to take place there. The quality of the place that emerges, almost as if out of happenstance, is what makes the Marina Barrage different from any other place in Singapore and lends it its unique public significance [...].

But very much aside from fitting into this grand vision for the city, the Barrage is also a piece of architecture that is intended to serve the public. The architects have cleverly integrated the seemingly conflicting requirements of an industrial

Marina Barrage, Singapore: Design Architect: Tierra Design (S) Pte Ltd; Architect: Architects Team 3 Pte Ltd, 2008.

(Photo: RDW Aerial Imaging, 2023, sourced on Alamy)

building and a public space. Traditionally, large pieces of infrastructure have a monumental and monolithic quality derived from the functional and programmatic requirements of assembling the massive equipment needed to sustain the life of a city. This lends it a scale that is very different from the more human proportions that one comes to expect of public spaces.[...]

Perhaps it is the location of the Barrage in close proximity to the city together with its relative inaccessibility and distance from convenient public transport that imbues it with its easy-going and almost idyllic charm, or perhaps it is the attraction of the wind and the views that bring people there. Whatever the case, the Marina Barrage can be said to be a rare example of a truly democratic and inclusive public space in Singapore.[...]

However, one often fails to observe one of the key drivers behind Singapore's rapid urban development—the nation's vast numbers of migrant workers. While the planners at the URA are responsible for the allocation and distribution of land and its functions, the actual realization of these buildings lay in the hands of an army of migrant workers. These construction workers are usually shipped in by the truckload to work at construction sites only to return to their dormitories in the night. Opportunities for leisure are few and far between.[...]

Marina Barrage then begins to hold a particular significance as a public space in our rapidly polarizing nation by remaining as a socially inclusive space. It is only at the Marina Barrage where a confluence of people, who may never meet in everyday life, can congregate to revel at the sights and take part in activities in a shared environment. There is a certain comradeship that comes from being able to look back at the city you live in and call home, even if it is only for a while.[...]

Winning Student Essay #2

To Pride from Prejudice: An Architectural Transition

Architecture has long been a testimony of society. It has shaped not only society's own identity, but that of its so-called "contradictions" as well. While the identity of the "accepted" collective continues to follow the norms and set up new ones, another identity is parallelly configured in the shadows discarded by the norm. The social needs of such individuals, although different, begin to be met outside of the accepted. This in turn links them to an alternate collective that finds solace in shared differences.

Over the years, a wide range of thought-provoking perspectives has been curated in the Berkeley Prize pool of essays. In the larger context of architecture being a social art and facilitator of community engagement, these essays have highlighted ideas and efforts for social upliftment of underprivileged communities across the globe—the homeless, street-children, squatters, slum dwellers, migrants, minority ethnic groups, destitute women, and differently abled.

These explorations have underlined the larger social responsibility for architecture to amend and rehabilitate inequitable approaches plaguing society. Communities have struggled and continue to struggle to live in cultures where being different is not accepted. Architecture has even tried to undo damaging practices in instances where differing communities were forced to accept extinct beliefs or worse, sacrifice their own to be acknowledged.

However, one such "contradiction" of society seems to have missed the attention of Berkeley Essay Prize authors so far. It has also largely been left unaddressed by architecture, especially in India: the third gender.

India's trans community is still struggling to find a voice and faces rampant social stigma. Negative perceptions and ostracism have pushed the community to the fringes of society and dire living conditions. Generally, they eke out a living by singing and performing at people's houses on important social functions such as childbirth and marriage. These are the only occasions when their visits are acceptable in people's houses. At all other times, they are shunned and left to seek the companionship of their like, forcing a close-knit community with practices that are uniquely their own. They endure violence, harassment, and discrimination, both at home and in public spaces, emphasizing that peripheries—even without distinction of social class—spell danger. Navigating this dichotomy is an everyday affair.

This is the situation of the trans community all over the Indian subcontinent. However, what distinguishes the Indian trans community from those in other parts of the world is, ironically, its high social status in ancient Indian society. Vedic literature includes references to a third gender or "third nature"—and recognizes

BP2021
First Place

THE TOPIC
Architects in Service to the Community

THE QUESTION
As a future architect, what is the best way you can serve the needs of your local community?

WINNER
Reva Saksena & Mallika Sarabhai
(Both in the Bachelor of Planning program at the School of Planning and Architecture in Bhopal, India)

EXPLORE!

See the complete text on the Berkeley Prize website

absence of procreative capability of a person as a natural process. In fact, it is so natural that Sanskrit language, apart from the masculine and feminine, has a third gender, the neuter gender or *napunsakalinga*. While Indian society was progressive about the acceptance of transgenders, much changed with the imposition of the Criminal Tribes Act in 1871 by the British. This denied the community basic civil rights and labelled them as "criminals" and their acts "a breach of public decency."

Fortunately, India has recently repealed the draconian law in a series of landmark decisions. The judgement grants legal recognition to the third gender, fundamental and socio-economic rights to all trans citizens and decriminalizes homosexuality among others. The most recent addition to the law has been the Right of Residence and penalties for offences against transgender individuals including denial of right of public passage or use of public places. This opens immense possibilities for architecture to mainstream this marginalized section of society and give shape to its dreams.

The authors have had an opportunity to study the life and living conditions of Indian trans-community in some detail.

The transgenders in India follow a unique set of traditions that have partly been dictated by their historical status and religious beliefs. Most transgender communities live in abject poverty in ghetto-like conditions. Although these

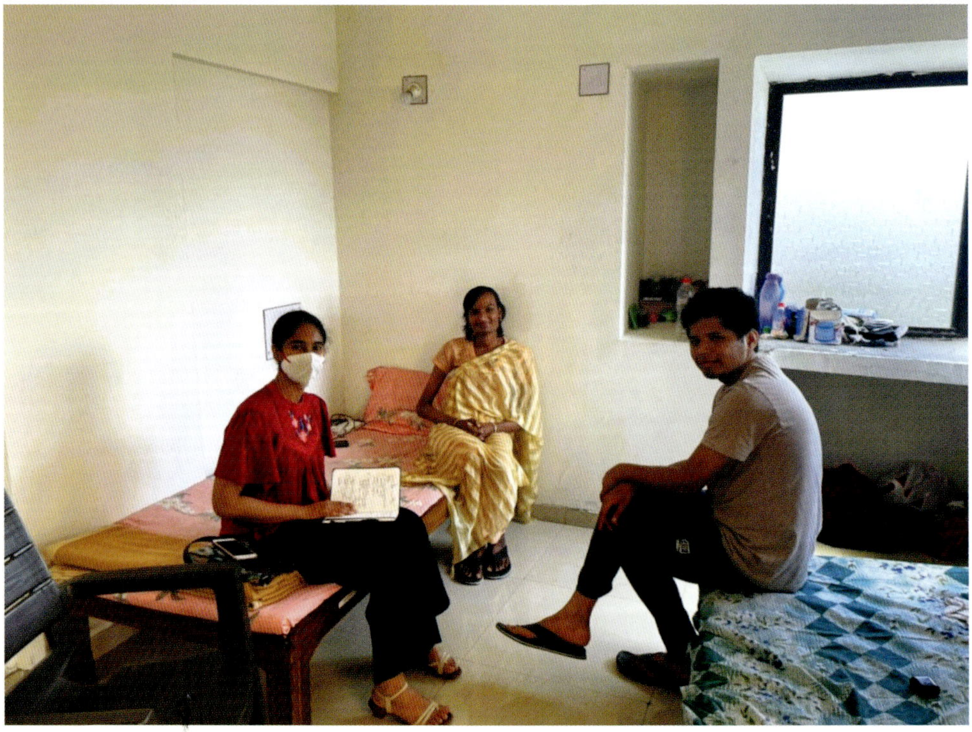

Aided by law, transgender people need not be afraid of shadows anymore. Reva Saksena, (masked) one of the student authors, with the transwomen, Paro (l) and Anshika (r) in a follow-up interview.

(Photo: Tushar Choudhary, 2022)

communities largely exist in urban slums, they are barely visible. By inhabiting spaces discarded by the system, this community has unconsciously generated its own living fabric.[...]

Although the community is close-knit, there exists some social structure. Localities in an urban area are divided, each belonging to a 'Guru'. Every Guru is then responsible for taking care of a community of '*chelas*' or disciples and running their collective accounts, which are used to support the community's daily needs. The 'Guru-Chela parampara' is an ancient Indian tradition. The *chelas* live together with their Guru in a '*Gharana*' or household. This is a rather closed building not more than two stories tall, with an obscure entrance leading to a small courtyard within. Most rooms open into a courtyard. Hardly any windows look outside. A pedestal at one end of the court defines the Guru's place.[...]

Architectural education and awareness can enable us to translate the trans-community's unique customs and requirements—cultural, sociological and economical—into habitable spaces. Architecture can conceive humanitarian solutions that harmonize requirements within inherent constraints and integrate them with practical standards. It has the power to convert abstract into concrete.

The trans-community's specific needs and social requirements on the one hand and the need to encourage their integration in the social mainstream are the dual challenges which an architect is challenged to meet. Aided by new aspirations of the trans-community, yet honoring its social setup, an architect has immense opportunity to evolve quality spaces.[...]

It is granted that Architecture may not directly be able to change social customs or break "accepted" social norms. But it can direct a society, through tangible and intangible cues, to reshape its perceptions of itself. Its very relevance lies in its potential to harness people's ideas that drive interaction and inclusiveness. The architectural expression is completely intertwined with society's aspirations and sensibilities. It holds the key to lead communities to their truest potential by instilling an emotion that may otherwise only be elicited from the self: Pride.

Pride is a complex emotion, as capable of creation as it may be of destruction. If realized collectively, pride may motivate change within a community to

"Transgenders wait for their turn for a dance performance in Calcutta, capital of eastern Indian state West Bengal, April 30, 2013. Several transgender and sex worker associations participated in an awareness program to encourage their acceptance in society."

(Photo: IMAGO Photo Agency, Calcutta, India / Xinhua News Agency, Beijing, China, sourced on Alamy.)

ameliorate its own circumstances. Reinforce confidence. Create opportunities to contribute and become relevant. If a community can truly own a space, engage with it and finally, as an epitome of their existence, take pride in it; that is the ultimate satisfaction for an architect. Trans-community in India is no exception.[...]

Winning Student Essay #3

A Vision for Aging In Rural Appalachia

BP2023
First Place

THE TOPIC
Architecture Designed for Aging

THE QUESTION
What are the major issues and the best design responses in your local community for the special needs of your senior citizens?

WINNER
Hayden Painter
(Bachelor of Arts in Environmental Design, School of Architecture, Montana State University in Bozeman, Montana, U.S.A.)

EXPLORE!

See the complete text on the Berkeley Prize website

A moment is delicate
A glint of frost in crisp dawn
What will become of us in time?

There's a place nestled deep in the foothills of Virginia's Blue Ridge Mountains that will never leave me. I always arrived well after sunset. My father would wake me as we turned into a gravel drive after hours of traveling on snaking country roads. I remember the sweet night air and the soft refrain of crickets. Moths flickered by a single porch light as we lugged our suitcases up to my grandmother's door.

My grandmother's name was Fonda. Her trailer sat rooted in the soil, at the base of a briar-choked railroad embankment. Out her kitchen window, past a handsome row of pines, the Shenandoah River marked the edge of her property. Over the years, I watched Fonda age right here—in rural Appalachia.

She would often reminisce over a life in the Appalachian Mountains, a region with a storied and misty history. Originally the home of the Cherokee people, settlement by primarily Scotch-Irish immigrants began in the 1730s (1). Today, the Appalachian region encompasses 423 counties in 13 states ranging from New York to Mississippi (2). The ridges and hollows have bred seclusion and traditionalism, and modern stigma paints the people of this place with coarse brushstrokes. Fonda paid no mind. She valued her home, her friends, and her family deeply. If she had her people, all was right.

However, what happens when we age? What happens to someone in a place like this, where winding mountain roads separate friends, where a withdrawal of industry and growing urbanization has bled the region of young people, where elderly females in particular experience high rates of poverty? Will they have support and companionship in later life?

I believe Fonda's situation is applicable to many older adults in this region. By sharing her story, I aim to posit a vision for the future of aging in rural Appalachia.[...]

Loneliness

In America, among older adults, loneliness has been identified as the most significant factor in predicting a lower quality of life. Loneliness has been linked to multiple chronic conditions including hypertension, coronary artery disease, metabolic syndrome, diabetes, and lung disease (3). After Fonda began experiencing isolation, she developed cardiac complications. Eventually her condition necessitated entry into a cycle of nursing homes and hospitals that would define her final years.

Fonda passed away in a hospital in February 2019. In the weeks before she passed, she pulled me close and whispered that she would rather be anywhere else. As beautiful as her home had been, its rurality turned the natural process of aging into isolation. This loneliness contributed to a decline in health, and her only option became the healthcare system.

My Grandmother was a wellspring of knowledge and kindness. Aging never detracted from all she had to offer. However, rural Appalachians are confined to three options in later life: aging in place, aging in nursing homes, and extended stays in hospitals.

This is a design problem. When considering aging, can we conceive a fourth option—one that guarantees companionship and purpose? A structure of living that is proactive rather than reactionary? Imagine a place where people age with optimism, reducing premature entry into eldercare. Just after Fonda passed, such a place was opening its many doors 60 miles away.

Cohousing

Emerson Commons is a multigenerational cohousing development in the mountain town of Crozet, Virginia. Described by residents as an "intentional neighborhood", 49 people live in 26 homes clustered on 3.5 wooded acres (4). Welcoming front porches face a common green, community gardens, a pool, a playground and a firepit. A historic farmhouse overlooks this communal yard and serves as a gathering place for meals, events, and game nights.

The community follows the Danish model of cohousing, where private, high-density homes are supplemented by beautiful common spaces and shared facilities. Modern cohousing started in Denmark in the 1960s, but in many ways, this model is a return to past living structures of Appalachia. When Fonda lived in the blue house, seniors and children took on roles of altruism depending on their ability. The elders raised my father and his brother, equipping them with skills and knowledge amassed over lifetimes in the mountains. In turn, when elders became frail, my father provided care and companionship.

Author Loyal Jones lists *"self-reliance... [and] familism"* as two guiding principles for Appalachians in his 1994 book *Appalachian Values*. (5) Those who moved to Emerson certainly exhibit these values through intentional investment in their community. What emerges from shared meals, facilities, activities, chores, and recreational spaces is a self-reliant community that is often described as a large family.
[...]

Healthy Homes

Trailers are affordable but do not qualify for federally backed mortgages and are subject to restrictive zoning. In addition, many mobile homes pose dangers to the health of seniors. In Fonda's case, her trailer received minimal daylighting, experienced wild temperature swings, and had horrible indoor air quality. My father discovered and removed a massive black mold infestation in her closet. Fonda once fell straight through the flimsy floor, the roof leaked, and the walls were barely insulated. Substandard construction and cheap materials are commonplace, but prefabrication can provide responsible and dignified solutions.

The University of Virginia's School of Architecture (UVA) in Charlottesville, Virginia, U.S.A. demonstrated the potential of modular prefabricated design in 2004. The project, called ecoMOD, started in 2004 under Professor John Quale. The goal was to design, build, and evaluate high-performance, affordable homes for low-income Appalachian residents. Quale's method hinges on buying bulk material, reducing change orders, and building with minimal delay and waste. Parts are trucked to the site, boomed into place and assembled quickly, reducing the cost of the construction, and thus, the overall cost of the home. (6)

In 2009, ecoMOD built a 990 square-foot, two-bedroom home in Charlottesville for $150,000—about 60% the cost of Emerson's "affordable" units. The ecoMOD design is near-zero energy, features super-insulated wall assemblies, a solar array, and a geothermal heat pump. Other projects have utilized green roofs, solar water heaters, and potable rainwater collection systems ("EcoMOD3"). These features support Appalachian values of independence, self-reliance, and connection with nature while reducing energy consumption. In addition, ecoMOD partnered with UVA's Institute on Aging, Jefferson Area Board on Aging, and UVA's Medical Automated Research Center to tailor designs to seniors.[...]

Vision

If these responsible designs were implemented in Community Land Trust-owned cohousing developments, older adults in rural Appalachia would benefit. These developments should be located in small towns bordering larger cities. Much like Emerson, residents could enjoy pedestrian access to town centers while still feeling "tucked away". Natural features like creeks, forests, and lakes would support physical and mental health. These communities thrive when they are multigenerational, and proximity to larger cities would accommodate a variety of residents; families, younger couples, and previously rural seniors. Landscapes should feature a communal gathering place, gardens, workshops, playgrounds, walking trails, and recreational opportunities for all ages and abilities. In these intentional neighborhoods, everyone has a place.

Of course, this lifestyle relies on compromise. Residents must relinquish some privacy and ownership to enjoy the benefits of social integration. This structure is not for everybody, but it can melt away the isolation that creeps through Appalachia's aging populations. If such a community existed during Fonda's lifetime, she would have wholeheartedly participated in its formation. Her generosity of spirit, wry sense of humor, and heartwarming soul food would have brought light to any intentional neighborhood. And in turn, she would have received the companionship she needed to shine her brightest.

Within the misty hollows and forested ridges of Appalachia, people will continue to live and age. As human beings, we will always require warmth. Like moths to the glow of a porch light, we're drawn to the company of others. We need confirmation that we matter to someone; that we're still visible. In the foothills of the Blue Ridge Mountains, a woman who mattered to me lived, aged, and passed. Across the country, many people are undergoing a kindred experience, and they all deserve the option of community.

NOTES

(1) Kehrli, Susan Downs. "Poverty or Promise? The Paradox of Appalachian Life and Values." Thesis, California State University, Dominguez Hills ProQuest Dissertations Publishing, 2005

(2) Appalachian Regional Commission, "About the Appalachian Region, https://www.arc.gov/about-the-appalachian-region/

(3) Theeke, Laurie A., et al. "The Experience of Older Women Living with Loneliness and Chronic Conditions in Appalachia." *Rural mental health* vol. 39, 61-72. 1 April 2015. doi:10.1037/rmh0000029

(4) https://www.emersoncommons.org/about-our-community.html#:~:text=Emerson%20Commons%20is%20a%20multi,everyday%20life%20in%20the%20neighborhood

(5) Jones, Loyal, and Warren E. Brunner. *Appalachian Values*. Jesse Stuart Foundation, 1994.

(6) "EcoMOD Project." *World Habitat Awards/Winners*, 2 May 2018; Ford, Jane. "EcoMOD3 Expands Modular, Sustainable, Affordable Housing Research." 20 August 2007. *University of Virginia;* Quale, John. "EcoMOD: Sustainable, Prefabricated and Affordable Housing Prototypes." *95th ACSA Annual Meeting Proceedings, Fresh Air,* https://www.acsa-arch.org/chapter/ecomodsustainable-prefabricated-and-affordable-housing-prototypes/

Winning Student Essay #4A

Thinking Water, Thinking Fluid

BP2019
First Place (Shared)

THE TOPIC
Architecture and Climate Resilience

THE QUESTION
What have architects done in the past and what can they do in the future to help reduce the negative effects of climate and climate change?

WINNER
Shahreen Mukashafat Semontee & Raquibul Hassan Bhuiyan
(Bachelor of Architecture students in the Department of Architecture at the Bangladesh University of Engineering and Technology in Dhaka, Bangladesh)

EXPLORE!

See the complete text on the Berkeley Prize website

Looking at the scorching sun, the farmer wiped off his sweat with the back of his hand. Humidity is a part of this regional climate. But today, it was more than usual, hinting at an imminent rain. After being torched from the hellish summer heat, people waited eagerly for the rains. The gusts of cold wind came first. The fields wobbled; water lilies in the pond fluttered like the pages of an open book. The farmer continued to work on his land on the river's edge. Like most of the villages in this region, this village has grown surrounding a river.

It started with a drop of water on his bald head. He looked upwards and smiled at the gathering of ominous clouds. The sky was clear just a moment ago. He let the raindrops cool down his body for a moment before taking shelter beneath a nearby tree. The parched land seemed just as thirsty, soaking in every drop of water. In between the rolling of thunder, children's joyful sound could be heard as they welcomed the rain with songs and dances. The feeble houses could barely resist the wind that was strong enough to dissolve the distinction between house and nature.

After a while, the dry earth did quench its thirst, turning into a magical green overnight. But the rain gave no sign of stopping. The water level seemed to go up and up, overflowing the river. The houses began to get submerged, what started as a blessing snatched away homes. Gradually the water subsided, leaving behind a trail of dismantled houses. The land was softer with silt, but the willpower of the people was stronger than ever.

They went back to assembling the pieces the very next day. Everyone became the builder of their own home. One by one all the neighbors joined hands. They survived the storm together and together they started to rise. Within days, all the houses got re-erected, as did their dreams. These habitual arrangements only demonstrate the existence of an age-old relationship between the people and water. They were well aware of the blessings that it brought; they were used to the seasonal floods despite its hardships. Living in the most dynamic and fluid landscape of the world, the hydrological dynamic had allowed the people to traditionally develop a particular building typology that empowered them to sustain their lifestyles adapting to this predictable change of seasons.

Our language might give a hint at how we view floods. In Bengali, the term *Borsha* refers to the normal rainfall and fullness of the rivers, and *Bonna* implies destructive flooding. These expressions reflect the awareness and mental presets of the common people to flood hazards. Being woven from an intricate network of river and canals—even our traditional art forms respond to this geo-cultural

Typical flooding conditions in Gaibandha, Bangladesh leaving houses partially submerged in water.

(Photo: Majority World CIC, 2004, sourced on Alamy)

region. The emotionally rendered *Bhatiyaali* songs speak for the longing for home of someone who is stuck in rain in a faraway land.

During days of heavy rain, village wives stayed indoors and painted stories with colorful stitch patterns in Nakshi-Kantha, denotively designed-quilt depicting the rich lived lives. The flood doesn't thwart everything completely. Their lives go on. These small but significant adaptations gave form to the local vernacular architectural style that has transcended without depending on a single architect to a state where the community become their own architect.

This architecture belonged to the inhabitants, craftsmen, and builders of rural Bangladesh, who understood, improvised and lived in harmony with the free-flowing nature. That at a time when the trained architects of Bangladesh were busy trying to build a newly independent country by designing stand-alone modernist buildings. So, the traditional architecture that responded to our climate was left in the hands of the local people. Passed down from generations to generations, their wisdom gave birth to the local architectural style. The design elements are old, but the simple rationales of the past still make them followed—affordable materials and re-*buildablity*.[...]

The straightforward solution in our mind for flood protection is to raise the house over the water level. As a result, traditional stilt houses are seen in some flood prone areas in this region. Built on bamboo stilts, they raise their homes safely above water. Sometimes, raising the earth below, several homesteads are elevated together above the surrounding fields. In 'Char'(island) areas, houses are built with light and cheap building materials that are locally available- bamboo, reeds, jute and thatch- being modular in size and ready to dismantle in case of a natural disaster. The thatched roofs bend down to protect the walls. The doors are built low to slow down strong wind. The use and recycling of these local materials made it possible for financially insolvent people to have a bare minimum protection against the flood. Here, the community fights together against the hazards, providing support to each other.[...]

Our conventional approach of regarding flood and monsoon as an impediment most probably comes from the British colonial rule. Unfamiliar with the unique chemistry of land and water in this deltaic region, they built dams and walls, creating a land versus water scenario. The measures taken by our government for flood protection, are still influenced by these colonial thoughts. All policies blindly adopt a land biased planning. Hard embankments and high walls are raised, but as the water gets even higher, everything overflows. Administration's costly efforts to protect from flood backfires and ends in chaos. The situation demands gradients, fluid occupancies and negotiated moments. In short, lacking in fluidity and dynamism, it needs flexible and ecologically attuned solutions.[...]

As the conventional methods are failing, the unpredictable nature of climate change needs an energetic latitude of imagination. Related professionals are challenged to come up with more creative and affordable solutions in our local context by merging modern technical knowledge with traditional building knowledge. So was the case with architect Kashef Mahboob Chowdhury, when he was designing a rural training center in Gaibandha. The client was Friendship, a non-profit organization. They work together with vulnerable people in remote communities in Bangladesh to help them transform their lives. The program brief was simple- a center for training, classes and meetings. But the architect wanted to take this idea further by "truly creating a center around which the wonderful activities of this organization would revolve, a place that will bring people closer" as told by the architect himself.[...]

Friendship Center draws on the two thousand years' history of the Buddhist monasteries and the monastic way of life still being lived by the local people. The center, looking inwards with its outdoor spaces as a series of courts, the fracture of forms and spaces appraise the elemental quality of our tradition and rootedness.

From far, its topographical intimacy with the attendant flood plain renders a complete invisibility. This single-story structure integrate itself subtly into the surrounding scenic beauty. As you approach closer, the wide orthogonal berm can be seen around, giving the feeling of a walled city and a sense of protection. Two raised walkways connect itself with the top of the berm. One acts as a monumental gate and other comprises a narrow auxiliary staircase access. As you descend through the 45-degree angled broad stairs, the journey into the orthogonal labyrinth starts. You might see an ongoing workshop going on, giving a glimpse of the service provided to the community. Sometimes, the workshops go on for a week or so.

A "private" zone serves as dormitory and refuge to the people who can stay then. The "public" zone comprises the administrative and training facilities. Glimpses of the courtyards catch our eyes through the brick tunnels, as if inviting us to explore further. At first, the courtyards and water bodies might seem secluded and scattered, but these spaces make us remind our traditional 'uthan' (court) and 'khal' (canal) of the village households. The spaces conform to our tradition of intimacy and community bonding. It makes you feel at home and at the same time connects with the people it provides service to. This feeling of simplicity and bareness was very essential for the purpose it was designed to serve. The space doesn't seem alien, nor does the lives and activities revolving around it. Community is what makes this center whole.[...]

Friendship Centre, Gaibandha, Bangladesh: Kashef Chowdhury – URBANA, Architects, Dhaka, Bangladesh, 2011.

(Photo: Afifa Afrin, 2016, sourced on Wikimedia Commons- Attribution Share Alike 4.0 International license)

Winning Student Essay #4B

BP2019
First Place (Shared)

THE TOPIC
Architecture and Climate Resilience

THE QUESTION
What have architects done in the past and what can they do in the future to help reduce the negative effects of climate and climate change?

WINNER
Muskaan Jain & Furinder Singh
(Bachelor of Architecture students at the School of Planning and Architecture in Bhopal, India)

EXPLORE!

See the complete text on the Berkeley Prize website

Designing For Climate and Change: A Paradigm Shift

"Architecture should speak of its time and place, but yearn for timelessness."
(Frank Gehry, Architect)

Introduction

Bhopal, the capital city of the state of Madhya Pradesh, India, was built on site of the 11th-century city of Bhojpal, founded by Parmara King Bhoj (1000–1055). It reached its height of culture, art, architecture, and public works under the enlightened rule of a 19th-century dynasty of Muslim women, which led to the rise of a unique mixed culture in Bhopal. Today, Bhopal remains a city of considerable beauty with its several natural and artificial lakes, marketplaces, magnificent mosques and palaces, and the new city with its verdant, exquisitely laid out parks and gardens, broad avenues, and streamlined modern buildings. Having a profound culture of indigenous tribes in Madhya Pradesh, Bhopal's history is largely dominated by the Mughal and tribal cultures. In the contemporary world, where the global push to urbanize and modernize has created new architectural ideas, initiatives by the state government and other social organizations have done a commendable job in reviving and preserving Bhopal's cultural past through its architecture.

"When you are building in a specific climate, in a place with a strong heritage, you can just walk in the streets and see the answers."
(Dr. Driss Kettani, Morocco)

The art of building construction is not only restricted to aesthetic structures but how those built-up spaces affect their users and the environment.[...]

Part 1

Gohar Mahal (built in 1820, by the first woman ruler of Bhopal, Gohar Aara Begum, also known as Qudisiya Begum) with its alluring fusion of Indian and Mughal architecture, was the first palace of Bhopal province, in which Gohar Begum resided for the latter half of her life, when her daughter was ruling the territory. Popularly known as the City of Lakes, Bhopal has an undulating terrain and small hills within its boundary, broadly separated by the Upper and Lower lakes. The Mahal is situated on the slope of one such hill, on the VIP road, facing the vast Upper lake.

"With its majestic traditional architecture, Gohar Mahal stands tall in an age where building concrete jungles is considered to be the latest trend"
(Arvind Sharma, event manager at Gohar Mahal)

Walking through the rustic doors of the palace, one enters the *Diwan-e-Aam* (House of Commons) having a courtyard, surrounded by colonnades supporting magnificent Mughal arches. With a single glance toward the upper floor, one observes stunning windows, niches, *jaalis* (perforated screens) and overhangs resting on intricately carved stone brackets. The other half of the palace encompasses the *Diwan-e-Khas* (Hall of Private Audience), having a centrally located fountain and arcades on all sides. On one of its facades, stands a massive gate with elaborate carving done in Indian rosewood. This hall reveals fine craftsmanship and was once used to welcome the special guests of royalty. To date, people stay mesmerized by the emotive story of Gohar Mahal as the captivating beauty of the palace speaks for itself and its past.

For a long time, this architectural marvel was left in ruins. The Ministry of Textiles of Madhya Pradesh Handloom and Handicrafts Vikas Nigam (Development Authority) and the Indian National Trust for Art and Cultural Heritage (INTACH) carried out its restoration collectively, rehabilitating it into an urban *haat* (market). The ambiance of the Mahal has attracted urban dwellers for several years, carrying forward the cultural legacy of the country in the form of textile, handicraft and local art exhibits.

Bhopal experiences a subtropical climate, characterized by cold and dry winters, hot summers and humid monsoons. Spread over an area of 4.65 acres, this three-story structure, constructed with locally available materials like mud, stone, and timber, withstands the fluctuating weather conditions with its solar passive design and perfect east-west orientation. Built on extensive contours, no cutting or filling of the site has been done. Most of this foundationless structure stands underground resulting in earth sheltering, which substantially controls the microclimate of the palace. Massive load bearing double walls built in Adobe mud bricks set using organic mortar and the double roofing system on the upper floor incorporate the property of thermal mass, thus radiating heat energy during cold winters and rejecting it during harsh summers.

The huge courtyards invite natural light and ventilation, thereby maintaining the pressure difference between hot and cold air throughout the year. The verandas along the colonnades and the overhangs above them help in preventing heat gain from direct sunlight. Presence of jaalis and hexagonal *jharokas* (wind catchers) help in regulating airflow within the structure, providing thermal comfort during the months of extreme humidity. The windows are adorned with a special kind of glass imported from Belgium, which allow diffused sunlight to enter the rooms while avoiding heat. All these techniques integrate successfully to boast the resilience of Gohar Mahal as a structure.

Looking into the past makes us realize that ancient architecture was much more climate responsive than its modern counterpart. In the period of post-modernism, with limitless resources, the focal point has shifted from developing environment-friendly buildings to extraordinarily grand engineering models.[...]

Part 2

The Museum of Tribal Heritage at Bhopal (the Tribal Museum) was completed in 2013. It was designed by the architects of Kamath Design Studio (New Delhi). Based on the concept by Shriram Tiwari, Director, Culture Department, Madhya Pradesh (*Editor's note: the State of India in which the City of Bhopal is located*), the basic idea behind its establishment was in the sense of a double-edged sword. On the one hand, its main purpose was to understand and represent tribal life; whereas on the other hand, its purpose is to transfer this knowledge for use by the developing civil society. The museum, therefore adopted an intensely different style of design, creating a pathbreaking alternative in the history of Indian museums. It provides an eloquent platform for the *tribal* to expand, evolve and make their existence be felt. It exhibits different aspects of lives of the tribal living in central part of India in the form of uniquely themed galleries. Each gallery depicts different features like culture, lifestyle, art, awakening and the concept of heaven and hell. The museum is a portrayal of rich tribal culture thereby promoting harmonious coexistence of tribal with urban.

Situated on Shyamla Hills, spread across 7 acres, the museum is a marvel of modern architecture inspired by tribal rhythms, geometries, materials, forms, aesthetics and spatial consciousness, with an emphasis on climate responsiveness.[...]

The structure has been built using locally available material, mainly constituting mud, stone and steel, giving the space a sense of indigeneity and authenticity. Instead of enclosing the whole museum into one solid building block, the architect has used semi-open spaces along with multilevel verandas which pierce into the built mass, inviting natural light and air into the building. The galleries, interconnected using narrow corridors, have double heighted ceilings, revolving chimneys and perforated screens on walls, collectively contributing to effective cross ventilation and stack ventilation, thereby maintaining proper air flow within the building. Large overhangs on the west façade of the building cut direct glare and excess heat of sun.

State Museum of Tribal and Folk Arts, Bhopal, Madhya Pradesh, India

(Photo: Biswarup Ganguly, 2024, sourced on Alamy)

The landscaping of the structure has been done using local forest species, which facilitate rain water harvesting, further helping in irrigation of the gardens. The presence of other elements like terracotta pots placed in courtyards and an artificial water body, which gets filled up during the monsoon season, help in regulating the temperature of the building. Considering the large scale of the project, incorporation of natural light and air into the building design has helped reduce its dependency on mechanical means significantly.[...]

The ultimate goal of building sustainable structures can be accomplished by practicing smart construction techniques, which involve considering climate as a major parameter and building in its favour. This requires an intimate study of the site, its climate and the impact of wind and sun on it, followed by the process of designing. Being heavily dependant on resources, the main target of the construction sector should be making use of locally available building materials and inherited construction techniques in order to achieve this objective. With the rise of modernism in architecture in the past few decades, millennia-old building traditions have been disrupted. By combining local traditional practices with the ever-evolving technology, designers would be able to create inspirational structures, which are not only aesthetic but also excel in the field of climate responsive architecture.

Looking at the pace of development today, it is essential for us, all practicing and future architects, to advance along with the society whilst having a deep knowledge of our roots. Only then will we be able to shape forthcoming architecture in a way that it serves as an asset to humans as well as the environment. After all, tradition and modernity are two faces of the same coin, which must coexist simultaneously.

"We have to know from where we are coming to know where we are going"
(Charles Correa, Architect)

Winning Student Essay #5

When Local Architecture Provides a Shelter

BP2016
Second Place

THE TOPIC
SHELTERING THOSE IN NEED: Architects Confront Homelessness

THE QUESTION
Who is doing what in your community to confront the issue of the men, women, young people, and children without any shelter? As both an individual and as a professional, how do you see yourself assisting in providing shelter to those in need?

WINNER
Zahra Mosaddegh Akrami & Ali Tabatabael Ghomi
(Students in the Faculty of Architecture and Urban Planning, Tehran University of Art in Keraj, Iran)

EXPLORE!

See the complete text on the Berkeley Prize website

"My grandmother lived in a house in the 'Bagh Khan' neighborhood, with fifty palm trees in its yard. A garden house, in which her fourteen grandchildren had fourteen swings with little unique worlds for themselves. Us boys, running around and being loud and carefree in the world we felt safe. And girls, you could always find them around our grandmother busy with their dolls. The garden house was truly a member of our family. Now, twelve years have passed since the destruction of our garden house in Bam's earthquake. Hamed points to a photo and says, "in this photo you can see us walking on rubble looking for our grandparents." He continues with a heavy heart, "I can still feel the burn in my bleeding fingertips while digging into the rubble to this day."

The Earthquake

In December 2003, in a cold winter dawn, an earthquake with a magnitude of 6.7 hit Bam, a city that lies on the southern plains of Iran. The official death toll was confirmed at 26,000. Over 90% of urban buildings were destroyed, leaving more than 100,000 people homeless. Until the arrival of tents and establishment of emergency camps, people settled around the fire in the ruins of their houses or at the dead-end alleys. After a few days several tents were set up to shelter people impacted by the earthquake. Due to the adverse weather conditions, the national and the local authorities decided to move affected families to temporary units until the reconstruction could be completed. By being the focus of national donations, Bam started to attract low-income and homeless families from other nearby towns and villages looking for financial aids and donations. This made the issue of housing even more complicated with two target groups seeking help, one the locals affected by the earthquake, and second the temporary financial migrants.

The government adopted different strategies to settle families in temporary units. The main approach was using prefabricated units as temporary shelters. Unfortunately, the development of prefabricated units was delayed, leaving people to live in tents for another few months in harsh winter. However, many survivors preferred to stay in tents and refused to move to camp sites located far from their destroyed houses. In addition, most of the survivors found living in prefabricated units challenging and unsuitable, with no sense of belonging most of the people could not accept units as their new homes.

Meanwhile and prior to construction of temporary units, a group of professionals from Iranian Housing Foundation Organization (HFO) took a different approach. HFO started building reasonable small shelters with the help of locals and using locally available material. The HFO is a governmental organization which is responsible for providing affordable accommodation to low-income families, and for post-disaster reconstruction work.[...]

After the Earthquake

Appreciating the importance of finding a prompt and practical way to build temporary accommodation for the people of Bam, HFO took it upon itself to overcome this challenge. The first step was to resolve the issue of construction material. Due to the scale of construction work, sourcing material for manufacturing prefabricated units was unfeasible and time consuming. Inspired by the history of the region, HFO engineers started to study old local methods of house building in the region.

By using readily available palm leaves and stems, HFO not only eliminated the cost and time required for manufacturing and transportation of prefabricated units, but also benefited from local knowledge and craftsmanship that was passed from a generation to another in the region. HFO engineers developed two types of fit-for-purpose designs benefiting from the light weight and flexibility of natural material. By using locally abundant natural resource, the project employed the craftsmanship of the community. While this provide HFO with an opportunity to utilize locals as laborers, the design was required to be simple and practical to be implemented by people with minimum to no construction background.

Using HFO designs, two types of shelters were built with maximum area of 15 square meters. In the first design, the structure was built from palm stems meshed together to form an approximate hemisphere. To create this frame, branches in the middle of palm leaves were tied together to create a weaved fabric approximately 10–15 centimeter in diameter. Each of these tied branches with length of 3–4 meters is called *Gasab*. Then each Gasab was firmly posted in the ground in 1 m intervals from each other on both sides of the structure.

The upper part of each Gasab was weaved and connected to the opposite Gasab. As the result, paired Gasabs would form a semicircle arch. Another set of Gasabs were used horizontally to bind and brace those vertical arches. These frames have a length of 5 meters and a width of 3 meters. Afterwards the structure was covered with palm leaves. The shelter had openings at both ends to access. Light and ventilation was provided from pores between the leaves. The same covering technique was used in the second design. However, the structure was made using four pieces of palm timbers.

One of the HFO goals was to involve survivors in the construction of shelters. The social and sustainable approach adopted by HFO has resulted in development of a design that was not only practical and safe, but also ensured the engagement of affected people in rebuilding their community. The design also enabled community to build their shelters in various configurations to address their specific needs, whether it was to cater their family size or flexibility with style. Various shelters with circular or rectangular plans and diverse covering textures were built. This resulted in construction of good quality shelters in timely manner. It was apparent that this could be only achieved with the effort derived from the people's sense of belonging to where they want to call home.[...]

While providing shelter for people who their homes were a one-off issue in case of Bam earthquake, it is an everyday concern of 15,000 homeless people of Tehran. The main anticipated cause of homelessness in Tehran is the migration of people from rural areas to urban areas in pursuit for a better life. In addition to financial difficulty, social pathologies such as drug addiction have also been one of the main contributors to this issue. With a population of more than 28,000, "Shoush" has been one of the worst suburbs in Tehran with respect to everyday violence and crime rate. Old families gradually moved out due to these problems. Shoush, while recognized as one of the oldest and culturally rich suburbs in Tehran, with 8,000 homeless it is probably the most impacted suburbs in Tehran in this respect.

All these social issues have resulted in formation of a secluded and isolated community from society that has attracted more homeless people to this neighborhood. Several schemes have been proposed to overcome issues in Shoush, some has been put to practice with little success while most have failed to improve the situation. Failing to address the social aspect of this problem and understanding the need for grassroots effort to solve the issue has resulted in failure of most of these initiatives.

Inspired by HFO local shelters, we believe temporary and cost-effective local shelters can be set up in the nearby hills where many of homeless people are gathered to spend the night. While we appreciate that this will not be "the" solution to their homelessness, it will offer a better-quality accommodation compared to shacks cobbled together from cardboard or plastic sheets which hardly last a single night. The humanitarian organizations fighting against drug addiction and homelessness in Tehran can take action on creating opportunities to build these shelters in feasible parts of the hills. Teaching construction techniques to homeless people is requisite for implementation of this proposal, so they can build shelters themselves. However, this proposal cannot be simply considered as a practical solution for Shoush homelessness issue until it is accompanied by social studies.[...]

Meanwhile, a number of NGOs in Tehran have recognized the social role of each individual in improving the homelessness issue. After having an unpleasant experience in Shoush neighborhood, Ali Heidari, a manager at an advertising company in Tehran, came up with the idea to create a group called "Ending Homelessness". He explains "I was carrying 15 meals for homeless people for the first time. When I got there, I was shocked by what I saw." He says "I walked to two people to put food containers next to them when I just realized they were dead. I saw them dead with my own eyes. In Tehran some people are starving to death!"

Although the motto for Heidari's group is to end homelessness, he understands that before building a shelter they should provide basic needs such as food, clothing and also a new attitude in order to return homeless people to society. He believes that the special condition of homeless people life has deprived them from all opportunities for participation in society. There is a strong and complex relationship between homelessness and social exclusion. Homelessness is caused by social exclusion and can also be the reason for it. Following the goal of ending homelessness, NGOs have focused their activities in areas such as health, education, employment, shelter and reintegration.

One of the activities that the NGO has started is placing kiosks next to a wall in different neighborhoods, which includes a refrigerator, wardrobe and bookshelf. People put their donated foods and clothes in it for destitute people. On the wall next to the kiosk is written "If you don't need it, leave it. If you need it, take it". Until now more than a hundred of "kindness walls" have been built in twenty-one cities. The NGO along with the weekly food distribution, tests homeless people for diseases such as HIV. Heidari says "after some time of communicating with homeless people and dealing with their issues, many of them have shown interest in overcoming drug addiction. [...]

The combination of the HFO design approach and the social motivation created by "Ending Homelessness" can help alleviate the homelessness issue. Motivating homeless people, especially the ones who try to quit drugs in order to find a shelter for themselves, will stimulate a passion for life. It is also a major step towards the improvement of their life quality. These shelters are not meant to be a permanent house, but a place where they can live while transiting to a better life. As Heydari says: "we are not doing anything special. We are just paying our debt to society. If we have homeless people in Iran, it's because at some point we were not caring enough about our people."

Mesh structure and covering of a local different emergency shelter made of palm stems and leaves.

(Photo: Provided by Zahra Mosaddegh Akrami & Ali Tabatabael Ghomi)

Winning Student Essay #6

BP2007
First Place

THE TOPIC
Making Social Architecture

THE QUESTION
What do you believe is the most needed project in your town that, when built, would better the social situation for a population in need? Please fully and clearly describe the project and why you feel it is so important.

WINNER
Sara Navrady and Erica Moore
(Final year students of undergraduate studies at the University of Waterloo School of Architecture, Cambridge, Canada.)

EXPLORE!

See the complete text on the Berkeley Prize website

The Oput Centre: From the Tree of Reconciliation to the Architecture of Healing

"On the way to Sudan, they forced us to kill many people. One morning a young boy was brought to us. We were told he had tried to escape.They had killed him. His body was swollen and cut from many beatings. We were told to chop the body into smaller pieces. Boys were given the heart and liver to eat. Girls were told to cook and eat the rest of the body parts. We did as we were told."
(O.R., age fourteen, abducted in February 2003)

"When the sun sets, we start to worry"
(United Nations Office for the Coordination of Humanitarian Affairs [UN OCHA], 2003)

For two decades, the Lord's Resistance Army (LRA) has made this nightmare a brutal reality for over 25,000 children in northern Uganda. Padibe is one of numerous towns in the Kitgum district that has seen the children of its surrounding villages snatched in the middle of the night. Predominantly of the Acholi population, these children are tortured, beaten, raped, and drugged into submission as obedient killers or sex slaves. In the period of one night, concepts of family, home, and childhood are transformed and replaced by a brutal nomadic lifestyle; violating their bodies, their emotional sensitivity and impressionability.

Recent peace talks between the LRA and the Ugandan government offer hope for the release of these young soldiers. However, there is little for them to return to: the village that was once their home lies in ruins with its remaining villagers evacuated to Internally Displaced People (IDP) camps in the wake of destruction by the LRA. Farmland has overgrown, camouflaging the charred remains of torched schools and homes. Many of Padibe's child soldiers were forced to participate in the destruction of their own community, and even the murder of family members. Upon their anticipated release, they will return with the fear of being outcast, harboring shame and anger toward a community that was unable to protect them, a community that has its own wounds to care for.

The Acholi people are uprooted trees, unable to take sufficient food from degraded soil lacking in nutrients. As a result, the tree fails to prosper, produce leaves, or bear fruit. We propose to build a vessel in which Padibe's broken community can recover its unity. In its most fundamental form as an institution and enclosure, architecture creates permanence and security, providing individuals with a sense of place. The Acholi culture of reconciliation is embodied in this beacon, the Oput Centre.

The Oput tree is the traditional symbol of the reconciled Acholi community, its deep roots fixing its position in the landscape. The primary event of *Mato Oput*, an Acholi ceremony of atonement and forgiveness, involves drinking a bitter drink made from Oput leaves. Committing to swallow all bitterness for the sake of restoring harmony is a symbolic gesture to re-establish balance in the community. Given the grave nature of this tragedy, this ceremony alone is not enough to restore social balance. Incorporating Acholi rituals such as Mato Oput, however, is an important part of helping the former soldiers and the rest of the community to begin to come together again. The Oput Centre provides a broad architectural threshold to enable this difficult human transition.

Forged by the hands of this community and adapted to their specific needs, we foresee the Centre to include medical services, rehabilitation for former soldiers, education facilities, and spaces to engage in community activities such as traditional music and dancing, theatre, and sports. As designers, we play a critical role in the healing process through our response to the mental and emotional conditions of the child, and how that affects our approach to the programmatic and spatial structures of the Oput Centre. [...]

"And now let me take you back, back to the moment my innocence was stripped from my body, to when my fingers learned the sharp, cold ridges of the gun, and my ears tuned to the wail of painful death...let me lead you into the darkness of that night." [...]

The purpose of the envisioned rehabilitation facility is to restore physical health and reclaim innocence while transitioning from a soldier to a child. A key aspect of this process is the sharing of experiences, a healing of memories. Many don't know how to grieve or forgive, and they risk falling into uncontrolled aggression, anxiety, and withdrawal. To provide a place to confide, heal, and resolve we will create spaces that encourage interaction. Here the children form a "family" that provides support until they are ready to join their own families. Like an average Ugandan family, 6 to 8 children live in a home together with one or two counselors, who provide additional support and security. [...]

The grim, long-lasting environmental and, therefore, human reality.

(Photo: Sue O'Connor, June 2007, sourced on Alamy.)

The rehabilitation process will be different for each child. In response, a variety of informal spaces within the home complex is required. This is achieved by overlapping the volumes of the rooms, to create pockets of space in different sizes that can open to the outside, have an elevated ceiling with a skylight, or be painted with calming colors to form special places. In visiting quarters nearby, parents and family members can stay overnight to encourage the rehabilitation process, and start the re-adjustment to family life. Once all the children have made the permanent transition back to living with their families, the homes at the Centre will be used by children who were orphaned during the war. [...]

The complex could also be adapted to serve young mothers who need additional spaces for taking care of the children they conceived while in captivity. Areas in between the homes become gardens for growing food or courtyards for dancing, while deep verandahs enable cooking, eating and gathering outdoors. With various gardens, groves, football pitches and play-spaces, nature is re-introduced as a healing presence in contrast to the unpredictable threat it presented while the children endured long days and unprotected nights in the bush.

Whether held in the captivity of the rebel army or in the confinement of IDP camps, the children of Padibe have also been deprived of basic, adequate education. The primary, secondary and vocational training schools of the Oput Centre branch out to the community, providing an opportunity for all of the children to reintegrate through their shared desire for knowledge. Instrumental in countering stigmatization, this helps to reintegrate the child soldiers with their peers in the community. [...]

As new ideas and concepts are shared within the school, the traditional ways of the Acholi culture must also be shared. The gathering banda is available to each member of the community, becoming an important place of passing on knowledge and traditions between generations. Also a setting for spiritual worship, it is a source for collective memory. Inspired by the traditional Acholi hut design, this gathering space is an elongated ellipse covered by a conical shaped roof. Light washes over two main structural walls curving to embrace each other, like two hands about to engage in a handshake. When shaking hands here in Uganda, both greeters take their free hand and hold their own elbow as a sign of respect, or they may take the other's hand with both hands as an added layer of affection, deepening the relationship. Physically, the *banda* is composed of two layers of walls that form both halves of the ellipse.

The main interior walls also extend outwards in both directions, and progressively disappear into the earth. The outer walls envelope the building on both sides, like the left hand, creating secondary spaces and entry thresholds that dissolve through the creative use of decorative vent-block. A slipping and overlapping of curving walls replaces doorways, while the absence of other openings promotes an inward focus. Symbolically, the gathering banda works as a coherent whole, composed of layers that represent the deepening of a relationship between all members of the community. Should a suffering child become defiant towards the elders in the community, this gathering space acts as a sanctuary for discussions; re-instilling in the child the value of traditional ways and important aspects of the Acholi culture, of which he or she will carry forward to the next generation. [...]

In the wake of tragedy, building takes on new meaning as a metaphor for reconstruction. Newly restored walls and roofs give rigidity and stability to a structure, and also form the building blocks of rebuilding the soul of the family, the community and the child. The walls of the Oput Centre bring help and hope to a people who are ready to build; ready to move forward. Scarred deeply by the tragedies they have lived through, the children and youth are nurtured and educated; moreover, they are given the ability to empower their community, become integral leaders in their society and evoke change. [...]

The rhythm of the drum resonates from deep within the gathering banda. It is a sound that wells up from the very depths of the soul...with innate meaning it finds its voice once again. Like a heartbeat increasing in strength, it calls to all who are around to "come with your song—come with your dancing—come, arise and greet the new dawn."

Winning Student Essay #7

A Day in the Life of a Wheelchair User: Navigating Lincoln

Architectural discourse has gradually become incoherent with the social and ethical needs of the contemporary city. With the relationship between theory and practice strained, lack of social relevance in design is ubiquitous. Practicing architects frequently regard theory as esoteric and non-transferable, whilst many theorists do not manifest their ideas into reality and build. With the connection gripping the precipice by its fingers, this paper is conceived; written to persuade, motivate, and encourage that there is real value in instigating ideas put forth in this paper. Concepts proposed are not only applicable to the city of Lincoln but are relevant and adaptable to all cities. Inspired by the architecture which has not yet manifested, it hopes to ignite the spirit needed to eradicate social inequities in urban design.

Albert Einstein is often quoted, probably apocryphally, as saying: "If the facts don't fit the theory, change the facts." In order to palpably grasp an understanding of what it is truly like to be physically disabled in Lincoln, I rented a wheelchair for one day to see for myself whether the facts fitted the theory. [...]

BP2013
First Place

THE TOPIC
The Architect and the Accessible City

THE QUESTION
Provide us with an overview of what is being done in your city to make it accessible to people who have physical disabilities. In your opinion as an architect, What More Can Be Done?

WINNER
Sophia Bannert
(Third year architecture student, University of Lincoln, Lincoln, United Kingdom)

EXPLORE!

See the complete text on the Berkeley Prize website

Alone and small in the street, my self-awareness heightens. Large swarms of hurried people part when they see me approaching. My whole identity has changed in the eyes of the city within minutes. My wheelchair is my fortress and the enemy. With its large spindly wheels as my first and only defense, they are also my burden. Jarred into an utterly complex version of what I formerly knew as reality, my eyes begin scrutinizing and dissecting the cobbled street surface ahead into zones which I can and cannot access. Never before had I seen the streetscape in such meticulous detail. Tiny height differences such as curbs and grooves between cobbles become mountains, cruelly halting progress and making small advances, exhausting. Whilst battling physical obstructions, I myself have become one. If the pavements were widened, perhaps disabled citizens wouldn't be seen as causing an obstruction. [...]

My wheelchair rattles and comes to a halt, jammed in between the quaint cobbles at the foot of steep hill; I cannot access any further.

Newly laid, flat cobble stones would alleviate this problem, whilst maintaining the historic beauty of Lincoln. A more level surface under foot will improve transitions for everybody. The installation of a funicular railway would bind the two city levels seamlessly, whilst becoming an attraction in itself. This has been discussed to improve the accessibility of Steep Hill by the city council but is as of yet just an idea. [...]

I make my way to a ramp situated at the back entrance of a supermarket, to buy lunch. After several attempts with different approaches, I still can't heave myself up the ramp. The incline is too steep. With a final attempt my wheelchair falls behind me and I am hurled out of the chair onto the cold, mocking, concrete.

This is a statement to all designers and architects. Within a mere few hours of navigating Lincoln in a wheelchair, my basic human rights have been breached more than once. Being denied the right to use a toilet as well as being unable to access a supermarket to buy food independently is simply unacceptable. The ramp's incline should be lessened, to fully integrate all users. [...]

Discussing accessibility with wheelchair users of the city offers another perspective. Michael has been bound to a wheelchair since childhood. Having lived in Lincoln all his life, he is well aware of the barriers present; He has mentally mapped out the streets in his head knowing exactly where he can and cannot access, with a shockingly small area in which he feels confident to travel within. He has only ever ventured up to the upper half of the city on several occasions and with enormous difficulty. This constructs a feeling of inferiority; only the physically fit can easily visit and exist in the higher land of the city.

He had longed to travel to the Usher Art gallery but had been wrongly informed that was inaccessible for the physically disabled. This illustrates a lack of information in the city regarding accessibility, leading to perceptions that the urban environment is unsafe. I believe that this can be greatly improved with local campaigning and media coverage. [...]

When observing disabled citizens in the heart of Lincoln, I note that their mere presence provokes undulating reactions from able bodied strangers. They swerve from being completely ignored, to being paid unnaturally full amounts of attention. Being either fully known or unknown, there is no comfortable middle ground of awareness. Swinging from two extremes illustrates how uncomfortable and inexperienced this society is in encountering people with physical disabilities. This unspoken barrier can be gradually removed with social activism and campaigning. More importantly, architecture has an absolutely essential role to play in breaking these stigmas down. If physical barriers are broken down, then the social barriers will quickly follow suit. Once our city is built for everybody then prejudices will vanish.

Cities are in a constant state of flux. In the pursuit of equitable progress in Lincoln, a project such as this will have to be tackled step by step, until the steps have been worn down into a ramp. It will require incremental yet substantial investment of time and capital. But before all of that, the first stride requires a heightened social awareness in society, expanding the boundaries of understanding, engaging citizens; realizing the collective need for a more accessible city. The larger the crowd of support; the louder the message; the more suitable the city will be for all, expressing a city belonging to everyone. [...]

Winning Student Essay #8

BP2000
First Place

THE TOPIC
Architecture as a Social Art

THE QUESTION
What role can architecture play as a socially responsive endeavor in the future? Discuss this in light of your examination of architectural history, theory, and your studio design experience.

WINNER
Nathan Koren
(Arizona State University, Tempe, Arizona, U.S.A.)

EXPLORE!

See the complete text on the Berkeley Prize website

"Architecture In Reverse: Building the Pyramid From the Top Down"

When considering the topic of "Architecture as a Social Art," I am immediately struck by the multiplicity of interpretations—more often conflicting than not—to which such a phrase might lend itself. The words themselves are ambiguous. What is "Social"? What is "Art"? In the practice of architecture (or should I say "Architecture"?) we are vaguely aware that these words imply some principles which our work ought to encompass, but the imprecision of the language itself leaves us without guidance. Architects with utterly oppositional philosophies can each claim passionately that theirs is the only truly social architecture, with both sides mustering copious amounts of verbiage to support their views. Debates have raged for a century, with no position declaring victory for longer than a moment. Today, the question of architecture's place in society yields such a bewildering diversity of responses that few even bother asking anymore.

In academia, however, the situation is worse. It is my experience that, lacking decisive examples of how social considerations play a role in the actual *practice* of architecture, today›s educational institutions are instead electing to dodge the question almost entirely. They are wholly unequipped, at least during the formative years of an architectural education, to impart any social ethics—even contradictory ones—to future generations of architects. Before delving into this critique, however, we must explore some of these potentially contradictory definitions of "architecture as a social art."

One definition of "social art" is *art that is created by a society*. By this interpretation, architecture has been an intrinsically social art throughout the majority of human history. In societies without a high degree of specialization, the ability to design and construct a dwelling was considered an essential survival skill. Even today, most dwellings are still built out of sticks or mud by the very people who will inhabit them. It is a decisively social phenomena: Evolved rather than dictated, vernacular architecture cannot be credited to any single individual, but to the collective intelligence, needs, and aesthetics of the society as a whole. Emerging from the group wisdom without pretension or self-consciousness, this art is nothing if not social. [...]

It is useful to define what *cannot* be considered social in this respect: namely, architecture that is incompatible with the needs, customs, and aesthetics of a society. Many examples of this "non-social" architecture can be found throughout the world, particularly in regions where more traditional cultures have found themselves all but forced to live in "universal style" housing and are struggling to adapt this new environment to their old lifestyle. [...]

Still, I think it is safe to say that if one wishes to address the role of architecture in society, the endless permutations of light falling on abstract geometry provide a very poor place to start.

Unfortunately, this is exactly where my architectural education began. Our first year in studio was spent wholly engaged in the abstract. Not only were we prevented from bringing social considerations to bear in our work, we were even discouraged from conceptualizing our designs as "architecture" in any respect. Issues of human scale were not to be considered. "Windows" and "doors" were to be thought of as "apertures" and "openings"; walls, roofs, floors, and the site itself were reduced to different kinds of geometric planes. All human considerations were to be cast aside for the sake of pure, unblemished, and utterly irrelevant formalism.

In the second year we were finally allowed to think in terms of the most basic architectural tectonics—"spaces" were allowed to be "rooms," "groundplane" slowly transmogrified into "site." On two occasions we were permitted to explore some programmatic notions—although these were still so limited and abstract as to preclude any precedent studies or real-world considerations.

The first semester of the third year retreated again from real consideration of place and program, as we were encouraged to develop somewhat theoretical structures using a more precise tectonic vocabulary. In one project, we were granted an actual site, although the careful investigation of it seemed to be regarded as optional. Now, in the latter half of the third year—six semesters into our architecture education—we have been given a project which requires deep and conscious interaction with the social sphere. We are now, at long last, being unambiguously introduced to the notion that *the inhabitants and location of a building, along with one's own social intentions, should be some kind of design determinant*. Three quarters of the way through our undergraduate education, we have finally been asked to consider Architecture as a Social Art.

This is too little, too late. Most of my classmates have already imprinted a definition of architecture that has nothing to do with its role in society. Others have tried from the beginning to interject notions of environment, culture, or economy into their process, but such actions are seen as rebellious, and have become increasingly tinged with cynicism and bitterness. I have certainly noticed this occurring in myself.

Why is the educational process failing so spectacularly? I believe it is because the *sequence* in which concepts have been presented is almost exactly the opposite of the way it ought to be. Psychologists speak of a «hierarchy of needs,» in which an individual›s physiological needs must be met before their social needs can be addressed, and their social needs must be met before self-actualization can be achieved. My education has attempted to build that pyramid from the top down, and it has not worked. Turning towards biology, we find the maxim "ontogeny recapitulates phylogeny"—in other words, that the development of an organism mirrors the evolution of the species.

The development of an architect should be no different. Our education should begin with a study of the historical *process* of architecture—not a rote memorization of various historical styles, but a thorough understanding of the many ways in which social and environmental determinants have shaped the built environment. This done, we should proceed study more contemporary ways in which the built environment has reciprocally shaped society, both by design and by accident. Finally—fully aware of the many roles that architecture can play—we might be ready to wrestle with the infinite subtleties of «volumes brought together in light,» and we would finally be equipped to do so within a meaningful, socially responsive context.

Winning Essay #9

"A Cathartic Architectural Language in A Democratic South Africa"

BP2018
First Place

THE TOPIC
Applying the Social Art of Architecture

THE QUESTION
What is the Social Art of Architecture?

WINNER
Wandilise Kona
(Bachelor of Architectural Studies student in the Department of Eng ineering and Built Environment at the University of the Witwatersrand in Johannesburg, South Africa)

EXPLORE!

See the complete text on the Berkeley Prize website

[...] The buildings under consideration for this year's Question, The Women's Jail by Kate Otten Architects and the Hector Pieterson Museum by Mashabane Rose Architects, are buildings that have exemplified architectural resilience in South Africa over the past decade, particularly in celebrating the fight against oppression in the post-apartheid South Africa. The buildings come into existence during a paradigm shift in the South African landscape—after the fall of the apartheid regime.

The emergence of the buildings in the new South Africa primarily deals with the redressing of their brutal political and architectural history. The social art of architecture, in this case, is the alteration of spatial meaning respectively. In architecture, however, the meaning of space is never defined in isolation its meaning is tightly tied to the coherence of its immediate ecosystem; its co-existing people, nature and artefacts, set of events and function which in architecture is termed as the "context" or "site."

In the given circumstances, the architect has rendered a disabling past with an enlightening function and intention through architectural intervention (e.g. a building). And through this design outcome, the architect has blurred unnecessary social thresholds within the given society. This social gesture then serves to indicate the architect is not designing on voided space but thoughtfully translating one spatial meaning to another. Hence the architect respectively is charged with outlining a new foundation for a democratically empowering future in South Africa through architectural spatial making.

The question of what the new architectural language will be in the post-apartheid South Africa must have been thought-provoking for spatial practitioners, particularly when it came to architectural spatial making that celebrates the fight against oppression in South Africa. I concluded that layers of spaces had to be peeled off to find what is pure, and to separate what is worthy of being celebrated from what is not; essentially informing newly designed spaces must have been quite tricky considering the drastic change in spatial use.

The design approach taken by Kate Otten Architects for The Women's Jail (TWJ) deals with the mentioned concern in various ways, attempting to appropriate a new extension in a historically brutal context. The Women's Jail as a modern office building is a new extension to the old British jail, and the jail ceasing to function as a prison is currently deemed as a national heritage site. One of the

Woman's jail at Old Fort Prison Complex, Constitution Hill, Hillbrow, Johannesburg, South Africa.

(Photo: Greg Balfour Evans, 2012, sourced on Alamy)

primary methods used to appropriate the new extension as a whole is the careful integration of its form and function, which to a large extent has much to do with how the building is experienced on a day-to-day basis—essentially informing its social significance.

Approaching TWJ from the west, I was struck by the distinctively walled precinct leading to its north-facing visitor's entrance. The first thought that came to mind was that there had to be a good reason for this; an intention by the architect to keep the internal space visually imprisoned from the public. This was where women activists were once imprisoned during the apartheid regime. The imprisoned space, housing a courtyard and new winged office spaces, is one of the most important spaces in this intervention, solely because of its spatial qualities and its cathartic storytelling.

The prohibited visual access to the courtyard space recreates a brutal scene that used to be, and the old perimeter walls serve to be a living testimony to the prison's function as a place of confinement. The outward form of the extension has been thoughtfully considered to depict a series of "cell" blocks that are symmetrically facing each other across the courtyard, what used to be the prison exercise yard. Consequently, the considered nostalgic form enhances its emotive storytelling through its materiality and function.

The new buildings do not seek to imitate but they 'touch' the old buildings 'lightly', thus retaining the integrity of both the old and the new, and the new contemporary shape helps define a new order of authority within the given space. In fact, what Kate Otten Architects have brilliantly achieved is blending the old and the new with 'light' walkways on either wing. This then creates a smooth transition from the old to the new, not just spatially but physically. The given transition ends with a grand statement—the third story of each office wing is projected over the north-facing prison wall. This gesture echoes the transformation of the old space, from a place of confinement to its new function as an expression of freedom and democracy.

As a poetic stance, the projection of the two buildings is purely thought-provoking, for the projection is said to resemble the nation's transition from a disabling regime to a resounding democracy. Hence this level of thoughtfulness has acquired the new office building with an eloquent contemporary look; having the new office wings hovering in triumph over their architectural history. [...]

The Hector Pieterson Museum is designed to depict a book or rather a spatial narrative, in which the narrative gives off its information through systematic

Courtyard Memorial, Hector Pieterson Museum, Johannesburg, Republic of South Africa.

(Photo: Greg Balfour Evans, 2012, sourced on Alamy)

circulation (a planned touring experience) and makes use of a number design tools and decisions in order to do so. And through this reading experience, the reader is projected in a time past. Approaching the given precinct from the south, the reader is welcomed by a gracefully exposed courtyard memorial – which is primarily situated where the students of 1976 were prohibited with open fire. Thus, the courtyard memorial has been dedicated to cleansing this spatial horror, and the reader can immediately note this dedication by the visual amenities MRA has provided for the public.

What is particularly impressive about the courtyard memorial is the simple use of various textures and change in levels in order to distinguish certain parts of its story from each other. Through this technique, the author or the architect has been able to create a legible narrative. On the south-west end of the courtyard, lies a particular rock memorial resting on the intersection of Kumalo Road and Pela Street. For instance, the rock sits on a circular gravel plane setting it apart from a paved surface area which progresses towards the courtyard's main exhibition platform. As the reader approaches this public display, he or she encounters a drastic change in ground level stepping down to the actual platform. Consequently, this forces the reader to experience a significant shift in attention as they engage with a primary aspect of the narrative with a bit more discretion.

The openness of the courtyard creates a sensation of invitation and belonging due to its generous accessibility, as opposed to its alienating memory, and this spatial quality is particularly cathartic for the students (and represented families) who once experienced the same space differently. This sacred landscape is accessible to an outdoor water feature resting behind a granite memorial platform—the main exhibition platform—displaying the bloodshed that was once experienced within the immediate context. The water running through this feature symbolizes the blood of the students that was shed in prompt of a democratic South Africa. This 'blood' spills into thin groves running on the lower level of the memorial platform linking it to an artificial river. The statement made by the architect here is that even though the students were brutally killed, with the intent to prohibit them from reaching their goal, their blood achieved it either way. What stands behind the water feature on the edge of Pela Street, are slate brick walls and pillars which are an expression of all the unknown youth that played a part in achieving democracy in South Africa. [...]

Conclusion

In summary, it is quite intriguing to understand how architecture can be utilized as a social catalyst by simply telling stories that have played a distinctive role in the course of our history as a nation and providing the public with humanitarian objectives. Kate Otten Architects and Mashabane Rose Architects deserve a standing ovation, for designing buildings that rooted themselves in their context and challenged their political history. This exhibits the power that architecture has in having an impact on the world at large, not to mention a nation. The social art of architecture should reach and touch the lives of the masses, and blur out unnecessary social thresholds as the sun would to flowers after a stormy climate. Hence the given architects allowed that which evolves to create this outstanding outcome.

In tribute to Jeremy Rose co-founder of Mashabane Rose Architects, Johannesburg, South Africa – 2015

BIBLIOGRAPHY

Joubert, 'Ora ed. (2009) *10 years +100 buildings.* Cape Town, Bell-Roberts Publishing.

Deckler, T. Graupner, A. Rasmuss, H. (2006) *Contemporary South African Architecture in a Landscape of Transition.* Cape To wn: Double Storey Books.

Damon, I. (2006) *Digest of South African Architecture. Linden*, Johannesburg, South African Institute of Architects (SAIA).

http://www.history.com/topics/apartheid

https://www.brandsouthafrica.com/south-africa-fast-facts/history-facts/womens-jail-111105

Traveling

The yearly-selected Prize Travel Fellows explore wide-ranging, socially conscious architectural projects in locales distant from their own.

Berkeley Prize semifinalists who select to compete for a Travel Fellowship are invited to submit proposals demonstrating how they would use the opportunity to travel to an architecturally significant destination, preferably to participate in a hands-on, service-oriented situation. This has been an exciting opportunity to explore a different part of the world and to participate in an organized project that will assist the winner in gaining a deeper understanding of the social art of architecture.

Travel Fellowship candidates have been asked to submit a proposal for a specific plan of travel and study away from their academic institution during their summer break. The Travel Fellowship provides a fixed stipend adequate to pay for round-trip airfare, and to pay for lodging, food, and incidentals during their stay—normally three weeks.

The requirements for the Travel Fellowship proposals are open-ended. The Berkeley Prize Committee has looked for both an understanding of the opportunity that is offered and an understanding of the possible ways in which the student's research into the current year's prize topic might be furthered by the travel opportunity. The winning students have been asked to write a report on their travels and to keep a photo diary.

The safety of the students in their travels has been of paramount importance to the Berkeley Prize. As is documented in the first report included here, however, not every contingency can be anticipated. Nor can the unexpected outcome be so rewarding from both a personal and academic perspective.

Excerpts from Selected Travel Fellow Reports

BP2023
Saavi Natekar
(Bachelor of Architecture student in the Department of Architecture at the School of Planning and Architecture, Bhopal, India)
For travel to Fez and Beni Oulid, Morocco (via Barcelona) to work as a volunteer on the Lam Alif Media Library project with Azi Chaouni Projects.

EXPLORE!

See the complete text on the Berkeley Prize website

Learning and Unlearning in Morocco

During my final semester of architecture school, just months shy of graduation, I stumbled upon an enticing opportunity: a fellowship in Morocco. [...]

Aziza Chaouni Projects (ACP), located in the Ville Nouvelle of Fès, became my haven. With a modest team of around ten designers, ACP tackled a myriad of projects. From day one, I braced myself for a departure from the conventional design approaches ingrained by my college curriculum. ACP's ethos placed users at the core of the design process, fostering collaborative solutions that resonated deeply with me.

My initiation into ACP involved crafting a design toolkit for upcoming workshops in Agadir. In 2023, the Regional Tourism Development Company (SDRT) of the Souss Massa Region invited ACP to spearhead ecotourism initiatives. These ventures aimed to blend innovative design with vernacular techniques, all while minimizing environmental impact. Our mission: to engage stakeholders, from elected officials to local communities, in a co-creative process to shape the future of three strategic sites: Boutbouqalt, Targua N'touchka, and Anmel. [...]

Marrakech, the final destination on my itinerary, held the allure of Jacques Majorelle's famed creation—the Majorelle Garden, a sanctuary of azure tranquility. Yet, our anticipated journey took an unexpected turn as catastrophe struck the city and the nation. A seismic upheaval, unseen in generations, shook Marrakech Medina to its core—a 6.8 magnitude earthquake that tore the ancient fabric of the

The scenes of the night as we slept on the ground of Jemma el-Fnaa square that night, oblivious to the extent of the devastation, the scenes around us were hauntingly surreal.

(Photos: Provided by Saavi Natekar)

city asunder, leaving behind a landscape marred by devastation. Once-stalwart structures crumbled, their echoes mingling with the cries of the afflicted in the maze of narrow streets now strewn with rubble.

What began as a personal retreat to Fès turned into a commitment to aid those devastated by the earthquake. Every night at the Market Square the trucks would assemble to collect any relief for the victims, from clothes to mattresses and even tents. Witnessing the outpouring of support from communities rallied my resolve to contribute to the recovery efforts.

In Douzrou, over 97 families lost their homes to boulders during the earthquake. Though lives cannot be restored, ACP is aiding in family rehabilitation. Homes were designed in modular form, using reinforced bricks for earthquake resilience and quick construction. The settlement layout, adapted to mountain terrain, retains the original contours, forming a stepped settlement plan with interconnected homes facing minor streets converging into larger community nodes.

In villages like Douzrou, where families lost everything to nature's wrath, ACP's initiatives offered a glimmer of hope. Through innovative design solutions, we aimed not only to rebuild homes but also to foster a sense of community resilience. As I bid farewell to Fès, my journey back to India was marked not only by a life-changing experience but a renewed perspective toward a design professional and the role we play in creating inclusive, resilient urban spaces. [...]

Images captured during the ACP team's visit to Douzrou vividly document their efforts to assess the damage and engage with stakeholders.

(Photos: Supplied by Saavi Natekar)

BP2019

Philipp Goertz

(Bachelor of Architecture student at RWTH Aachen University, Aachen, Germany)

EXPLORE!

See the complete text on the Berkeley Prize website

For travel to the Architectural Association London's Visiting School in Tokyo, Japan for their "Ring of Fire" course that explores innovative new ways of designing shelters to respond to natural disasters in a 40,000 km area of the Pacific Ocean; and to Kyoto, Japan for self-guided research on construction techniques in traditional Japanese buildings.

"What is it that we really require from the scientist and technologist? We should answer: We need methods and equipment which are cheap enough so that they are accessible to virtually everyone—suitable for small scale application; and compatible with man's need for creativity. Wisdom demands a new orientation of science and technology towards the organic, the gentle, the nonviolent, the elegant and beautiful." - E.F. Schumacher

I start my final report with the very same quote as my Travel Fellowship proposal. It sums up the agenda and main objectives of my trip to Japan. The first objective was to understand whether participation in the construction process by its future inhabitants may result in identification with the house; and how far this factor may influence a building's resilience and sustainability. The second objective was to develop how digitalization and computer-aided technologies in combination with low-tech analogue approaches could be beneficial to the idea of participation. And the third objective was to understand the role of traditional clay and adobe constructions and its modern implementation in terms of sustainability and resilience. [...]

This idea of resilience and sustainability through aesthetic and absolute carefulness in design manifested during my visit to Kyoto. Rengeji Temple and the Katsura Imperial Villa endured in perfect conditions—not due to unbreakable materiality but because it deeply touched people's emotion and, therefore, became worth to maintain and care for.

This very same idea applies to the thatched roofs, that I visited in the backcountry of Kobe. Ikuya Sagara san, a thatcher, invited me to his house in Ogo. He generously showed me some of his works and even let me assist on construction site. I still doubt my contribution to the progress on construction, but he still invited me to come back to Japan and work with him.

A common thatched roof lasts about thirty years. Especially the parts that are exposed to wind, rain and snow a lot will start to rot—the roof needs to be fixed. Due to its thickness and the natural properties of material and construction, only the very top layer of the roof needs to be replaced completely—the layers beneath can be reused in the construction of the new roof which then again will last for thirty more years. This periodical maintenance seems to be much more valued in Japanese culture today than in what I have experienced so far in Germany.

Interesting to me is the fact that humans seem to be much more willing to accept the need for maintenance in circumstances were the reasons are understandable and the effect of restauration becomes visible and therefore graspable. A thirty-year-old thatched roof may start to leak at certain points and moss will start overgrowing certain parts—visible effects that after refurbishment will be removed. Here, the effect of invest in workforce and capital becomes evident immediately.

What on first sight appears to be a weakness—the fact that adobe, clay, straw and various other natural materials are ageing under the influence of external forces like the weather can become its invaluable strength. Touched by aesthetics and the approachability, people care for the construction and seem to be willing to accept the need for on-going maintenance.

Conclusion

In the moment a building is constructed its decay begins. Participation in the construction of a building and therefore understanding its construction strongly increases inhabitant's affection and willingness for ongoing maintenance. A house that lasts 150 years due to ongoing maintenance is much more sustainable than any supposedly super sustainable house that is demolished 30 years after its construction.

Digitalization and computer-aided technology can be a great tool enabling people to experience the joy of construction. It enables us to find small-scale and very individual solutions without great monetary means. It is, by its nature, a very democratic tool and therefore accessible to a great majority of people. Constructions in adobe, clay and straw can benefit from digitalization and computer-aided technology. Building practice no longer becomes the exclusive field of a few highly specialized experts occupied with erecting more and more complex constructions but an occupation of the public—of everyone.

Architecture then again becomes "accessible to virtually everyone—suitable for small scale application; and compatible with man's need for creativity," not in some romanticized way that teleports us back into long-gone times, but in a modern and yet human way that makes use of all the great advantages of technology while never abandoning its original purpose: to serve the well-being of humanity.

Perhaps adobe, clay and straw—Japanese aesthetics as well as every construction, built with thought and great care, is the answer to urgent necessities in terms of sustainability and resilience as it orients itself towards "the gentle, the non-violent, the elegant and beautiful."

I would like to investigate more into clay and straw and timber constructions. Not necessarily because I believe they are the only answer to a worthy and sustainable living, but because they appear to be materials of great potential that can strongly benefit from newest technology. The very material properties of clay can educate us to build better buildings and maybe to live better lives.

Philipp assisting in the thatching of a roof.

(Photo: Provided by Philipp Goertz)

BP2018
Sneha Varghese

Bachelor of Architecture student, Department of Architecture, National Institute of Technology Tiruchirappalli (NIT Trichy), Tiruchirappalli, India

For travel to Barcelona, Spain to attend the CITY 2018 Conference organized by the International Academic Forum; and to Maseru, Lesotho to participate in a hands-on, "In-Loco Workshop" for renovations of an orphanage through RISE International.

EXPLORE!

See the complete text on the Berkeley Prize website

'Are you nervous?'
As the length of my to-do list grew shorter, and that circled date on my calendar grew closer, I heard that question more and more from my concerned friends and relatives. I truthfully answered, 'All of it is too new for me to be scared.'

I knew that during my trip would be I swept up in exhilarating novelty. But I also knew that unless I could comprehend that novelty I wouldn't be able to absorb from it. I spent the months preceding my travel researching more about the spatial and cultural contexts of Barcelona and Maseru. At opposite ends of the development spectrum, Barcelona was a city globally upheld as a beacon of inclusive and creative urbanization while Maseru was the capital town of an African country still trying to rid itself of millstones like poverty, HIV and unemployment. Like hooking prologues, the imagery I formed beckoned me to uncover and indulge in the stories of these cities. [...]

Barcelona

For Barcelonans public space design is political. They recognize the integral role these spaces play in promoting democratic interaction of diversities, fostering identity and citizenship, supporting the domestic spheres of life, and facilitating entertainment and relaxation. Therefore, since the 1980s they have demanded, created and cherished these spaces which usually front buildings of communal significance like churches, markets, and cultural institutions. This positioning establishes a symbiotic relationship of activation that contributes to the success of these spaces. [...]

The most enviable character I found as I strolled through these streets was the degree of unabashed expression and agency. The sometimes-garrulous graffiti, the posters of cultural events, the banners with political cries are all indications of that mobilization which works through a rich network of resident associations, social enterprises and civic organizations. Barcelona thrives because participation is a way of life here. The people care enough to be involved. It's not that they are not afflicted by conflicts: the influx of tourists has eroded many neighborhoods into tourist products, long term residents are often smoked out by increasing rents and living costs, increased immigration has brought with it problems of xenophobia and racism. They recognize these shortfalls, announce their aspirations and toil for their realization. The city makes them feel like they belong and in turn they work untiringly for it. [...]

The IAFOR City2018 conference themed *Fearful Futures* was held over three days at the University of Barcelona and NH Collection Constanza. To be in company of professors, practitioners and students of diverse disciplines from all over the world and to be exposed to their ideas, findings and enquiries was one of the most academically enlightening experiences I have ever had. I shall now provide a brief overview of a few of the many sessions and my primary takeaways from them. [...]

Though the mere experience of Barcelona urban planning had imparted vital lessons on facilitating inclusivity it was imperative that I back my observations as an outsider with the perspectives of citizen experts. I therefore met with Maria Roser of the Collectiu Punt 6, which is a cooperative social enterprise of feminist architects, sociologists and urban planners who aim to democratize planning by including gender issues. The following is an excerpt of my interview with her. (*Editor's note: questions only, follow*)

Could you give me a brief of your organization's projects and the methodologies you adopt to achieve you goals?

Would you say that Barcelona is gender inclusive?

Is Barcelona safe for women? Which is a better strategy for women safety: security or autonomy?

What are the methods to ensure that meaningful participation, especially of vulnerable groups takes place? [...]

Lesotho

To the uninitiated, the African continent represents a bleak picture: provincial people, dry landscapes, arcane beliefs, poverty and disease. A place that's needs fixing. Most people feel impelled by altruistic responsibility toward it; a responsibility that sometimes arises from an intrinsic presumption of their superior human condition. [...]

The next morning (after her arrival) I met Adrian who was the other international fellow participating in the workshop to provide renovations to God's Love Centre orphanage. An architect from Malta, he too was eager to discover what the next few days would hold. Daniela took us to the site and introduced us to Luca, the project architect. He, along with the local fellows welcomed us into the team. They gathered around us, cracked jokes, shared their quirks and kick-started what was to be a joyride of a workshop. [...]

Nearing the orphanage, we could hear the laughter of the children from the street itself. It was vacation time for the children, which meant that they were always out and were always playing. The orphanage itself was a small concrete structure with two rooms, one hall and a kitchen. There was a container which was being used as a school and a store house at the edge of the site. The place was stretched to its maximum capacity, crammed with children of all ages and only a handful of staff supervising them. Showing us around the house, Luca pointed out the portions that required urgent attention. This included the front yard too, where a vegetable garden, a swing, a septic tank and toilets were haphazardly positioned.

On the second day, Luca asked me to go to the existing site and come up with a design outline for a play-castle that would help structure the front yard. Kobo, an architect fellow volunteered to help me. We began by measuring and marking the perimeter. Soon the kids gathered around us curious to find out what was happening. On hearing that it was for a play-castle they excitedly began to throw in ideas and suggestions. They shared how currently it was too sunny for them to play because of the orientation of the swing and the lack of trees. The

God's Love Centre orphanage, Maseru, Lesotho

(Photo: Provided by Sneha Varghese.)

boys said they wanted more space to play football, while the girls complained that they didn't have enough space to play their games. The environmental factors hindering their play had driven them to play in front of the storage shack. I spent the rest of the day working on their inputs and coming up with a simple L-shaped play castle design that would establish a corner and define their space. I also marked out landscaping to soften the sunlight and improve the usability. [...]

The weekend that followed was one of the most fun filled I have ever had. Visiting the Thaba Bosiu cultural village, the hangout spots of the fellows, having traditional Basotho food and going horse-riding for the first time, I couldn't help but envy the Basotho people's proclivity for fun. I found myself immensely comfortable in their company, loving their energy and finding concurrence with their tastes. It was the beginning of friendships and the making of memories that I will always cherish.

I had only one day left, and that impending end made me savor the labor more. I spent it working on the roof of the orphanage, fixing the holes with waterproofing membrane against the beautiful backdrop of the Lesotho skies. The last day ended more quickly than I thought and as I bid my goodbyes to the children and to the fellows, I couldn't help but feel the pang of separation. [...]

BP2011
Diana Mihai
Ion Mincu University of Architecture and Urbanism, Bucharest, Romania

For travel to a workshop sponsored by Architects Sans Frontieres-UK in Jammu and Kashmir, India.

EXPLORE!

See the complete text on the Berkeley Prize website

On a scorching morning in mid-July, I embarked on a three-week journey for my Berkeley Travel Fellowship in India. I took advantage of a long lay-over in Istanbul to visit Basilica Cistern, a subterranean structure that dates back to the Byzantine age. After changing three planes, I arrived in Leh where I joined the other workshop participants. As Leh is situated at an altitude over 3,500 meters, we had to take complete rest for three days in order to avoid altitude sickness.

Week 1: Introduction

The workshop began with an introduction of *Architects Sans Frontieres*-UK's philosophy, the NGO responsible for facilitating the workshop in Leh. We learned that the organization aims to help Building professionals develop their skills of working with people by setting up multidisciplinary teams and exposing them to challenging contexts. Our group consisted of seventeen members with backgrounds ranging from architecture to building surveying.

Later, the introduction was followed by a screening of *Ancient Futures: Learning from Ladakh*, a film based on the eponymous book written by Helena Norberg-Hodge. Founder of the International Society for Ecology and Culture, Norberg-Hodge was one of the first people to arrive in Ladakh after it opened for tourists in 1975. The film depicts the traditional culture of Ladakh that remained unchanged for centuries until modernization took its toll. Previously a self-sustaining and strong culture living off the goods of the land, Ladakhis are now dependent on external resources and violence is on the rise. Nothing spells globalization

"View of Old Leh from the Namgyal Tsemo] hill, with the Indus River valley and the Stok mountain range (part of the Zanskar range) in the background. Stitch of 3 horizontal images." Leh is the joint capital of the Ladakh union territory in northern India. The town is located in the valley of the upper Indus River.

(Photo: Stegop, 2016, sourced on Wikimedia Commons, Creative Commons Attribution-Share Alike 4.0)

quite like the all-too-familiar T-shirt with a frowning Che Guevara available for purchase at the foothills of the Himalayas.

Subsequently, the first week's activities were divided between participatory design work at the Government School for Girls in Leh and field trips to the surrounding villages, where we focused on four thematic areas: Culture and Heritage, Learning Environments, Safety and Sustainability. To facilitate our interaction with the students, Sarah Ernst, one of the workshop coordinators, presented the idea of Participatory Rural Appraisal, an approach meant to involve the local community in the design process by sharing information through mapping of ideas and collaborative discussions. This way we were able to find out details of the students' life in and outside the school. Tsering Tashi, the Physical Education teacher, explained that most of the students come from faraway villages in Ladakh and they stay with relatives while studying in Leh. We were surprised to find out that during winter, the school is closed for two and a half months, due to the harsh weather. [...]

Week 2: Design & build

On the second week of the workshop, we started to work effectively at the Government School for Girls in Leh. First, we were divided into three groups. Drawing on what we learned in the previous week, each group had to develop proposals for the school with different time frames for implementation:

- Short term group (1 week): proposal for a display and seating area;
- Medium term group (2-3 months): proposal for a new toilets block, based on an improved Ladakhi traditional toilet;
- Long term group (1-2 years): proposal for retrofitting the school, meant to serve as a model for improving similar buildings.

As part of the short-term group, my team mates and I started work by selecting a site on the school's grounds for our proposal. We decided on a site in the proximity of the library, considering the request of the students for a reading space in the courtyard. Equally important in deciding on this site was its perspective towards the playing field and the presence of a small bed of flowers, a rarity in the school's courtyard. [...]

Despite being set in a high-altitude desert, the school strives to be self-sufficient by having solar panels that supply energy and a solar panel water pump. Another

Main building on the SECMOL campus.

(Photo: Mrladakh, 2003, sourced on Wikimedia Commons, Creative Commons Attribution-Share Alike 3.0)

impressive feature was the toilets block. Drawing on the traditional compost toilet, suitable for a harsh climate where year-round functioning flush toilets are virtually impossible, the back wall of the composting space is made out of a large sheet of steel painted black. This helps create an updraft that draws the smells out through horizontal vents at the roof level.

While the Druk White Lotus School was a great lesson in sustainability based on traditional and modern solutions, we discovered similar principles implemented at a fraction of the cost at an experimental campus called SECMOL (The Student's Educational and Cultural Movement of Ladakh). Located in the Indus valley near Phey, this school admits around 40 students and aims to prepare them for adult life by making them responsible for their surroundings (they take turns preparing meals in the kitchen, maintaining the school grounds and taking care of animals).

Moreover, sustainability is taught through playful experiments like the solar cooker (a simple structure made out of mirrors, that can be used to boil water), as well as through a scheme of recycling the waste material produced on site. A low-cost passive solar system has been applied successfully - plastic sheets are used to soak up the sun, only to be rolled over the windows during the winter to keep the buildings warm. [...]

Exploring Chandigarh, Jaipur and New Delhi

After the workshop in Leh, my Berkeley Travel Fellowship continued with visits to three important Indian cities: Chandigarh, Jaipur and New Delhi.

I reached Chandigarh after a four hours train ride on the Kalka Express from New Delhi. Once I stepped out of the train station, my preconceived idea of what a city should look like was dismantled while facing a seemingly endless mass of vegetation, with no buildings in sight. The contrast with the bare landscape surrounding Leh couldn't have been bigger. My first impression of the city as a sprawling forest with tarmac covered roads increased on the taxi ride to the Chandigarh College of Architecture.

Despite the heavy car traffic, there was hardly anyone on the sidewalks and the buildings were concealed by greenery and fences. At the college, I had the privilege of meeting Mr. J. P. Singh, the dean of the school, who led me on a tour of the studios and advised me on how to make the most of my short time in the city. Despite being met with knowledgeable smiles when I expressed the desire to explore the city on foot to get a better sense of its atmosphere, I walked from the college to the Chandigarh City Museum. [...]

Subsequently, I visited Jaipur, the eighteenth-century walled city built by Maharaja Sawai Jai Singh II. As the historical city's layout was inspired by a nine-part mandala, a grid of avenues divides the city into nine sectors. It was interesting to notice how, in contrast to Chandigarh's typical sector, the commercial areas are disposed along the main streets, protecting the residential areas nestled in the middle of the block. From the main streets, alleyways provide access to multistoried residences called havelis, typically organized around one or multiple courtyards. Consequently, this has generated a vibrant urban atmosphere, as well as a gradual transition from the public areas towards private space. [...]

Finally, my last stop was in New Delhi. After having to change my plans of visiting the part of the city designed by Edward Lutyens, I visited Qutb Complex, a group of Islamic monuments located in Mehrauli, one of the seven ancient cities comprised in contemporary Delhi. The oldest monuments of the complex date back to the twelfth century, marking the beginning of Muslim rule in India. One of these monuments is Qutb Minar, a five stories-high tower showcasing Indo-Islamic architectural motifs. The different stages of construction are highlighted by the use of different type of materials, with red and buff sandstone being used for the first three stories, while the last two were built out of marble. In fact, red sandstone was the preferred building material for the rest of the complex's monuments. [...]

BP2006
Andrew Amara

(Bachelor of Architecture student, Makerere University, Kampala, Uganda)

To attend the 12th annual United Nations World Urban Forum (WUF12) convened by the United Nations Human Settlements Programme (UN-Habitat) in Vancouver, Canada with programs/activities including the Growing Up in Cities (GUiC) program; World Youth Forum; UN HABITAT World Urban Forum; and the Global Design Studio.

EXPLORE!

See the complete text on the Berkeley Prize website

As I arrived at Vancouver Airport, I couldn't help wondering what the next few weeks would be like. This was my first travel experience outside Africa: over 18 hours of travel from Uganda, across the Mediterranean, Europe, and the Pacific Ocean to reach Vancouver. I had expected that there would be somebody to pick me up from the airport, but instead I was given directions on how to find my way around, so I was on my own. Friends and family back home find this hard to believe. [...]

Canada is so different from Uganda, from the food to the built environment. The landscape is animated by the ocean, rivers, mountains, and forests. The city center is a spread of high-rise blocks that sit next to the waterfront. Back home, not more than 10 buildings rise higher than 10 stories; in Vancouver, cars are parked in

View over Kampala, Uganda. A few high(er)-rise buildings can be seen towards the upper right.

(Photo: Simisa, 2009, sourced on Wikimedia Commons, Creative Commons Attribution-Share Alike 3.0)

View of downtown Vancouver taken from the Vancouver Lookout at Harbour Centre.

(Photo: Bobanny-"assumed, based on copyright claims," 2007: sourced on Wikimedia Commons - Creative Commons Attribution-Share Alike 3.0)

6-story buildings. Buses run on electricity. Many things are automated: a machine sells me soda, a machine does the laundry, a machine takes me upstairs. It took a while to get used to a grid of streets that look almost the same. It is a wonder that I didn't get lost!

Growing Up in Cities (GUiC)

Over my first weekend in Vancouver, I took part in the Growing Up in Cities (GUiC) sessions. GUiC is an action research initiative that involves young people as co-researchers in evaluating their neighborhoods and working to implement change. The first few days were really cold although the sun was up and shining. Eventually the weeks became warmer.

I got to meet interdisciplinary, multi-sectoral teams and young people from various parts of the world, who are working to understand and transform their urban environments. Part of the agenda was to learn about each other's projects; what works and what doesn't in young people's participation in research planning and action.

For instance, GUiC New Zealand showcased how they are trying to empower and involve the children on the Cook Islands in planning for the shoreline. The youth from South Africa were tackling urban issues by looking at the social problems caused by HIV AIDS. [...]

World Youth Forum

Soon after the Planners Congress, we joined the over three hundred international youth delegates in the World Youth Forum. Many shared ideas/inspirations, set intentions and engaged meaningfully in various activities. Participants split up into groups with different focuses: health care, environment, leadership, gender and indigenous issues. We deepened our creativity and developed new capacities. At the end of the three days, we made strong recommendations to the UN HABITAT and leaders from around the world.

What I appreciated the most about the forum was the informal setting—free and fun. Such a setting nurtured understanding. For instance, one sunny evening my group went trekking along the beach analyzing the intricate ecosystems along the shore line and discussing several ways of protecting our environment.

In between the conferences we would take tours through Vancouver: visiting gardens, parks, communities and entertainment centers. Water Street (Downtown Vancouver) became one of my favorite spots. I would escape there, in search of a hot Ethiopian meal, sit by the street bustling with activity, or just walk under the shade. The people are very friendly; even the bus drivers greet me. [...]

World Urban Forum (WUF)

The World Urban Forum began on June 19. About 10,000 participants from over 100 countries gathered in Vancouver for the Third session of the UN Habitat-WUF to discuss a way forward on world's state of rapidly growing cities: under the theme *Our Future - Sustainable Cities - Turning Ideas into Action*. The urban agenda highlighted inclusiveness, with balanced participation from the public, private and civil society sectors. Ministers, mayors, academics, community-based organizations, non-governmental organizations and the private sector shared ideas and experiences on what would improve the quality of life in the world's cities. In addition to keynote speeches, there were dialogue sessions, roundtable meetings and networking events.

The global urban population will increase by approximately two billion reaching close to five billion in 2030. How will our cities accommodate this additional two billion people? What city forms are we contemplating? What density and what physical reach are we expecting? What quality of life are we seeking in cities? [...]

It was agreed that there is need for parties—local, state and provincial governments, citizens, the private sector and civil societies—to involve themselves further in urban development, and to work harder to solve urban challenges. This drive must be characterized by innovation and municipal leadership. Partnerships and relationships need to be built in an inclusive manner to better understand the challenges and develop practical solutions. It was noted that transparency and accountability is vital. The public needs to be informed of the problems and of the steps being taken by the governments to address them.

Particular emphasis was placed on the needs of women, youth and people with disabilities. There was a strong participation of women and youth. [...]

Global Studio Vancouver (GSV)

With new insight from the World Urban Forum, we then began the Global Studio Vancouver (GSV) design workshop. GSV brought together ninety students, teachers and practitioners of architecture, planning, landscape architecture, industrial design, community development and international relations from over fifteen countries.

It was a constructive, stimulating and challenging atmosphere: different participants, different backgrounds and regions, different approaches, each one contributing innovative ideas, sometimes through heated debates or roundtable discussions. [...]

The workshop focused on participatory design and planning approaches, and culminated in an event to engage the public in a dialogue on possible futures. A Future Directions Forum was also held. In addition, GSV participants developed *"pps:r"* (people, places, situations, response), a public art exhibit on Hastings Street, one of the major corridors in the city. [...]

We took part in a series of orientation programs to give us a better understanding of the urban fabric and heritage of Vancouver. Founded in 1886, Vancouver has a relatively short history. Over the years, plans for housing, services, transportation, finances and infrastructure have played key roles in making Vancouver a city that respects the environment and provides residents with opportunities to live, work and prosper. There are residents from around the world speaking more than 70 languages, thriving neighborhood communities, a downtown core, and a broad-based economy.

The city also has extensive public consultations in planning and decision making. It was new and impressive for me to see how this works because, back home in Uganda; a public building will go up without any reasonable public discussion. Vancouver has managed to create a vision of the city as a great place to live, work, shop and play close to home; a city that seeks to become sustainable by integrating economic, ecological and social impacts in decision making. [...]

Global Studio Vancouver Challenges:

Can participatory design and planning contribute to improving people's lives?

Can Global Studio put its skills at the service of communities?

Can Global Studio add value to the already much investigated downtown eastside?

Can Global Studio help turn ideas into action?

Can Global Studio develop skills and knowledge that participants can take home and apply?

We broke up into five teams to work on five Community Projects with local community organizations.

The Five Participating Community Organizations:

VANDU (Vancouver Drug Users) women's group

Vancouver Aboriginal Friendship Center

Strathcona Revitalization Committee

Waterfront Coalition

Chinatown Revitalization Committee

Initial Questions:

What do people like/dislike about the area?

What would improve their lives?

What physical changes would help improve their lives?

Does the group have a vision for the future?

What is the political/planning/historical context? [...]

The time I spent in Vancouver was truly memorable. As I boarded the plane at Vancouver Airport, I couldn't help wishing I could carry the whole set of workshops and experiences back to my classmates in Uganda.

Andrew Amara is now a member of the Berkeley Prize Committee.

BP2004
Adriano Pupilli

(Bachelor of Architecture student, University of Sydney School of Architecture, Sydney, Australia)

For travel to Barcelona, Spain to attend *Forum of the Cultures Barcelona 2004* to gain an understanding of its core themes: Cultural Diversity, Sustainable Development, and Conditions for Peace; and to attend *Arquitectura 3000* to gain understanding of its core themes: Mind, Land, and Social.

EXPLORE!

See the complete text on the Berkeley Prize website

Walking the old streets of Barcelona, a living breathing city, one cannot help sense the richness of the surrounding social and built fabric, as if it speaks of the people it serves, exuding their messages, ideas and dreams. A continual dialogue, an evolving architecture, which if allowed to flourish, tells the story of people and place; present, past and future. Layers of flaking paint, stone and graffiti record time and events analogous to growth rings of tree-trunks or sedimentary layers of stone. This universal dialogue, its development by people via the creative adaptation of urban built-form and the resulting inclusive elements of the city that have evolved will be presented to the reader for evaluation. These notes attempt to explore issues facing Barcelona's displaced, particularly youth, and the nature of self-help architectural solutions developed as a response, looking specifically at: the adaptation of borrowed/recycled space and materials and their function in housing the displaced, the integration, interaction and role of *centros sociales* or social centers within the surrounding urban fabric. Ultimately this report seeks to initiate global dialogue on the implications of a human approach to the provision of affordable and sustainable housing in one's own city, investigating the potential of this movement to alter non-ethical city development, architectural process and the architect's relevance to a greater humanity.

A street artist scrawls *Bien venidos a Karcelona* (1) across a blank wall in the inner city, a simple message to passing tourists and locals alike. Another paints a delicate eye and a quotation on stone ruins, *unos roban, otros matan por dinero... otros violan la educacion, destrui enpaises pobres....y yo me dedico a escribir textos!!* (2), presenting the importance of informal expression in keeping the actions of political leaders in check. [...]

These forms of expression greatly enrich the experience of inhabiting or passing through Barcelona's built environments, however in some cases, go further to create an altogether new environment, by which people informally adapt an existing one. For example, in the *barrio of Gracia*, community groups within each street organize an annual fiesta whereby inhabitants of each street collect an array of recycled CD's, bottles, paper, milk cartons... assembling these materials in creative arrangement. Together with local musicians and actors who perform on makeshift stages, the community imaginatively transform their streets into diverse and surreal landscapes utilizing local and renewable resources, each street competing yet complementing each other, the adapted built environment continually interacting with the bustling human traffic. Importantly, the informal adaptations of the built environments discussed above, contribute enormously to the richness of the city fabric and its relevance to Barcelonan people; speaking to its inhabitants as inhabitants communicate in return, perhaps simply by the act of reading or choosing to ignore a message. However, the greater role of informal adaptation of borrowed/ recycled space and materials in facilitating appropriate shelter solutions to displaced populations in the city also became apparent throughout field research in Barcelona, selected cases will now be discussed. *(Editor's note: The report continues here with descriptions and discussions of the Placa de la Vergonya (3); Can Masdeu; Le Castillo(5); Anarko Piena Cultural; Cyber Forat; and Miles di Viviendas. The commentary of Anarko Piena Cultural, as follows, is particularly interesting.)*

Anarko Piena Cultural Center

Walking up a small lane from Placa de la Vergonya a small pink sign stopped me: Tienda Gratis or Free Shop. An oxymoron such as this commanded another glance at the building that it addressed. Anarko Penya Cultural is a highly socially and politically orientated social center, providing free accommodation to its diverse inhabitants, importantly however, it also provides a most impressive array of free community services to the surrounding urban poor neighborhood who are continually under threat of displacement due to inner-city development discussed earlier. Previously a theatre and ballet school before its abandonment many years ago, the building and its occupants now provide free language, painting and dance classes, gymnasium facilities, hold regular community theatre productions, political discussions, demonstration organizations and disco tech parties.

Joseph, a young occupant of the house explains that "we have been in good terms with the twelve property owners over our two and a half years of occupation", they are permitted to stay rent free due to major repairs they have performed on the house, recycling what was an unusable space into an affordable home and community nucleus. They now continue to repair and maintain the property as part of their agreement with the landlord to be the caretakers in exchange for its free use. [...]

As one of the primary objectives of the Barcelona travel fellowship, I attended *Forum of the Cultures Barcelona 2004*.

A forum showcasing the complexity of the world's people, habitats and their interaction with each other has the potential to be a great event, increasing global consciousness, leading towards cultural acceptance and peace. However, after three visits to the Forum, the dialogue of peace, cultural diversity and sustainability shouted loudly by glossy brochures and banners littering the Forum, became lost by the contradicting and underlying economic objectives of the venture. Had objectives been clear and honest from the outset and the city's people more involved in decision-making and brainstorming the Forum, perhaps it may have been a different species with genuine messages relevant to both Barcelonan and foreign guests.

However, the Forum did provide the invaluable opportunity to compare approaches to addressing displacement, ethical city development and sustainability in Barcelona. Grass-roots approaches, such as the adaptation of space and materials to house people affordably and with a high level of autonomy, delivery of education, support services and entertainment to the neighborhood by community-run social centers, were compared with more formalized approaches used by the Forum and city. ...The human movement presented by the above case studies

Facade of the *Anarko Piena Cultural Center*, Carrer de Sant Pere Més Baix, Barcelona, Spain. The photo dates from 5 years after Adriano's travel. An even later 2011 image shows the façade completely rehabilitated and the structure apparently once again in use as a public theater.

(Photo: "Color sépia," 2009, sourced on Wikimedia Commons - public domain.)

demonstrate a working alternative to the delivery of affordable and appropriate shelter to displaced youth of Barcelona. It became evident that other minority groups also depend on this form of community support and housing to survive in Barcelona, although not as prevalent. While social centers are not without any problems, at times suffering a lack of personal and tenure security, overcrowding and privacy, internal disputes regarding personal/cultural differences, these centers have demonstrated their capability to provide socially, financially and environmentally appropriate housing to occupants with essential elements not mirrored by formal models investigated. Importantly, their role as community nucleus was not emulated elsewhere, providing support services that retain a sense of bartering, sharing and dignity rather than a sense of shame in the receipt of a handout.

This discourse is presenting many questions to socially conscious architects, planners and engineers as it is undeniably altering the process by which the marginalized are choosing to be housed and supported in Barcelona, the architect's role evolving to stay relevant. [...]

If formal methods of development and community support are to evolve to become less prescriptive, more resourceful with our city's finite resources and inclusive of all who inhabit our urban landscapes, a decentralized human approach seems a sensible solution. By utilizing this process architects can begin re-establishing their relevance to serving a greater humanity, a relevance that too often seems lost in the race to submit proposals for the next luxury hotel or apartment block, importantly making a positive step towards ethical and sustainable city development, and the city as habitat for all.

NOTES

(1) Welcome to Car-celona.

(2) One robs, others kill for money...others violate education, demolish poor districts....and I dedicate myself to writing

(3) Plaza of Shame

(4) The Castle

(5) Outdoor Cinema

Adriano Pupilli is an emeritus member of the Berkeley Prize Committee

Directed Community Service

An opportunity for students to compete for a stipend to join existing charitable programs in their local communities.

The Goals

During 2020 and 2021, BP Travel Fellowships were suspended due to the pandemic. Substituted was the opportunity for BP essay semifinalists to compete for stipends to join existing volunteer programs in their local communities or to initiate one of their own. In either case, the hope was that the proposal would reflect the content of their BP essays for that year.

The proposal required that the student focused on one of the following two options:

1. **To develop a detailed action plan indicating the specific steps needed to develop a new community service program linked to some aspect of architecture or the built world.**

2. **Volunteering with an on-going community service program and/or organization of the student's choice linked to architecture or the built world.**

The overall goal of the Community Service Fellowship was to further the student's understanding and application of the social art of architecture by allowing them hands-on participation in an organized project in the field. A concurrent goal was to provide the students with examples of how possibly to start their own programs in the future as a way of giving back to their community.

Selected students received a stipend of up to $3,750 sufficient for the proposed program costs. The following synopses describe the winning students' projects.

The Winning Students

Winta Assefa, studying in the Bachelor of Architecture program at Addis Ababa University, Ethiopia, received a stipend to design and produce a prototype for a new generation of individual booksellers' "Mobile Libraries."

Ipsita Choudhury, studying in the Bachelor of Architecture program in the Department of Architecture and Planning at the School of Planning and Architecture, Bhopal, India, received a stipend for "Making Home a Livable Place" as a volunteer with Better Bhalswa, Delhi, India to help co-create a program. The purpose of the program, *Worth in Waste*, is to create visible change for the heavily impacted community of over 200,000 marginalized people living at the Bhalswa dump site through place-making and light infrastructure interventions.

(Editor's note: See also, IN PRACTICE: The Emerging Professional Lives of the Top Student Winners below. Gunraagh Singh Talwar, BP Essay Prize Winner 2021, formed and has led the Better Bhalswa initiative.)

Hadiya Javed, studying in the Bachelor of Architecture program in the Architecture and Planning Department at NED University of Engineering and Technology, Karachi, Pakistan; and **Swaleha Javed**, studying for a Bachelor of Science in Psychology in the Institute of Professional Psychology at Bahria University, Karachi, Pakistan, received a stipend to volunteer with ModulusTech, the first team in Pakistan to devise a sustainable yet affordable flat-packed housing solution designed to provide adequate living conditions for potential users—the bottom 40% of the population in urban cities like Karachi.

"The focus of this project is to create a prototype that can help the young booksellers in Addis Ababa, Ethiopia, display and sell their books more comfortably and efficiently. Many of these booksellers carry those books in their hands, holding up to fifty books per hand. Carrying this many books has long-term repercussions for booksellers' physical health."

(Photo provided by Winta Assefa)

CODEC team in conversation with Nirmol Dada (center) and his wife, Shujota Didi (r) at the site.

(Photo: CODEC Program and Knowledge Management team, 2022)

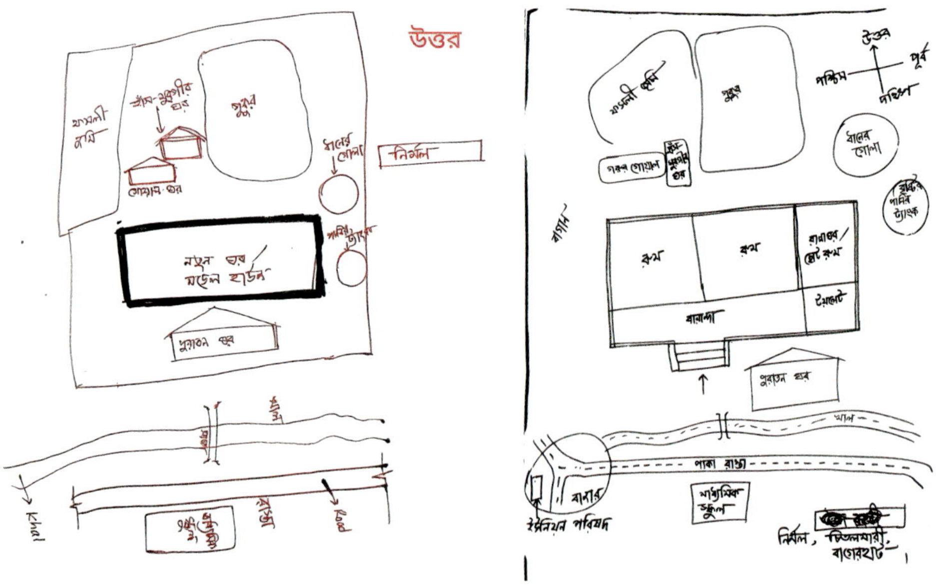

Primary drawings for the family.

(Illus.: CODEC Program and Knowledge Management team, 2022)

Final plan under construction, showing pierced masonary wall to allow for air circulation.

(Photo: CODEC Program and Knowledge Management team, 2022)

Nowshin Matin, studying in the Bachelor of Architecture program in the Department of Architecture, Faculty of Civil Engineering at the Military Institute of Science and Technology in Dhaka, Bangladesh, received a stipend to join the CODEC—Community Development Center—in Khulshi, Chattogram, Bangladesh, as a volunteer member of the Knowledge, Management, Program Development, and Technical Team, specifically involved in helping to facilitate the implementation of the CODEC Affordable Resilient Housing Piloting Initiative.

Gauri Patra, studying in the Bachelor of Architecture program at the Gautam Buddha University in Noida, Uttar Pradesh, India, received a stipend for "Fundamental right to the city for the invisible," working with Aashray Adhikar Abhiyan (NGO) as a volunteer providing support for the homeless population in Shakarpur, Delhi, India.

Michal Romaniuk, from Poland and studying in the Bachelor of Architecture program at the Manchester School of Architecture, United Kingdom, received a stipend for "Reinterpreting the Modernist Heritage of Warsaw," a project to conduct a series of workshops to determine community desires for future neighborhood projects.

M.S. Srinivas, studying in the Bachelor of Architecture program at the School of Planning and Architecture, Delhi, India, received a stipend for "Proposal to Volunteer with Social Design Collaborative," a community-driven architecture practice, to learn about ameliorative design and inclusive planning.

EXPLORE!

Read the full Community Service reports

Initiating Local Competitions

The Berkeley Prize Architectural Design Fellowship and its diverse results.

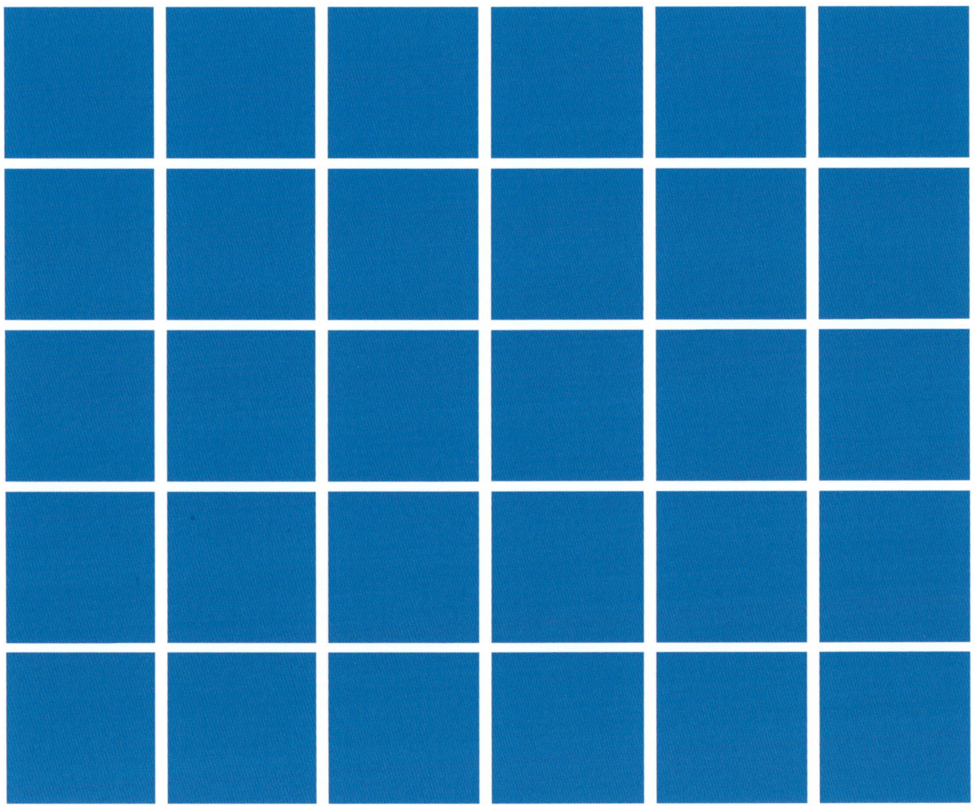

The Goals

This Architectural Design Fellowship has offered undergraduate architecture students the opportunity to stage a local or regional architectural student design competition for the benefit of the student's community. The goal is toward furthering the exploration of the meaning and potentials of the social art of architecture. The competition topic is required to be based on some aspect of the students' essay that was submitted in response to the year's Berkeley Prize topic.

The students awarded the fellowship have been provided with funds to stage the local competition and to provide individual cash prizes for the winners. Prospective competition hosts are asked to name a faculty or administrative advisor within their academic institution to review the competition. He or she agrees to assist the students with any professional guidance needed to make the competition a success.

It is up to the students, however, to decide the scope of the competition, how they intend to publicize it, establish the entry requirements, establish a time schedule, select judges, and determine the awards. Students are asked to provide the Berkeley Prize with periodic updates on the progress of their competition and a final report on the results, all of which are posted on the Berkeley Prize website.

This fellowship was available between 2008–2011. In all, six fellowships were awarded to one- and two-person teams.

Excerpts from Two Select Final Reports

Preeti Talwai

University of California, Berkeley College of Environmental Design, California, United States

EXPLORE!

Read the full Design Fellowship report

The InFORMal Competition, 2011

The University of California, Berkeley is known for its longstanding tradition of commitment to social issues in architecture, and accordingly it is on this campus that the Berkeley Prize was established. Today, amidst growing concerns that this social aspect of its Environmental Design fields is eroding, I am glad to state that this year's final entries for the *InFORMal* competition sponsored by the Berkeley Prize re-introduced a sensitive and nuanced understanding of the social art of architecture.

The two finalists for the competition prepared 36″ x 72″ design boards for a final presentation and judging. They then showcased them to a four-member jury. Based upon the work and the presentations, the awards were decided.

Rebecca Hui, a junior majoring in Urban Studies and Business at UC Berkeley, was awarded first place and $1,500 for her exceptional investigation of Gulbai Tekra, Ahmedabad. This slum, known as "Hollywood" to the locals, is a significant site for the creation of statues of Lord Ganesh for large-scale autumn export during the Ganesh Chaturti festival. Rebecca visited, thoroughly documented, and carefully analyzed the informal inhabitation of this artisan population in the slum. Her interviews with the inhabitants were evidenced by a small video that she presented as well as an eye-catching range of diagrams and photographic documentation that charted various social factors at the site.

Synthesizing all of this information, Rebecca proposed an intriguing solution of adding an overpass to the existing site—juxtaposing the informal with the formal in a well thought out manner. She accompanied this larger design gesture with other proposed changes, such the materiality of the statues. The presentation of this work was impressive, with first-rate graphics and a holistic understanding of the competition's goals.

Zoey Espinoza, a third-year student majoring in Architecture at UC Berkeley, was awarded second place and $1,000 for her outstanding work on the BART Station Plaza at 16th Street and Mission Street in San Francisco. She focused on the participants of the weekly nighttime "Poetry Slam" that occurs there and implemented a design intervention that helped foster this event, an integral part of this site.

With painstaking attention given to both social factors and technical aspects of the site, such as acoustics, Zoey altered the site to better accommodate the Poetry Slam while still preserving its essence. The information gleaned from her ethnographic methods—a combination of interviews, observation, and immersion in the space—was evident in her extremely detailed understanding of each facet of the site and event and was realized through excellent diagrammatic representation and design.

Her design measures, which included a stage, seating, and dynamic waste receptacles, were considerate of the existing conditions and celebrated informality—a unique take on the competition brief. Relating to a space in her immediate community, Zoey provided a wonderful insight into an essential but much-overlooked area in San Francisco's complicated urban fabric. [...]

When taken together, the disparate sites explored by these two finalists are truly compelling. While the site-specific social conditions are literally oceans apart, these entries demonstrate that the significance of informal, socially disenfranchised inhabitants to society's civic character is universal. Though both students contented differently with complex issues, there was an underlying acknowledgement and appreciation of these communities that was refreshing to witness.

The judges overwhelmingly felt that all work was commendable, and it sparked interesting conversation within the jury. I wish to thank the Berkeley Prize, and specifically Ray Lifchez, for sponsoring these contestants and affording me the opportunity to engage in this endeavor and think more deeply about the use of space by those groups who are often discounted in design. The experience has been truly remarkable.

The local competition poster.

A SLUM CALLED HOLLYWOOD
Gulbai Tekra-Ahmedabad, India

I first stumbled upon "Hollywood" when I got lost on a rickshaw in Ahmedabad, India. The things I noticed first were typical of your gawky foreigner: tents made from corrugated metal, livestock frolicking about, and half-naked children running around. What struck me most were the infinite stacks of elephant statues lined up on the street. But the sight of the slum was a strange contrast against the bordering commercial districts and the luxury cars that honked the slum. When I asked my friends about the slum, they told me locals called it "Hollywood," but that it was formally called Gulbai Tekra. I am not entirely sure the story behind the name "Hollywood," but my theory is that the sight of this slum is so contrasting against the two commercial districts nearby that it appears to be a painted set-up you would only find in Hollywood.

I returned regularly to learn more about the Gulbai Tekra. Gulbai Tekra's sustenance revolves around building elephant statues resembling the Hindu god, Ganesh. Employment? Making Ganesh. Religion? Worshipping Ganesh. Education? How to make Ganesh. Dwellers produce 30,000 Ganeshes per year, sell them for 90 USD, and made 23 USD in profit. Labor wages are set at 5.60 USD per statue. The statues are formed out of Plaster of Paris mixed with coconut fiber. The community was mostly comprised of immigrants from the rural villages of Rajasthan, a state in northern India.

Despite Gulbai Tekra's flourishing community and activities, the general perception was quite negative, and many felt that the area needed to be "cleaned up" (quoted from comments in a forum). On the other end, slum dwellers share with me the government's efforts to evict them due to the environmental hazards that the traditions that surround the celebration of Ganesh cause. Every year in September, thousands will immerse Ganesh statues in the water-bodies of India to celebrate the creation and destruction of life. Unfortunately, the ritual consequently releases whopping amounts of toxins when the statures dissolve. While environmental consciousness is a priority, I felt there were greater reasons beyond this for such severe evictions. I also came to learn there were plans to widen the streets when I saw red arrows drawn on the walls of houses, which marked the extent by which the street will be widened. I was haunted by one dweller's statement: "In two months, my house will become a bus stop."

Driven by the urgency of the slum's removal, I was convinced to record the dweller's stories. I created a questionnaire to learn about each dweller's background and story. I was also interested in abstracting notions of "happiness," and executed this by asking the dwellers to give me a number from 1-10 that reflects their happiness. Based on that number, I gave them the numbers of flowers and photographed them. I also surveyed the perceivably higher-income individuals found in the commercial streets near Gulbai Tekra, and proceed to "map happiness" across the different income groups. Through these ethnographic interviews, I hoped to gain an empathetic point of view to the priorities that shaped the inhabitants of the slum and the perspectives of strangers outside the slum.

"A Slum Called Hollywood" by Rebecca Hui: part of her competition entry.

Design Drivers

NOT ECO-FRIENDLY

To avoid the reasons for eviction, the most obvious priority is to find substitutes for current statue-making materials and ensure that the process is environmentally friendly.

SOLUTIONS:
- Use unbaked natural clay
- Produce stone-based reusable statues
- Use paper-mâché

EVICTIONS

Red arrows in slum dwellers' homes mark the extent in which their houses will be destroyed. A celebration of the slum's culture may convince the greater community of its values.

SOLUTIONS:
- Economic Vitality: Turn the main street into a celebratory marketplace and opportunity for economic vibrancy
- Cultural Vibrancy: Allow the marketplace to be an open canvas for the community of artists

HIGHLY UNSANITARY

There are no sewers and animals are allowed to run rampant, causing piling of fecal matter and frequent outbreaks of sanitation-related diseases.

SOLUTIONS:
- Animal corrals
- Canted elevation to drain rainwater
- Underground water collection system

TRAFFIC CONGESTION

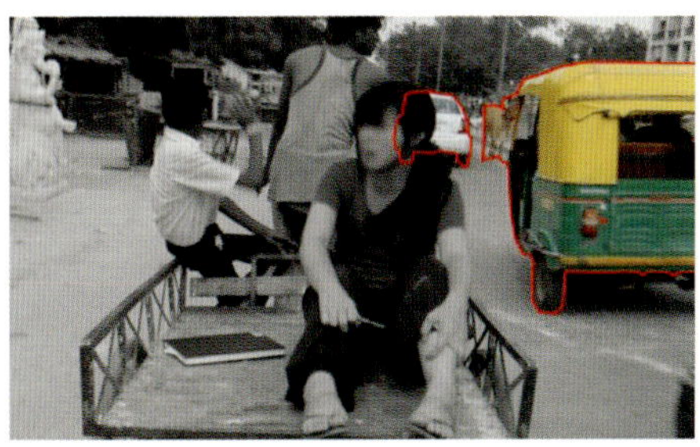

Slum dwellers ebb in and out according to the levels of traffic, an unsafe habit that is perceived as a nuisance to commuters.

SOLUTIONS:
- Elevate the street for the through traffic while keeping the existing level, in order to separate commuters and dwellers

Robert Unger

Bezalel Academy of Art and Design, Jerusalem, Israel

EXPLORE!

Read the full Design Fellowship report

The Water Towers: New Perspectives Competition, 2010

The initiative to create a national competition on the subject of conservation and repurposing of Israel's disintegrating water towers has come at the right time, as reflected in the competition results and the interest it has sparked.

The inherent characteristics of the water towers in the country's landscape and the sweep of nostalgia for the general public, combined with the growing awareness in Israel of the efforts of conservation, created the perfect atmosphere for architects as well as the general public to look at the water towers as potential for revival, rather than an object belonging to the past.

The jury examined the entries for nearly forty works, searching for the right balance between several values which sometimes collide: local community needs, daring originality, sensitivity to the existing structure, and above all, in-depth research.

The winning proposals were generally those that dealt with the surrounding urban tissue surrounding the towers, and successfully set the tower back into the center with respect to its past.

The competition was open in two categories—students and young architects—a decision which brought more submittals, and showed that experienced planners have greater sensitivity to the existing environment, as well as a higher level of research and presentation abilities. On the concept side, students were mostly more original and even revolutionary, bringing ideas which spark the imagination in terms of how to take a fresh look at an existing tower and what can become of it, in a contemporary manner.

As expressed by the jury members, many of the works dealt more with the landmark, with the symbol of a water tower rather than with the water tower itself, in its physical, material evidence, which is old and fragile, having been built decades ago in reinforced concrete. An important realization was that education to conservation in Israel is lacking, resulting in projects which are sometimes alienated from their own history, and therefore from their immediate environment.

On the shoulders of many good people, this project has grown beyond any expectation and attracted architects, designers, nostalgia-lovers, photographers, conservation activists, government representatives, municipal officials, national newspapers, television and websites, and most importantly the public.

The peak of the project was the exhibition, closing on 1 January 2011, a good date to end this portion of the project and begin the next step—establishing an archive of the hundreds of photos and tens of documentation files gathered in the past months, and, with the help of the Israeli Society for Preservation of Heritage

Sites, pushing forward the actual realization of the concept to re-use the water towers and bring them back to the public.

This, of course, is dependent on local municipalities and water corporations, but thanks to the buzz created by the exhibition, I am optimistic. Since the first days of the competition, I said to myself: if even one of the water towers receives a new function and returns to serve the community as a place to meet, relax or communicate, I have done my share.

I would like to thank the Berkeley Prize for giving me a chance to make a change.

ISRAELI STUDENT WINNERS

First Prize: Public Park and Shaded Bench in Givat Shmuel by Nitzan Bartov & Rita Zheleznyakov

"In the last two weeks of 2010, the winning proposals, as well as historic photos and posters, and the documentation files, were exhibited in a Jaffa port hangar. Thousands of visitors attended the exhibition, which received wide coverage in national media—radio, TV and press. Since April 2011, the works have been exhibited inside a water tower in Kiryat Tivon, which has been renovated and re-used as an art gallery. Two academic seminars were held on the topic of conservation of water towers, and several tours to the water towers of Tel-Aviv were held. All activities were publicly open for free. The competition and exhibition were made possible with the funding and help of many good people and organizations."

ICOMOS

2010 berkeley prize

The local Water Tower competition posters in English and the home country language, Hebrew.

EXPLORE!

Read all of the full Architectural Design Fellowship reports here.

In Practice

The Emerging Professional Lives of the Top Student Winners

The Goals

If there is one common thread to the Berkeley Prize's winning students' yearly submittals, it is that each one of the students is committed to a social life, one in which other people's needs and desires are at the forefront of what they do. A better, people-centered architecture is the ultimate design goal of the Berkeley Prize. A better, people-centered worldview is equally important to the former students as their professional lives demonstrate.

For both the 20 and 25th anniversary celebration of the Berkeley Prize, we asked all of our top winning students to tell us—in a minimum number of words and a few illustrations—how their subsequent professional lives developed. We received a number of responses among winners of the Essay Prize, Travel Fellowship, and Architectural Design Fellowship prizes. A variety of these is shown here in chronological order. All show how the social art of architecture can and does work in the "real" world.

Particularly striking from all these responses is the sheer variety of ways in which student prize winners integrate an evidence-based approach to design into their personal and professional lives. Some have also applied what they have learned to collateral fields in equally interesting ways. Seven of the students have become Berkeley Prize Committee Members in recognition of the depth and quality of their growing professional work.

The idea of the Berkeley Prize—and to some extent this book itself—is twofold:

First, to demonstrate that there a social art of architecture component to any work future practitioners might undertake.

Second, that there are a variety of successful avenues to pursue to be both architecturally creative and people oriented.

Particularly satisfying from an academic standpoint is the excitement the winning Berkeley Prize students exhibit about their work. The more current work of these past students can be traced further on social media. This continuing and growing work encompasses the direct application of lessons learned to building projects; becoming part of the public administration of urban and rural development; pursuing further academic pursuits and/or becoming public advocates for the application of these "new" approaches to design; and, in several instances, by teaching an even newer generation of architecture students. All are prime examples of how on-the-ground research has successfully led to the delivery of practical solutions for pressing social problems.

If there is one common thread to the winning students' goals after the university, is that each and every one of the students is committed to a social life, one in which other people's needs and desires are at the forefront of what they do. Since its founding, the Berkeley Prize has been guided by this overriding objective. Our goal is to discover ways to eliminate the false dualism that has emerged in architecture between social concerns and creative design, and between people-driven design and object-driven design.

Architecture is more than just design. It is about people *in* design.

Selected Winners' Professional Lives

Responses celebrating the twentieth anniversary (1998–2018) and the twenty-fifth anniversary (1998–2023)

Andrew Amara

Uganda, Essay Prize and Travel Fellowship winner, 2006

My architecture degree taught me how to design steel, glass and concrete: how to detail buildings and specify materials. I was on course to a "flashy" profession. But my participation in the Berkeley Prize as a student opened up my eyes to the human element of what architects do: we are supposed to touch lives, and transform lives by improving access to quality spaces and shelter. It also showed me that PARTICIPATION from local communities yields better results in design.

The realities of slums and disorganized settlements in my home towns of Uganda is a people in timber shacks, no access roads, poor sanitation, open sewers that flood when it rains, and a host of related socio-economic challenges. This reality pushed me to study urban planning and development.

Andrew Amara, 2006 BP Essay and Travel Fellowship winner (and, now, BP Committee Member), leading a workshop as the Director of TownBuild to engage local families in Nabweru, an impacted suburb of Kampala, Uganda, towards developing affordable and sustainable shelter, 2016.

(Photo: TownBuild team members.)

I now run an urban development program where we engage low-income households in improving access to sustainable housing. I also lead an architecture practice we were explore innovations in various award-winning projects across the country. As a Berkeley Prize Committee member, University instructor and alumni leader, I continue to mentor students on career and the importance of finding ways to impact society.

(As of 2024, Andrew is Principal Architect at Studio Flame in Kampala, Uganda that offers services in architecture, engineering, and urban planning.)

Andreea Movila

Romania, Travel Fellowship 2015

My 2015 Essay Prize submission answered the theme of "Architects Confronting Poverty" with a case study from my country, Romania. It was not the first time I participated in an essay competition, but the first time I approached the theme of architecture as social art, which transfigured my life afterwards in an unexpected way.

I subsequently won a Travel Prize, and returning from my travel I convinced the Dean of my architecture school that a contest for architecture students from Romania focused on social problems in the country would be very necessary. He invited me to come with a proposal, including the rules, jury, and prizes. In 2015, we organized the first edition of the contest.

This is now a nation-wide essay competition called the "Architecture of Alterity" *(Alterity: "Otherness")*. The competition, directed at architecture students throughout Romania, focuses on architectural responses to social problems in the country.

(As of 2024, Andreea lists her current role as, Publisher, SHAREarchitects: "Our experience of over 25 years in the Central and South Eastern European market positions SHARE Architects as one of the most active events network in the region, a source of constantly updated information, supporting the continuous training of specialists and the promotion of young talent...Each year, SHARE Architects forums have been in pursuit of excellence in the fields of architecture and construction, improving the quality and complexity of its dynamic events with each edition.")

Delma Palma

United States, Travel Fellowship 2014

I am an architect and urban designer who designs mixed-income communities in some of the most impoverished areas of the United States. At the firm where I work, my co-workers and I work with many entities, such as city housing authorities, public planning departments and private developers, to deconcentrate the poverty that was exacerbated by the way public housing was developed in the 1950s and '60s. Through designing mixed-income communities we help cities and neighborhoods become more resilient socially, economically, and physically.

(After her Berkeley Prize fellowship and her graduation, Delma Palma was hired as an architect and urban designer at the firm of Torti Gallas + Partners, located in Washington, D.C., United States. Their motto is "Architects of a Better World." While there, she was author of an in-depth article for the firm, *"Resilience in Housing Diversity."* See, https://tortigallas.com/ideas/resilience-in-housing-diversity. As of Spring 2024, Delma is a visiting scholar/lecturer at Hunter College, New York, U.S.A.; and Vice President of Design and Construction, Empire State Development (ESD), New York, "leading the design vision of New York State's economic development projects and integrating the State's community, climate, and housing goals into ESD's real estate projects.")

Sophia Bannert

United Kingdom, Essay Competition Winner, 2013

In 2017, I won the Royal Society of the Arts (RSA) *Inclusive Living Brief* for my project Bee-Able. Bee-Able is a system designed to tackle inaccessibility in the city, aiming to make our cities more inclusive and accessible for everybody, via satirical design interventions, accessibility rating and way-finding technology. This was a direct result of the research undertaken for my Berkeley Prize essay written in 2013.

Charles Fadem

United States, Essay Competition Winner 2000

I am currently the Director of Interior Design at Board & Vellum Architecture in Seattle, United States, but my work focuses on experiential design, which transcends the architecture, landscape, and interior design disciplines. Experiential

Fuel Coffee & Books, Capitol Hill, Seattle, Washington, U.S.A.

(Photo: Another Believer, 2023, Wikimedia Commons - Creative Commons Attribution-Share Alike 4.0)

and interior design focuses most on the story of interaction with architecture on a human scale. We believe that the social activity in a space activates and completes it, and in this way, there is no question that design is a social art. More than just design, there is no more social art than conversation. We have both a podcast called B&V Radio, as well as regular community "Night School" events, where we invite the public to join us in the discourse of design.

Aparna Ramesh

India, Essay Competition Winner 2014

After my graduation in May 2015, I headed off to Bangalore where I worked as an architect with a small studio office. It was in Bangalore that a few architect friends and I had the opportunity to meet the young and enthusiastic team of Guardians of Dreams, a city NGO working passionately to improve the life outcomes of young orphans and street children. Working within the constraints of time and money while attempting to skillfully translate the NGO's vision, and more importantly, the children's ideas and aspirations first onto the drawing board and consequently, into a real-world, three-dimensional building was the most challenging yet fulfilling task. For direction and inspiration, I frequently revisited the field notes and research for my 2014 Berkeley Prize essay, "The Architecture of a Healthful Learning Environment."

Nicole Graycar

United States, Travel Fellow 2008 (BP Committee Member)

I am a consultant on Carnegie Mellon University's new CMU-Africa campus in Rwanda, which aims to lead the region in technology education. Back in Pittsburgh,

Article and photo essay by Nipun from *"Reinforcing a Labour of Love,"* published in @futurarc, December 2022, telling the story of how a Buddhist nunnery in Nepal was rebuilt after the devastating earthquake of 2015.

(Photo: Nipun Prabhakar)

I am helping Carnegie Mellon become the first anchor tenant in the largest undeveloped site within city limits. The riverfront property, once home to steel mills and currently surrounded by a depressed community, will be at the forefront of sustainability and community engagement.

Nipun Prabhakar

India, Essay Competition Winner, 2014

In January 2017, I started working in Nepal as a consultant architect for Hunnarshala. We worked with the Tibetan refugee nuns, rebuilding their meditation houses, which fell during the earthquake of 2015. After the project was finished, I was invited to work in Kathmandu on post-earthquake rehabilitation where Hunnarshala is working with a local organization, Lumanti. I am currently working there, helping people with designing and building earthquake-safe houses.

(Nipun, as of Spring 2024: "I'm an independent photographer and a community architect and designer, working with various South Asian indigenous communities at the intersections of ideas, artefacts, folklore, and the built environment. Collaborators and clients include the New York Times, Washington Post, Rest of World, FuturArc, Goethe Institute, Aga Khan Trust for Culture, Aga Khan Documentation Center, MIT, CISCO, People's Archive of Rural India. I've also collaborated with professors and projects at universities like Massachusetts Institute of Technology (MIT), US; Cornell University, US; Institute of Development Studies, UK; University of Michigan, US; and Kyoto University, Japan—all for various research and documentation projects.")

Benard Acellam

Uganda, Essay Prize Winner 2010; BP Committee Member

Designing for and with people and the environment. I have been involved with the Berkeley Prize since 2010 when I participated in the Essay Prize competition as a first-year architecture student. The knowledge acquired through participation in five competition cycles and subsequently through involvement in reviewing the student submissions as a committee member has greatly shaped my understanding and practice of architecture and urban planning.

In a nutshell, the prize birthed and grounded my belief that architecture should be about people, and that consideration for the environment is of utmost importance. I continue to translate this knowledge into practice chiefly through ensuring that people's needs, desires, aspirations are at the center of the spaces and places I create, and that I design with the environment.

Working in a developing country context such as Uganda provides a myriad of problems but also opportunities to tailor architectural solutions that show that people and the environment matter. My professional life as an architect is about tackling these challenges and opportunities one through each project I undertake. As an educator, it also means sharing my approach and beliefs with students and inspiring them to develop their own thoughts about design and its role in society. The Berkeley Prize remains an invaluable source of inspiration and knowledge in my career in practice and academia.

(As of 2024, Benard lists his work as including both his role as an Assistant Architect at DE-ZYN FORUM LTD, and Assistant Lecturer in Architecture at Makerere University, Kampala, Uganda.)

Winta Assefa

Ethiopia, Community Service Fellow 2021

I'm named Winta—pronounced the way British people say "winter"—and I'm a Saudi-born architect, visual artist, and storyteller currently based in Addis Ababa, Ethiopia.

I participated in BP2020 at a time when I had to rush work for my final year of university, and I had no idea how, or if, I would practice architecture after graduation. But for around a month, I highlighted quotes from different students' essays, printed them out, and reviewed them again before writing my essay. It was inspiring and somewhat intimidating to see architecture students express themselves so well through writing. I still remember how mesmerized I was by 2004 winner Angela Nkya's way with words when I first came across her essay.

The announcement changed a lot of things for me. I'm still an indecisive night owl who has difficulty leaving her house. But since then, I've been able to go on a non-traditional path with the skills I gained from architecture school. This includes working with teams to create socially conscious designs and teaching people how to communicate visually, among other things.

Philipp Goertz

Germany, Essay Prize Winner 2019

Back in 2018, when I was writing my essay for the Berkeley Prize, I stumbled upon a book called *Small is Beautiful: A Study of Economics as if People Mattered* by E.F. Schumacher. Its content strongly influenced me on my trip to Japan, which I owe to the Berkeley Travel Fellowship, and that left me with deep gratitude for the joy felt discussing architecture with like-minded students as well as being able to visit beautiful clay-plastered architecture.

During my time working on the essay and my visit to Japan, I felt that in architecture there is the possibility to genuinely engage with people and create a world in which people matter. This attitude carries on in my architectural works. Recently, I won with a friend the second prize in a student competition, in which we worked on the transformation of Berlin Siemensstadt. Today, four years after my trip to Tokyo, I am working on my thesis project at RWTH Aachen University, Aachen, Germany. And again, there is Schumacher's book next to me. My thesis deals with a deeply troubled place in the city center of Aachen that I seek to make a place in which people matter.

Khushali Haji

India and U.S.A., Essay Prize Winner 2020

I'm very proud to be a recipient of the Berkeley Prize. The process of writing and researching the essay helped me understand a lot about where my interest professionally lies. Researching the communal history city with an architecture student helped us both broaden our understanding of how buildings fit into their political and historical contexts. It helped us understand that architecture and urban design, far from being apolitical, are always rooted in the conflicts or politics of their time, and how much of an impact these buildings themselves have on the community that uses them.

Currently as a researcher, writer, and theater artist, I always attempt to be critical in the questions I ask, of the answers I find and how I present them to my audience. The prize (along with significant financial aid) helped me understand my voice and interest in writing on socio-political and personal narratives in cities in the South Asian context.

Ghina Kanawati

Lebanon, Essay Prize Winner 2018

Four years ago, when I was still a third-year undergraduate architecture student, I decided to dust off my writing skills and participate in the Berkeley Essay Prize competition. I felt lucky that 2018's essay question was broad, challenging, and applicable to my hometown: Beirut.

I weaved the knowledge and experience I collected into a heartfelt essay that won second place. Among the many things the award gave me was an incredible confidence boost in my potential and what I can offer my community as a professional.

The Beirut Port blast occurred just after my graduation on 4 August 2020. Soon after, I was on the wounded streets of the city I got the chance to write about, participating in recovery projects to help my city stand back on its feet.

These experiences led me to my current work position as an architect and researcher at CatalyticAction, a charity that empowers vulnerable children and their communities through participatory built interventions in public spaces across Lebanon. We co-design these interventions through a process that engages the

Project review with clients in Lebanon, masked during pandemic.

(Photo: Provided by Ghina Kanawati)

community members in participatory activities enabling them to take ownership of their spaces. The most rewarding feeling is when a child feels heard and happy to see a project to which they contributed become a reality. I'm proud of the impact we are creating and excited about what the future holds for me.

Oprah Omeka

Kenya, Essay Prize Winner 2022

The Berkeley Prize broadened my knowledge and interest in the social art of architecture through exposure to projects globally that have explored social inclusion in architectural design. I appreciate the role local communities play in shaping architectural spaces through their customs and lifestyles. Therefore, I aim for careers in architecture and architecture-related fields that give room for consistent collaboration with clients and occupants of spaces to design new long-lasting and evolving spaces, renovate existing ones, and develop a network of like-minded individuals for future projects.

I am currently self-employed as a freelance photographer in Nairobi, Kenya. I like to understand how people think and why they think the way they do. Interacting with them in organically occurring situations and photography sets gives me the opportunity to see their perspectives.

Ushna Raees

Pakistan, Travel Fellow 2018

The Berkeley Prize was one of the best experiences of my life. It inspired me to pursue a career that focuses on community development and social art of architecture. In my professional practice, I still try to apply my Berkeley Prize essay, *"idea i-e: Communicating with the Society through the Social Art of Architecture."*

I'm currently working at *arcop Associates, Architecture and Urban Planning,* Delhi, India as project architect on several school projects sponsored by AKDN (The Aga Khan Development Network) and AKESP (The Aga Khan Schools, Pakistan) in different districts of Gilgit Baltistan and Chitral. All schools are currently under construction. Although the primary intent of their design is to promote youth education, the flexible design of the schools also aims to facilitate and benefit the community in terms of cultural enhancement and agro-biodiversity. They offer an alternative approach to learning through smart and experiential spaces.

The program accommodates smart classrooms, e-library, multipurpose halls, auxiliary spaces, and enclosed corridors with incidental and interactive learning

The Society for Protection of Ancient Buildings, non-profit organization headquartered in London, United Kingdom.

(Photo: Provided by Hadas Rix)

spaces. The flexibility of spaces allows the appropriation of program throughout the day by engaging people of all age groups, fueling to an improved and connected living for the community. The use of vernacular materials creates a sense of place and belonging, amalgamating the building with its context. The main idea revolves around uplifting the entire community, encapsulating social sustainability through design intervention.

Hadas Rix

United Kingdom, Travel Fellow 2005 (Past Member, Berkeley Prize Committee)

As the Berkeley Prize Travel Fellowship winner in 2005, I attended the International Union of Architects (UIA) conference in Istanbul and participated in the first global studio. The workshop in Zeyrek, a deprived neighborhood and a World Heritage Site, introduced me to concepts such as gentrification, preservation versus restoration and social engagement in practice. This early career experience had a life-changing impact and for many years I supported the Berkeley Prize as a reviewer.

In the following year, my B.Arch. final project focused on social architecture in a deprived neighborhood. The project won first prize in the Israeli Planning Association student competition. Following my conservation experience in Zeyrek, I founded a conservation consultancy in 2010 and was privileged to promote cultural heritage and design the restoration of significant buildings as a conservation architect.

The Berkeley Prize provided me with the confidence to write about architecture, and I have prepared over 50 reports and heritage statements on listed buildings and heritage sites. In 2019, I moved to the UK to complete an MSc in Historic Building Conservation at the University of Bath. My dissertation on issues of authenticity when conserving historic imitative crafts was published in two papers in the *Journal of Architectural Conservation,* published by Taylor & Francis.

(As of 2024, Hadas lists her responsibilities as: "Construction Project Manager at University of Bristol, Bristol, United Kingdom.")

Reva Saksena

India, Essay Prize Winner 2021

I recently completed my undergraduate architectural program. My thesis project was entitled "Social Inclusiveness through Design: Development Centre for the Transgender Community at Vadodara, India." This was an extension of the research undertaken for my Berkeley Prize 2021 Essay.

I reached out to NGOs, volunteers, and members of the Transgender Community who helped test the feasibility of my essay and further my design proposal, albeit theoretically, into a valid architectural realization. While conducting interviews and documenting the community's living conditions, I realized the valuable contribution of community participation in making architecture a truly social art. The outcome was an architectural model for the trans community, designed as an "in-transit" complex to support community members to develop necessary skills of economic value until they can become independent and live with pride. The model caters to the essential needs of the trans community: safety, privacy, and "own" space.

Through the Berkeley Prize, I learned that the idea of a community is formed by the association of people with each other, people with their spaces, and spaces with their surroundings—a concept that has driven me since and inspired me to become a more conscientious designer.

I hope that I will be able to take my architectural model to the wider architecture community and influence decision-makers in the government or elsewhere.

(As of 2024, Reva lists her responsibilities as: full-time Architectural Designer at Populous in Delhi, India. "Populous' reach stretches across Asia Pacific with regional headquarters in Brisbane, and offices in Beijing, New Delhi, Singapore and Sydney.")

Gunraagh Singh Talwar

India, Essay Prize Winner 2021

Editor's note: The Bhalswa landfill, located in North Delhi, has a colossal mountain of trash that reportedly receives over 50% of Delhi's waste. The area also numbers over 200,000 residents.

Every year, as an architecture undergraduate, I would write for the Berkeley Prize. This was an opportunity for introspection and to reflect on my thinking as an aspiring architect. In the first instance, with the Travel Fellowship, I was building with Gambia in a community-building initiative. This was my unlearning, imbibing in me greater nuances of building—as a verb over noun—with the ability to shape a greater space than tangible.

The prize and its annual prompts also raised me to question conventions, be it worldly concerns or our professional practice. Believing us to be "mediums to change," since 2020 I have led a bottoms-up initiative for Bhalswa, Delhi, India. As professionals skilled in multidisciplinary domains, we are fantastic collaborators for driven teams. Adopting unique lenses through collaborations, my team has developed an ecosystem of solutions for our movement called *Better Bhalswa*.

Devising solutions in space and beyond, I bring value through design strategy. In a profession obsessed with the act of building, I am an architect who is yet to build their first building. I still think I've built a lot, and for this, I have much to be thankful for.

(As of 2024, Gunraagh lists his activities as "part-time Next Generation India Fellow," an initiative by CEEW—Council on Energy, Environment and Water, New Delhi—and the United Nations Foundation. "As a fellow in the Sustainable Cities thematic, I will continue my efforts in re-imagining India's urban spaces focusing on transforming cities into more inclusive, resilient, safe, and eco-friendly habitats.")

It has long been clear that obtaining a degree in architecture does not always lead to a career in designing and building physical structures. Studying the social art of architecture can lead to a host of other related and equally valuable and socially conscious pursuits. This is made abundantly clear by the biographies of Preeti Talwai and Nathan Koren who focus on different collaboration issues; and Anusha Narayanan, who with her partner now runs a marketing company.

"This is a photograph from July 2021 when we were trying to revamp a park space with residents of Kalandar Colony at Bhalswa. We engaged children and youths in the community as our primary stakeholders/user group for the pocket park. The drawing (being held up by the youth in the background) was an initial concept for an entryway that we were designing for the park. This engagement meeting discussed the design, and we took a photo upon deciding to go ahead with it."

(Photo: Gunraagh Singh Talwar)

Preeti Talwai

U.S.A., Architectural Design Fellow 2011 (BP committee member and 2018 BP Juror)

I am currently working as a User Experience Researcher at X (formerly Google[x]), the innovation lab of Google. I conduct qualitative human-centered research that helps vet futuristic ideas and determines which are worth pursuing. I study human needs, attitudes, motivations, and behaviors across different domains and ecosystems.

The core values of the social art of architecture—in which the Berkeley Prize catalyzed my interest—have been central to my work after college. At X I am the only researcher with an architectural background. I bring a deep investment in conducting physically contextualized research and investigating human-environment relationships, with a belief that all technologies must be understood within socio-spatial ecosystems.

The critical perspective, empathy and humanism, and conviction in socially engaged and purposeful design drive my work every day. To me the most exciting thing about the social art of architecture is its universal significance to almost any discipline, while the biggest challenge is a lack of awareness. I hope that by continuing to work in non-architectural fields, I am able to open industry minds to social and environmental questions, and help shape more humanistic and socially driven approaches toward building things for people.

Nathan Koren

United States/United Kingdom, Essay Competition Winner 2000

I'm now less interested in architecture as a social art, and more interested in society as an architectural art. Before architecture school, my thinking was shaped by architects and planners with diverse but compelling narratives for how societies and their environment reciprocally shape each other. But for me, practicing architecture offered few ways to put this sensibility into action.

I quit architecture, moved to the UK, got an MBA, and joined a company that develops autonomous vehicles. After half a decade working as their liaison to urban planners and policymakers, I realized that aligning all the interests to create true infrastructural change was a fundamentally collaborative activity—that is, a social process—but the tools people used were too isolating and individualistic, inhibiting innovation.

Therefore, I founded two software companies, both focused on different collaboration problems: Futurescaper, a collaborative foresight system that is now used by the United Nations to map out contentious and subjective issues amongst many people, and Podaris, a cloud-collaboration platform for transport planners. My hope is that these technologies will allow a greater number of collaborators to shape their futures and their environments.

Anusha Narayanan

India, Architectural Design Fellow 2008 (Berkeley Prize Committee Member)

(Partner, *Fish Do It* Consultants LLP, Mumbai Area, India. *Fish Do It* is a strategy, content and design business.)

We are consultants and project planners for events, and marketing and brand communications. On a daily basis we work with small and nimble, and big and traditional businesses. We have designed magazines, produced branding and event collaterals, curated content for conferences, run editorial platforms and consulted with brands on strategy and content.

We have also designed digital solutions for brands, which involves wire-framing, designing back- and front-ends, liaising with programmers, and dealing with tech and data on a daily basis. Perhaps that sounds like a lot of words, but it involves the same things as does architecture: analyze, plan, design, collaborate, execute, and make sure we leave behind a robust system—whether organizational or digital—or just a workflow for teams to use in future.

5

The New Faculty

The Berkeley Prize Teaching Fellows and the Dialogue They Have Started

Introductions to the Teaching Fellows' Courses

The Berkeley Prize Teaching Fellows and the Dialogue They Have Started

Mid-way through its history, the Berkeley Prize decided to expand its outreach directly to those who teach architecture. The primary goal of the Teaching Fellowship was to support innovative thinking by architecture faculty as they focused their students' attention on the social, behavioral, and physical characteristics of the users of the buildings and spaces they design. More than this, the Teaching Fellowship presented a unique opportunity to attempt to provide a largely complacent academic community around the world with an outline of how to teach the social art of architecture and to explore why it is overwhelmingly not taught in schools.

EXPLORE!

Read more about the Teaching Fellowships.

The Berkeley Prize Committee distributed "A Request for Proposals" to a good portion of the world's architecture schools. We alerted the architecture blogs, mined our extensive mailing list, and advertised the opportunity on our archival website. The response was good for the first year of a prize program. From those proposals we selected a first cohort of five fellows and an associate fellow.

The selected faculty were asked to overlay a dedicated social art of architecture perspective to one or more of their existing courses for a full year of classes. What this meant and how it was to be accomplished was left mostly to the inventiveness of the individuals. All were awarded a healthy stipend in support of their added responsibilities.

Since the first of the eventual two Teaching Fellowship years coincided with the 2013 Berkeley Prize topic of *The Architect and the Accessible City*, the committee elicited the help of Elaine Ostroff, a renowned figure in the Universal Design movement whose archives are now held by the Smithsonian Institution, to act as a sounding board for the work of the fellows themselves. (See her Introduction to BP2013 in Part 3 above.) She extended this role into the second year of the experiment.

Much of what we did was to talk. We conducted monthly conference calls with all of the year's fellows as a group, held one-on-one conversations with the participants, and finally requested written interim and final reports for each semester's work from all of the fellows.

The commentaries of the first appointed fellows show that they all agree on one principle: accessibility is, first and foremost, about an inclusive architecture that does not develop special, code-related responses for one client group or another, but that creates a built environment in which everyone is equal. This is, at heart, a definition for people-centered design. Within this community of agreement, however, exists a great range of perspectives, all of which are informed by the special context in which each of their courses are taught.

Initially, our main interests were focused on results, rather than process. As the first year of the fellowship progressed, we realized that the process of re-orienting the course of study itself required more attention. For the second fellowship year, we reduced the number of appointed fellows to three and took much more care in discussing how exactly they might go about adjusting their classes to accommodate the new social perspective.

The second Teaching Fellowship reflected the 2014 topic of *The Architect and the Healthful Environment*. We encouraged prospective faculty to consider how best to transform students' thinking about the role of the built environment as a powerful forced for health. The emphasis on the healthful environment could be explored in any context and address the widest range of potential users of a space.

All of the 2024 fellows and their students show how, when faced with talking about architecture in non-traditional ways, not only does the process of teaching change, but the interests and motivations of the teachers and students themselves change. The subject of the "healthful environment" puts these issues in stark relief, but they point to the same conclusion: the attitudes of students about what is important in design and what is merely transitory style can readily and rightly be influenced by the context in which each course is taught.

In teaching this "Design for a New Age," especially interesting is the introspective nature of the selected faculty. The focus is not the student work and the student achievement, although that is significant and holds lessons of its own. It is about how the lives of the faculty themselves change when faced with talking about architecture in non-traditional ways. The specific subject matters put these issues in more stark relief, but they are the same issues that can be asked in any human-centered design process. By supporting investigations into these teaching changes in diverse settings and situations, the Berkeley Prize has both augmented other more rigorous academic research efforts, but also opened new avenues of study.

Rather than only dealing with metrics and three-dimensional form, the new faculty were asking questions about everyday life and its interaction with the buildings we use and inhabit: Where is the entrance and how does it provide a beacon for all those looking for it? Once inside, how does the building greet the owner or visitor? How are the occupants' everyday activities served and enhanced by the design of the building? Where is the window-seat in which you can retire to quietly read a book? How is a place best designed to accommodate such moments of human life?

What was accomplished during the two years is both exemplary in its breadth and its depth. From Hong Kong to India to Palestine to Serbia to Scotland to Singapore to Uganda, and to the United States, faculty from around the world showed identical interest in far more than just form, more than just geometries, but in the exploration of the meaning of architecture itself through its social roots. While doing so, they necessarily confronted larger-scale issues of proving relevance and gaining acceptance from their peers while simultaneously attempting to generate interest among students. Equally important were seemingly smaller-scale issues of how exactly, for instance, to identify, utilize, and maintain the services of user/experts.

The success of these initial Teaching Fellowships was clear; how to extend this success into the future, less so. The Berkeley Prize did not have the resources required to systematically coordinate the work of the Teaching Fellows within the structure of the prize, nor to provide the kind of ongoing, thorough assistance in their course programs that was desired and requested. Rather than accept these limitations, it was decided not to renew the Teaching Fellowship after 2015.

The reflections from all the Berkeley Prize Teaching Fellows point to the benefit of exploring the potential of many more programs like this one to the teaching and learning of people-centered architecture. The following selected introductions give a glimpse of what new social art of architecture courses might include. They are a first step in this academic evolution.

2014–2015 ACADEMIC YEAR
TEACHING HEALTHFUL ARCHITECTURE

The Prompt

Reflecting on the 2013 Berkeley Prize Essay question, the Teaching Fellowship encourages faculty to consider how best to inspire students to see an additional role of the built environment as including the potential to serve as a powerful force for health. This emphasis on the "healthful environment" can be explored in any context and should address the widest range of potential users of a space.

2013–2014 ACADEMIC YEAR
Teaching Universal design

The Prompt

To reflect the Berkeley Prize topic of The Architect and the Accessible City, the emphasis of this year's Teaching Fellowship is placed on a specific client group: those with physical and mental disabilities. This includes the disabled who use the building or space, those who visit the building, and those in the general public who might, at a future time, need to be accommodated.

At the same time, your proposal might address another client group altogether, or address a design issue other than buildings. Your specific and unique approach to tackling the complex issue of Universal Design should be at the heart of the Fellowship application. In your proposal you agree to teach the studio(s) you are now teaching, but now taught with an emphasis on Universal Design.

Excerpts from Selected Introductions to Teaching Fellows' Universal Design Courses

Ajay Khare, Ph.D.

Founder-Director of the School of Planning and Architecture, Bhopal, India, for his course, "Universal Design for Cultural Interface at Sacred Site of Ujjain in Madhya Pradesh, India."

with Rachna Khare, Ph.D.

Professor and Dean (Research and Faculty Affairs) at School of Planning and Architecture Bhopal.

Ujjain is one of the seven sacred cities for Hindus and presents diversity in true Indian context. Apart from the rich tapestry of myths and legends, the city has witnessed a long and distinguished history with rich traditions. The city is a famous pilgrimage and visited by several people to pray for good health and well-being, and a large number of them are vulnerable and deprived. This is also a site of mass Hindu pilgrimage or bathing festival called Kumbh or Simhasta.

Our institute, School of Planning and Architecture (SPA), Bhopal, is an autonomous institution of Ministry of Human Resource Development, Government of India. Supporting its Charter to be a socially aware institution, a multidisciplinary Center for Human Centric Research (CHCR) is housed at SPA-Bhopal. In accordance with its objectives, the CHCR conducted this design studio for Berkeley Prize Teaching Fellowship.

Universal Design is not part of the regular curriculum in most architecture schools in India, including our own institute. Subjects like environment psychology, barrier-free environments, human-environment studies, and sociology are taught separately as theory courses and are remotely connected with architecture design studio. This one-year long Berkeley Prize Studio provided us an opportunity to explore ourselves as universal design educators, and find a place in the existing pedagogy.

EXPLORE!

Read all of the full 2013-2014 reports.

Note: All texts date from the year when the Fellowships were awarded.

Ujjain User Study, 2013-2014

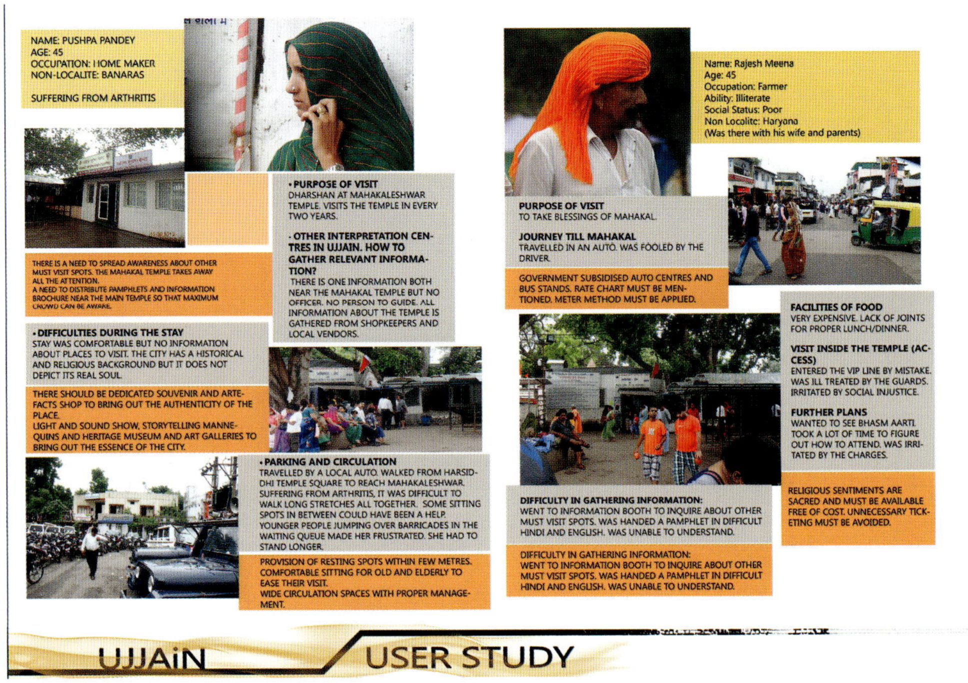

Eve A. Edelstein, Ph.D., Associate AIA

Associate Professor, University of Arizona College of Architecture, Planning and Landscape, Tucson, US, for her course, "Expanding the Universe of Design: Applying a Neuro-Architectural Process to Create Accessible Cities," in collaboration with the University of Arizona Disability Resource Center. Building on her background in both architecture, neuroscience, and anthropology and with the use of emerging simulation and behavioral tracking technologies, Edelstein explores the neural bases for attributing value to architectural design and uses such advances to develop principles that may be applied in design thinking and in practice.

The Berkeley Prize Teaching Fellowship provided the opportunity to demonstrate that the neuro-architectural process could be merged with universal design objectives in an existing undergraduate design studio. A "Neuro-Universal Design" curriculum was created for third year design studios in tectonics (fall semester) and land ethics (spring semester), spanning the 2013–2014 academic year at the School of Architecture, College of Architecture, Planning & Landscape Architecture (CAPLA) at the University of Arizona, Tucson. The cohort comprised 63 Bachelor of Architecture undergraduates, six architectural design faculty, and the Berkeley Prize Fellow—a faculty member in architecture, planning and landscape architecture, who is also trained in clinical neuroscience, anthropology and architecture.

In order to provide iterative and in-depth interaction, user/experts from the staff of the Disabilities Resource Center (DRC) at the University of Arizona and a faculty expert from the Interworks Institute, College of Education at San Diego State University joined in lectures, discussions, field trips, studio critiques, and juries. Together, they represented user/experts with expertise in:

1. Design and architecture;
2. Neuroscientific research-based design;
3. Assistive technologies; and
4. Environmental equity.

A series of lectures by the DRC and invited user/experts discussed the philosophy and impact of equitable design. The concept that architecture can and should "flex" to meet the continuum of human needs was introduced, in contrast to design philosophies that demand people "bend" to built settings. The politics of design equity was highlighted, challenging students and faculty to consider for example, if the "poetics of stairs" should supersede the "politics of space." The disability resource faculty attended studios, mid-term, and final juries, providing iterative feedback and insights to inspire equitable design, prompting students to consider the balance required in design for social equity.

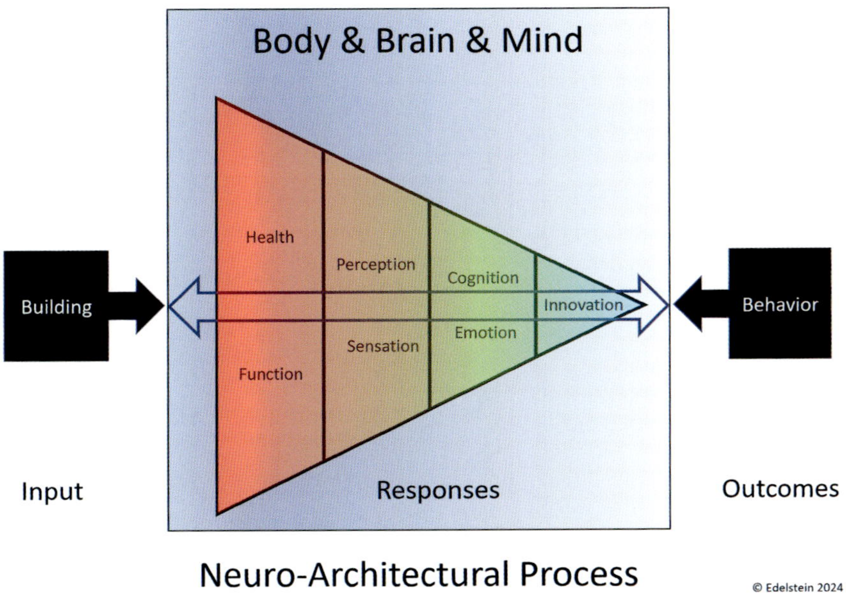

Buildings, Brains, and Behavior

"A flow diagram using a conceptual framework derived from the scientific method, links the physical stimuli of a built setting as the input to the responses of the body, brain, and mind, yielding behavioral output. A feedback loop between all elements represents the complex interaction between physical and human outcomes." Collaborators: Caren Sax, Ed.D, San Diego State University, California, U.S.A. and Amanda Kraus, Disability Resource Center, University of Arizona, Tucson, Arizona, U.S.A.

(Edelstein's updating of her original diagram that appeared in her article, "Research-based design: New approaches to the creation of healthy environments." World Health Design Journal, October (2013): 62-67. She is now one of the Clinicians for Design & School of Medicine, Stanford University, Stanford, California, U.S.A.)

ESALA students set-up shop in the community to start a dialogue with residents about what they want for a new community development, 2014. Part of the events surrounding the Commonwealth Games in Glasgow, Scotland, United Kingdom.

(Photos: Alex MacLaren)

Alex MacLaren, RIBA

Design Tutor, Edinburgh School of Architecture and Landscape Architecture (ESALA), Edinburgh, United Kingdom, for her courses on "Social Housing" and "Civic Futures." MacLaren focuses on how Universal Design can be integrated into real-time projects that start—and sometimes falter—as a result of otherwise well-intentioned community and student interaction.

Two design studio courses were run this year, each with approximately 30 students. In each case, students met individually with tutors once a week over 11–12 weeks, and attended a further weekly group seminar or lecture. Students worked in designated studio space hosted by the university and were encouraged to work there every day in addition to the mandatory twice-weekly studio meetings.

The first semester, entitled "SOCIAL Housing," asked second-year students to design a housing block of 24–30 units of mixed tenure, over four floors. The second-semester studio was entitled "Civic Fabrication: [Per]Forming Communities." This semester began by introducing students to the local environment, and most importantly, introducing them to members of the local community living or working in that environment. We asked students first to imagine a future for this area, then to design a piece of architecture which would support "civic" development in that future. Usual academic "crits" were replaced by design review seminars where we asked students to present their proposal back to the community members at the middle- and end- of the semester.

Post-graduation, students have been offered the opportunity to rework their projects voluntarily for inclusion in a community exhibition in the area, also to be built and staffed by students. Students will receive no academic reward for their participation this summer activity. However, there has been significant student support for this initiative, perhaps because re-presenting their work in this is a way of addressing that frustration of the conflicting demands of the user-experts invited to the studios and the standing requirements of academe.

The physical safety of participants was addressed through routine risk assessments, but the mental impact of this experience on students and on user-experts was more of a concern than had been anticipated. Some students found the local environment to the site unnerving and found communication difficult. One of the user-experts was similarly uncomfortable and intimidated by their initial visit to the university. These feelings caused some individuals to behave unpredictably, leading to concerns over physical safety.

The experience to date suggests that this approach has huge pedagogic value and enhances the learning experience, but at the risk of diminishing the traditional "academic achievement" of students when compared against standard assessment benchmarks. However, the long-term benefits of educating future architectural professionals in this way may reap far greater societal benefits later.

Making space for communication between students and user-experts, and specifically allocating time for non-confrontational communication, and orchestrating this, prior to any direct review of work, was essential in addressing the above.

Faiq Mari (Associate Teaching Fellow)

Teaching and Research Assistant, Department of Architecture, Faculty of Engineering, Birzeit University, Palestine. Mari, 2013 Berkeley Prize 2nd Place Essay winner, is at the start of his life in architecture and teaching. As a Teaching and Research Assistant, he is an active participant in helping to broaden his school's understanding of the goals and potentials of teaching the social art of architecture. Mari also participated in the activities of the other prize fellows during his first year of teaching. His final report describes that year.

Introduction

We enter architecture school and start losing sense of time and place. Too much work and too little time to pause and ponder the real reason we are actually studying. As years pass by, one project after another, we start to feel an increasing gap forming between us and our surrounding reality.

This was at least my own experience. During my recent years as an architecture student, I have always felt a gap between architectural education and its surrounding context. It was often a very indirect relation that we had with the community we designed for, and under the many layers of theories and analyses lied a very limited understanding of the human we designed for. Seldom was it that architecture was seen as a tool of real change on ground.

But does architecture have to be taught this way?

My experience in my first year as a teaching and research assistant was my trial in answering this question.[...]

Mock-up of accessible kitchen constructed as part of course at SPA Bhopal to test design assumptions, 2014.

(Photo: Provided by Faiq Mari)

Some months before I was appointed a teaching and research assistant, I participated in a competition that shaped the year ahead: the Berkeley Prize Essay Competition.

It was an opportunity for me to delve into my deep conviction of architecture as a social art. During the process of writing my essay, which talked about disability in Palestine from an architectural perspective, I came to understand the importance of inclusive design, and the great power and responsibility an architect has in enforcing it. My conviction of architecture as a social art developed and solidified. The direction I would take as an architect became clearer.

In my essay I discussed the important role of education and awareness-raising in achieving the rights of the disabled. I had stressed the potential of architects and architectural education in this regard. As I was about to start my job as a teaching and research assistant, I began to formulate a plan to apply this through my own career.

As a result of his exemplary work, the Prize also funded Faiq's participation as a representative to the presentation and awards meeting for the *2014 Indian National Student Design Competition: Inclusive Design for Cultural Interface in Pilgrimage Sites* sponsored by the School of Planning and Architecture, Bhopal. His reports describe both his Berkeley Prize Fellowship and that experience.

Architect Faiq Mari is now a Doctoral Candidate at ETH Zürich, Switzerland (German: Eidgenössische Technische Hochschule Zürich; English: Federal Institute of Technology Zurich) through the Institute for the History and Theory of Architecture.

6

Conclusions

What has been done.

What needs to be done.

How possibly to start doing it.

The emphasis must be on place, not studio;

User/experts must become an integral part of the learning environment;

Different standards must be adopted for course outcomes and student evaluations;

Social scientists must be (re-)integrated into the design process; and

The idea of *empathy* must be consciously incorporated into all facets of the work of the architecture studio and classroom.

What Has Been Done

If attempting to *teach* is a conceit, then trying to facilitate *learning* certainly has its own host of issues. How exactly do you energize students—all of us—to accept that there are untrodden avenues of research, the results of which could dramatically impact the way in which we normally view a building project. Architecture, that oddly positioned discipline somewhere between mechanics, art, and everyday life, asks us to do exactly that.

There are many contradictory indicators in the world today. Billions of people requiring, at the very least, shelter. Hundreds of millions of people with the ability and desire to go beyond shelter to search for an environment providing something beyond the bare minimum of protection from the elements. Tens of millions able to consider the built world as both adaptable and designable and curious enough to build accordingly. And, finally, a limited number who have the ability, freedom, desire, and resources to respond to all of this and say, "Let's create something wonderful."

This final group are normally (and nominally) the traditional focus of design students, architectural educators, and finally, architects of the future. There is nothing wrong with this. It is perhaps, however, a narrow scope for such a universal issue. Architecture is exactly that: a reality that effects each and every human being at many levels throughout their lives.

The idea of a "social art of architecture" is not fully understood, let alone accepted by schools of architecture or the profession of architecture. As the Berkeley Prize has shown, the *social art of architecture* asks simply that people and their everyday issues become a primary focus of concern and design. But how?

The preceding work provides some clues. The scholars have provided proof of a large arena of opportunities for academic research in furthering architecture that does not start and stop with the traditional *form* and (hopefully, although often not) *function* trope. The students from around the world in large numbers have, through their hands-on research, confirmed that there is a world outside the studio filled with people whose everyday lives interest them in any number of ways as a prelude and basis for design. Finally, the faculty have shown that they can adapt their syllabi and methodologies to provide guidance and direction in approaching these supposedly "new" arenas for architectural education.

This is what has been done. What *needs* to be done is an entirely different question.

World Trade Center Transportation Hub, New York, U.S.A., Santiago Calatrava, architect, 2016. It's about the people...and the (everyday) built world that can enrich our lives.

(Photo: Benjamin Clavan, 2022)

What Needs To Be Done

If the Berkeley Prize has only shown one thing, it is that the methodologies of architectural education and that of the social sciences are still far, far apart. Few, if any students, have returned Prize proposals and subsequent essays with documentary evidence of something the students learned about the lives of the people that were the focus of their inquiries. Clearly, there is incidental information and randomly collected evidence supporting their written suppositions. There has not been one student response that started or stopped with the words: "We interviewed 10, 20, 50 people representing a cross-section of the community and asked them the following questions..." Or, "After visiting the site of our inquiries, we did a thorough (even a passing?) literature review of potentially pertinent research."

We urge students to interview residents, other users, city officials, the architects and planners responsible for the buildings and urban sites about which they were writing and to tell us about their thoughts and responses to the students' questions. At best we receive one or two vague statements. These unfortunately are often also lacking context. This is not to say that the undergraduate students' effort and their subsequent written documents are without merit; it is simply that such research is beyond their capacity or, more likely, their comfort zone.

Architecture students are self-selecting. They look at wonderful and beguiling buildings and say, "I want to do that." What *that* is, clearly fills libraries of books on the subject. The bottom line is that young architects are normally, and primarily interested in architecture as product, not as process. Definitely aesthetics, sometimes the program, and at the far—and opposite—end of the spectrum, human-centered research. This is not necessarily bad.

Architecture and the social sciences are seemingly two different academic disciplines. As many times as the need for cross-fertilization might overlap in the built world, architects have not entered the world of design to become sociologists, anthropologists, and/or psychologists. And the same, vice versa. How to bridge this wide gap between architecture and the social sciences is fraught with issues. What is the relationship between architecture and society? What should it be? Can architecture actually improve society? How exactly does relatively small scale architectural interventions inform large-scale change? Does the desire for an *art* of architecture preclude or override such critical engagement in any case? How can architecture students be motivated to at least explore these questions?

A concise summary study of the history and current status of research into social and behavioral studies in design was recently published by two respected scholars in the field. Every major name, every major research project, every major conclusion is documented. Two hundred pages of dense type, including a chapter documenting a very relevant case study is presented in detail. A few photographs, some charts, references, contributor biographies. All very academic and within its stated scope, an excellent body of work. I would project that very few practicing architects, even if they know of the book, will read it. And, the only way you would get an undergraduate architecture student to even open the covers is if a specific portion was assigned as a requirement for a course. Asking students for an entire read would be beyond any architecture faculty member's wildest dreams.

The half-century trajectory of Berkeley's College of Environmental Design is a case study. In the late-1960s and through the mid-1980s, the school's faculty were consciously augmented by cross-disciplinary researchers from the social sciences. This hiring program was essentially an experiment. The new faculty would provide their own courses, sit in on reviews of student projects, and sometimes attempt to re-generate existing lecture courses along the lines of social research. By the 1990s, most of these faculty had retired or left for greener, more disciplined(?) pastures. The fault, if one could call it that, lay on all concerned: the faculty, the students, the administration, the professional discipline of architecture itself. Even the growing (begrudging?) acceptance of the need for post-occupancy studies (POS) and concerns for sustainable design are treated as secondary issues.

Part of the cause for this is the economic model of the profession of architecture itself. Traditionally underpaid and over-worked, the profession does not see a financial benefit of hiring architecture students "additionally" trained in—or even on a conversational level with—the social sciences. If anything, such students are seen as potentially lacking in the everyday computer drawing skills (and perhaps age-old sketching abilities by hand) for which they are normally hired.

The late twentieth-century introduction of computer-aided design on a large scale that eventually overtook the entire field of architecture seems to have been the final death knell to such *social* widening of the design process within the office setting. This has included pre- and post-occupancy studies of their on-the-ground projects. Aside from the fact that architecture firms spent precious tens of thousands of dollars retrofitting their practices for the computer age, only the largest and most visible firms could even contemplate paying employees to provide, let alone integrate, a wider social context for their hard-fought projects.

Two negative trends have resulted. Social scientists and architects are unable to communicate in valuable ways within the academic setting. The profession as a whole is not interested and/or cannot afford such a widening of the work of the architect.

Primary among reversing these trends is the idea that the teaching of architecture itself needs to, once again, further evolve. It is not just acknowledging the importance of people-centered design, but introducing ways in which such

Biblioteca Latino-Americana Victor Civita (Victor Civita Latin American Library) in the Latin America Memorial, São Paulo, Brazil, 1989; Oscar Niemeyer, architect. A world of imagination that does not just exist in books.

(Photo: Benjamin Clavan, 2014)

people-centered research can become part of the everyday catalogue of architectural studies. There is certainly a growing body of work by architects who focus on the users, not just the creation of geometries of form. There is also a growing body of work amongst those documenting such efforts. Recent anthologies document case studies of people-oriented design. When these examples focus beyond communities-in-need and the dispossessed, the overall message seems to be that architecture can and should become a major part of the pathway to solving and resolving social issues worldwide. Perhaps.

Much of this conclusion is based on the widening acknowledgement of such worldwide issues of over-population resulting in an ever more widening lack of shelter for all; mis-use and mis-handling of energy generation and consumption; climate change; the propensity for more and more global health issues. The list goes on. These existential issues of survival and their subsequent effects on the built world, both apparent and not-so-apparent, have clearly filtered to an ever-growing cohort in the academic arena. This all points to the need for a widening of the discussion of architecture.

How Possibly To Start Doing It

The first step is that you need to acknowledge the problem. The problem with architectural education is more a matter of what it is, rather than what it is not. At the primary level, the problem is that students and many faculty still see architecture as a two-dimensional subject starting and ending with the study of form. This is not surprising, given that the *starchitects* of the 21st century who to a person revel in the manipulation of geometries, partially as a result of technologies allowing such forms to be designed and built. This in itself is not necessarily bad, nor should such travels into the geometric stratosphere be abandoned. It is important to note that architects have been attempting this throughout history with or without computer-aided design.

As the Berkeley Prize has shown, the question is not only whether the form is correct, but more importantly, does it serve the people for whom it was designed at multiple levels. Providing sheer drama is one aspect of satisfying human desires. It is clearly not the only one, nor the only one that architecture can provide. All of this points to the question of acknowledging the role and wide universe of what we commonly refer to as the user.

If you design a residence, the primary users are the individuals who will reside there, but there are any number of wider users. These include the neighboring residents, the town or city at large, the workers who built the residence, the building supply chain that provided the materials for the structure, and the city officials who permitted the project. There are others. Now, expand a single residence to an apartment block and the list of users increases. Cross over to other building types such as retail stores, shopping centers, office buildings, public buildings, religious buildings and the list of users expands even further. All of these users are part of the design project, whether acknowledged or not.

Architecture faculty need to accept this proposition and determine how best to respond to it. Architecture students need to be directly exposed to some if not all of these users. It is not simply about a building program document. It is about actual people living their lives in any number of ways. All kinds of people with all kinds of similarities, all kinds of differences, and as a result, all kinds of needs. The social sciences provide a platform for studying, understanding, and finding ways to respond to these differences. On the surface, it seemingly makes *teaching* more difficult. At the same time, it can also make learning more interesting.

There is much in this book directly and indirectly about "Universal Design." This is partially a function of the larger discussion within architectural academia about the purpose of studying and adopting the methodologies of the social sciences. It also points to a bias toward more prosaic questions in the profession of architecture concerning how to adequately provide accessible buildings as required under growing legal requirements. As a result, in the United States, Universal Design still has a certain stigma of supposedly being reflective of only one particular interest group: those with disabilities. In Europe, and Asia particularly, the term has been widely accepted as having a much broader meaning and purpose.

My own reaction to this issue is to stress the idea that what is being implied by the use of any of the collective terms: Universal Design, Human-Centered Design, Design for All, etc., is actually part of the larger study of the *social art of architecture*. It is, at heart, about us as people and how we maneuver our way not only through the built world, but through life itself. Creating wonderful architecture is only a (thankful) by-product of this journey. The very fact that we are able to talk about architecture in this way, which is partially a result of all the academic research and studies that have led up to it—including the work of the Berkeley Prize—is in itself a proud accomplishment.

Clearly, the work and output of the scholars, the students, and the faculty who have been associated with the Prize points to the need to more systematically investigate a series of large-scale changes that would be required to fully implement the teaching of the *social art of architecture*. These requirements pose a dramatically different approach to the teaching of architecture and the preparation of teachers of architecture as both are structured today. First and foremost, it opens the door to the question of value, of what works and what does not, of what is good and bad. Inside the academy, it questions the accepted dogma of subjectivity and neutrality in traditional teaching, particularly as it applies to subjects of taste and perception in architecture. Outside the academy, it requires a willingness to explore subjects outside the traditional realm of architecture.

In the end, what the Berkeley Prize is about is an attempt to explore specific ways to bridge these divides. There are architecture scholars ready, able and willing to discuss the issue. There are clearly any number of students who accept and are interested in the opportunity to provide community service through architecture and, in the process, fully embrace architecture's human dimension(s). There are faculty who are searching for ways to integrate social science approaches to the study and implementation of the work of future architects. Finally, and most importantly, there is clearly a public interest and need for all of this dialogue and action: A *people-centered* architecture—the true Social Art of Architecture.

Coming full circle:

Chorsu Bazaar, Tashkent, Uzbekistan. Tradition meets modernism. Chorsu derives from Persian, and means "crossroads," or "four streams." This immense, blue-domed structure, completed in 1980 is located on the site of damaged or destroyed markets dating from medieval times. Designed in the "Soviet Modernism"-style by Vladimir Azimov, Sabir Adylov et al., the market allows daily activities that wonderfully reflect the life of the 14th century as well as the 21st century.

[Photo: Benjamin Clavan, 2014]

Nothing is lost: not beauty, not individuality, not academic freedom, nor the necessity and willingness to experiment with form and function.

The wonder of it all is that there is everything to gain.

Opposite: An unusually quiet passageway in the bustling Medina Quarter, the original walled city of Marrakesh, Morocco. The Medina dates to the 11th century and its walls and winding streets were originally designed for security. This contemporary and contemplative view speaks to the Medina's role as a place for people to wander, explore and discover...and to live one's life to the fullest, not quite knowing what comes next. What better metaphor for "It's About the People!"

[Photo: Benjamin Clavan, 2007]

[NOT] The Back Matter

Those Who Have Made the Berkeley Prize Happen

The Berkeley Prize Committee

Emeritus Committee Members

Further Readings on The Social Art of Architecture

Further Readings on The Social Art of Architecture

A selection of books and articles focused on the subject of this book. These investigations are *Façana de la Penya Cultural Barcelonesa* mostly by authors associated with the Berkeley Prize and/or friends of the Prize from the U.C. Berkeley's College of Environmental Design. This list, in an arbitrary order of preference, serves as essentially a starting point for further investigation of the social art or architecture.

■ ■ ■

The Timeless Way of Building

Christopher Alexander, Oxford University Press, 1979. This is a heart-felt introductory volume in a long series of books produced by Alexander and the Center for Environmental Structure. The CES was an independent environment research, theory and design consortium focused on the built environment and the way we live, located in Berkeley, California, U.S.A. Alexander was a former Emeritus Professor at the U.C. Berkeley College of Environmental Design (CED). He was the lead author of a number of unique books that can be seen as primers on the social art of architecture and a new way of looking at the built world in general.

Along with Sara Ishikawa, Murray Silverstein, Max Jacobson, Ingrid Fiksdahl-King, and Sholmo Angel, the Center's *A Pattern Language: "Towns-Buildings-Construction,"* Oxford University Press, 1977 is a focus of their life-long efforts. This is a "catalog of 253 *patterns* that cover everything from the layout of cities down to the layout of rooms." Whereas *The Timeless Way* can be seen as an introduction to all of his and the Center's work, *A Pattern Language*—as both advocacy and a methodology—has become a worldwide field of study in itself. Their approach has been applied, for instance, to resolving intricate issues and creating new developments in computer science.

(The Center is now functioning as the "The Christopher Alexander & the Center for Environmental Structure Archive," located in Berkeley.)

Design and the Public Good: "Selected Writings, 1930-1980 by Serge Chermayeff

Edited by Richard Plunz, The MIT Press, 1982. Forty essays, articles, and lectures by this architectural innovator who was an early proponent and lifelong practitioner of what would eventually become known as the social art of architecture. Among his writings is *Community and Privacy: "Towards a New Architecture of Humanism,"* that he co-wrote with Christopher Alexander (see above) in 1963.

Design Like You Give a Damn (1): "Architectural Responses to Humanitarian Crises"

Edited by Architecture for Humanity, Metropolis Books, 2006.

Design Like You Give a Damn (2): "Building Change from the Ground Up"

Edited by Architecture for Humanity, Abrams, 2012.

Each volume showcases public buildings, housing and environmental projects by approximately 70 different designers and firms from around the world who are dedicated to the proposition that it is first and foremost *about the people*.

The Power of Pro Bono: "Forty Stories about Design for the Public Good by Architects and Their Clients"

Edited by John Cary and Public Architecture, Metropolis Books, 2010. Public Architecture is a national non-profit founded by Jon Petersen and for which John Cary served as executive director from 2003-2010. The forty pro bono projects showcased in the book ranging from housing, health, education, arts, etc. demonstrate how architecture itself is and should be treated as a "social act."

Design for Good: A New Era of Architecture for Everyone

John Cary, Island Press, 2017. As showcased by Melinda Gates in the Foreword to the book, architecture is about the power and dignity of design. The core chapter titles say it all: "Buildings That Heal;" "Shelter for the Soul;" "Spaces that Enlighten," "Places for Civic Life," "Raising Expectations", and "A Call to Expect More."

(John Cary is an emeritus Berkeley Prize committee member.)

Rural Studio: Samuel Mockbee and an Architecture of Decency

Andrea Oppenheimer Dean, Princeton Architectural Press, 2002.

Samuel Mockbee and the Rural Studio: Community Architecture

David Moos, ed., Birmingham Museum of Art, 2003.

The Rural Studio, founded in 1993 by architects Samuel Mockbee and D.K. Ruth, is an off-campus, design-build architecture studio run by Auburn University School of Architecture, Planning and Landscape Architecture (Auburn, Alabama, U.S.A.). Students learn first-hand about the social responsibilities of the profession of architecture by working on a yearly basis with poor communities in rural west Alabama to provide needed low-cost homes and buildings.

Palaces for the People: "How to Build a More Equal and United Society"

Eric Klinenberg, The Bodley Head, an imprint of Vintage, 2018. In this deeply thoughtful and cross-disciplinary book, sociologist and best-selling author Klinenberg demonstrates how the well-built world has the power to create a social infrastructure that can foster a "more equal and united society."

(Eric Klinenberg was one of the four jurors for BP2020, "Designing Civic Buildings: The Architect Works With A Team.")

Revisiting "Social Factors:" "Advancing Research into People and Place"

Georgia Lindsay and Lusi Morhayim, Cambridge Scholars Publishing, 2015. With an introduction by Galen Cranz, who for decades taught social and cultural perspectives on architectural design at Berkeley's CED, this book presents a series of essays by well-known figures in the study of social factors in architecture. Of special interest is the new (revised?) perspective from several decades after the initial thrust for such studies.

(Georgia Lindsay and Lusi Morhayim are both Ph.D. graduates of the CED... and students of Galen Cranz.)

New Commitment: "In Architecture, Art and Design"

NAi Publishers, 2003. The first in a series of *Reflect* books. Essays by 30 contributors, primarily from the Netherlands but with worldwide outreach, focusing on commitment to social issues in the creative world. Separated into two categories of "Reflections" and "Positions," this is an interesting collection of writings, both for its focus and as a primer on European thinking on the subject.

Architects' People

Russell Ellis and Dana Cuff (eds.), Oxford University Press, 1989. In fourteen different essays, leaders in the study of the social art of architecture, including several from Berkeley's College of Environmental Design, "examines the people and social life lurking in the architect's imagination." A primer on how architects view the people for whom they design, where these concepts originate, and how they affect the architecture they create.

(The authors were among the core group of faculty of the CED who propelled the school as the premier academic institution studying and advocating the social art of architecture.)

■ ■ ■

Rethinking Architecture: Design Students and Physically Disabled People
Raymond Lifchez, University of California Press, 1987. This book received a great deal of attention by reviewers for its focus on bringing the disabled into the architecture school design studios as on-the-spot consultants. The greater message was that the students needed to get out into the community to focus first on people—and how to do that.

Design for Independent Living: The Environment and Physically Disabled People,
Raymond Lifchez and Barbara Winslow, Whitney Library of Design, 1979. One of the first books to tackle head-on the complexities of designing for and designing with disabled persons. This is first and foremost a "how to" book. For those who wanted to probe further, the book is a guide to sorting out difficult design issues by talking and working directly with those who will be the direct beneficiaries of any architectural intervention.

"Designing for Health: Teaching the Social Art of Architecture."
Benjamin Clavan in *Health for All: "Cultural, Operational & Technological Influences Proceedings, International Union of Architects - Public Health Group + Global University Programs in Healthcare Architecture (UIA-PHG+GUPHA) Annual Conference, Dalian, China, May, 2015,* edited by Romano Del Nord. Published by TESIS Inter-University Research Centre, University of Florence, Italy, 2016.

"Teaching the Social Art of Architecture: The Transformation of the Studio from Object-Centered to Human-Centered Design."
Benjamin Clavan, in *Proceedings, 5th International Association for Universal Design (IAUD) Conference, Fukushima and Tokyo, Japan, November, 2014.*

■ ■ ■

FOR MORE ON THE BERKELEY PRIZE

"The Berkeley Prize: Those Who Make it Work,"
Benjamin Clavan and Raymond Lifchez in Places Journal, 18(2), 2006.

"Competing to Learn: The Berkeley Prize and the Social Art of Architecture,"
Raymond Lifchez and Benjamin Clavan, in Places Journal, 17(1), 2005.

...

ADDITIONAL RESOURCES

Reconstructing Architecture: Critical Discourses and Social Practices
Thomas A. Dutton and Lian Hurst Mann (eds.), University of Minnesota Press, 1996.

Universal Design, A Methodological Approach: A Pathway to Human-Friendly and Elegant Architecture
H. Froyen, Institute for Human Centered Design, 2012.

The Scope of Social Architecture
C.R. Hatch (ed.), Van Nostrand Reinhold,1984.

Architecture for People
Byron Mikellides (ed.), Holt, Rinehart and Winston, 1980

Architecture School: Three centuries of educating architects in North America
Joan Ockman (ed.), MIT Press, 2012.

The Favored Circle: The Social Foundations of Architectural Distinction
Garry Stevens, MIT Press,1998.

Strategies for Teaching Universal Design
Paul Welch (ed.), Mig Communications,1995.

Those Who Have Made the Berkeley Prize Happen

Raymond Lifchez (1932–2023), founder, chair, and benefactor

Ray ended his long and distinguished teaching career as an Emeritus Professor of Architecture and City & Regional Planning at the University of California, Berkeley's College of Environmental Design, where he taught undergraduate design studios and writing seminars for 50 years. In 1976, he received the university's Distinguished Teaching Award; in 2002, the Association of Collegiate Schools of Architecture Distinguished Professor Award; and in 2008, the Berkeley Citation.

His publications include *Design for Independent Living: The Environment and Physically Disabled People* (Whitney Library of Design, 1981, with Barbara Winslow); *Rethinking Architecture: Design Students and the Physically Disabled* (University of California Press, 1987); and *The Dervish Lodge: Art, Architecture, and Sufism in Ottoman Turkey* (1992). He received a Community Service Citation from the Bay Area Book Reviewers Association for *Rethinking Architecture*, and an American Book Award Nomination for *Design for Independent Living*.

In addition to sponsoring the Berkeley Prize, Ray established the Lifchez Professor of Practice in Social Justice in CED's Department of Architecture; the Judith Lee Stronach Memorial Lectures on the Teaching of Poetry, which are published by U.C. Berkeley's Bancroft Library in conjunction with the University of California Press; The Judith Lee Stronach Baccalaureate Prize in the College of Letters and Science at U.C. Berkeley; the Judith Lee Stronach Undergraduate Summer Scholarships at the CED; the Berkeley Seminars in Modern Jewish Culture at the Center for Jewish Studies, Graduate Theological Union, Berkeley; and the Percival and Naomi Goodman Fellowship at the Buell Center for American Studies, Columbia University, New York.

In 2018, Lifchez was named a recipient of the Ed Roberts Award from the renowned Center for Independent Living in Berkeley. The award honors pioneering individuals who have made major contributions to the independent living/disability rights movement in the United States and internationally.

Ray received a Master of City Planning (U.C. Berkeley); Master of Science in Architecture (Columbia University); Master of Arts in Art History (Columbia University); and a Bachelor of Architecture (University of Florida).

Benjamin Clavan, Ph.D., Architect, coordinator and website editor

Benjamin is one of the founding members of the Berkeley Prize and has been responsible for the day-to-day operations of the Prize for much of its history. Working closely with BP chair, Ray Lifchez, these responsibilities have included a leading role in the development of the yearly prize topics; recruiting the invited jury members; interacting with the 60+ committee members; guiding the editorial content and look of the prize's website; and helping to organize, oversee, and participate in the review and selection process to determine the winning students. Over the past few years, he has traveled worldwide to attend conferences and deliver lectures on the topic of achieving people-centered architecture and the role the Berkeley Prize has played in furthering this goal.

Benjamin is Principal of BENJAMIN CLAVAN, ARCHITECT, located in Los Angeles, U.S.A. and Valencia, Spain. The residential and commercial projects of his firm—all smaller scale, hands-on, people-oriented projects—have been showcased in design magazines and featured on television. In different periods of his professional life, he has also been active as an architectural writer and journalist and his research and commentary—both popular and scholarly—has appeared in various publications.

Dr. Clavan has previously been involved in civic affairs, particularly as they intersect with urban design issues. Over the years he has served as an appointed Member of the West Hollywood, California Planning Commission, the West Hollywood Public Facilities Commission, and as a publicly elected member of his Los Angeles neighborhood's Community Council and Chair of its Land Use Planning Committee.

He holds a PhD in Architecture and a Master in Architecture (University of California, Berkeley), a Bachelor in Architecture (University of Virginia), and successfully completed the Diploma in Architecture program (The Bartlett, University College London) as a non-degree student.

Thea Chroman, administrator

The part-time, day-to-day manager of the Berkeley Prize and a BP committee member since 2007, Thea has been responsible for much of the direct student interaction for the prize. Her full-time work is as a housing policy analyst at the state of Oregon's Department of Land Conservation and Development (Salem, Oregon, U.S.A.). Her efforts are focused on reducing barriers to housing production and delivering equitable housing choice to Oregonians.

Editor's note: My thanks go to Thea, first for making the Berkeley Prize actually function for all of these years, and more recently being involved with the creation of this book and helping to act as a sounding board as it progressed.

Thea previously served as the assistant director at the University of Oregon Wayne Morse Center for Law and Politics in Eugene, Oregon. There she worked primarily with undergraduates who are interested in leadership, public service, and social change. Among her accomplishments there, she curated programming that connects students with opportunities, helped provide them with a broad introduction to ideas around the meaning of democracy, supported their civic engagement, and assisted in launching them into their post-college careers.

Also a public radio producer, Thea's reporting on education and urban planning in the San Francisco, California Bay Area garnered accolades including the Society of Professional Journalists Sigma Delta Chi award for Best Radio Documentary; the Society of Professional Journalists Mark of Excellence (Region 11); and multiple Gracie Allen awards, among others. As associate producer at KALW Public Radio in San Francisco, she was responsible for the daily news show script, wrote grants, and always won the holiday Pie-Off.

Thea's student planning work won the Student Achievement in Planning award from the Oregon chapter of the American Planning Association. She was a Fulbright Berlin Capitals Fellow and was a finalist for the NPR Kroc Fellowship. Thea has a B.A. in Sociology from Mills College in Oakland, California and an M.S. in Media Studies from the University of Oregon. She is also completing coursework for a Master of Community and Regional Planning at the University of Oregon. In Oregon, she serves on the boards of directors of Ditch Projects and the Eugene Science Center.

Editor's note: My further thanks go to Jessie who has been instrumental in making the prize a functioning international reality and for helping sort through the intricacies of 25 years of BP documentation, particularly with regards to the many illustrations for this book.

Jessie Canon, webmaster

Jessie has been responsible for creating and maintaining the prize's online presence and an ever-increasing Berkeley Prize history database since 2004. He is a seasoned web development professional with over twenty years of experience across diverse roles. From his role as a Lead PHP Web Developer at The Tactile Group in Philadelphia, US, to his influential tenure at MDLinx, M3, US, he has consistently delivered innovative solutions using various technologies. His career highlights include directing web development teams, implementing departmental policies, and collaborating closely with stakeholders to deliver quality projects on time and within budget. He has been responsible for creating and maintaining the prize's online presence and an ever-increasing Berkeley Prize history database since 2004.

Linda Helen Lamé, financial manager

Helen has for many years been responsible for dealing with the day-to-day financial aspects of the Berkeley Prize. This has been a large task that has included participating in the budgeting and disbursement of the operating costs for the prize. In addition, she has served a major role in the complicated distribution of the individual student prize awards around the globe. All of this has been accomplished in close association with the prize team. She is a full partner in the prize's overall success. Long-time assistant to Ray Lifchez, Helen is now one of the trustees of the Raymond Lifchez Revocable Trust.

The Berkeley Prize Committee

The Berkeley Prize relies on the input from an extensive group of reviewers located worldwide, representing both the academic and professional world of design and the social sciences. Without their yearly contributions of time and effort, the Berkeley Prize could not function.

Benard Acellam
Elaine Addison
Andrew Amara
Sangeeta Bagga, PhD
Erick Bernabe
Aleksis Bertoni
Paul Broches, FAIA
Himanshu Burte
Ellen Chen
Thea Chroman
Benjamin Clavan, Ph.D.
Roddy Creedon
Popo Danes
Howard Davis
Charles Debbas
Lynne Elizabeth
Teddy Forscher
Dorit Fromm
Thomas Gensheimer
Ann Gilkerson
Alex Gonzalez
Nicole Graycar
Zachary Heiden
Ocean Howell, Ph.D.
Neelakshi Joshi
Rachel Kallus
Daniel Karlin
Thomas-Bernard Kenniff.
Barbara Knecht
Aboubacar Sidiki Komara
Scott Koniecko, AIA
Malini Krishnankutty
Raymond Lifchez
Ian Mactavish
Christine Macy
Padma D. Maitland
Faiq Mari
John Q. McDonald
Jason Miller
Anusha Narayanan
Maire O'Neill Conrad
John Parman
Helaine Kaplan Prentice
Ushna Raees
Clare Robinson, Ph.D.
Patty Rose
Daves Rossell, Ph.D.
David Salazar
Magdalena Saura
Corey Schnobrich
Anthony W. (Tony) Schuman
Arijit Sen, Ph.D.
Murray Silverstein
Avikal Somvanshi
Preeti Talwai
Philip Tidwell
Robert Ungar
Leslie Van Duzer
Jan Wampler, FAIA
Matt Werner
Cynthia Whitehead
Keith Wilson
Friedner Wittman, Ph.D.
Bahram Hooshyar Yousefi, Ph.D.

EXPLORE!

Read the committee members' full biographies

Emeritus Committee Members

Stanford Anderson
Christopher Ategeka
John Cary
Kim Dovey
Thomas A. Dutton
Roberta Feldman
Nicole Graycar
Lance Hosey
Michael Keniger
Keith Mitnick
Angela Nkya (deceased)
Phillip Ong
Elaine Ostroff
Victor Santiago Pineda
Adriano Pupilli
Hadas Rix
Rafi Sega

berkeley prize

www.BerkeleyPrize.org

↗ Cave of Horrors, Dead Sea Scroll rescue dig

LIFE PRINCIPLES
FROM THE
NEW TESTAMENT

AMG
PUBLISHERS

Following God through the BIBLE

Cease Striving

BOOK 1

Mendy Clark, D.Ed.Min.

Following God

CEASE STRIVING
BOOK 1

ISBN 13: 978-1-61715-527-7

Manuscript editing, text design, and layout by Rick Steele Editorial Services
http://steeleeditorialservices.myportfolio.com

Cover illustration by Daryle Beam/Bright Boy Design

Printed in the United States of America
2021 First Edition

Cease Striving is dedicated to those most profoundly and daily affected by my ignorance of God's sanctifying grace (Gal. 3:3):

To my dear husband Stan, and our four precious gifts from the Lord,
Lindsey, Jenna, Maegan, and Tyler.

May the God of all grace continue to revive and restore the years the locust has eaten.
I love you all more than words!

ACKNOWLEDGMENTS

I would like to acknowledge the precious women on the Transforming the Heart Ministry Team, the Women's Bible Study groups at Chaffee Crossing Baptist Church in Fort Smith, Arkansas, and Charlottesville Community Church in Charlottesville, Virginia, for their participation, helpful comments and prayerful suggestions as they participated in the pilot study of this workbook.

Mendy Clark

MENDY CLARK (DEd Min, Southwestern Baptist Theological Seminary) is a Bible teacher, author, retreat speaker, educator and discipler of women. She is the founder, executive officer and lead teacher of Transforming the Heart Ministries. Transforming the Heart is a ministry dedicated to making disciples by equipping and training them using the biblical framework established in the all-sufficient Word of God.

Preface

"Cease striving and know that I am God."

Psalm 46:10

More than likely, if you've picked up this workbook, something in the title caught your attention. Maybe deep down, you are willing to admit that there is a striver within, and you seek rest for your soul.

Perhaps it's more than that. Maybe you have reached the end of yourself and have been crying out to the Lord for help. Striving to live the Christian life has made you anxious, joyless, and weary even to the point of exhaustion. If this is where you are, I understand entirely. It's what I call the "white-flag moment," when all of the sudden, in my head, a white flag goes up in frustration and exhaustion, and all I want to do is quit!

How do I know so much about striving? Let's just say the Lord, in His grace, has been rescuing me, from me, my entire life! Unknowingly, I spent the first twenty-five years of my walk, striving to live the Christian life in my flesh and failing miserably.

If this describes where you are, one thing is sure; the grace of God has placed this workbook in your hand. Notice I mentioned the grace of God explicitly because God's work of grace is the exact opposite of man's striving! Basically, this workbook is about two things:

God's Grace

and

Man's Striving

Be prepared as you walk through this study in Galatians, to see how Paul addresses and answers where man strives to be like god regarding salvation. You will see these areas specifically addressed in the questions Paul asks the Galatian believers, namely:

- Did you receive the Spirit by the works of the Law, or by hearing with faith (3:2)?
- Having begun by the Spirit, are you now being perfected by the flesh (3:3)?

If you consider Paul's first question, you will see that he is referring to man's salvation, in particular, justification. And in the second question, Paul is clearly referring to sanctification. Let's

face it: there is an inherent desire to be "savior" in each of us, and it entered the human race at the Fall.

In this workbook, you will discover why people strive, where it enters into the heart of humanity, what and whom people strive to be, and how it manifests itself in our relationship with both God and humanity. You will also discover that God's work of grace through the Gospel of Jesus Christ is the only remedy for such striving.

Throughout the Book of Galatians, Paul admonishes believers who are struggling because false teachers have come in with the lie that man can be justified in religion and sanctified through his work of religious activity. In other words, the message of the false teacher is that salvation, whether referring to man's justification or sanctification, is achieved by Christ's work plus man's work. Paul warns that adding anything to God's work of grace, whether it is Christ's finished work on the cross, or the work of grace now by His Spirit through His Word, is a different gospel.

This workbook has been written:

- To those brave enough to admit that they love themselves more than God and others in far too many areas of their heart.
- To those who are willing to acknowledge that they are in desperate need of a Savior!
- To those who are ready to wave the white flag of surrender in their heart and willingly allow God be God in their life.

If this description fits you, this is a divine appointment with the one true God. I am convinced, once you truly see God's grace, you will cease striving!

My prayer as you proceed through the study is, "Save us, O Lord, from striving to accomplish Your kingdom work in the flesh, rather than simply yieldingly and obediently allowing You to do Your kingdom work through us."

Final Note: To be able to fill in all blanks in this workbook, you will need access to the New American Standard Bible (1995 edition).

MENDY CLARK

CONTENTS

Lesson 1

Laying Some Groundwork: Part One

GOD'S GRACIOUS INVITATION

Man was not created by God to strive. He was created to know and fellowship with the God who had created him. In essence, man was created to rest in Him and His gracious provisions. If you look closely at Psalm 46:10, you will discover that man's rest is directly connected with knowing God as the God revealed in the truth of His Word. Do you know the one true God as He is revealed in Scripture? Or have you created a god in your image? A god who looks like you, thinks like you, and responds the way you would if you were godlike.

So, what happened? From where does striving come? How did it enter into man? To understand what happened, we must turn to the Book of Beginnings—Genesis and specifically, look at chapters 2–3.

A close observation of Genesis 2 reveals a perfect situation. Man, created by God for God, was placed in a garden that He had planted (Gen. 2:8). In fact, the splendor and magnificence of the garden would be surpassed only by the presence of the one, who would walk with man in the garden in the cool of the day (Gen. 3:8). Can you even imagine what that must have been like?

Furthermore, there were amazing and gracious provisions from the LORD God in that garden.

1. Let's look at Genesis 2:8-9 and answer the following questions:

Who planted the Garden, according to verse 8?

____

How are the trees of the Garden described in verse 9?

a. ______________________________

and

b. ______________________________

In Genesis 2:9, we read that the Lord God caused every tree in the Garden to grow. Noting the description of every tree as "pleasing to the sight" and "good for food" is essential. If we keep reading, we discover that the Lord God names two trees in the middle of the Garden.

What does He specifically name the two trees in the middle of the garden (v. 9)?

---

and

---

2. Now read God's instruction to Adam from Genesis 2:16-17. Fill in the appropriate blanks from Scripture:

"From ____________ tree of the garden you may eat ____________________;

BUT from the Tree of the Knowledge of Good and Evil, you ___________ ___________ ______________,

For in the day that you eat from it, you shall ________________ ____________."

Interestingly and most significantly, man is never commanded not to eat from the tree of life. In fact, it is His most vital provision. Man is instructed by God to eat from any tree that is in the garden with only **one** exception, the tree of the knowledge of good and evil (Gen. 2:16-17). He was forewarned, in the day man eats from it, God said, he would surely die (v. 17). Do you see that had man obeyed the LORD God, he would have eaten from the tree of life?[1]

We must pause here, or we will miss the grace of God. Do you see it? We know from Ephesians 2:8, that the good news of salvation is by grace through faith. Oftentimes, we view this as a post-Fall verse only. However, if you look closely, you will see that salvation by grace through faith was, in fact, pre-Fall. Pastor and author, Paul David Tripp, defines grace in this way, stating, "God's call to obey is itself a grace. In this call, He is actively rescuing you from you."[2]

Keep in mind that **grace** has everything to do with God saving man. God's warning to Adam was His grace in action. Moreover, it was His **invitation** to life. Grace, then, in its simplest definition, is God's invitation of life to man.

So, if grace is God's invitation of life, what is faith? Faith is man's **response** to God's invitation of grace. In its most basic definition, and for the purpose of this study in Galatians, when you see the word, faith, consider these three things, and in the order they are listed:

- A firm conviction of God's Word
- Personal surrender to God's Word
- Obedience to God's Word[3]

If you look closely, you will discover that the Spirit of God is the one who convicts our heart (mind, will, and emotions) by using the Word of God. In essence, this is God's grace in action. It's His invitation of **grace**. Once our hearts have been convicted with the Truth of God's Word, we will either surrender our wills and obey (faith), or we will refuse to surrender and disobey (unbelief). Do you see that grace always precedes faith and both are gifts from God (Eph 2:8)?

Had Adam and Eve responded in surrender and obedience to God's invitation of **grace** before the Fall, they would have been **saved by grace through faith**. In essence, salvation by grace through faith was not Plan B. It was God's plan all along.

---

1. For a more in-depth look at Genesis 2-3, see my workbook entitled, *Created to Bow*, (Maitland, FL: Xulon Press, 2011).
2. Paul David Tripp, *New Morning Mercies* (Wheaton, IL: Crossway, 2014), January 27 excerpt.
3. W. E. Vine, *Vine's Expository Dictionary of Old and New Testament Words* (Grand Rapids, MI: Fleming H. Revell, 1981), 71.

Tragically, we know that Adam and Eve's response to God's invitation of grace was a refusal to surrender and obey (unbelief) because they chose to listen to the voice of the serpent rather than the voice of God. In fact, the enemy proposed an alternate plan, one that would promise life as god but end in certain death. Let's explore his plan.

3. Look at Genesis 3:1 and record what the serpent is doing to the woman?

In Genesis 3:1, we read that the serpent spoke to the woman. In the next question, record what he was saying to her.

4. What did the serpent ask the woman in Genesis 3:1?

Did you notice the serpent questioned the Word of God? If you compare the serpent's question with what God said in Genesis 2:16, you will discover it is the exact opposite of what God said.

5. Now, record the serpent's second statement to the woman in Genesis 3:5.

"For God knows in the day you eat from it your _______________ will be opened,

and

you will be ____________ ___________."

Do you see that the serpent's statement is placing doubt on the character of God, specifically the goodness of God? In other words, God is holding out on you. He is withholding something that would result in your good. Their eyes would be open for sure—but tragically, to evil. However, this also meant that their eyes would be closed to good (God), which is a description of the spiritual blindness that entered when man fell. Do you see the exchange? Do you think the alternate plan was better?

6. Now, record the description of the tree of the knowledge of good and evil from Genesis 3:6.

a.

b.

c.

7. Now, go back to the description of every tree in the garden from Genesis 2:9? What makes the tree of the knowledge of good and evil such a temptation? In other words, what is added to the description of all the other trees in the garden?

8. What makes the Tree of the Knowledge of Good and Evil such a temptation? In other words, what is added to the description of this tree that was unlike the other trees in the Garden?

Do you see it? Weren't all the trees described as being "pleasing to the sight" and "good for food"? The answer is a resounding, "Yes!" Then what information was added about the tree that made it too difficult to pass up? Was it not their desire to be like God? Isn't that still man's greatest desire?

The serpent had placed doubt upon God's Word and God's character. Keep in mind, the serpent, whom Jesus described as the one who, "steals, kills, and destroys," is still speaking today (Jn. 8:44; 10:10).

You might ask, "How can I know that the enemy is speaking to me even today?" One particular way to know is to ask yourself two questions that find their origin in the garden:

1. Are my thoughts putting doubt on God's Word?
2. Are my thoughts placing doubt on God's character, and in particular, His goodness?

If the answer is, "Yes," to either or both of the questions, I can assure you based upon the authority of God's Word, it is the enemy's voice that is controlling your thoughts!

Let's review how the serpent spoke to Eve in Genesis 3:1-5.

1) He placed doubt on God's Word, stating, "Indeed has God said, "You shall not eat from any tree of the Garden" (Gen. 3:1). The exact opposite of what God said (Gen 2:16)!

2) He placed doubt on God's character, stating, "God knows that in the day you eat from it your eyes will be opened, and you will be like God, knowing good and evil" (Gen. 3:5; emphasis added). In other words, God is holding out on you. He is not really a good God. The biggest lie ever told by the "father of lies" can be found in the phrase, "you will be like God" for no created being (whether angelic or human) will ever be like God Almighty!

MAN'S RESPONSE: UNBELIEF

So, what did Eve do with the information she had just been given? Did she go to the LORD God while He walked with her in the garden in the cool of the day? Sadly, Genesis 3:6 tells us what she did next, stating, "When the woman saw that the tree was good for food, and that it was a delight to the eyes, and that the tree was **desirable to make one wise**, she took from its fruit and **ate**, and she gave also to her husband and he **ate**" (emphasis added).

Note: Up until Genesis 3:6, the fall of mankind had not occurred. The temptation to sin is not sin! Remember, Jesus was tempted in the wilderness, and yet, He was without sin (Matt. 4:1-11). Oftentimes, we forget that. The sin did not occur until Adam and Eve acted upon the enemy's temptation and **ate**. In fact, the earthly rebellion recorded in Genesis 3:6 did not originate in the garden.

So where did the lie that a created being (whether angelic or human) could be like God originate if not in the garden? Ezekiel 28:12-19 and Isaiah 14:12-14 record the heavenly rebellion, which occurred prior to Adam and Eve's time in the garden.

The same desire to be like God had arisen in one of God's created beings before the Garden as well.

9. Look at Isaiah 14:12-14. Notice and record the five "I will" statements made by the created angelic being, Lucifer in verses 13-14.

a. I will ____ (v. 13).

b. I will ____ (v. 13).

Note: The stars of God are a metaphor for the other angels. Think about it: Who alone sits on the throne?

c. I will ____ (v. 13).

Note: Who do you think sits in the recesses of the north in the heavens?

d. I will ____ (v. 14).

Note: Oftentimes, the clouds served as a metaphor for the presence of Almighty God (Ex. 13:21; 24:16; 40:34).

e. I will ____ (v. 14).

Did you happen to see the final "I will" statement made by Lucifer? Isn't he essentially saying in his heart, "I will be like God Most High!"? Insanity! Absolute Insanity! And the insanity continues. Since the Fall, man is still striving to be like God rather than knowing that there is only ONE GOD!

WHAT IS THE ROOT ISSUE?

Consider the following illustration to gain insight into the magnitude of the root issue that entered into the heart of man at the Fall. Study this illustration for it will show up throughout the entire study of Galatians.

The Unsaved Person

Flesh Is in Control

↓

"I will be like God!"

The Saved Person

The Spirit/Human Residual Flesh

↓

"I am God!"/"I will be like God!"

The stick figure on the left represents a man or woman without Christ. Do you see that the dominating factor in the heart is the flesh, which says, "I will be god!"? The man without Christ desires to be his own god.

However, when Christ comes to live within a person by His Spirit, although indwelt by God, there remains that person's residual flesh. The residual flesh still says, "I will be god!"

Although a total impossibility and sheer insanity, this dominating pride to be like God reigns in the heart of an unbeliever, and sadly can still reside and rear its ugly head within the heart of those who are His. Whether the desire to be like God has total dominion, as is in the case of an unbeliever, or it is given power when we, as believers, choose to disobey God's Spirit, the flesh's desire to be like God is a result of the Fall and will remain a constant enemy for the believer until glorification.

You see, when the believer is glorified, the struggle to be like God will be over, for then, those who are in Christ will see Him as He is—in all of His glory—as God! And we will know for certain we are nothing like Him! He alone is God!

For now (while in the process of sanctification), every believer, who is indwelt by God's Spirit understands the struggle within between the Spirit and the residual flesh (that so desperately wants to be like God).

Man, in his flesh, continues to strive to be like God rather than knowing that He alone is God. The greatest deception, which is as old as the garden, is to believe the lie that man can strive to be like God, when in actuality, in striving, he is actually striving with God, and as a result, striving with man as well. Think about it. If the flesh of man is trying to be like God, there is no true fellowship with God or one another. Two people attempting to be like God will inevitably collide with one another. Do you see the insanity? Deep within, do you sense the strife?

WHERE IS THE ROOT ISSUE?

As we have just discovered, the root issue is man's desire to be like God. So then, where exactly does the root issue reside, and what is the motivating factor behind man's desire to be like God? In this next section of the study, we will look at where that root dwells and the motive behind man's desire to be like God.

Keep in mind as we progress in our study that the root issue is man's core problem, or that which remains after all of the "layers" have been peeled. In other words, the root issue is what I like to call, "getting to the source" of the problem.

Let's begin this portion of the lesson by looking at where the sin of pride (man's desire to be like God) originated and took root. Let's start with its origin by re-reading Isaiah 14:12-14, which as we learned earlier, is a reference to Lucifer's rebellion against God.[4]

10. Begin by reading Isaiah 14:13. Record with whom and where the sin of pride originated?

____________________________ __________________________

11. Now, look at Mark 7:20-23. Record where Jesus said that all sin resides (v. 21)?

____

12. What did Jesus say proceeds from the heart of man who has said, "I will be god"?

a. ____ h. ____________________________________

b. ____ i. ____________________________________

c. ____ j. ____________________________________

d. ____ k. ____________________________________

e. ____ l. ____________________________________

f. ____ m. ____________________________________

g. ____

Now, look at the following illustration to explain what Jesus said in Mark 7:21-22:

---

4. For a more detailed look at Lucifer's rebellion, you may want to refer to Chapter 2 in my workbook entitled, *Created to Bow.* (Maitland, Florida; Xulon Press, 2017), pp. 15–39.

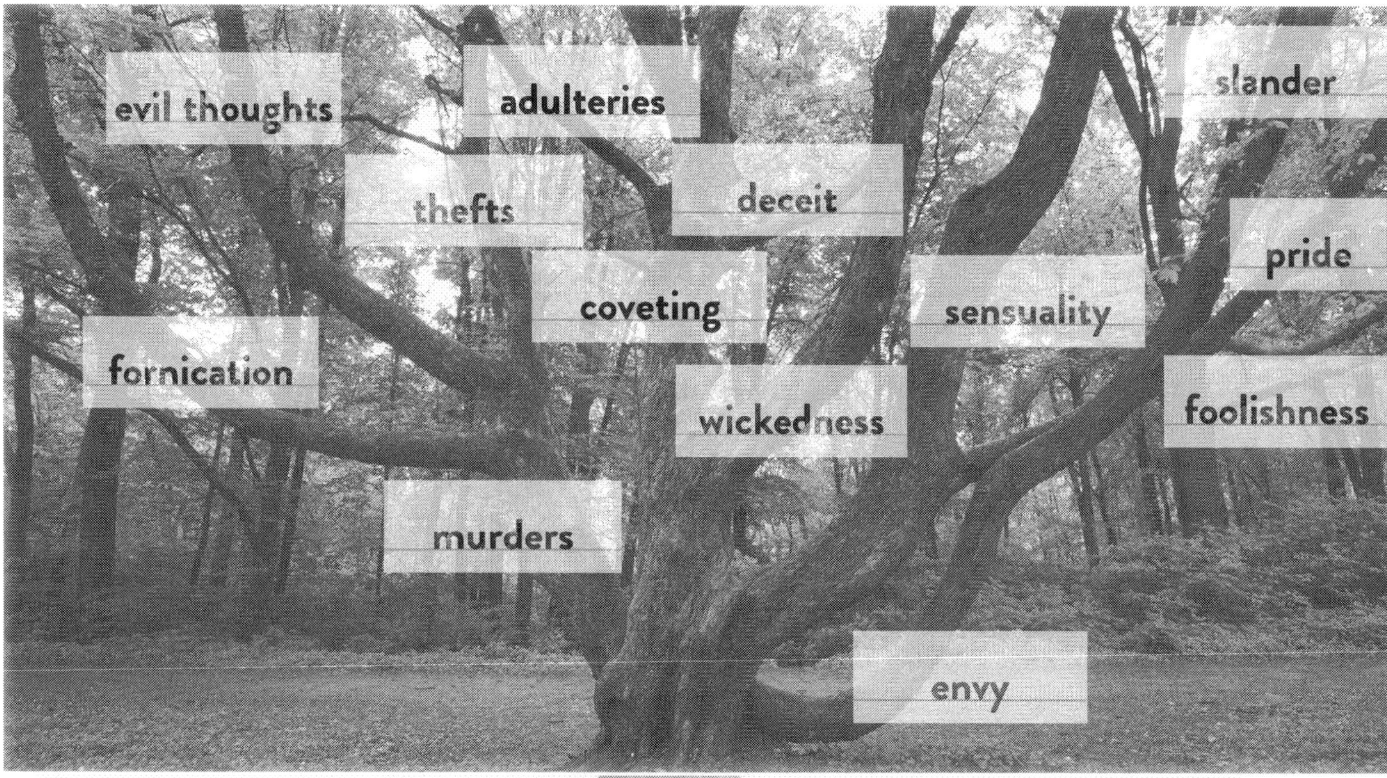

Let the branches of the tree represent the thirteen sins mentioned explicitly in Mark 7:21-22. The roots, then, would represent man's heart (Mark 7:21).

So many times, the focus is placed on the sin(s) of an individual (the branches of the tree). When that happens, our focus is in the wrong place as we are feebly attempting to treat the symptoms and not getting to the real issue—our hearts. Sadly, humanity, in an attempt to be like God, has become adept in efforts to treat the consequences and symptoms of the Fall, but until we see the source of the issue, we will never see our true condition and need for a Savior. Only the Creator of the human heart can save and transform it.

However, man, in his attempt to be like God, strives in futility to treat, rehab, or cut down the branches. As god, we are either trying to fix ourselves or have some other human being save us, right? Wouldn't it just make more sense to let the Savior rescue and transform the roots?

13. There is one more verse we will need to consider concerning the heart of humanity. Look at Jeremiah 17:9. How is the heart of humanity described?

    a. ____

    and

    b. ____

14. Now read Jeremiah 17:10. Who alone can know your heart? ____________________

Note: A synonym in Scripture for man's heart is his soul. Therefore, these words can be used interchangeably. The heart (soul) of man is comprised of his mind, will, and emotions. The conscience also resides in the heart of man and serves as the moral regulator of his soul.

A simple illustration is helpful, so picture it this way:

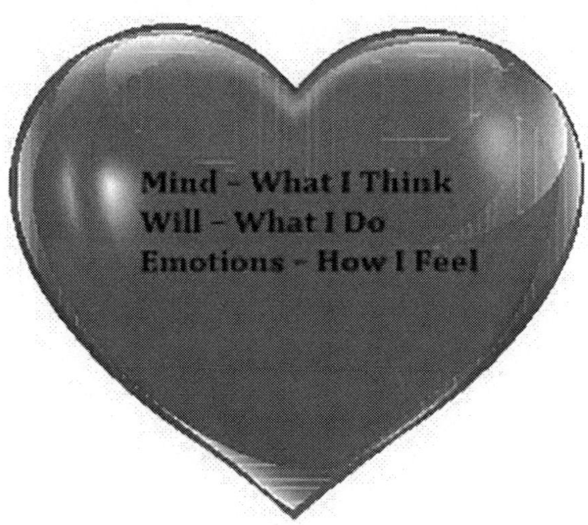

Do you see the importance of the heart (soul) of humanity? Do you see that the heart is the place where human desire to be like God was first exposed and then after the Fall took up residence?

15. Now, look at 1 Peter 2:25. What is Jesus called in reference to the heart (soul) of humanity?

____

and

____

16. What do these two descriptions imply about the heart (soul) of humanity and the God who made human hearts?

WHY THE ROOT ISSUE?

We have looked at the root issue, humanity's desire to be like God; its residence, the heart of humanity; so now, let's look at the motivating factor behind the issue. To do so, we will look in Scripture and let Jesus tell us just as He told one of His closest followers while He was on earth, Simon Peter.

Specifically, the focal verses for this portion of the lesson will be John 21:15-17. After examination of these three verses, you will be asked to examine three questions, three answers, and three commands. Most importantly, within these verses, you will discover the underlying motive of Peter's heart (and ours) when Peter failed the Lord.

However, before we can examine the verses in John, we must first look back at the context in which these verses are vitally connected and can be better understood. What went wrong? What was the cause of Peter's failure? How could this have happened to someone who had fellowshipped and walked so closely with Christ?

As you begin to lay the biblical foundation, you will discover that although the act of failure can occur in an instant, many things led up to Peter's denial of Christ. In other words, there were warning signs. You will see clearly that the root issue resided within Peter, specifically within his heart.

Sadly, Simon Peter was so sure of his heart and his love for the Lord that he chose to ignore God's Word. Thankfully, the Lord Jesus did not leave him in his failure but chose to rescue Simon from Simon. Upon closer examination, we will focus on a merciful Savior as well as a broken and grieved disciple in need of repentance.

Watch as the Shepherd and Guardian of our heart lovingly and graciously restores one of His closest sheep from epic failure. As you survey Simon Peter's failure, see that you too are a Simon in constant need of rescue, repentance, and restoration. There is a Simon lurking in all of us. It entered at the Fall. In fact, it answers why we desire to be like God.

You will see that each section is divided into topics. Pay careful attention to the topics for they depict a specific order and reveal Simon Peter's heart (mind, will, and emotions).

Upon completion of this lesson, I can assure you, if you will allow the Holy Spirit, He will reveal things you have never seen. I know He did this for me. I will never look at these verses the same way again. Let's get started.

17. We will begin laying the foundation by looking at each gospel separately. Record the facts from each gospel, and then we will compile all of the information to see the whole.

Laying the Foundation

Matthew's Gospel

Jesus' Word to the Eleven	**Peter's Response**
Matthew 26:31 ____________________________	Matthew 26:33 ______________________________
____	____

Jesus' Word to Peter	**Peter's Response**
Matthew 26:34 ____________________________	Matthew 26:35 ______________________________
____	____

Mark's Gospel

Jesus' Word to the Eleven	**Peter's Response**
Mark 14:27 ______________________________	Mark 14:29 __________________________________
____	____

Jesus' Word to Peter	**Peter's Response**
Mark 14:30 ______________________________	Mark 14:31 __________________________________
____	____
____	____

Now watch carefully as Luke gives additional information of Peter's denial just before the Lord's prediction.

<u>Luke's Gospel</u>

First, note what the eleven are discussing following Jesus' prediction of Judas' betrayal and prior to Jesus' conversation with Peter.

Luke 22:24. What are the eleven "disputing"? ____________________

Luke 22:25-30. Briefly, how does Jesus respond? ____________________

Now notice who Jesus singles out, in particular, following the dispute concerning the identity of the greatest among them.

Jesus' Word to Peter	**Peter's Response**
Luke 22:31-32 ____________________	Luke 22:33 ____________________
____________________	____________________
____________________	____________________

Jesus' Word to Peter

Luke 22:34 ____________________

____

Note: In Luke 22:31, the Greek word for "demanded" means to obtain permission by asking. Literally here, it means, "to claim back for oneself."[5] If you look at Satan's request, did you happen to notice to Whom he must gain permission? Who is ultimately in control here? You see, the pride in Peter's heart has been exposed, and the enemy knows it! Finally, the Lord will use the Enemy for His glory (as Peter will strengthen the brethren afterward), and for Peter's good to both expose and rid Peter of his deceptive pride.

<u>John's Gospel</u>

Jesus' Word to the Eleven	**Peter's Response**
John 13:33 ____________________	John 13:36 ____________________
____________________	____________________

Jesus' Word to Peter	**Peter's Response**
John 13:36 ____________________	John 13:37 ____________________
____________________	____________________

5. Spiros Zodhiates, *The Complete Word Study Dictionary* (Chattanooga, TN: AMG Publishers), 598, Strong's #1809.

Jesus' Word to Peter

John 13:38 ___________________________________

____

Do you see that Jesus' warning from His Word was an invitation of God's grace to His disciple? Did Peter respond in faith? Now, read Luke 22:32. For what did Jesus pray specifically? Peter's ____________________.

Part One: Simon Peter's Heart

Simon Peter's Thoughts (His Mind)

Using the information that you have just gathered, answer the following questions.

18. Did you notice every time Jesus addressed the eleven, one, in particular, was the first to speak out? Which of the apostles was quick to respond to Jesus first? _________________________________

19. By what name does Jesus address Peter in Luke 22:31?

Note: In Hebrew the name, Simon, literally means hearing. The repetition of address places emphasis and importance.

20. Does Simon hear what the Lord Jesus is saying to him? __________

Note: Every time Jesus warns the eleven that they would "all fall away," the Greek verb form translated "all fall away" is in the passive voice, which indicates that the subject(s) would be acted upon. In other words, there was no doubt that they all would fall away.

Similarly, every time Jesus predicted Peter's denial, the Greek verb in the earliest manuscripts uses the middle voice, which signifies that the subject would both initiate and participate in the action. In other words, Peter would willingly choose to deny Him.

Note of Interest: Prior to the death of Christ, God's Spirit would not indwell man until Pentecost. We see evidence of God's Spirit in the Old Testament, as He would come upon a man for a time, but He would not abide within man's heart until Christ had finished His work on the cross.

Therefore, without God's indwelling Spirit, all that was within man was his flesh. Left to our flesh, man will only and always fall away and deny Christ. In other words, only God, residing within man, can cause man to obey. It is God's indwelling Spirit who keeps us from falling and denying Him. Sadly, Peter, in his attempt to be like God, and relying solely upon his flesh, would not listen and obey what Jesus forewarned and had to discover the truth about his inability and weakness the hard way.

21. Now think about it, when Peter tells the Lord Jesus that "he will never fall away," what is he implying...

About himself?

About the other disciples?

About the Lord's Word?

Do you see that Peter thinks more highly of himself than the other disciples and God's Word?

22. Where is Simon Peter's confidence and dependence?

23. Now read Luke 22:32. How is the Lord Jesus predicting Peter's repentance and restoration? Be sure and note the cause of Peter's repentance and restoration, which, by the way, will have nothing to do with Peter!

24. What is Simon Peter's mindset before the denials? ___________________________

SIMON PETER'S ACTION (HIS WILL)

Now that we have established Simon Peter's thought processes prior to his failure, let's see how that mindset led him to act in sin.

25. Fill in the blanks below.

What did Simon Peter do?	**What did Jesus say/do?**
John 18:10 -________________________________	John 18:11 _____________________________________
____	____

Do you see that the flesh of man always opposes God's Plan?

What did Simon Peter do?	**What had Jesus said?**
John 18:15 __________________________________	John 13:36 ____________________________________
____	____

Simon (which means hearing) heard the Word of God but refused to ______ His Word.

Now let's summarize briefly what happened:

What did Simon Peter do?	**What did Jesus do?**
Matthew 26:69-74	Luke 22:61________________________
Mark 14:66-71; Luke 22:55-60	________________________
John 18:16-18; 25-27________________________	

26. Do you see how Peter's self-confidence led to self-effort?

    a. Where did Simon Peter's self-effort (striving) get him?

    b. What did his flesh accomplish?

Now that we have examined Peter's mindset and consequent actions, let's look at the emotional state in which Peter was left for a time.

SIMON PETER'S EMOTIONAL STATE (HIS EMOTIONS)

27. Look at the following verses as we continue to examine Peter's emotional state, which resulted from his thoughts and actions.

What did Simon Peter do? Record Peter's emotional state in each blank.

Matthew 26:75

Mark 14:72

Luke 22:62

John 21:17

Do you see immense grief as he wept bitterly? Truly there is no pain so intense as grief. Watch, however, in this next section of study, as we see Jesus lovingly reinstate His failed disciple and spiritual leader (John 21:15-17). Notice that this part of the lesson is also divided into topics. Pay close attention to the order, or you will miss the biblical way of true repentance and restitution.

Part Two: The Gift of Repentance and Restoration

As we begin this portion of the lesson, we must understand that repentance, which involves both rescue and restoration, is a gift from God. Therefore, as we review Peter's condition, we must first understand that only the Lord can grant repentance as a gift of grace. In other words, Peter cannot repent (rescue or restore) himself back to God. If he could, Jesus would not have had to come and die.

So what is Simon Peter's condition? We have spent quite a bit of time looking at the state of his heart before his denials of Christ. But what did our loving Lord do afterward?

28. Look at Mark 16:7. Contextually, the angel appeared to the women who had come early resurrection morning to anoint Jesus' body (Mk. 16:1-6). What does the angel instruct? Notice, in particular, who was singled out?

Now we find the disciples, and specifically requested Peter, in Galilee, just as the angel instructed. And what do we see Peter doing? He and the other disciples have gone back to what they knew and did best—fishing. However, despite all of their training and self-effort, it has resulted in NOTHING!

But wait, who do we see awaiting the disciples on the shore? Do you see that He is the one always coming after and pursuing His own? Notice in John 21:9 what was waiting for them when they arrived at the shore—a charcoal fire. Make no mistake. The word for charcoal fire is used only twice in the New Testament; here in John 21 and John 18:18.

29. Was Jesus re-creating a scene: and if so, for what purpose? Any thoughts?

Concerning the significance of the charcoal fire, New Testament scholar, Gerald Borchert, states, "It is almost as though the evangelist is affirming the well-known concept that for a person to become right with God and gain a sense of release from the past sense of rebellion that that person should face the reality of where the deviation or sin occurred."[6]

There are those who teach, where repentance is concerned, that what is in the past should remain in the past. However, the re-creating scene in John 21 illustrates otherwise. Notice, however, it is the Lord re-creating the scene of failure and not something Peter has conjured up for himself nor something that one of the other disciples had decided. Make no mistake; the Lord is not doing this to harm Peter but to rescue and restore Peter. Any time He brings back our past, you can be assured, He is doing so to rescue and restore us from ourselves. Notice also, the public arena in which Peter failed is the public arena in which he will be granted repentance (rescue and restoration).

Now, let's look at what Jesus does to offer biblical repentance (rescue and restoration) to His failed disciple. There is a pattern to note here.

THREE QUESTIONS

6. Gerald L. Borchert, *John 12–21 Vol. 25B*, (Nashville, TN: Broadman & Holman Publishers, 2002), 333.

First, notice it is Jesus who addresses Simon Peter. Keep in mind that Jesus is not asking Peter questions in order to find out information for Himself. He knows all things—especially the heart of man! However, whenever the Lord asks a question, His questions are for the benefit of the one being asked. In other words, there is something that He wants Peter to see and know.

30. What do you see about the Lord in His questions? Look at Romans 2:4 to help answer this question. Do you see that the questions the Lord asks are His _______________ leading Peter (and you and me) to repentance?

31. What does our kind and gracious Lord Jesus ask Peter first in John 21:15?

Question #1:

a. How does Jesus address Simon Peter?

b. Why do you think He addresses him in this way (each time)?

Note of Interest: The word, *agapao*, is the Greek word used here for our English word, "love." Agapao, by definition, involves the direction of the will. When used in reference to God, it is "God's willful direction toward man. It involves God doing what is best for man and not necessarily what man desires or deems as best."[7]

Furthermore, the Greek construction of the phrase, "more than these," is stated in a similar degree. In other words, Jesus is comparing Peter's love with something. Commentators vary in their thoughts as to whether "these" are in reference to the fish, the disciples, or something else.

c. To help determine the meaning of the phrase, "more than these," look at Mark 10:29-30. With this information provided, what is Jesus asking Simon, son of John?

d. With what two things does the Lord Jesus compare the list?

1) ______________ sake and the _________________________ sake

Notice how the Lord Jesus equates Himself with the gospel.

Question #2: Now, look back in John 21:16. What does Jesus ask Simon, son of John?

Some may wrongly assume that Jesus asked Peter the same question. But if you look closely, you will discover that this is not a comparative question. Similarly, though the Greek word, *agapao* (love) is the word used in the second question.

7. Spiros Zodhiates, *The Complete Word Study New Testament Dictionary* (Chattanooga: AMG Publishers, 1993), pp. 64-66.

a. What is Jesus asking Simon, son of John, in this question?

Question #3: Now once again, what does Jesus ask Simon, son of John, in verse 17?

Note: In this last question by our Lord, the original Greek text presents a different word for love, phileo, which is defined as a dear friend or brotherly love.[8]

For a third time, it appears Jesus is asking the same question, but once again, there is a slight variation because a different word for love (phileo) is used.

b. What is Jesus asking Simon, son of John, in this third question?

32. As you survey the three questions, and you remember the questions are not for the benefit of the Lord Jesus, but Simon Peter's advantage, what do you see in the series of questions? Record any insights below.

Weighing in on the series of questions, Dr. Borchert states,

> *Peter experienced a major undoing (cf. Is. 6:5, KJV) of his self-assertiveness because Jesus asked him the third time (21:17) about his love. The third time did it. Imagine again the scene as the evangelist framed it: a charcoal fire and three questions about Peter's relationship with Jesus. It hardly takes a genius to relate this event to that of the denial. Facing up to oneself is a traumatic experience.*[9]

What about you? Has the Lord allowed you to be placed in circumstances or with people who are pressing or squeezing you? Has your response resulted in failure like Peter's? Has the Lord brought questions to your mind? Are you experiencing the trauma of facing up to yourself? Could He be inviting you to repentance and restoration?

THREE ANSWERS

Now that we have examined Jesus' probing questions, let's look at Simon, son of John's answers.

---

8. Ibid. 1445.

9. Borchert, *John 12–21* (Vol. 25B), 335.

Answer #1: How does Simon, son of John, answer Jesus' comparative question (v. 15)?

*Note: In each of Peter's answers, the Greek text uses the word, phileo (love).

Answer #2: How does Simon, son of John, answer the second question Jesus asked (16)?

Answer #3: On the third question, how does Simon, son of John, answer the Lord?

a. To what does Simon, son of John, appeal each time he is asked about his love for the Lord?

Hint: Lord, ______________ __________________ ...

b. What do you see in the appeal Peter gives to the Lord here versus the appeal he made prior to his denials? Is there a difference? If so, explain.

33. Notice the third time Jesus questioned Peter's love, his emotional state is identified and recorded. What do you see here? Any thoughts?

So now that we have looked at the three questions and answers, let's examine the Lord's three commands to Peter.

THREE COMMANDS

Note: The word, "command," is used because the verb tense in each statement by the Lord is present imperative active. The imperative mood indicates a command, and the present tense indicates continuous action on Peter's part.

34. Record the three commands given by Jesus to Peter.

Command #1 ____ (v. 15).

Command #2 ____ (v. 16).

Command #3 ____ (v. 17).

35. For a better understanding of the commands, and what each command has to do with Peter's (and our) love for the Lord, look at the following cross-references for help. Record what Jesus clearly stated.

a. John 14:15

b. John 14:21

c. And finally, look at the contrast stated in John 14:23–24. What is contrasted in these verses?

Do you see why Jesus is questioning the love of Simon, son of John? Do you see that the commands of the Lord Jesus involve a love for God, which, in turn, affect others? Didn't Peter just reveal the truth about the heart of fallen man?

Now think back to the garden and about what happened. Wasn't the LORD God asking Adam the same question? Didn't the two trees in the middle of the garden represent the same question? "Adam, do you love Me?" or "Adam, do you love yourself?" Sadly, we know the answer.

In Ecclesiastes 1:9, we learn that there is nothing new under the sun.

What happened in the garden that day? Adam and Eve wanted to be like God.

Why did this happen? Adam and Eve loved themselves more than the God who had created them.

Where did this happen? Physically, in the garden, which the LORD God had made. Spiritually, in the heart of man, which the LORD God had made.

Look at the following illustration as an example of what has been stated thus far. The two trees represent two choices. Under each tree are the root issue and the underlying motive in the heart of man.

TWO TREES REPRESENT TWO CHOICES

You are God!	I will be God!
I love You!	I love Myself!
I will surrender my will to Your will (Word)!	I will not surrender my will to Your will (Word)!
I will obey You!	I will not obey You!
You, alone, are Good!	I can be good like God!

Do you see that Adam and Eve's response to God's invitation of grace was not faith; instead, man chose to believe the voice of the enemy, and we rejected God's Word?

In our refusal to surrender and obey God's clear and stated Word (Gen 2:16-17), we rejected life and chose death. You don't have to look far to see the repercussions from declining God's invitation of **grace**?

Now, post-Fall, separated from God, all of mankind is born dead in transgressions and sin (Eph. 2:1), and our greatest need is a Savior! That's why I love Ephesians 2:4, which begins, "But God, being rich in mercy, because of His great love with which He loved us..." continues to extend His invitation of grace through faith to us today.

As you look at Ephesians 2:4, do you see who He is as God and the motivating factor of His heart? Quite the opposite of our futile attempt to be like God and our self-love wouldn't you say?

Do you see that man's insane desire to be like God still exists today? Is it difficult to fathom the reason why? If honest, wouldn't we all have to confess that deep down, we love ourselves more than God and others? In fact, for every person who has ever lived since Adam, (with exception to the Lord Jesus Christ), this is the root issue and motive.

If you think about it, you can trace every sin ever committed to this one root issue, "I will be my own god!" because the one motivating factor resonates, "I love myself!"

Go ahead. Try to think of one sin that cannot be traced to this root and connected motive. I have spent hours trying. When you peel off all of the layers, you will discover, as I have, the flesh is perfectly summarized by the desire to be my own god because deep down, I love myself! This is true of all flesh, except for the one who was and is God, who loved His Father (and us) more than His own life—Jesus Christ, the righteous!

So, in a nutshell, humanity was not created to strive with God for God's place as God. Our strife entered the moment we declared that we would be our own god, ultimately proving that we loved ourselves more than the God who had created us.

Therefore, for the purpose of this study, when the flesh is mentioned, think of it in this way:

The flesh says, “I will be god!”

The motive of the flesh, “I love myself!”

Isn’t this still the mindset of the flesh today?

Keep these things in mind as we proceed in the study.

Lesson 2

Laying Some Groundwork: Part Two

In this second part entitled "Laying Some Groundwork," we will look at two groups of mankind (unbeliever and believer), and more specifically, at their heart as it is revealed in Scripture. But first, we will look at the heart of all mankind as created by God.

THE HEART OF ALL MANKIND

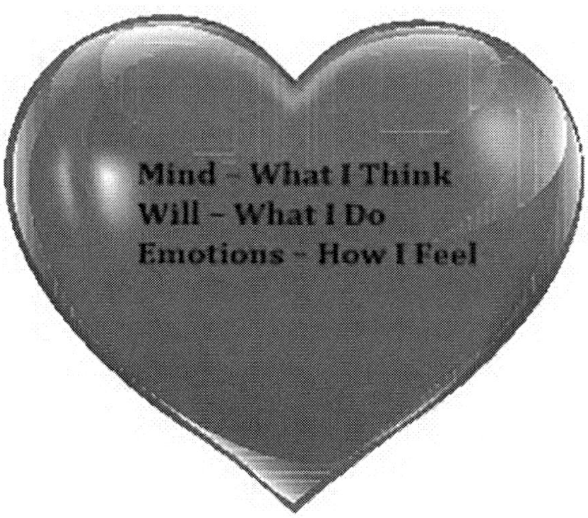

Note: The heart of man (soul) is comprised of one's mind, will, and emotion. The conscience, or moral regulator of the soul, is also located in the heart of man.[10]

God created the heart of mankind with the same components. However, the source that controls/reigns over the heart is the difference maker. If the source is our flesh, this will affect what we think, which in turn, will determine what we do, and consequently, how we feel. However, if the source is Christ's Spirit, He will cause us to think biblically (truth), which will determine what we do and how we feel. Sadly, those who think the flesh is in control are sorely mistaken; in fact, they are deceived. The Enemy is behind that lie! In reality, he is the power source behind the flesh (internal influence) and the world (external influence).

Note: Personally, one of the most helpful definitions of the word, "mind," comes from *Baker's Dictionary of Theology*, which states,

> *The English versions of the Bible express a variety of emotional, volitional, and intellectual movements by the one word, mind. If controlled by the Holy Spirit, the mind displays the right attitude to God and to one's fellow man (Lk. 10:27; Rom. 12:2; 1 Cor. 1:10), and the mind thus bent on the service of God is contrasted with the flesh (Rom. 7:23, 25). The mind of the believer may be controlled by 'the flesh' (Col. 2:18), but such perversion of the mind is ascribed more to the unregenerate (Rom. 1:28; 2 Cor. 3:14, 4:4; 2 Tim. 3:8).*

10. Spiros Zodhiates, *The Complete Word Study New Testament Dictionary* (Chattanooga: AMG Publishers, 1993), pp. 819, 1494.

The mind, therefore, is in itself neutral, and its moral quality is determined by the power to which it is subject (emphasis added).[11]

WHO IS IN CONTROL OF YOUR HEART?

1. Look at 1 John 3:10.

Notice that we are either children of _______________ or children of the ________________.

Did you notice that there are only two options?

Since there are only two, let's explore them both. We will begin with the child of the devil.

2. Let's begin by looking at Ephesians 2:1–3 and answering the following questions:

How does Paul describe our state (spiritual condition) prior to (or apart from) salvation in verse 1?

In what are we dead? In _____________________________________

and

In _____________________________________

Describe the walk of those who are dead in their trespasses and sins (vv. 2–3)?

According to the ____

According to the ____

Live (walk) in the ____

Do you also see that those who are dead in their trespasses and sins live under the dominion and control of these three enemies?

- The world (system)
- Satan
- The flesh

11. Everett F. Harrison, Geoffrey W. Bromiley and Carl F. H. Henry, *Baker's Dictionary of Theology* (Grand Rapids, MI: Baker Book House, 1988), 355.

Note: Satan has an internal and an external avenue through which he works, namely: the flesh and the world. The unbeliever is under the dominion of Satan. Sadly, the person who thinks they are their own masters has been tragically deceived, for there is not a third option in Scripture. You are either a child of God or a child of the devil (1 John 3:10). Heartbreakingly, the one who thinks he is his own master will one day discover that they were just a pawn in the Enemy's hand.

What are those who "live in the lusts of the flesh" doing, according to verse 3?

1) Indulge in the ____

2) Indulge in the ____

How are the lost (unbelievers) described by nature, according to verse 3?

______________________ of ______________

3. Now, look at 2 Corinthians 4:4 and answer the following questions:

How are the minds of the unbelieving described and who is doing this to them?

__________________ by ____________________________________

Notice what they cannot see specifically?

4. Now, drop down a couple of verses and read 2 Corinthians 4:6. Where, specifically, is the light of the knowledge of the glory of God visible?

5. Now, read 1 Corinthians 2:14 and answer the following questions: [**Note:** The natural man is the man without God's Spirit].

Does the natural man accept or understand spiritual things (the things of God's Spirit)? ________

How does the natural man view the things of the Spirit of God?

Why does the natural man not accept the things of the Spirit?

Now, let's compare the natural man with the believer.

6. Let's begin by reading 2 Corinthians 5:17. What is the man in Christ called?

A __________ ________________________

7. Now, look at Romans 8:9. [Notice, Paul is writing to believers in this verse]. Fill in the blanks below:

"You are not in the ____________________ but in the ____________________, if indeed the Spirit of God ________________ ________ __________. But if anyone does ________ have the ____________________ of ____________________, he does ________ ______________ to ________________."

8. Now, turn to John 14:23. **Note:** Just before His death, Jesus stated,

"If anyone loves Me, he will keep My Word; and My Father will love him, and we will ____________________ to him, and make Our ____________________ with him."

9. Now, turn to 1 Corinthians 3:16 where Paul asks the believers a question, stating,

"Do you not know that __________________ are a ____________________ of God and that the __________________ of _______________ dwells _________ you."

10. As you look back over Romans 8:9, John 14:23, and 1 Corinthians 3:16, who makes the man in Christ a "new creation"?

So then, who is missing in the life of an unbeliever? ____

Look at the following illustration for a visual of what you have just read in Scripture:

The Unsaved Person
[The Unbeliever]

Human Flesh is in Control

The Saved Person
[The Believer]

Christ comes to live within people by His Spirit.

↓

The Spirit/Humanity's Residual Flesh

Fill in the following blanks as Scripture describes the heart of each:

<u>The Unsaved Person</u>

<u>The Saved Person</u>

Mindset - ________________ (Rom 8:6)

(Heart)

________________ toward God
(Rom. 8:7; Col. 1:21)

Mindset – ________________

(Heart) and

____
(Rom. 8:6)

Note: The word, "mindset," as it is used in Romans 8:9, can be a synonym for the word, heart (soul).

Heart: More ____________________ than all else

and

desperately ____________________
(Jer. 17:9)

Heart: ________________Heart

and

________________ Spirit
(Ezek. 36:26)

Known only by ________________ (Jer. 17:10)

Note: We do not need to have our old hearts rehabilitated or behavior modified. We need a heart transplant!

Fill in the blanks as Scripture describes the characteristics of each:

The Unsaved Person

The Saved Person

Characteristics of The Flesh

None ____________________________ not even one:

None ____________________________

None ___________________________ God

All have ____________________ aside (from God)

Together have become ______________________

None who does _____________________

Does not ________________________ God (v. 18)
(Rom. 3:10–18; Ps. 14:1–1–3)

Characteristics of The Spirit

Spirit of the _______________ (He is God!)

Spirit of ___________________________

Spirit of ___________________________

Spirit of ___________________________

Spirit of ___________________________

Spirit of ___________________________

Spirit of the ___________________ of the
LORD (Isa 11:2)

Notice that the heart and characteristics of each are:

The Unsaved Person

Toward Self
Loves Self

The Saved Person

Toward God
Loves God and Others

What about Sin?

In the unbeliever, sin is a state of being;

therefore, sin reigns!

Sin remains (in residual flesh);

but it does not reign!

The Flesh Says,	**The Spirit Says,**
"I will be like God!"	"Only One God: Father, Son, Spirit is God!
"I love myself!"	"I will love the Lord my God with all of my heart."
	"I will love my neighbor."
"I have a plan!"	"God has a plan from eternity past!"
"My will be done!"	"Your will be done."

Keep in mind, when you pray, "Thy will be done," you are also saying, "My will be undone."[12]

Surrender and obedience put my will to death.

12. Elisabeth Elliot, *On Asking God Why* (Grand Rapids: Fleming H. Revell, 1989), 101.

THE RESCUING GRACE OF GOD

As you look over the illustration of the heart (mindset) and the characteristics (utter depravity) of the man or woman without God, do you see man's desperate need for a Savior? Do you see that a God who is rich in mercy (Eph. 2:4) has rescued us by His grace through faith (Eph. 2:8)?

When describing what happens to the man or woman who has been rescued by God's redeeming grace, I love the words of the late New Testament scholar, Kenneth Wuest, who states, "The new life is a **Person** within a person, living out **His life** in that person (emphasis added)."[13]

As you read Dr. Wuest's definition, do you see that apart from Christ, man is incapable of living the Christian life? No amount of striving in our flesh can accomplish what God requires, which is God. In other words, it takes God in man to know God, to please God, and to glorify God in the manner He alone is worthy. As you look at the visual of the believer, do you see why Paul called the believer a "new creation" (2 Cor. 5:17)?

Furthermore, if you look closely, you will discover that new life begins with a person. The person is none other than Jesus Christ, who is Life (Jn. 3:3,7; 14:6; 1 Jn. 1:1–3). He has come to live within an individual by His Spirit (Rom. 8:9; Gal. 3:2–3).

Did you notice that the Person, Jesus Christ, is living His Life through the individual who is willingly surrendered and obedient to His Word? Isn't that precisely what Jesus did while on earth? He willingly came to surrender and obey the Father's plan from eternity past because He loved the Father (John 14:31). However, unlike us, He did so perfectly, always, and completely.

As you look back at the illustration of the believer, do you see that the believer must still contend with the residual flesh within? Upon receiving Christ (justification), His Spirit came to live within; however, that does not mean that the flesh has totally and completely been eradicated. It means that the fleshly nature no longer is the dominating power within.

Let's pause for a moment and look at what happened at salvation. It will be vital throughout this study to remember that when Scripture speaks of our salvation, it is always in the perfect tense. The perfect tense is a Greek verb tense that we do not have in the English language. When defined, the perfect tense is a completed action in the past with present and future results of the action. In this case, the action by God is rescuing man.

Therefore, when Scripture speaks of our salvation, we must consider all three tenses, namely: past, present, and future.

Consider the following information for a more concise understanding:

THE RESCUING GRACE OF SALVATION

Tense	Theological Term	What Happened?
Past	Justification	"I have been saved from the PENALTY of sin."
Present	Sanctification	"I am being saved from the POWER of sin."
Future	Glorification	"I will be saved from the PRESENCE of sin."

Always bear in mind that salvation is wholly a work of God the Father, God the Son, and God the Holy Spirit. Grace always precedes faith. The wages of Adam's sin in the garden that day brought death. Remember, you too were once dead in your transgressions and sin (Eph. 2:1). Dead people are not asking for help. An outside source—Life—was necessary. All then that man can bring to his salvation is his sin and desperate need for a Savior. This is

13. Kenneth S. Wuest, *Wuest's Word Studies From the Greek New Testament: Galatians, Volume One* (Grand Rapids, MI: Wm. B. Eerdmans Publishing Co., 1972), 71.

true whether we are talking about sin's penalty, power, or presence. No matter the tense of our salvation, man is completely dependent on Him!

In contrast, the man or woman who has not been saved remains under the penalty, power, and presence of sin. You might say sin reigns! As we have discovered, the man or woman without Christ does not have the Spirit residing within; therefore, that person's fleshly nature is the dominating power or force within (Rom. 8:9). We know that "If anyone does not have the Spirit of Christ, he does not belong to Him" (Rom 8:9). Ironically though, he does not belong to himself either. As we have discussed, "The children of God and the children of the devil are obvious" (1 John 3:10). Therefore, the one without the Spirit of Christ actually belongs to the devil. A sobering thought isn't it?

However, for the man or woman who has been redeemed by God, having been justified by grace through faith, he or she is now being sanctified. Sanctification is that process, whereby God's Spirit using the Word, is revealing places in our heart where the flesh is dominating in an area of our heart. In other words, whereas the flesh is the dominating power in the unbeliever, the flesh can still rear its ugly head and can have power over the believer in a specific area of the heart. These areas are places where we have said in our heart, "I will be like God because I love myself!" Every sin, whether it involves a sin of a believer or the sin nature of an unbeliever, can find its root in these two statements.

In reality, the flesh of a believer looks no different than the flesh of an unbeliever. For instance, our residual flesh still contends with God's Spirit. The flesh, whether in reference to the believer or unbeliever, does not seek God, because the focus of the flesh is self. Therefore, if the believer is seeking God, one can easily determine that it is the Spirit of God within causing that desire because human flesh (believer or unbeliever) will not seek God.

Likewise, for example, consider the fear of the Lord. If a person has the fear of the Lord, you can rest assured that is God's Spirit because the fear of the Lord is one of His seven-fold characteristics listed in Isaiah 11:2. Therefore, He is the cause. Man, in his flesh, has no fear of God (Gal. 3:2; Rom. 3:18).

We read in Scripture and will study in the Book of Galatians about the war between the flesh and the Spirit (Gal. 5:17). We even sing about this tension from within.

For example, within the hymn entitled, "Come Thou Fount of Every Blessing," contains one of my favorite stanzas. In fact, this stanza explains the war that is waging within the believer between the residual flesh and God's Spirit. Only a believer knows this struggle from within. The section reads,

O to grace how great a debtor

Daily I'm constrained to be!

Let Thy goodness like a fetter,

Bind my wandering heart to Thee.

Prone to wander,

Lord, I feel it,

Prone to leave the God I love;

Here's my heart,

Lord take and seal it;

Seal it for Thy courts above.[14]

---

14. Words by Robert Robinson, "Come Thou Fount of Every Blessing," *Hymns of Grace* (Los Angeles, CA: The Master's Seminary Press, 2015), 104.

Don't you, at times, feel the propensity to wander? That, my friend, is evidence of our residual flesh. Praise be to God, someday, we will not be able to sing this stanza in our glorified state!

As you read the last part of the hymn above, do you see that the Lord is the one who seals our heart? Let's see how Scripture backs this statement up.

1. Look at Ephesians 1:13. With whom does the Lord seal us? ___________________________

So, if we belong to the Lord Jesus, and He reigns in our heart by His Spirit, what influence then, can the enemy via our residual flesh and/or the world have on our hearts? What does that look like?

2. Let's begin answering the first question, "What influence can the enemy have on a believer's heart?"

Did you notice, the word, "influence," rather than the words "possession" or "dominion"? The Spirit of God and the Enemy cannot reside in the same heart! However, the Enemy can influence the heart of a believer. He does so through the avenues of our residual flesh and the world. Our flesh, (our desire to be god because we love ourselves) is the internal influence whereby the enemy gains access to our soul (mind, will, and emotion). The world, (its desire to be god and its love of self) is the external influence whereby the Enemy can gain access.

Now, as to the second question, "What does this look like in a believer?" or better stated, "How can this happen to a believer?"

As a review from the previous lesson, Ephesians 2:8 states that we are saved by grace through faith. You will recall that grace is when the Spirit of God (who resides within the believer) takes the Word of God and speaks truth to our hearts. In truth, when this happens, we have just experienced the grace of God! You may also remember that grace is the invitation from God to respond in faith.

Also keep in mind, faith, by definition, has three components:

- A firm conviction (Holy Spirit) of God's Word
- Personal surrender of your will to God's Word
- Obedience to God's Word[15]

Do you see the necessity of the order? Do you see the first component of saving faith begins with the grace of God as His Spirit takes the Word of God and convicts our heart? When this occurs, man has just been invited by God to respond by surrendering his will and obeying God's Word.

However, as we have seen, man does not always respond in faith. Sometimes, the believer will choose unbelief, which is diametrically opposed to faith. Unbelief is when the one under the conviction of the Holy Spirit and God's Word refuses to surrender his will and obey God.

When unbelief is the response to God's grace, the believer has just said, "No" to God's Spirit and God's Word, and "Yes" to his flesh (or the world). The unbeliever has no power source within. Therefore, he will habitually respond in unbelief.

The believer, however, has the power source within. Herein, is where and how the struggle begins over an area of our heart.

Anytime God's Spirit illuminates His Word in the mind of a believer, grace has been extended. In other words, God is inviting the believer to respond in faith (surrender and obedience). He is not asking the believer to muster up faith or strive in one's flesh to surrender and obey, He is asking the believer to let Him do it! In other words,

15. W. E. Vine, *Vine's Expository Dictionary of Old and New Testament Words* (Grand Rapids, MI: Fleming H. Revell, 1981),

only God's Spirit can cause us to surrender and obey God. In essence, if you are a surrendered believer, you are letting Christ live His life through you.

Consider the following illustration:

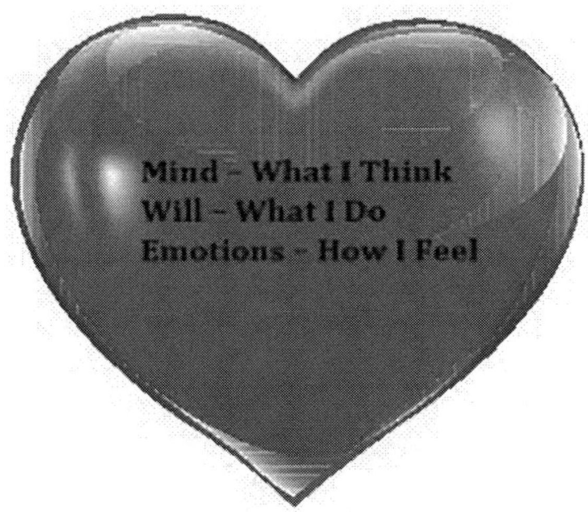

THE RIGHT-SIDE-UP HEART

A believer whose mind is Spirit-led (using God's Word), and who is willing to surrender and obey will exhibit emotions in keeping with the fruit of the Spirit (love, joy, peace...). This is the heart of a man or woman who the Lord can use for His glory.

However, when the believer says, "No" to God's Spirit and God's Word, and "Yes" to his flesh (or the world), something happens in the heart of the believer. In other words, the moment you and I refuse to surrender our will and choose to disobey God's Spirit and His Word, our hearts flip upside-down. Now, all of a sudden, emotions, such as fear, anger, shame, guilt, and so forth, are leading our hearts.

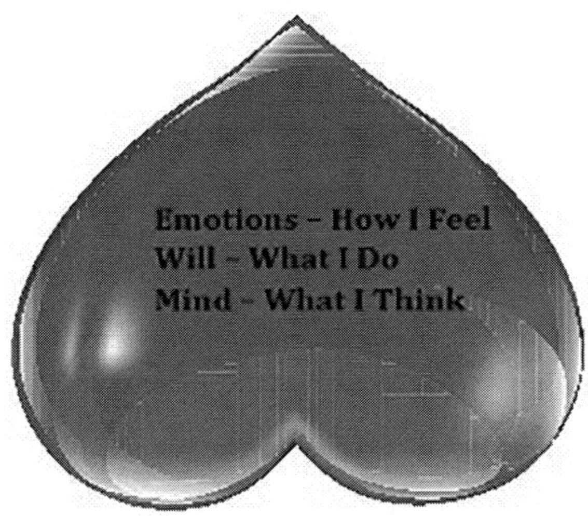

THE UPSIDE-DOWN HEART

Notice from the illustration, the heart that is flipped upside-down is emotion driven, which in turn, directly affects the will (what a person does or does not do) and the mind (what a person thinks).

When I find that my heart has flipped upside-down, I know the Enemy (who comes to steal, kill, and destroy) has gained influence over an area of my heart whether it was through the avenue of my flesh or the world's influence

over me, and he has rendered me useless (unfruitful). He cannot have my heart, but I can allow him to render me useless to the Master, who died to control my heart. When this happens, the Spirit of God is grieved or quenched.

Has this ever happened to you? Maybe you find yourself at this moment thinking, "That describes my heart right now!"

When this happens to me (notice that I said, when), I know it is time to cry out for the Savior to save me from sin's power. Every time I cry out, He comes to deliver me. When I ask Him what that would look like in my life, the Spirit of God is faithful to bring to my mind His Word. Scripture declares that the Word of God is profitable for four things:

- Teaching (I need to be instructed)
- Reproof (I am off-track)
- Correction (I need to get back on track)
- Training in Righteousness

In 2 Timothy 3:17, we discover the purpose, so that the man (woman) of God may be adequate, equipped for every good work." If we were to explain the word, good, we would see that Jesus defined it in Mark 10:18. When called, "Good teacher," Jesus answered, "Why do you call Me good? No one is good except God alone" (emphasis added). Therefore, the word, good, is to be associated with God alone. Only God's Spirit in us can do good work. Our job is to surrender and obey.

Invariably, the Lord will show me my heart (and only He can—Jeremiah 17:10) when I am in His Word. James says that His Word is like looking into a mirror (James 1:23). His Spirit is faithful to bring to my mind where I am in need of reproof and what I need to do to correct what He has just revealed by His grace. In essence, God's Spirit is inviting me to respond in faith in some area where I have gotten off track.

As I surrender and obey what He has just shown me, (and He will show you what that looks like in your life), my heart is then flipped right-side up, again. Now, I can think biblically. His Spirit is, once again, leading my heart and causing me to walk in the truth of God's Word. Now, that I am walking in the Spirit, I will not carry out the desires of my flesh (that are in direct opposition to His Spirit and His Word). Doesn't that sound like Galatians 5:16–17?

You may be thinking, but what if I have not sinned? What if I am the victim of someone else's sin? What if my heart has flipped upside-down due to a tragedy? Rest assured that whether it is my sin, the sin of another, or just the by-product of living in a fallen world, the same thing applies.

In Colossians 2:6, Paul reminded the Colossian believers that just as they had received Christ Jesus the Lord (justification), they were to walk in Him (sanctification). Just as we were justified by grace through faith, we are now being sanctified by grace through faith. He is the initiator, and we are the responders. Furthermore, He is the one who gives us the faith to respond, proving, salvation is wholly a work of God!

Some situation or person has gained power or control over your heart rather than God's Spirit. I can always tell this has happened in the area of my emotions. When God's Spirit is in control, there is fruit.

The more His Spirit controls our hearts, the less we will carry out the desire of the flesh (Gal. 5:16). Isn't that what John the Baptist said after meeting Jesus when he stated, "He must increase, I must decrease" (John 3:30)?

Therein is the process of sanctification—less of us, and more of Him! Are you cooperating with God's Spirit as He reveals the truth about your heart through His Word? Or is your flesh the dominating factor in your heart right now?

Will you let Him save you?

Keep these truths in mind as we head into the Book of Galatians. You will discover, as the Church in Galatia did, that the war between their flesh and God's Spirit is real and personal.

In fact, right off the bat, you will discover that the hearts of the Galatian believers had been turned upside-down by the false brethren, known as the Judaizers, who had come into their fellowship preaching a different gospel (Gal. 1:6). You will see that their minds, once dominated by truth, had been led astray, leaving their hearts greatly disturbed (Gal. 1:7). However, the Spirit of God will use the Word of God (Paul's letter) to remind them of the truth of the one true gospel so that their hearts can be set upright once again in order that they be "adequate, equipped for every good work" (2 Tim. 3:17).

Lesson 3

The Transforming Message of Grace

By now, you have probably picked up on the overarching theme of this study, which is grace. As stated in the preface of this workbook, grace is the exact opposite of striving. Until this study, I did not realize that the first time the word "grace" is recorded in Scripture is in Genesis 6:8. This first occurrence is in reference to Noah and in the context of judgment and salvation.

The verses before the word "grace" set the context. Genesis 6:5 states, "The LORD, seeing that the wickedness of man was great on the earth and that every intent of the thoughts of his heart was only evil continually" (emphasis added). Can you see in this verse the depravity of man?

Moreover, we are told that the wickedness was so great that the Lord was grieved in His heart that He had made man (Gen 6:6). And then, one of the most merciful statements in all of Scripture follows man's condition and the Lord's gracious response, stating, "BUT Noah found favor (grace) in the eyes of the LORD" (emphasis added). There it is. The first mention of the word we know as grace. The specific Hebrew word used here, hen, "stands as the fundamental application of unmerited favor or regard in God's sight."[16]

Do you see that Noah had done nothing to earn the favor of God? If you keep reading, you will see that Noah responded in faith (surrender and obedience) to the grace of God's invitation, which he had been extended. This grace by faith was Noah's salvation from the righteous judgment of a holy God on this wicked and perverse people. The ark would represent or become a type of the Savior to come. By definition, a type is a picture in the Old Testament of a New Testament truth.

Equally as interesting to the first place where the word grace is used, is the number of times the word is actually stated. According to Strong's Concordance, the word favor (grace) is used sixty-four times in the thirty-nine books that comprise the Old Testament.[17] And not every use of the word in the Old Testament is in reference to God. (Sometimes, it is used as man finds favor with man.)

Also intriguing, the word "grace" is stated only six times in the gospels. Although the word itself is rarely used in the gospels, we know the **person** of grace is the theme of the gospels.

However, the apostle Paul uses the word "grace" eighty-nine times in his thirteen letters. The message of salvation by grace through faith is the theme of all of Paul's letters. But instead of taking my word, let's take the time for you to see this truth for yourself.

A LOOK AT THE MESSAGE

1. Let's start by looking at the beginning and end of each of the thirteen letters Paul wrote under the inspiration of God's Spirit. A careful observation will reveal the theme Paul consistently uses as a bookend for each letter.

16. Warren Baker and Eugene Carpenter, *The Complete Word Study Dictionary Old Testament* (Chattanooga, TN: AMG Publishers, 2003), 354

17. James Strong, *The New Strong's Concordance of the Bible* (Nashville: Thomas Nelson Publishers, 1990), pp. 351, 430–431.

a. Romans 1:7 ______________________ to you

and

____

from God our __________________________

and

the Lord _______________ __________________

Romans 16:24

---

b. 1 Corinthians 1:3 ______________________

and

____

from God our __________________________

and

the Lord _______________ __________________

1 Corinthians 16:23

---

c. 2 Corinthians 1:2 ______________________

and

____

from God our __________________________

and

the Lord _______________ __________________

2 Corinthians 13:14 The ______________________ of the Lord Jesus Christ

The ______________________ of God

The ______________________ of the Holy Spirit

Do you see the Trinity in this verse? Can you see the role of each?

d. Galatians 1:3 ______________________

and

____

from God our __________________________

and

the Lord _______________ __________________

Galatians 6:18

e. Ephesians 1:2 ______________________

and

____

from God our __________________________

and

the Lord _______________ __________________

Ephesians 6:24

f. Philippians 1:2 ______________________

and

____

from God our __________________________

and

the Lord _______________ __________________

Philippians 4:23

---

g. Colossians 1:2 ____________________

and

____

from God our ________________________

Colossians 4:18 (final four words) ____________ __________ ______________ ________________

h. 1 Thessalonians 1:1 ____________________ to you

and

____

1 Thessalonians 5:28

---

i. 2 Thessalonians 1:2 ____________________

and

____

from God our ________________________

and

the Lord __________ ____________

2 Thessalonians 3:18

---

j. 1 Timothy 1:2 ____________________,

and

____

and

____

from God the ________________________

and

Christ Jesus our ________________

1 Timothy 6:21 (final four words) ____________ __________ ______________ ________________

k. 2 Timothy 1:2 ______________________,

and

____

and

____

from God the __________________________

and

Christ Jesus our ________________

2 Timothy 4:22 (final four words) _____________ ___________ _______________ __________________

l. Titus 1:4 ______________________

and

____

from God the ____________________________

and

Christ Jesus our _____________________

Titus 3:15 (final five words) ____

m. Philemon 1:3 ______________________

and

____

from God our __________________________

and

the Lord _______________ __________________

Philemon 1:25

---

2. Now, having looked at the beginning and end of every letter Paul wrote, what is the one word/theme you see repeated over and over again?

Note: The repetition of the word, "grace," is called an *inclusio*. An inclusio is a literary tool used in biblical studies to highlight or emphasize a repetitive word, theme, or phrase in Scripture. When an inclusio is present, everything within the letter is used to describe, support, and explain the repeated theme.

Therefore, since grace is the theme of all of Paul's letters, everything written in between describes, supports, and explains the bookend of God's amazing grace. In fact, if you were to study all thirteen of Paul's letters, you would discover that each letter is divided into two sections. In between the bookends of God's grace, you will discover how people are called to respond in faith.

If we were to grammatically look at Paul's letters, in the first part of all thirteen, we would see that the verbs primarily used are in the indicative mood. The indicative mood, in Greek grammar, indicates statements of fact. However, if we were to look closely at the second portion of his letters, we would observe that the verbs used are predominantly in the imperative mood, which signifies commands to obey.

Take the Book of Romans, for example, which can be divided into two clear segments, specifically: Romans 1—11 and 12—16. In Chapters 1—11 you will find the indicative verbs. In this segment of Paul's letter, statements of fact are used to communicate man's depravity, Jesus Christ our Savior, salvation by grace through faith, God's sovereignty, and so forth.

However, in Romans 12—16, there is a marked shift. Now, the verbs are in the imperative mood signifying commands to obey. In other words, the first part of the letter contains facts about who God is and what He has accomplished on our behalf, and the second portion includes information on how we are to live. In light of who God is and what He has done, our response should be faith (surrender and obedience). The second portion of the letter is possible only because of the first part—who God is, and what He in His grace has done for us. You will notice that who God is and what He has done is always connected with man's need. This is a repeated pattern in all of Scripture.

Therefore, in summary, the statements of fact (first part) are comprised of who God is and what He has done. The commands to obey (second part) contain our response. Do you see it—salvation by grace through faith? Grace is God's invitation to Himself, who He is and what He has done on our behalf. Faith is man's response to surrender and obedience. In other words, because of who God is (indicative facts), and because He lives in the believer, man is able to respond in surrender and obedience to His commands. Grace must precede faith; otherwise, man would be left to strive within himself to obey God's commands. The entire Old Testament is filled with stories of man striving to obey God and falling short, only to prove over and over again, that man is in desperate need of God!

3. Notice again, as you look over the pattern in all of Pauls' letters to the church where grace originates? Who is the source of grace?

4. Where is man in regard to the grace of God? ____

The truth that grace originates in the Godhead and humanity is merely the recipient cannot be overstated. In fact, it is part of the definition of grace. Maybe you are familiar with the acrostic, which defines grace as:

G – God's

R - Riches

A - At

C – Christ's

E – Expense

As doctrinally sound and as clever as this acrostic is, there is something overtly hidden. Something that apart from His grace, we are unable to see on our own, and has taken me years to discover. This is something the church at Galatia needed to discover, which is why Paul wrote the letter. Furthermore, it is something I believe, every child of God must eventually realize in the process of sanctification. My prayer is that it will be something you too will discover in the progression of this study.

In order to discover the hidden factor within the acrostic, let's look first at the life of Saul (who would later become known as the apostle Paul) since he is the human author specifically chosen by God to reveal this life-giving message of grace.

A LOOK AT THE MESSENGER

Truly the gospel message in which Paul was entrusted to deliver to the Gentiles is a message of grace. In essence, Paul was chosen by God to be His messenger of grace. You may be thinking, "Why Paul of all people?" What would qualify Paul to become God's messenger of grace? After all, wasn't he in great opposition to the message of grace prior to his conversion? We will look more intently into his transformation in the next lesson, but for now, let's look at his testimony of grace years after his conversion.

(**Note:** You will notice that I will refer to the apostle Paul as Saul at times. For purposes of this study, Saul is a reference to his pre-conversion, and Paul is post-conversion. Similarly, when I am referring to his pre-converted state, I will refer to him as Saul).

5. Let's begin by looking at Saul's (Paul's) impressive resume in the flesh. Turn to Philippians 3:5–6. List the seven credentials in which Paul could have boasted in his flesh:

1) ______________________________

a. Now, look at Genesis 17:11–12. What do you see?

____

____

2) ______________________________

a. Now, look at Deuteronomy 14:2. What do you see?

____

____

3) ______________________________

Benjamin was the twelfth son of Jacob. His mother was Rachel. His father named him Benjamin, which means, "son of my right hand." The right hand in Scripture is always the hand of favor (Gen. 35:18). The first king of Israel, Saul, came from the tribe of Benjamin (1 Sam. 10:19–24). Similarly, Queen Esther and her uncle Mordecai were from the tribe of Benjamin (Esth. 2:5). Both were God's chosen instruments to preserve the Jews in Israel's history.

Furthermore, when the twelve tribes of Israel divided, the tribe of Benjamin linked with the tribe of Judah to form the Southern Kingdom (1 Kings 12) also known as Judah.

4)

a. Look at Acts 26:4–5. What do you see?

5) "as to the law" ____

a. Look at Acts 22:3. What do you see?

b. Now, look at Acts 23:6. Not only was Saul a Pharisee but he was also a

6) "as to zeal" ____

Did you happen to notice that everything on Saul's pre-conversion list was physical and outward as opposed to spiritual and inward (heart)?

6. Let's pause for a moment to investigate Saul's pre-conversion zeal. Look at the following cross-references and record his zeal and how far he was willing to act.

a. Turn to Acts 7:58 to discover the first mention of Saul in Scripture. What is Saul's zeal accomplishing? (You will have to read Acts 6:8—7:57 to establish context).

Traditionally, the one to whom the robes were laid was the one who was not only consenting, but also, the one overseeing the act. Do you see that his zeal included a willingness to commit murder, if necessary?

b. What do you learn about Saul's zeal in Acts 8:1?

c. Notice how Saul's zeal is being demonstrated in Acts 8:3. What do you see?

d. Now look at Acts 22:4–5. What do you see?

Think about it. If Saul targeted both men and women, where did that leave their children?

e. Look at Acts 26:9–11. What do you see here?

Who does this sound like?

f. Look again at Acts 22:3. What do you see in regard to zeal?

Who was the object of Saul's zeal (or so he thought)? _____________

Do you see the trap of deception?

7) "as to righteousness, which is in the Law" ___________________________________

Did you notice that Saul (Paul) is not claiming sinlessness? He is boasting in his righteousness, which is in the Law, and as it compares with others. Doesn't that sound a lot like our flesh?

7. Now, look at Isaiah 64:6. What did scholarly Saul clearly not remember?

Furthermore, consider that a Pharisee, which means, separated ones, took pride in their own righteousness and were adept at judging others for their lack of righteousness.

Now, if you look at Saul's (Paul's) qualifications, you can understand why God chose him right? Wrong. In fact, if you look closely at Saul's (Paul's) credentials, they are the **exact opposite of grace** because the antonyms for grace are works, religion, and the flesh!

Furthermore, although Saul's lineage, education, and zeal were impressive, do you see that he was still spiritually blind, separated from the God he was trying so hard to please, and desperately in need of God's grace?

You might think that his qualifications in the flesh disqualified him for the message of grace. From man's perspective, you would be right. BUT GOD . . . rich in mercy . . . (Eph 2:4)!

8. Now look at 1 Timothy 1:12–15 and answer the following questions:

a. What do you learn about Paul at the very beginning of verse 12?

Note: A measure or way to tell if someone is operating from grace or works is a heart of thankfulness and gratitude! It is the evidence of grace!

b. What do you learn about the Lord Jesus Christ from verse 12?

1)

BECAUSE:

2)

3)

Note: The active voice is used for the Greek verb, translated "strengthened," meaning, the subject, Jesus Christ, performed the action. Likewise, both the verbs, "considered" and "putting," are in the middle voice, meaning the subject, Jesus Christ, both initiated and participated in the action! In other words, Paul is giving all of the glory to Jesus Christ, which is where it belongs at all times!

Note of Interest: The Greek verb translated "considered" literally means, "to lead the way/to go before." Also note, Paul did not put himself into ministry.[18]

c. How does Paul describe his former way of life, according to verse 13?

1)

2)

3)

By the way, all of these characteristics are nouns, which signify a state of being.

d. While in this state, what was Paul shown (v. 13)

Note: The Greek word translated "shown" is in the passive voice, meaning that the subject was acted upon from an outside source (God). Moreover, in the New Testament, when the Greek word translated "mercy" is used in the passive voice, it can literally be translated, "to obtain salvation."[19]

e. Why was Paul shown mercy according to verse 13?

18. Spiros Zodhiates, *The Complete Word Study New Testament Dictionary* (Chattanooga, TN: AMG Publishers, 1993), 707.
19. Ibid., 563.

Paul is stating his condition as one who lacked a saving knowledge of Jesus Christ.

f. What was more abundant than Paul's ignorance and unbelief, which led to his activity of blasphemy, persecution, and violent aggression?

1) ______________________________

with

2) ______________________________

and

3) ______________________________

Note: Grace, faith, and love are all nouns; therefore, they represent a state of being.

Now look at Romans 5:20. What do you see about sin and grace in this verse?

____

____

g. In whom are these three states of being found? ______________________________

h. What, according to Paul, is the trustworthy statement deserving (worthy) of full acceptance?

#1 – Jesus Christ ______________________________

#2 – I ______________________________

Note the order! When we truly see who Jesus is and consider why He condescended to come into the world, then, and only then, can we see ourselves as we truly are—in dire NEED of a SAVIOR! Have you seen Him this way? Do you see grace in Paul's statement?

Another evidence or by-product of true grace is humility and great joy!

When grace gets ahold of you, you will find yourself like Paul. You will be overwhelmed with a joyful, thankful, grateful, and humbled heart as you recount the magnitude of who He is, what He has done, and how blessed you are to call Him Lord and Savior. You will begin to know what it means to be in Christ.

So, let's go back to our definition of grace. Do you see that the hidden element in the acrostic is you! In other words, grace most assuredly is God's riches at Christ's expense. But did you notice that you and I are not in the acrostic? Like Paul, all that we can contribute to grace is our sin, desperate need, frailty, weakness, and humanness.

So, for clarity's sake and purpose of this study, we will view grace from two perspectives. The definition of grace will be a lot like the trustworthy statement deserving of full acceptance:

#1 – Jesus Christ is God's Lavish Merit/Provision

#2 – I have – No merit on my own!

ON A PERSONAL NOTE

Many years ago, I memorized the acrostic for grace. It became my pat answer along with my "go to" definition, "unmerited favor." I have spent years learning how to define grace. Through diligent study, I could have told you the Greek word for grace, as well as expound on its definition, using many biblical references for support. But it was not until recently that the Lord, in His infinite grace, has taken the concept of grace from my head and placed it where it belongs—at the core of my heart. The gift of His grace has been nothing short of a life-giving gift that has been transformational, to say the least!

The late pastor and author, Wayne Barber, while giving his testimony, summed up my testimony beautifully when he stated, "I grew up understanding Christianity from a works' perspective. It was all up to me!"[20] After all, I thought and was taught; Christ is living in me. Therefore, I should be like Christ, right? I should be able to live the Christian life, right? I would hear the Word taught and think, "I need to do that! I will just have to try harder!" Do you see it? The words, "I should, I need to, I will just have to..." was the trap I found myself in for many years, and sadly, I had no idea.

You see, grace is the opposite of works and religion. By all rights, and unbeknownst to me, I was a striver, and the tendency of my flesh is to strive even now. Somehow in my mind, I had confused striving with seeking, and worse, I didn't realize it. I was a sucker for lists like, "Five Ways to Have an Effective Quiet Time," or "Ten Things to Help Improve Your Prayer Life." Believe me, when I say, I tried them all. I was trapped in this performance-based mentality.

Graciously, the Lord revealed this to me when I was writing *Created to Bow*. The subtitle was a perfect description of the trap from which He was setting me free—the trap of fear, perfectionism, and control.

The message of grace is difficult for a person who strives. Hopefully and prayerfully as we walk through the Book of Galatians together, this former striver can help shed light on what that looks like. It's a trap for sure. And sometimes I find myself edging toward that trap door again. And sadly, sometimes, I find it is too late, and once again, the trap door has shut with me inside. Thankfully, at least now, I do not have to stay there long. In His grace and mercy, He rescues me!

If you, like me, have found yourself in the trap of striving to please or merit God's approval or worse, the praise of people, this study is for you.

---

20. Wayne Barber, *Living Grace* (Nashville, TN: Broadman & Holman Publishers, 2005), ix.

Lesson 4

The Transformed Messenger of Grace

PAUL'S TESTIMONY
Acts 9:1–19

In the last lesson, we just mentioned Saul's conversion. So, in this lesson, in order to grasp the magnitude of God's grace in Paul's life, we must take the time to examine what happened when Saul (his Hebrew name) was transformed into Paul (his Greek name). How did Saul, the religious and zealous Pharisee, change from striving to please and earn God's favor (grace) to actually becoming the recipient and messenger of God's amazing grace?

As you proceed through the lesson, watch closely as you discover two diametrically opposed plans. In reality, Saul's plan is disguised in religion. Consider how Saul's plan is wrought in deception as he attempts to please God by terrorizing the Lord's Church. In essence, Saul's plan is ultimately antichrist because he is against the Lord Jesus Christ and His Church (see 1 John 2:18). You might say that Saul is like a present-day terrorist in his attempt to please "his god," because in reality, he is actually opposing the one true God.

Thankfully, the Lord in His infinite grace and mercy, also had a plan, which will ultimately, prevail. Keep these things in mind as you proceed through the lesson. Marvel at our kind and gracious God as He rescues Saul from Saul and the Enemy's deceptive trap.

Begin this lesson by reading about Saul's conversion in Acts 9:1–19 and answer the following questions:

1. What is in the heart of Saul according to verse 1? ______________________________

and

____

2. Who is the target of Saul's hatred according to verse 1?

3. Who is really the target of Saul's hatred according to Jesus (v. 4)? ________________________

Now, let's review for a moment. You will recall that the heart (soul) of man is comprised of his mind, will and emotion. That being said, obviously Saul's mind was filled with hatred, right?

4. What did his hatred against Jesus Christ cause him to do according to verses 1b–2?

Notice that the early church was called, the Way. Look at John 14:6 to discover why. What do you see?

Do you see that the opposition is really against the Way, the Truth, and the Life?

5. What does he hope to accomplish with these letters (v2b)?

Note: Do you see that Saul has a plan? Remember in Saul's mind, he is doing all of these things for God. When, in actuality, he is working against God and His Plan. To be specific, his attacks are against Jesus Christ. You see, Saul is deceived. Sadly, he is really just a pawn in the hand of the enemy. He is on the enemy's mission and following the enemy's plan, which is always against Jesus Christ.

6. So, if his mind is filled with thoughts against Jesus Christ, and his will is causing him to act on his thoughts, what do you think has filled his emotions? In other words, how do you think he feels?

7. Who is his anger really toward?

Who is getting the brunt of his anger though?

Anger is an emotion that can destroy others as well as the one who is owned by it.

Anger can be displayed in two ways:

1) Anger turned inward results in depression.

2) Anger turned outward results in outbursts.

Do you see that the target of anger for a person who is depressed is self, resulting in self-pity? This person is always the victim. Likewise, if the anger is turned outward it will affect other people and he/she leaves victims in their wake. Either way, the person who is angry is never at fault and rarely even sees this is within!

Furthermore, the mindset of a person with anger issues (whether it is turned inward or outward) is actually against God. The enemy of your soul does not care which action (inward or outward) you choose, as long as you do not discover that he is the true source and that your anger is really against God.

In Saul's case, do you see that his anger is actually against the person of Jesus Christ, who is God? Satan is the source and Saul does not know it. And because his anger is turned outward in violence and rage, the disciples of the Lord Jesus Christ are his victims.

Look at the following two charts for a visual to help you understand Saul's mindset.

The Two Faces of Pride Manifested in the Flesh[21]

The Enemy

The **Source** of Pride

↙ ↘

Angel of Light ↓ The Roaring Lion

The Flesh

The **Sin** of Pride

↓

ANGER

↙ ↘

Self-Pity	Self-Confidence
Depression	Fits of rage/ outburst of anger
Self-Destructive	Destroy others

Both bound in the web of fear, perfectionism, and control.

Also, in the case of Saul, keep in mind that the Jewish mindset believes that there is one person who is the LORD God. The Jew either knows nothing or rejects the concept of the Trinity: Father, Son, and Spirit, One God—Three Persons. Saul thinks he is protecting and defending the one true God! In his mind, (and the mind of every Jew apart from Christ), Jesus is not the Messiah, and therefore not God. In fact, this is the case with every other religion of the world as well. Every world religion in the world (other than Christianity, of course) rejects that there is one way to the Father—His Son, Jesus Christ (John 14:6).

21. For more information regarding "The Two Faces of Pride in the Flesh," see my workbook entitled, *Created to Bow* (Maitland, FL: Xulon Press, 2017), pp. 158–187.

Now look at the two "Faces of Pride" as displayed through the enemy of the world's system:

The Two Faces of Pride Manifested in the World[22]

The Enemy

The **Source** of Pride

↙ ↘

Angel of Light	↓	The Roaring Lion

The World

The **Sin** of Pride

↓

ANGER

↙ ↘

Religion	Rebellion
Has a "form" of godliness but denies its power	Ungodly
Self-righteousness	Unrighteousness
Works/Performance/ Merit Based	Overtly Riotous/Sinful Acts

↘ ↙

Self-glorifying

Self-gratifying

Critical/Judgmental of others

↓

Both bound in the web of fear, perfectionism, and control.

22. *Ibid.*, pp. 188–215.

Whether the Enemy gains access through the flesh or the world makes no difference to him. Sadly, humanity does not know that underlying it all, the Enemy is the source of deception. He is the one that is at war against God and has been from the beginning.

Unbeknownst to Saul, and every other man/woman apart from God, he is in the snare of the enemy and he is doing the will of the enemy (2 Tim. 2:26). Thankfully though, Saul is about to have his eyes opened by the outside Source of Truth! Let's go back to Acts 9.

8. What happened suddenly as Saul was approaching Damascus (v. 3)?

9. What was Saul's response according to verse 4?

Note: This will be all of creation's response when they see Jesus someday (Phil. 2:10). It is our rightful place in the presence of the King!

10. What did Saul hear (v. 4)? ________________________

11. What did the "voice" say (v. 4)?

Note: Jesus knew and called Saul out by name. His sheep hear His voice. He calls them out by name (see John 10:3). Jesus Christ came after Saul when he was not looking for Him, and in fact, was actually radically going against Him. Oh, what a gracious Shepherd!

12. Now look at Revelation 1:12–17a, where you will discover a description of the glorified Lord Jesus Christ by the apostle John, who has been exiled to the island of Patmos because of the "word of God and his testimony of Jesus" (Rev. 1:9). Using these passages, answer the following questions:

What does John hear in verse 12?

As you consider the description of Jesus in His glorified state, pay close attention to the description of His eyes and His face. What do you see?

His eyes were like ____ (v. 14b)

His face was like the ____ (v. 16b)

What is John's response in verse 17a?

13. Now, as you look at what happened to Saul and compare it with what happened to the apostle John, what do you see?

Could Saul be seeing the glorified Christ?

I think so!

14. Now let's go back to Acts 9. What does Jesus tell Saul he is actually doing in verse 4b?

Note: The Greek verb translated "persecuting," means, "to prosecute and pursue with repeated acts of enmity."[23] Interestingly, the antonym means, "to guard, defend, and protect."[24]

Keep in mind, Saul thinks he is actually guarding, defending, and protecting God. Do you see the trap of deception he is in? Remember, the definition of deception is to say one thing but do another. Oh, how we need the Lord's perspective (Word) to keep us from deception!

15. Did you notice that Jesus did not say, "Saul, Saul, why are you persecuting My church (disciples)," which was actually, in a literal sense, what was happening. Why do you think Jesus answered Saul in the way that he did? Any thoughts?

Does it comfort you to know that God views the persecution of His Church with the persecution of His Son? In other words, in God's eyes, they are one and the same.

16. What question does Saul ask the Lord Jesus (v5)?

*Isn't this the age-old question every man is asking?

17. Notice Jesus' answer is direct. How does He answer Saul (v. 5)?

What specific name did Jesus present to Saul? The name, Jesus, by definition means, Savior, Deliverer, Rescuer. By stating His Name, Jesus is revealing God's Plan to save. In essence, He is inviting Saul to Himself.

18. Let's pause and look at the name, Jesus, for a moment. Go to Luke 1:26–33 and answer the following questions:

---

23. Spiros Zodhiates, *The Complete Word Study Dictionary New Testament* (Chattanooga, TN: AMG Publishers, 1993), 474.
24. *Ibid.*

Who sent the angel Gabriel to Nazareth (v. 26)?

What was Mary instructed to name the son whom she was to bear (v. 31)?

So, in essence, who named Jesus?

What else was Mary told about Jesus in verses 32–33?

He will be ________________________

He will be called the ____*

The Lord God will give Him the _____________________ of His father David.

He will _____________________ over the house of Jacob (Israel) forever.

His kingdom will have __________________________________.

Note: If you have ever done a study in the Bible on the names of God, you would discover two things about each name God reveals, specifically: **1)** God's character, attributes, and nature, and **2)** humanity's need. The name God reveals always coincides with man's need.

When Jesus answered by stating, "I am Jesus," what is He revealing to Saul about Himself and Saul?

Although Saul knew all of the Old Testament names by which God had revealed Himself to humanity, he was in the process of discovering that every name culminated into this one name—Jesus. Humanity's greatest need since creation is for the one who created him/her. Likewise, man's greatest need since the Fall is for a Savior!

19. Now let's look at the next thing Jesus said in Acts 9:6. List His instructions to Saul.

a. ________________________

b. ________________________

and

____

(The Greek word translated "told" is in the passive voice. which means that the subject is being acted upon).

Notes of Interest: Let's pause here for a moment, or we will miss something significant. The specific Greek verb, along with the tense, mood and voice is packed with meaning and very important.

Although the tense, mood, and voice of a word can be intimidating, persevere in your study to gain understanding.

Take it slow so that you can absorb what is being communicated. The English language is not as specific, but the Greek language is a very specific language.

For example, the verb's tense, mood, and voice leave no question in regard to who is responsible for the action and who is being acted upon. This is vitally important, especially if the topic of discussion is our salvation. Man can take credit for something the Lord God alone is doing if we are not careful. By taking the time and effort to methodically look at the meaning of a specific word, we can discover who is responsible for what.

For me personally, this has made a huge difference so that I am not trying to take responsibility for something only God can do or being upset with the Lord because He is not doing what I should be doing. It has been both enlightening and liberating to say the least! So now, let's dig deep.

First, the word, "rise" (Gk. *anistemi*) is a synonym of the same word used in Matthew 28:6, to describe what happened to Jesus Christ when He arose (*egeiro*) from the dead!

Now consider that the word, *anistemi*, is an aorist imperative passive verb, meaning:

Aorist tense: it occurred at a point in time

Imperative mood: it is a command

Passive voice: the subject is acted upon!

With this information, what do you see about Jesus' identity as Savior, coupled with the passive verbal command to, "rise (*anistemi*)," in Acts 9:6?

Note: Jesus, the Risen One, will be the cause of Saul's ability to rise. In essence, He was saying, "I will raise you." Jesus was in the process of raising Saul from spiritual death to life.

20. Now skip down to Acts 9:8, and let's look at the synonym, which reads, "And Saul got up (*egeiro*) from the ground, and though his eyes were open (*anoigo*), he could see nothing."

Note: The verb (*egeiro*) used here is aorist indicative passive, meaning,

Aorist tense: it occurred at a point in time

Indicative mood: it is a statement of fact

Passive voice: the subject is acted upon

Furthermore, the word "open" (*anoigo*) is used as a metaphor meaning, "to open the understanding of the mind, to cause to perceive and understand."[25] The word, *anoigo*, is a perfect participle passive verb meaning:

Perfect Tense: An action in the past, with present, and future results (of the action).

Passive Voice: The subject is being acted upon (from an outside source).

Also keep in mind that whenever our salvation is mentioned in Scripture the perfect tense and passive voice are always used.

25. *Ibid.*, 186.

With all of this information provided, how do you interpret Acts 9:8, which reads, "And Saul got up (*egeiro*) from the ground, and though his eyes were open (*anoigo*), he could see nothing"?

Do you see that the ability to see/hear God comes from God?

21. Now, let's consider the men who were traveling with Saul. Look at Acts 9:7. What do you learn about Saul's traveling companions?

Do you see that the call to follow Christ Jesus is an individual call?

Those closest to you may not see, hear, or understand what the Lord Jesus is saying to you personally?

22. Now, describe the condition in which Saul is left following his encounter with the Lord Jesus (vv. 8b–9).

23. What is Saul doing these three days? To answer this question, look at what the Lord Jesus tells Ananias in verse 11b. What do you see?

Saul is ________________________

Note: Prayer, by definition, is dependence upon God. Saul has been laid low. He has been made to come to the end of himself by a kind and loving God who is pursuing him. Although physically blind, his spiritual eyes have been opened. And from now on, rather than striving to please God in his own strength, he will spend the rest of his life bowed at the throne of grace receiving mercy and finding grace to help in time of need (Heb. 4:16). Beautiful picture of amazing grace!

Now that we have examined the Lord Jesus' divine appointment with Saul, let's look at His encounter with a disciple from Damascus named, Ananias. By the way, Ananias' name means, "Jehovah has dealt graciously" (emphasis added).[26]

24. Begin by reading Acts 9:10–16 and answer the following questions:

How does the Lord reveal Himself to Ananias (v. 10)? ___________________

26. Zodhiates, *The Complete Word Study Dictionary New Testament*, 155.

What are His instructions to Ananias (v. 11–12)?

1) ___________________________

Note: This is the same word used with Saul earlier in verse 6, but this time, it is not used metaphorically. It is used in a literal sense. The active voice is used, meaning Ananias will perform the action rather than passive as in Saul's case. In other words, the word, arise, although the same word, is simply a command to get up. One might conjecture that the Lord came to Ananias while he was praying.

2) Go to the street called ____

3) Inquire at ____

Why? "...for a man"

from Tarsus named Saul,

he is ___________________________

and

he has seen in a ________________

a man named Ananias ____________________________________

and

____

so that he might ____.

What do you see about the Lord's instructions to Ananias?

Is He not a God of specifics?

How does Ananias respond at first (v. 13)? Do not just copy the verse, read it and summarize not only what is being said, but also why he is saying it.

WHAT ABOUT YOU?

Has the Lord ever given you instructions from His Word that are very specific, but prove to be costly and cause you great fear?

Look at the instructions He gives to all of His disciples in Mark 8:34. What do you see and how do they coincide with what He has just told Ananias?

How does the Lord answer Ananias (vv. 15–16)? Notice it has nothing to do with Ananias and everything to do with His plan (from before the foundation of the world). The same is true today. What do we learn from the Lord about His plans for Saul?

Notice His one word of instruction to Ananias? ________________

Why? Now record His plans for Saul.

Note: The word, instrument, is the Greek word, skeuos, which pertains to hollow vessels for containing things. However, in this verse it is used figuratively of the human body, that is, clay, frail, feeble.[27]

Now, look at Isaiah 45:9 for a greater understanding of the figurative use of this word. What do you see?

By the way, the word, quarrel, in the Hebrew language literally means, "to strive"![28]

What will this chosen instrument do in regard to the Lord Jesus, according to Acts 9:15?

Note: The name Saul had spent his life rejecting up to that point, is the name he will proclaim for the rest of his life. In fact, isn't he still proclaiming the name of Jesus to you and me today?

Now record specifically with whom Saul will bear His name?

____

____

____

27. *Ibid.*, 1293.
28. Warren Baker and Eugene Carpenter, *The Complete Word Study Dictionary Old Testament* (Chattanooga: AMG Publishers, 2003), 1051.

If you were to read through the Book of Acts, you would discover that each time Paul gives his testimony it is before these three audiences.

4) What else are we told about Saul and his life (v. 16)?

Did you notice that Paul's suffering is a must? In other words, it will be necessary. Please do not let that statement confuse you or cause unnecessary fear. We will explore the concept of suffering more and more as we proceed in this study. In fact, it will make perfect sense to you, and you will agree with its purpose and welcome the results. (Notice I said, results and not the suffering itself).

Furthermore, have you ever thought about what words like this do to the "health, wealth, and prosperity" false gospel that is so prevalent today?

25.Now, let's conclude the lesson by reading Acts 9:17–19 and answering the following questions using these verses.

What did Ananias do immediately after the Lord's instructions (v. 17)?

Notice how Ananias addressed Saul. What do you see?

Note: By addressing Saul as his brother, we see an inclusive term that denotes family and relationship.

What twofold purpose does Ananias tell Saul he was sent in verse 17b?

1)

2)

Note: The word translated as "filled" is the Greek word, pimplemi, which, in this verse, is used metaphorically to mean, "to be filled with something, that is, to be wholly imbued, affected; influenced with or by, as with the Holy Spirit."[29]

Furthermore, the verb used is in the aorist tense, which means at a point in time; and, the passive voice is used, which means that the subject, Saul, was acted upon. In other words, the Spirit of God is doing the filling.

Ananias is merely the instrument or vessel used by God for God to accomplish His work. Saul is the recipient of the action, which God is performing. Do you see that God is the one accomplishing all that is happening to both Saul and Ananias? In His grace, He allows us to join in His work as He continues throughout history to complete His eternal plan. Now that's grace!

29. Zodhiates, *The Complete Word Study Dictionary New Testament*, 1175.

What immediately happened to Saul when Ananias obeyed the Lord (vv. 18–19)?

"And immediately there fell from his eyes something like ____________________

and

he __________________________ his sight

he arose

and

was ___________________________________

and

he took ___________________________________

and

was ___________________________________."

As you ponder the verses above, look at a couple of places in Scripture that serve as excellent cross-references in order to gain insight into what was happening to Saul.

1) Look at 2 Cor. 4:3–6. What do you see?

Do you see that Paul uses the term, "scales," in Acts 9, but in 2 Corinthians he speaks of a "veil." Whether he uses the term scales or a veil makes no difference because the outcome is the same. Those whose eyes are veiled cannot see Christ (or themselves accurately) until God in His grace, removes the veil.

2) So, where is the glory of God revealed or unveiled according to 2 Corinthians 4:6?

Now, look at Romans 6:4 to help explain Paul's baptism. What do you see?

Note: The word, "baptized," literally means, "to immerse in or wash with water in token of purification from sin and spiritual pollution."[30]

What an amazing picture in the physical realm (vv. 18–19) of what had happened to Saul spiritually (vv. 5–6, 8). Keep in mind that Saul's baptism had not saved him; rather, his baptism, like every baptism, was an outward sign of an inward reality. From this point on, Saul would identify himself with those who had put their faith and trust in Jesus Christ. He had been buried with Christ in baptism, represented by a liquid grave (water) and raised up (a picture of being resurrected from the dead state that he was in) to walk with Him in newness of life (Rom. 6:4).

30. *Ibid.*, 310.

As you have examined Acts 9:1–19, have you seen the grace of a loving and kind God as He rescued a "religious" man from self-righteousness, self-striving, self-confidence, and self-deception, which sadly led to self-assurance? Have you discovered that the basis of a "religious" person is self?

Remember this deception entered in the garden when Adam and Eve (and by extension, humanity) chose to believe the lie that he/she could be like God. In that moment of temptation, rather than love the Lord our God with all of our heart, humanity chose to love ourselves.

Now, after studying the conversion of Saul, can you see why the Spirit of God chose him to be the human author of words like...

> For **by grace you have been saved** through faith; and that <u>not of yourselves</u>, it is the **gift of God**; <u>not as a result of works</u>, that no one should boast. For we are His workmanship, created in Christ Jesus for good works, **which God prepared beforehand**, that we should walk in them" (Eph 2:8–10; emphasis added).

Do you sense that these words are the beautiful testimony of a man who has been rescued from striving to grace?

Can you see why his only boast is in Jesus Christ?

Lesson 5

The Messenger, Message, and Recipients of Grace

GALATIANS 1:1–5

Although we have spent quite a bit of time laying the essential groundwork for our study, it is finally time to open the Book of Galatians. Someone once said, Galatians is just Paul writing the Book of Romans angry. The more I study the Book of Galatians, the more I concur. However, I can also assure you that the anger you will pick up on in this letter is righteous anger that comes from the Lord. That's because righteous anger always results in compassion. Righteous anger comes from a heart filled with God's Spirit, motivated by God's love and great mercy. As most assuredly you will discover, it is the kindness of God that leads man to repent (Rom. 2:4).

For Paul, this letter is personal. He is writing to his spiritual children, and he is upset. Someone and something have come, infiltrated the church, and are causing his spiritual children to get drastically off track. In fact, Paul calls the "someone" false brethren (Gal. 2:4), and the "something" a different gospel (Gal. 1:6). The stakes could not be higher for Paul, and he will not just sit back in silence. He is writing to confront his spiritual children, and it doesn't take long for him to get straight to the point (Gal. 1:6).

In this lesson, we will begin by taking a close look at the first five verses in Chapter 1. It will not take long to see the reason Paul has written this letter or see why he is upset (Gal. 1:6). However, watch carefully in these first five verses as Paul immediately begins to address the issues at hand. What appears to be a "common" Pauline letter of introduction is loaded with foundational truths and weighty reminders of the gospel of grace.

THE MESSENGER OF GRACE

Let's start by reading Galatians 1:1–5 and answer the following questions.

1. With what word does the letter begin? ____________________

Although it may seem strange to us and unlike the letters we send today, (where typically we sign our name at the end), in ancient times, it was customary for the author to identify oneself at the beginning of a letter.

2. Now, let's look closely at Paul's introduction of himself. Pay close attention to how Paul describes himself to this church. In doing so, you will gain insight into what is going on in the church of Galatia (or any of his other letters) as well as the purpose of the letter. With that stated, how does Paul identify himself to this particular church?

Paul, an ____________________

Note: The word "apostle" literally means to send as an ambassador. In general, an ambassador is someone who is sent with a message from his/her authority. However, the word "apostle" speaks more to the designated office for one who had been called by Christ Himself. There is no continuity of the office of an apostle since there is no place in Scripture where the churches are instructed to ordain apostles.[31]

31. Spiros Zodhiates, *The Complete Word Study New Testament Dictionary* (Chattanooga, TN: AMG Publishers, 1993), 238.

3. Notice how Paul describes his apostleship in verse 1. What does he say?

Not - ____

Not - ____

BUT Through ____

and

____

Notice how Paul carefully presents who sent him and who did not. You know from having completed the previous lesson in Acts 9 that Paul is referring to his Damascus road encounter with the living and glorified Jesus Christ. You also are aware of the fact that although Paul (Saul) had a plan, God also has a plan! Thankfully, we know whose plan prevailed. God's plans will not and cannot ultimately be thwarted (Job 42:2).

4. Now, as you look back at how Paul described himself, what might the churches in Galatia be questioning?

Oftentimes, the messenger can become the target of criticism as doubt is placed on his character or his word. Basically, his credibility is under scrutiny. This tactic, no doubt perpetrated by the false brethren but designed by the Enemy, served to ultimately sabotage the message. Remember, Paul's message is the gospel of grace, and he is God's chosen instrument to deliver this message.

Doesn't this remind you of what happened in the garden with Eve? The serpent placed doubt on both the character and the Word of God. Be aware that he still works the same way today with God's true messengers.

THE MESSAGE OF GRACE

Now, watch as Paul quickly turns the attention from himself to focus on the issue at hand, the gospel of grace.

5. Let's begin by recording what Paul stated about God the Father (v. 1)? What additional information did Paul add?

Whether you realize this or not, every word Paul is choosing to use has significant meaning. The statement that God the Father has raised Jesus Christ from the dead speaks to the New Covenant. In other words, the Old Covenant has been fulfilled in the person of Jesus Christ. They are no longer under the works of the Law but under the New Covenant of grace. Keep that in mind as you proceed because this seemingly added phrase is actually addressing a heretical message that had crept into the churches in Galatia.

6. Notice Paul is not alone (v. 2). How does he label those with him?

Knowing Paul's credibility is under attack, why do you think Paul is letting the churches in Galatia know that there are others with him called the brethren?

THE RECIPIENTS OF GRACE

7. Who are the recipients of the letter according to v. 2b?

Now, let's pause here and look at the establishment of these churches from Acts 13, and in particular, Acts 13:13–14. As you read along, follow the route Paul and Barnabas took on their first missionary journey to Galatia. The map can be beneficial, especially if you are a visual learner.

Notice as you read along that the places they visited are in the southern portion of Galatia. Most commentators believe that the churches, which were established during Paul's first missionary journey, are the recipients of this letter.

I found it very helpful to record the following references in the margin alongside the place on the map, which is below:

Acts 13:1	Paul began in Antioch (Syria)
Acts 13:4	From Antioch (Syria) to Seleucia and from Seleucia to Cyprus
Acts 13:5	While in Cyprus, Paul went to Salamis
Acts 13:6–12	From the whole island (Cyprus) as far as Paphos
Acts 13:13	From Paphos to Perga in Pamphylia
Acts 13:14	Paul in the synagogue at Antioch (Pisidian)

Do you see that the first missionary journey is located in the southern portion of Galatia?

8. As we continue to pause, let's look at some crucial facts using Acts 13:14—14:28, which will be very helpful as we look at the churches in Galatia. Answer the following questions from Acts 13:13–52 in particular.

When Paul and his companions entered into a city, where did they typically go on the Sabbath (Acts 13:14; 14:1), and to whom were they looking to address (13:16; 43)?

Where? ____

Who? ______________________________ specifically, you who _________ God.

Notice: Paul began with the Jews, and in particular, men who had a fear of God because a fear of the Lord is a characteristic of the Spirit of God that God alone can bestow (Is. 11:2).

Note: There is a lesson here for everyone who desires to tell others about the grace of God through Jesus Christ. I learned quite a while ago from pastor and author, Henry Blackaby, to, "look and see where God is already at work and then join Him."[32] Do you see that in this way, He is the Leader and the Initiator, and we are the followers and responders? Isn't that the pattern for discipleship Jesus taught (Mark 8:34)?

Now, look at Acts 13:15. What do you see? In other words, what are they offering Paul?

Now, let's take a close look at what Paul presents. Let's begin by re-reading Acts 13:17–23. Watch the progression as Paul begins to preach Jesus Christ and remember the synagogue officials had just read from the Law and the Prophets. Allow me if you will, to trace the Old Testament counterpart of the message in brackets:

17 The God of this people Israel chose our fathers, [Genesis]

and made the people great during their stay in the land of Egypt, and with an uplifted arm He led them out from it. [Exodus]

18 For a period of about forty years, He put up with them in the wilderness.

[Leviticus, Numbers,Deuteronomy]

19 And when He had destroyed seven nations in the land of Canaan, He distributed their land as an inheritance—all of which took about four hundred and fifty years. [Joshua]

20 And after these things, He gave them judges until Samuel the prophet. [Judges]

21 And then they asked for a king, and God gave them Saul, the son of Kish, a man of the tribe of Benjamin, for forty years. [1 Samuel]

22 And after He had removed him, He raised up David to be their king, concerning whom He also testified and said, "I HAVE FOUND DAVID, the son of Jesse, A MAN AFTER MY HEART, who will do all My will.' [2 Samuel]

32. Henry Blackaby, *Experiencing God* (Nashville, TN: LifeWay Press, 1990), 15.

23 From the offspring of this man, according to promise, God has brought to Israel a Savior, Jesus... [Matthew, Mark, Luke, John]

Do you see it? The Old Testament Scriptures they were reading that day transitioned from the Old Covenant to the New Covenant, culminating in the Savior—Jesus!

And if you keep reading (Acts 13:24–41), you will discover that the life, death, and the witnessed resurrection of the Lord Jesus Christ, as proclaimed in the Gospels, was foreshadowed throughout the entire Old Testament. In essence, Paul's entire message, which he had taken from the Old Testament, finds its fulfillment in and points directly to the Lord Jesus Christ!

Now, look specifically at Acts 13:38–39. What is Paul proclaiming? Be specific.

Therefore, let it be made know to you, brethren, that:

1) through Him ____ (v. 38)

and

through Him ____ (v. 39)

from ______________ ______________________

from which you could **not be freed**

↓

through ______________________________

Could the message be any clearer? At first, it appears as if Paul is contrasting the Lord Jesus Christ with the Law of Moses? But the Law is good and came from God, right? The answer is a resounding, "Yes!" Jesus came to fulfill the Law of God (Mt. 5:17). So, what is being contrasted? Is the Law of Moses the issue, or is the issue with man's inability and attempts in his flesh to keep the Law? Wouldn't this message confront the religious leaders, who, by all outward appearances, have kept the Law?

Now that we have looked at the message of grace Paul has delivered, let's look at the response. How do the people respond according to Acts 13:42?

Read Acts 13:43 to discover in what Paul and Barnabas urges the people who have heard to continue? What do you see?

Now, record how the Jews responded to the message of grace. Look at Acts 13:45–46. What do you see and what did they do?

When the Jews refused the gospel, where did Paul and his companions turn (13:46)?

So how did the Gentiles respond, according to verse 48?

What resulted in the preaching of the gospel of grace, according to verse 49?

Again, how did the Jews respond in verse 50?

Look closely at Acts 13:51–52. How did the disciples respond to the rejection and subsequent persecution that resulted from the message of grace?

Note: One might think that Paul and his companions would have been filled with depression and great sadness, which would be true if they were operating in their flesh. But they were not. They were filled with joy because of the indwelling and empowering Holy Spirit.

Remember, you can always tell if you are operating in the flesh (by striving) or in the Spirit (by grace) by looking at the results. If there is joy, gratitude, thanksgiving, and humility, then you are being Spirit-led—no matter the response or outcome.

If you were to keep reading, you would see the same message of grace and the response it produced throughout the entire region of southern Galatia (Acts 14). Sadly, the persecution turns violent in Lystra (Acts 14:8, 19). However, throughout each of these places where the message of grace is taught, some will respond in faith. As a result, Paul will leave behind a group of believing men and women who will comprise the churches throughout the region of southern Galatia, and it is to these churches Paul is addressing his letter to the Galatians.

Now let's get back to the Book of Galatians and the message of grace.

THE MESSAGE OF GRACE

9. Let's look again at the theme of Galatians (and every other letter Paul penned). Again, what do you see in Galatians 1:3?

a. ____________________

and

b. ____________________

from ____________________

and

____

Note: Keep in mind that there are two kinds of peace. First, there is the peace with God. This peace is based solely and entirely upon God, because man, without God, is not at peace with God; rather, sin has separated him from God. Peace with God is a term of relationship, and therefore, accompanies our justification.

Second, there is the peace of God, which emphasizes fellowship with God and others. This is the peace we can forfeit when we allow sin(s) to separate us from fellowship with our Lord God; which, in turn, will always affect our fellowship or lack thereof with other people. Therefore, the peace of God is a term of fellowship associated with our sanctification.

Consequently, a person who is in Christ cannot lose peace with God; but the peace of God can be forfeited when we have sinned against God or another. The peace of God can be restored when God grants us the ability to repent, and we surrender and obey.

As we have defined the word, "peace," you will notice that the word, "grace," always precedes it. Behind the order of the words in Scripture is a foundational truth. In other words, the order of the written words matter!

In this case, for example, our state of peace, whether it is with God or of God, is dependent on the grace of God. In other words, the grace of God is appropriated by God alone when we come to Him with no merit, no striving, as we really are, which is in need of Him. The grace of God is His Son, who lavishly provides both the peace with God and the peace of God.

This is the message Paul is trying to communicate. He is building the foundation of God's grace and subsequent peace so that he can show them where they have gotten off track.

10. To help us better understand what Paul is doing, look at 2 Timothy 3:16–17. What is the purpose of all Scripture?

    a. ________________________________

    b. ________________________________ We are off track.

    c. ________________________________ Here's how to get back on track.

    d. ________________________________

Why? What is God doing? Look at 2 Timothy 3:17. What do you see?

"... so that ________________________________

____

11. Do you see the order in 2 Timothy 3:16? Remembering that the order of the words matters. What is Paul doing in the letter's introduction? **Hint:** Look at the first purpose mentioned in 2 Timothy 3:16.

____

12. Now, let's go back to Galatians 1:4–5 to see what Paul needs to re-teach the churches in Galatia. From what foundational truths have they veered? Notice Paul begins with the Lord Jesus Christ and God the Father. Of what does Paul remind the churches in Galatia?

THE LORD JESUS CHRIST

↓

1:4 who ____

that He ____

out of this present ______________________

according to ____________________________

and

____

1:5 to whom be

____

forever. Amen.

13. Look closely at the gospel of grace in verses 4–5 and answer the following questions:

What is man's state/condition?

Do you see that man is in sin and needs to be delivered?

Who gave Himself to deliver humanity?

Whose plan (will) was the Lord Jesus Christ fulfilling?

As you look at Galatians 1:4–5, can you see the simplicity of the gospel message? Never confuse the fact that the simplicity of the gospel for man rests entirely in the profoundness of the God who provided it.

14. Now, let's look at some cross–references in Scripture that will help explain the statements you just read in Galatians 1:4–5. Record what you see by each reference.

a. Simply record man's state/condition.

Ephesians 2:1 - ____

Romans 5:6 - _______________________________

Romans 5:8 - _______________________________

Romans 5:10 - _____________________________

Colossians 1:13 - ____

One of the most comprehensive places to see man's lost state (depravity) is in Romans 3:10–18. As you read these verses, what stands out most to you?

On a personal note, while looking again at the depravity of man from Romans 3:10–18, I saw something I had never quite seen before, or at least not as clearly.

For me, this time, the focus became:

None righteous

Not even one

No one seeks God

No one understands

None who does good

Not even one

No fear of God

Do you see it? The key repeated word and phrase, "None" and "Not even one." As I looked at the list I had made, I saw for the first time in these passages—NO MERIT! I guess you could say this time around the Lord allowed me to see these verses through the eyes of grace! Amazing, isn't He?

b. Who gave Himself to deliver man?

John 10:15, 17–18

c. Whose plan (will) was the Lord Jesus Christ fulfilling?

1) John 4:34

2) John 5:30b

3) John 6:38

4) John 17:4

Although not an exhaustive list of references, can you see how Paul is laying out the gospel of grace in Galatians 1:4–5 in what appears to be the introduction of the letter? Clearly, Paul is re-teaching the churches in Galatia the gospel of grace in all of its simplicity.

15. Now, one last assignment in this lesson, go back to Paul's initial message to the churches in Galatia found in Acts 13:17–39 and compare the message he first preached with Galatians 1:4–5. What do you see?

As you think back to 2 Timothy 3:16 again, and remember the four purposes of Scripture listed, what comes after teaching? Keep this in mind because what Paul says next in his letter is clearly a rebuke!

Record Paul's next words in Galatians 1:6

And with this thought, we will continue in the next lesson.

For now, continue to soak in the truths of the simple, yet the profound gospel of Jesus Christ. Meditate this week on the definition of grace.

Think about the Father's loving plan.

Consider the magnitude of the name He gave His Son, Jesus—Savior, Rescuer/Deliverer!

Recall the state from which you were and are being rescued.

If that thought doesn't cause **humility**, **gratitude**, **thanksgiving**, and great **joy**...then something is drastically wrong. Remember, these are the byproducts of the **gospel of grace**!

Maybe you read these words and think, "The byproducts listed above do not describe me right now. In fact, if I were to be totally honest, I am quite the opposite!" Maybe you too have fallen under the influence of a different gospel? If so, there is good news! Keep studying!

Lesson 6

Distorted, Deserting, and Disturbed

GALATIANS 1:6–10

In our last lesson we looked closely at the introduction of Paul's letter to the churches in Galatia only to discover in the opening verses a clear reminder of the gospel of grace, which they had already received (Acts 13), but had apparently either forgotten or chosen to ignore in their disturbed state (Gal. 1:7).

In this lesson, and with typical Pauline fashion, he will address the issue head-on. The problem at-hand was critical because false brethren, known as the Judaizers, had infiltrated the church with a distorted message. This different gospel had caused the Galatian believers to respond in desertion, which was leaving them greatly disturbed (Gal. 1:6–7).

Do you see their heart (mind, will, and emotions) in the paragraph above? Their minds had been inundated with a false message (also known as a lie) that had caused them to respond in their will by desertion, leaving their emotions greatly troubled.

Moreover, a close inspection of Paul's other letters, (including the two addressed to the problematic Corinthian church), would reveal that Paul always began by expressing a heart of gratitude and thanksgiving for the church he was addressing. However, the Book of Galatians is different, making the letter unique.

Paul's heart is troubled because their hearts are troubled. After all, his spiritual children were in danger, and like any loving spiritual father, who senses his children are in danger, Paul gets straight to the point. Herein is where we will begin.

Let's get started by reading Galatians 1:6.

1. Notice, without hesitation, Paul addresses the issue. What had the Galatians been doing?

Notice Paul did not say that they had deserted an idea/concept, or even an opinion/viewpoint, but a person—God!

By using the term, "deserting," Paul is painting an alarming picture. The word, "deserting," is a military term used to describe a person who defects from his post. In other words, it means to go AWOL (or absent without leave).

If we are not careful, we may miss the magnitude of the betrayal because the defector or deserter is not merely leaving God, but they are joining the enemy. You see, to turn from God leaves only one other option, which is to turn to the enemy. Have you ever thought of sin in that way?

2. How does Paul feel about what they are doing (v. 6)? ______________________________

Note: The phrase, "I am amazed . . ." could just as easily be translated, "I am shocked!" Interesting choice of words, isn't it? Instead of being amazed by God's grace in their life, Paul is amazed by their quick desertion of Him.

3. Pause to consider again just how the Galatians were called (v. 6)?

". . . by the _________________ of ____________________"

Keep this phrase in mind as you read the letter and remember that there are two components to the definition of grace: **1)** God's part, where He makes lavish provision through the Savior, Jesus Christ; and **2)** man's part, where there is no merit! In fact, all that man can ever bring to salvation (whether in reference to justification, sanctification, or glorification) is our sin, our humanness, our weaknesses, and our constant need for a Savior.

4. For what had the Galatians so quickly deserted the grace of Christ (v. 6)?

Note: In its simplest definition, the word "gospel," means, to bring or proclaim the good news.[33] Furthermore, the term, "different," is translated from the Greek word, heteros, which means, "of another kind, in another form, of a totally different kind."[34]

5. What was Paul's assessment of the "different" gospel (v. 7a)?

Note: There is only ONE gospel—Jesus Christ! Do you see that to add anything to Jesus Christ, in regard to salvation (whether it involves justification, sanctification, or glorification) is to say, Christ + _______________ saves?

Do you see that the blank makes it a different gospel, no matter what one places in the blank?

6. As we continue reading Galatians 1:7, notice some had come into the church.

a. What were they doing to the Galatian believers? ________________________________

Note: The word "disturb" (*tarasso*), means, "to stir up trouble by agitating."[35] When used in a figurative sense as it is used here, it means to unsettle the mind. Doesn't this help to explain what happens when lies enter into a mind filled with truth and peace? Do you see why the enemy is called the author of confusion (1 Cor. 14:33)? Did you happen to notice that the desertion began in their mind?

b. What had they done to the gospel of Christ? ________________________________

Note: The word "distort" (*metastrepho*), means to go in the exact opposite direction. Shedding additional light, the antonym means to guard, keep, and preserve.[36] Keep this in mind as you consider what some were attempting to distort!

---

33. Spiros Zodhiates, *The Complete Word Study New Testament Dictionary* (Chattanooga, TN: AMG Publishers, 1993), 669.
34. *Ibid.*, 665.
35. *Ibid.*, 1366.
36. Zodhiates, *The Complete Word Study Dictionary New Testament*, 972.

Notice also the phrase, the gospel of Christ, because the good news of Jesus Christ is the target or the aim of a false teacher. Remember that behind every false teacher, there is a false message, and a false salvation because the underlying source is the father of lies (John 8:44). Therefore, for the false teacher, Jesus Christ is the issue.

7. Look at the following cross-references to discover why the enemy of our soul would target Jesus Christ specifically. Record what you see.

John 14:6

Acts 4:12

John 10:9a

1 John 5:11–12

1 Timothy 2:5

Herein lies the issue. The gospel of Jesus Christ is exclusive. There is one Way, one Name, one Door, one Life, and one Mediator. (And there are many more references to consider because every single book in the Bible points to Jesus Christ.) Paul's concern could not be more critical because to miss Jesus Christ is to miss God.

8. Now, turning back to Galatians 1, watch as Paul continues to warn the Galatians about this different gospel. Read verses 8–9 and answer the following questions:

Who might bring a different message?

(v. 8) ___________________________________

(v. 8) ___________________________________

(v. 9) ___________________________________

Note: The New American Standard Bible uses the word, "though" (v. 8) but a more specific translation would be the word, if (*ean*), which implies uncertainty. Could Paul be using a literary tool to emphasize the absurdity that he or an angel from heaven would preach a gospel contrary to Jesus Christ?

Also notice, if you look closely at the list of potential messengers, whether human or angelic, both belong in the category of created beings and as such, they in no way have the authority to change or alter the Creator's message or plan in any way. In fact, only a fallen angel or human would have the audacity to attempt to change God's message or plan. Isn't that a more plausible explanation for a different gospel?

Tragically, throughout time, Satan has not ceased to use man and/or fallen angelic beings in his attempt to distort the message of grace. Whether his instruments are willful or deceived, one of his greatest tools he uses is religion, which finds its foundation in human achievement.

Consider, for example, the false teachings of Mormonism and its chief messenger, Joseph Smith, who had an alleged encounter with an angel named Moroni in the mid-nineteenth century. According to Smith, the angel Moroni was the keeper and guardian of what he called the golden plates. Smith professed that Moroni led him to discover the plates, which contain the teachings upon which the Book of Mormon is based. However, if you look closely at the *Book of Mormon*, you will discover that Joseph Smith inserted himself and his views throughout its pages because he surmised that the Scriptures were lacking in sufficiency and needed his insight.

Sadly, Mormonism is just one of many false teachings today. In fact, any religion that adds to or subtracts from Christ is a false system. Believers beware! For as long as the father of lies (John 8:44) remains, there will be false teachers who will preach a false message and offer a false salvation. This is the message Paul is writing to warn the Galatians because the consequences are condemning.

According to Paul, what would be the severity of preaching a gospel contrary to the message he had originally preached?

Let him be ___________________________________.

Note: The word Paul uses here, "accursed" (*anathema*), is a strong word of damnation. It literally means to be given up to the curse and destruction.[37] In essence, Paul is using strong language to warn anyone who preaches anything other than Christ alone will be damned to hell. There is no more straightforward or understandable way to say that to reject the grace of God, which is Jesus Christ, is to damn oneself to hell.

Now think back to the last lesson where we examined Paul's message to the churches in Galatia. Look again at the central focus of his message in Acts 13:23, 28–30, 37–39? What do you see?

Can you see God the Father and Jesus Christ in these verses? That, my friend, is His invitation of grace! Do you also see the exclusivity of Jesus Christ in Paul's first message? Can you appreciate what's at stake? Paul is reminding the Galatians that nothing has changed!

37. *Ibid.*, 148.

Why do you think Paul repeats the warning in Galatians 1:9? Why say the same thing twice? Any thoughts?

Think about it. When you want to get something significant across, especially to your children, do you ever repeat yourself? What if the information is a matter of life or death? Would you reiterate that warning? Remember, he is talking to his spiritual children.

9. Now, let's look at the question Paul asks in Galatians 1:10. For clarity's sake, we will break it down into two parts: 10a and 10b.

What does Paul ask the Galatians in 10a?

Did you realize there are only two options? Isn't that true? Do you see that the answer is mutually exclusive; meaning, that by choosing one option, you automatically disregard the other? Therefore, if a person is seeking the favor of another person, he is not seeking the favor of God. So, is it really about a person, and if so, which person?

Isn't seeking the favor of men really about you? Sadly, it is for me.

10. Now, record Paul's next question in 10b.

As I look at these two questions, I see two facets of the same issue. One answers what the problem is and the other answers how this is accomplished or what it looks like. In other words, striving becomes the means of how I seek the favor of other men. And even worse, if you peel off all the layers, the one I am most striving to please is actually me! Yuck! Even writing that makes me sick!

Isn't it true, that at the end of the day, seeking the favor of man, and striving in our flesh to please man is really about us? This is true of every man. Remember, it is the root issue that entered at the Fall.

11. Now, let's look at a couple of cross-references where Jesus said the same thing, and notice, each time, He was addressing the religious Pharisees. Record what you see.

a. John 5:44

b. John 12:42–43

Now, let's pull this all together. Man seeks the favor of other men by striving to please them so that man can get the glory that rightfully belongs to God alone. In essence, we are all thieves seeking what rightfully belongs to Christ alone.

Consider the picture of our salvation. Jesus is hanging on the cross between two thieves. These two thieves represent all mankind. Each lived their life striving to be their own god because each loved themselves most. Both thieves wanted His glory as God. Truly the bent of each man's heart is to rob Him what is due Him alone—glory!

Similarly, both thieves represent the two responses to the gospel message. Both were given a front row seat to witness the grace of God as He suffered and died between them. One thief responded in faith and went to be with Him in Paradise. The other responded in unbelief and chose eternal separation. These two responses still represent how man responds to God's gracious invitation of grace even today. Which thief are you?

12. Now, let's look back again at Galatians 1:10. Fill in the blanks provided.

Paul states, "For am I ____________________ seeking the favor of man or of God?

". . . If I were __________________ striving to please man . . ."

a. What do you see?

Isn't that what Paul did before he met Christ?

b. How does Paul answer (v. 10b)?

Deep-down within the text, Paul is describing his former way of life (seeking the favor of man and striving to please man) and introducing his new life as a bondservant of Christ. So, what does it mean to be a bondservant of Jesus Christ?

Here is where we must pause to examine the word, bondservant, or we will miss a vivid and beautiful picture of what it truly means to be in relationship with Jesus Christ.

My favorite definition comes from the late theologian and Greek scholar, Spiros Zodhiates, who defined the term this way, stating, "A bondservant (*doulos*) is a slave who is in a voluntary and permanent relation of servitude to another, his will being altogether consumed in the will of the other."[38]

13. To gain an even better understanding of the word, let's look back in the Old Testament, where the Lord God established the conditions necessary to become a bondservant. Turn to Deuteronomy 15:12–17 and answer the following questions:

How long would a Hebrew man or woman sold into slavery serve (v. 12)?

What happened on the seventh year (v. 12b)?

How was the servant to be sent away (vv. 13–14)?

What purpose did the years of service and the freedom offered serve, according to verse 15?

Now watch what happens in verse 16, for this is where and why the word "bondservant" is established.

1) What does the servant say to his master when his time of service is completed?

Did you notice that it is a matter of the servant's will? In other words, it is a choice. This is a voluntary decision.

2) Why does the servant not want to leave his master?

a) ____

and

b) ____,

since he ______________ ______________ with the master;

Can you see that the difference maker is not in the slave, but it's in his master?

What external sign was used to mark this occasion according to verse 17?

38. *Ibid.*, 483.

Note: An awl was used to make a large hole in the ear. The hole would have been larger than a pierced ear; it would be visible for all to see easily. The hole served as a sign, not so much for the bondservant, but for his Master! Those who would see the bondservant would think, "Wow, that man is blessed. He must have a loving Master!"

How long would the servant be a bondservant (v. 17)? ___________________

Now look back at Zodhiates' definition. Do you see the definition beautifully described in this illustration? Can you see that the motivating factor is love, specifically for the master? Do you see it also includes the master's household? But where did the love he had for his master and the master's household originate? Was it not first in the master's love for his bondservant?

Isn't this an amazing picture of Paul's new life in Christ? No more seeking to earn the favor of God, and no more striving to please man, which was just a facade, for Saul to promote Saul and all for Saul's glory.

From the moment Saul encountered the glorified Christ on the road to Damascus until the time Paul was ushered into His very presence, Paul's life was willingly, voluntarily, and lovingly forever devoted to His Master and the Master's household, which included the Galatians he was warning. Now that's amazing grace!

THREE THOUGHTS IN SUMMATION:

Firstly, as I read Galatians 1:6–10, I could not help but think back in Scripture to another very similar scenario. Let's go to Exodus 32, where we will find another time when God's people, Israel, quickly deserted Him.

To quickly place the chapter in context, it is essential to know that the events in Exodus 32 occur approximately two months after the Lord God had rescued Israel out of four hundred years of enslavement to Pharaoh in Egypt.

In Exodus 32, the children of Israel are growing worried and impatient, as Moses has not returned from Mount Sinai, where the Lord God had summoned him to receive the Ten Commandments. We are told that the people assembled around Aaron, and said to him, "Come, make us a god who will go before us; as for this Moses, the man who brought us up from the land of Egypt, we do not know what has become of him" (Ex. 32:1).

As you continue to read verses 2–6, you will discover that Aaron fashioned a golden calf, and the people offered burnt offerings and peace offerings, and "the people sat to eat and drink, and rose up to play" (Ex. 32:6). The Hebrew word for "play" (*sahaq*) literally has licentious sexual overtones.[39] In essence, the Israelites turned their idolatrous worship into a drunken orgy.

14. Now, look at what the LORD God said to Moses in Exodus 32:7–8. List the things you see about the Israelites. What do you see?

15. Now, as you consider what the Israelites did in Exodus 32, how does this compare with what was happening in the churches in Galatia?

39. Warren Baker and Eugene Carpenter, *The Complete Word Study Dictionary Old Testament* (Chattanooga, TN: AMG Publishers, 2003), 946.

16. Now, read Jeremiah 2:13. Watch how the LORD God describes what His people were doing in Jeremiah's day. What do you see, and how is this a depiction of what the Israelites and the Galatians were doing (and we too are capable of doing even today)?

Secondly, as I think about the characteristics of a bondservant, I am reminded of what Jesus said when asked by the Pharisee, "Teacher, which is the great commandment in the Law?" (Mt. 22:34–36)? Of course, the Pharisee was testing Jesus.

17. You will find the account in Matthew 22:36–40. How did the Lord Jesus answer?

1)

And then Jesus answered again, except this time He equated the second commandment with the first with only the order to differentiate. In other words, the first commandment must be true for the second one to be remotely possible.

Jesus then answered, "The second is like it. . . ."

2)

18. Did you happen to notice the end of the second command, which states,

"You are to love your neighbor as ___________________________________" (v. 39)?

What is Jesus telling us about ourselves? What does He know about us that we either don't know or refuse to admit? He's right, you know.

19. What is the importance of these two commands (in the order they are given) according to Jesus (v. 40)?

Do you see the correlation between the bondservant who loves his Master and loves the Master's household? Do you see the significance of the order?

20. Now read 1 John 4:19–21 and answer the following questions:

a. Why do you love the Master?

b. What do you see in verses 20–21?

Isn't John saying the same thing Jesus said in Matthew 22:36–40? And isn't Deuteronomy 15:12–17 just a picture of them both?

Think about it:

It takes God to love God.

It takes God to love others.

It takes God not to love ourselves!

And finally, another way to look at what Paul is saying in Galatians 1:6–10 is to consider that there are two gospels: one saves, the other does not! One gospel is based on divine accomplishment, and the other gospel finds its basis in human achievement.

Look at the following visual illustration of the statements just made.

Two Gospels

Saving Grace	Non-Saving Merit
↓	↓
Divine Accomplishment	Human Achievement
Christ ALONE!	Christ + ________________

Now, consider the fact that you can put anything in the blank space representing human achievement. Even if you were to put "holy" things in the empty blank, you would still be adding to Christ. And if you were to peel off the layers, you would see that no matter what you are adding, the root issue, in the end, would ultimately be about you!

Throughout this letter and this study, keep in mind that salvation has three tenses. So, whether we are talking about justification, sanctification, or glorification, the message is still Christ alone!

You may be asking at this point, but what about our part? Don't we play a role in this salvation somewhere? The

answer is a resounding, "Yes!" But the part we play is not, nor will it ever be the role of Savior! Where grace is involved, we find ourselves as human beings, vulnerable to weakness, sin, and in great need. And in this state, the message points directly at the heart of our pride, which is why men hate it so much.

Remember the root issue that entered at the Fall. Man's greatest desire was to be like God because we love ourselves so much. And whether the heart of man is dominated by pride, as in the case of an unbeliever (who needs to be justified), or within the residual flesh of the believer (who is in the process of being sanctified), mankind is still striving to take the lead role. Sadly, we want His place and His glory.

In reality, issues arise because we do not like our role in salvation, which by the way, we chose when we failed to surrender our will and obey God in the Garden. We chose death rather than the tree of life, and apart from God's amazing grace, we would have remained in that condition for all eternity.

At times, we scoff at the role of the bondservant because we love ourselves more than the Master. Inherent within every fallen man is the desire to play the role of the Savior. At least, I can sadly say with all honesty, this can be true in my life.

We will talk more on this issue as the study continues but for now, let's close the lesson by looking at one final passage in the Book of Philippians where we find the ultimate bondservant, Jesus Christ.

21. Read Philippians 2:5–11. Prayerfully thank the Lord Jesus Christ for taking the role of the bondservant on our behalf. Remember, the motive for the place He willingly, voluntarily, and lovingly chose finds its basis in the love He had for His Father and the Father's household. We are the mere benefactors of such amazing grace and immeasurable love. Now, if that doesn't evoke praise, joy, thanksgiving, and immense gratitude, I do not know what will!

Feel free to record your words of praise and adoration using Philippians 2:5–11 in the space below.

A brief summary of Galatians 1:1–10, in light of our stick figure, which represents the believer:

<u>Theology</u> (Galatians 1:1–5)	versus	**<u>ME-ology</u>** (Galatians 1:6–10)
Jesus Christ		* A different gospel
raised by God the Father		* Disturbs the mind
from the dead		* Distorts the gospel of Jesus Christ
gives grace		* Adds ME to the equation
and		
peace		
gave Himself for our sins		* Appeals to MY flesh
delivers us out of this present evil age		* Agrees with the world's mindset
according to the will of		* Seeks the favor of man
our God		* Strives to please man
and		* Leads to ruin
Father		

As you look at the chart and the visual above, do you see Galatians 1:1–10?

Did you notice that Paul began his letter to the church in Galatia with God? You see, it really is all about Him, and the Galatian believers have forgotten that truth. Grace subtracts you and me from the equation, which is why our flesh hates it. In fact, grace subtracts everything except God from the equation. Only God can save man!

Notice also that we are merely the recipients of God's gracious gift of salvation. We are the ones lacking and in need of grace and peace, which only God can give. We are in sin and need of deliverance. This is our state. This is what we bring to salvation. Do you see that we are in desperate need?

So, what is the issue in Galatia? A different gospel has come in and distorted the true gospel of Jesus Christ. This false message has disturbed the believers causing confusion and doubt. If not corrected, it will render the church useless.

We must keep in mind that although Jesus Christ indwells the believer by His Spirit, there remains residual flesh until glorification. The sanctification process, in which we find ourselves, lies between the already (justification), and not yet (glorification), and our residual flesh, and the fact that we are still in the world greatly lends to our propensity toward the "ME-ology" doctrine.

The unbeliever lives under the "ME-ology" doctrine. It rules and reigns supreme. Worst of all, the "ME-ology" doctrine is just a deceptive lie from the enemy because, in actuality, the god of this doctrine is Satan himself.

However, the believer, although no longer under the domination of the "ME-ology" mindset, can still find himself or herself tempted or in the snare of its lie. The residual flesh that remains explains the tension within the believer. There is a continual battle raging in the heart of a believer between God's Spirit and our residual flesh. Do you sense it?

Remember, our flesh still wants to be god! Our flesh still loves self more than God or anyone else. Although justified (having been saved from the penalty of sin), we are still in the process of being saved (sanctification). Sanctification is the process whereby the Spirit of God, using the Word, invites us by grace to respond in faith (surrender and obedience). Scripture declares that our faith is what causes us to overcome the world and our residual flesh (1 John 5:4).

Paul is warning the Galatian believers not only to remember God's initial invitation of grace, and how they responded in faith, but also to keep on reminding them that they are still in the process of being saved by grace through faith. Sadly, instead of overcoming, the Galatian believers are being overcome, which is why Paul is writing with such intensity.

Notes

Lesson 7

Transforming Grace

GALATIANS 1:11–24

As we continue in the first chapter of Galatians, we find ourselves in a very strategic place as Paul defends himself. In this lesson, we will look at the reason Paul is on the defense. Keep in mind that some have come to disturb the church and distort the gospel of Christ (v. 7). These false brethren, to whom Paul is referencing, are also known as Judaizers. The Judaizers were a group of Jews who emphasized the Law, particularly regarding the Sabbath and circumcision. These men were accusing Paul of disregarding both in order to please man rather than God.

Fundamentally, the Judaizers had come in with an agenda to place doubt on Paul's apostleship, which in reality, was nothing more than a flaming dart from the enemy aimed straight at Paul's message—the grace of Christ. In theory, if the preacher can be discredited, then the gospel he preaches is also in question. The attack for Paul was personal. However, his defense, although personal, will not end in his glory but the glory of another person—Jesus Christ.

Paul refused to take credit for the gospel he had received because he had done nothing to receive it. In fact, as you have already seen, he was doing everything in his power to destroy it.

1. Let's begin the lesson by reading Galatians 1:11–12, and answering the following questions.

    a. What does Paul remind the brethren about the gospel he was preaching in verse 11?

Note: The Greek word translated "preached," is in the passive voice, meaning that the subject, Paul, had been acted upon. Similarly, the specific prepositional phrase, "according to," comes from the Greek word, *kata*, which means, "down from."[40] In other words, Paul was telling the brethren that the good news he had preached to them did not originate with him. In fact, the gospel had come down from heaven, and he was merely the instrument God was using to proclaim it.

2. What does Paul remind the brethren in verse 12? First, state the two negatives and then the positive:

I did not ____

Nor was I ____

BUT

I received it through a ______________________________

40. Spiros Zodhiates, *The Complete Word Study New Testament Dictionary* (Chattanooga, TN: AMG Publishers, 1993), 822.

3. Now look at 1 Corinthians 11:23a. Where did Paul get his message? What do you see?

4. Now, as you re-read Galatians 1:11–12, summarize the things that Paul wants the brethren in Galatia to recall (v. 11a) about himself and the gospel message he had preached to them?

As we continue to the end of chapter one, you will discover that verses 13–24 form a unique message. In fact, these verses, which comprise Paul's defense, actually become his personal reminder to the Galatian believers. You see, the false brethren who had come into the Galatian church had maligned both Paul's character and message.

In no uncertain terms, Paul will defend himself but not in the usual manner of argument. Typically, when people sense they are under attack, they will narrow in on the argument with things that bring them the most merit and value, right? They will boast in achievements and highlight strengths, correct? They will vehemently proclaim innocence and the fact that they are right.

At least that is what I do when I sense I am under attack and attempt to defend myself in a matter of contention. Sadly, when this happens to me, my propensity, far too often, is to justify myself, prove my innocence, go on the defense, proclaim to be the right one, speak of my own merit, and so forth.

Do you see the key repeated words, me, I, myself? When words like this are coming out of my mouth, the Lord, in His kindness, is allowing me to see what is in my heart; for according to Jesus, from the abundance of the heart, the mouth speaks (Lk. 6:45). That's when I realize I am in a trap!

Watch, however, as Paul's defense of himself rests solely on the grace of God and has absolutely nothing to do with him. In fact, rather than defend himself, Paul will own his sin and failure. Observe as he declares his guilt, rather than innocence, and owns his unrighteousness rather than justifying himself. Learn as Paul's defense is nothing more than a testimony of grace as he takes the place of the guilty sinner and places all his faith in the one who resides within—Jesus Christ.

Moreover, watch as Paul ends with the glory of the Lord Jesus Christ. In other words, rather than hide, cover, or blame, Paul shares his greatest sin and failure, and in doing so, Christ receives all of the glory. Don't you want this to be your defense?

So, to understand Paul's defense, we will divide the rest of the lesson into three parts, which will comprise his testimony. The three divisions are as follows:

- Paul's manner of life before Christ
- God's call and revelation of Christ to Paul
- Christ in Paul

If you look closely at the three parts and place your name where you see Paul's name, you can see that this too, is your testimony and the testimony of everyone who is genuinely in Christ. Let's get started.

PART ONE: PAUL'S MANNER OF LIFE BEFORE CHRIST

5. Let's begin by reading Galatians 1:13–14 and answer the following questions:

    a. First, note what his former manner of life was **in**? ____________________ (v. 13).

Note: The term, Judaism, describes the religious system held by the Jews, whose main emphasis was placed on circumcision and Sabbath keeping.[41] The Pharisees, the sect to which Paul belonged, were responsible for keeping and watching over the Law of Moses. They were the example of how to live. You will remember, the name Pharisee, literally means separate ones.

Furthermore, you may not know that in addition to the Law of Moses, the Pharisees had added 613 commands to the Scriptures to which they tediously and meticulously strived to adhere (at least outwardly). This, in a nutshell, describes Paul's former manner of life.

So now, with this additional information, describe Paul's former manner of life in your own words. What do you see? Where is the emphasis and focus placed for someone who defines his former manner of life with the phrase, "in Judaism"?

    b. Where did Paul's former manner of life in Judaism lead him? What was his agenda concerning the church of God (v. 13)?

    c. What was his desired plan for the church (v. 13)?

    d. Now, who does that sound like? Who is the head of a "religious" system whose agenda is persecution, and whose end goal is to destroy? ____________________

    e. Of what were the churches in Galatia either ignorant or forgetful? Look at Ephesians 6:12 for the answer.

Do you sometimes forget this truth? I know I do.

    f. In his former manner of life, how did Paul compare with others in Judaism (Gal. 1:14)?

"I was ______________________________ in Judaism

__________________ __________________ of my contemporaries . . .

being more ________________ ________________ for my ancestral traditions.

41. *Ibid.*, 779.

Note: There was a famous historian in Paul's day named, Josephus, who recorded that the traditions of the elders were considered more desirable than the words of the prophets.[42] Think about the magnitude of deception when more value is placed on the traditions of the elders rather than the words of the living God.

Isn't this what is happening in every false religion?

g. Now, as you look at Paul's former manner of life using verse 14, what do you see?

....

In other words, who was Paul's former god? ________________________

Unbeknownst to Saul, who was ultimately his former god? ____________________________

Now, let's keep reading in Galatians 1:15, where we will see a very significant word: **BUT.** In fact, it will prove to be the most significant but in Paul's life, and in ours as well.

PART TWO: GOD'S CALL AND REVELATION OF CHRIST TO PAUL

Watch closely as Paul recounts how his plans became abruptly interrupted with His plan for Paul's life. Let's begin by looking at this most pivotal verse from various aspects. We will start with the one who is initiating it all—God the Father.

6. What three things specifically do you learn about the Father in verse 15?

a. ....

b. ....

c. ....

By the way, the verb tense in each case is in the active voice, meaning that the subject, the Father, is performing the action! Do you see that God set Paul apart, through His grace and that God through grace called Paul and was pleased to reveal His Son to him?

Note: A Pharisee, by definition, means "separate one." Pharisees notoriously would strive to set themselves apart; but when you read verse 15, you see clearly that it is only the Father who can set apart.

7. Now, let's examine this same verse (v. 15) by looking at Paul. What do you learn about him? You may have to give some thought in your responses here, for the facts may not be as obvious. Keep in mind, however, that Paul is merely the recipient of God's saving act.

a. ....

b. ....

c. ....

Did you see that Paul, as the recipient of grace, had been set apart from the womb, had no merit to offer for his salvation and no knowledge of the true grace of God, which is in Jesus Christ? In other words, Paul's salvation was totally a work of the grace of God!

42. *Ibid.*

More importantly, do you also see that from this point forward, Paul's manner of life has changed from being in Judaism to be in Christ? He now has a new identity.

8. Now, look at what God's purpose (plan) for saving Paul included in verse 16a. Why did God call Paul, and for what was he set apart (v. 16a)?

As you think about this pivotal point in Paul's testimony, do you see that in that one moment in time, on that road to Damascus, God rescued Paul from the enemy, out of the world, and from Paul's flesh? Do you realize He has done and continues to do the same thing for you and me even today?

Although Paul is specifically addressing the topic of justification in Galatians 1:15, isn't this truth also relevant in the life (sanctification) of a believer as well? Isn't it the Father's good pleasure to reveal His Son to us, and in us daily? Will He not do so in the pages of His Word by the power of His Spirit?

On a personal note: I remember many years ago when the Spirit of God took the Word of God to open my eyes to the truth in Galatians 1:15. You see, even as a believer, I had spent many years hiding, covering, and blaming others for past sin in my life. I carried a lot of guilt, shame, and anger as a result. I remember lamenting the fact that much of what I carried was a result of the ignorance of God's Word.

Publicly, especially at church, you would have never known; but privately, I would spend hours lamenting my past sins, all while being rendered useless under its weight. Herein is where I learned to strive. Maybe if I would pray more, have a longer quiet time, do more good things, work harder in my church—just maybe that would make the guilt disappear.

Sadly, the sin I could not forget had power over me no matter how many times I had confessed it. In my anger, I even blamed the Lord. Why hadn't He warned me? He could have stopped this from happening—right? And then the Father, in His kindness, opened my eyes to Galatians 1:15 through the testimony of Bible study teacher and leader, Kay Arthur.

I remember listening intently as Kay shared her testimony. You see, I thought that because she had been entrusted with such a powerful gift of teaching God's Word that her life as a believer must have been perfect. Surely, she had done everything right. And if her life had not been perfect, surely the Lord could use her because of all of her Bible study training, right? Wrong. None of these things qualified her for God's grace.

In fact, her testimony was the exact opposite. Her testimony is just another example of God's amazing grace, and all that she could bring to her salvation was sin, brokenness, and rebellion. She shared the heartbreak of how as her walk with the Lord grew more and more intimate, her guilt deepened. She also shared how deeply she lamented the wasted years of her life and how the Lord used Galatians 1:15 to heal her heart. By placing emphasis on the Father, His timing, and His pleasure at the revelation of His Son in her life, she sensed immediate relief. He had revealed the Son to her at just the right time.

The same had been true in my life. Except, rather than the need for justification (from sin's penalty), I needed relief from the power that sin had had on my life as a believer. The many years I had spent as a spiritual baby, ignorant of His Word, had taken a toll as I continued to fail miserably on many fronts.

Similarly, every woman I have ever counseled over the years has lamented years of time wasted in guilt, shame, and intense anger. Some had made statements, through many tears, like "If only I had known this when my kids were still at home." When I hear these words, the Holy Spirit gently reminds me to take them to Galatians 1:15, where He used these same words to heal my heart so many years ago. I cannot begin to express the joy that is

experienced as I watch the Lord in His kindness and grace reveal the same powerful truth of His saving grace and lift the heart and countenance of yet another one of His children. It's truly amazing, this grace!

So, what happened next in Paul's life? From Judaism to Christ, what does that look like? Paul explains in verses 16b–24, which we will examine in the third section of this lesson.

PART THREE: CHRIST IN PAUL

9. As Paul so frequently does, he begins the next part of his testimony (Galatians 1:16b–17) by stating what he did not do and then records what he actually did. What do you see?

    a. With whom did Paul <u>not</u> consult?

        1). ___________________ and ________________

        2). Nor did I go up to Jerusalem to those who were ________________ before me.

    b. Where did Paul go? ____

    c. Now, look at verse 18 to discover how long he spent in the Arabian Desert? ____________________

    d. Any thoughts in regard to the number of years Paul spent alone with the Lord Jesus?

....

....

When I read "three years," I immediately thought about the three years of training the apostles had with Jesus while He was on earth. Interestingly, when the Lord Jesus wants to reveal Himself, He takes His disciples to Himself.

WHAT ABOUT YOU?

Has the Lord ever tucked you away to a quiet, lonely, isolated, and dry place? Could it be so that He can teach you something about Himself? Maybe your desert has been in the form of an illness or the loss of a spouse, whether through physical death, or even the death of a marriage. Maybe you're experiencing a new season in life that has left you alone. Oftentimes, we are sent to the desert kicking and screaming only to discover that the time He has allotted for you has been orchestrated to bring you in a little closer to Himself. There are things we learn in the desert that we would never see or know in the crowd.

At some point in the life of every disciple, there will be desert times alone with the Lord Jesus. If you find yourself there now, ask the Holy Spirit to illumine His Word to you as to the purpose of this time alone with Him. Lean into this time. Don't resist what He has allowed.

Be aware that another voice may show up in the desert. Be on guard against the voice that tells you the Lord has forsaken you, or that He is punishing you. Words that bring condemnation are <u>not</u> from Him—the Lord convicts. There is a vast difference between conviction and condemnation. Words of condemnation bring no hope, and there is no peace. The voice of conviction, although sorrowful, always brings peace and great hope in the Lord.

Ask the Spirit to cause you to bring the Lord Jesus the glory He is due, even in this isolated place. Every place He leads His disciple has purpose as He orders our steps (Ps. 37:23). You will discover that all the paths of the Lord are lovingkindness and truth (Ps. 25:10) even the paths we would never have chosen on our own. I can promise you that He has not brought you into the desert to hurt you; instead, He is beckoning you to Himself. It's an invitation to grace. How will you respond?

And watch, as Paul's time in the desert was not wasted, but it will be used to minister to others. Now, let's continue with Paul's testimony in Galatians 1:18b.

10. Where did Paul go after his time with the Lord (18b)? ____________________________

Why did he go? ____

How long did he stay? __________ days.

11. Who else did Paul see while in Jerusalem (v. 19)? __________________________________

Note: James, the Lord's half-brother, became the head of the church in Jerusalem. He is the human author of the Book of James. He was later stoned in AD 62.

12. And now, when you come to a place in Scripture like Galatians 1:20, you must ask yourself, "Why is this here?" What is Paul saying, and why is he saying this? Any thoughts? **Hint:** Romans 8:16 may be helpful.

Isn't Paul calling God as his witness? Wouldn't the Spirit of God within the Galatians bear witness with the truth of what Paul was saying as well?

13. Where did Paul go after leaving Jerusalem, according to Galatians 1:21?

__________________________ and __________________________

Note: The capital of Syria is Antioch, where Paul and Barnabas were later sent out on their first missionary journey (Acts 13). The mention of this would have placed the Galatian churches in context because this was when they were established.

Paul's mention of Cilicia could be traced in Acts 15 and 18 as he continued to preach the gospel. Basically, Paul was explaining to the Galatians his spiritual journey from its inception to when he had brought the gospel to them, and where he was sent after them. In other words, in God's grace, His path for Paul and the gospel included them!

14. For another look at what Paul is recounting in Galatians 1:17b–21, read Acts 9:19b–30. Many scholars believe that the three years in Arabia are recorded at the beginning of verse 23, which states, "And when many days had elapsed . . ."

As you read this section, note some of the details Paul left out of his account to the Galatians.

And finally, turning back to Galatians, let's observe verses 22–24, as Paul brings his defense to an end. Watch as Paul masterfully brings everything back to the one who alone deserves the glory.

15. Read Galatians 1:22–24. Notice, when you get to verse 24, you will read, "And they were glorifying God because of me" (emphasis added). Note that a better translation would read, "And they were glorifying God in me" (emphasis added).

As you look at what Paul is saying in these verses, and consider the better translation of verse 24, what do you see?

As I considered these verses, I thought about the testimony of the late former attorney and advisor to President Richard M. Nixon. His guilt and high crimes against the government landed him in prison, where Jesus Christ found him, called him to Himself, and transformed his life in the desert of that prison.

The man to whom I am referring is Chuck Colson. You see, Jesus Christ had a plan for this man's life far greater than the one he had spent a lifetime building for himself. Unbeknownst to him, God had set him apart from before the foundation of the world, to preach the gospel of God's amazing grace to thousands of prisoners. And in obedience to Gods plan for his life, he would do so until his death through the ministry he was entrusted, called Prison Fellowship.

In the prologue of his book entitled, *Loving God*, Colson describes a particular Easter Sunday, while invited to speak to a large group of inmates, the moment he realized the paradox and grace of God in his own life. As you read his conclusive statement, think about how it correlates with Paul's defense in Galatians 1:13–24. Colson writes,

> *As I sat on the platform, waiting my turn at the pulpit, my mind began to drift back in time... to scholarships and honors earned, cases argued and won, great decisions made from lofty government offices. My life had been the perfect success story; the great American dream fulfilled. But all at once I realized that it was not my success God had used to enable me to help those in prison, or in hundreds of others just like it. My life success was not what made this morning so glorious—all my achievements meant nothing in God's economy. No, the real legacy of my life was my biggest failure—that I was an ex-convict. My greatest humiliation—being sent to prison—was the beginning of God's greatest use of my life; He chose the one experience in which I could not glory for His glory."*
>
> *Confronted with this staggering truth, I discovered in those few moments in the prison chapel that my world was turned upside down. I understood with a jolt that I had been looking at life backward. But now I could see: only when I lost everything I thought made Chuck Colson a great guy had I found the true self God intended me to be and the true purpose of my life.*
>
> *It is not what we do that matters, but what a sovereign God chooses to do through us. God doesn't want our success; He wants us.*
>
> *He doesn't demand our achievements; He demands our obedience. The kingdom of God is a paradox, where through the ugly defeat of a cross, a holy God is utterly* **glorified**. *Victory comes through defeat; healing through brokenness; finding self through losing self.*
>
> *Of course, our success-mad, egocentric culture cannot grasp that crucial truth. It is understandable only when the false values that obsess us are stripped away, sometimes in the midst of our most abject failures. Surely that was so in my life . . .*[43]

43. Charles W. Colson, *Loving God* (Grand Rapids, MI: Zondervan Press, 1987), pp. 21-25.

WHAT ABOUT YOU?

Does God's grace mark your testimony (both justification and sanctification), or do you boast in the things you have done and are doing? Are you deceived into thinking that you were justified by grace through faith; but now, your sanctification is all up to you?

Is your testimony limited in scope to a one-time event in the past or does it include this ongoing process called, sanctification, where we find ourselves being saved from the **power** of sin? Are you still allowing the Lord Jesus to use your weakness, humanness, sin, and failure for His glory?

Let's be honest, we all have things in our life we would like to erase, forget, or do over. One truth the Lord has continued to show me in regard to this amazing grace is that in order for the Savior to be seen, I have to be willing to confess my need and cry out for a Savior, and as He leads, to share that with others.

In other words, there are times I may not look so good. In fact, there are times I look really bad. In reality and all honesty, there are still times I choose not to act or respond very well. In essence, I need a Savior! I must remain open and willing to allow Him to choose those experiences in which I cannot glory—for His glory!

A lost and imprisoned world needs to see that kind of Savior!
A believing, yet bound, follower of Jesus Christ needs to see that kind of Savior too!

TRANSFORMING GRACE

A brief summary of Galatians 1:11–18, in light of our stick figure, which represents the unbeliever and believer:

Saul

IN JUDAISM

1:13 Persecuted the Church of God

Tries to destroy the Church of God

1:14 Can advance beyond contemporaries
and
countrymen

More extremely zealous for ancestral traditions

FLESH = STRIVING

Paul

IN CHRIST

1:11 Gospel preached (passive voice in Greek)

1:12 through revelation of Jesus Christ

1:15 Set apart (active voice) by God
from mother's womb
Called (active voice) through His grace

1:16 Revealed (active voice) His Son in me

↓

That I might preach (passive voice) to the Gentiles

GRACE = NO FLESH

GOD'S INVITATION

↓

SALVATION = By **GRACE** through **FAITH**

↓

PAUL'S RESPONSE TO GRACE (FAITH)

1:16 Did not immediately consult
with flesh
and
blood,

Not Flesh

BUT

1:17 Did not go up to Jerusalem to the apostles

BUT

Went to Arabia for three years (v. 18).

Spirit

↓

led by Spirit into the desert
taught by Christ

A NEW CREATION

Note: Did you notice before meeting Christ, the dominating source in Saul's life was his flesh? Did you also notice that Saul's identity was in Judaism? Do you see the striving involved?

Did you happen to notice that the striving is against God, His church, and others? Who is this really about? The answer is Saul. Saul loves Saul. What you are seeing in the life of Saul is pride. Pride is the reason for the fall of humanity that took place in the Garden of Eden. Pride wants to be like God. Pride loves self more than God and others.

Moreover, the pride in Saul's flesh was manifested in the world through religion. No matter what religion you follow, whether Judaism, Hinduism, Buddhism, Atheism, and so forth, the enemy does not care. You may be a professing Muslim, a Baptist, Methodist, or Catholic. The Enemy does not care as long as you are <u>not</u> in Christ. Do you see that religion is just a mask for the flesh?

WHAT ABOUT YOU?

In what is your identity? Are you hiding behind the mask of religion? Believers are not immune. Remember, we still have residual flesh! Keep that in mind the next time you find yourself striving.

Note of Interest:

The passive voice means that the subject is being acted upon.

The active voice signifies that the subject is performing the action.

Lesson 8

The Controversy: Circumcision

Before we progress any further in our study of Galatians, we must stop and address the issue that Paul will be confronting, specifically in Chapter 2. As stated in the previous lesson, a group of people known as the Judaizers had come into the churches in Galatia, placing doubt on Paul's apostleship and message of grace.

Their agenda was to disturb the Galatians and distort the grace of Christ by adding the works of the Law to the message (Gal. 1:7). The Old Testament and more specifically, the works of the Law, were the main issue; however, circumcision became the primary work of the Law upon which they focused. In other words, they were preaching Christ + circumcision = salvation. Therefore, they were proposing a different gospel than the message of grace Paul was preaching.

Because we know that Scripture is the best interpreter of Scripture, and in order to do due diligence, we must look at the first place the word, circumcision, appears in Scripture. Therefore, this entire lesson will be devoted to the issue at hand—circumcision. Why was it established? Why is it not included if it is a requirement in the Old Testament? Is it necessary, and if not, why not? Could the Judaizers have a point? The answers to these questions and more are found in His Word, so let's start at the beginning in Genesis 17, where the word circumcision is first mentioned.

But before we get started, we need to do a little catch-up in the life of Abraham to place the events of Genesis 17 in context. Keep in mind as you proceed through the lesson that this is not an exhaustive look at the life of Abraham. We will merely be glancing at the major events of his life of faith.

With all that in mind, the first mention of Abram (his name before the Lord changed it to Abraham) can be found in Genesis 11:26 where we can trace his genealogy to his father, Terah, and even as far back as the line of Shem (Gen. 11:10) and his father, Noah (Gen. 9:18).

Following the brief overview of his genealogy in Genesis 11:26–32, we pick up on the details in Genesis 12, where Abram was seventy-five years old when the Lord first spoke to Abram and told him to leave his country, his relatives, and his father's house and go to the land He would show him (Gen. 12:1). The grace of God is proclaimed as the Lord God promises to make Abram a great nation and to bless all the families of the earth through Christ (Gen. 12:2–3).

Keep in mind Abram was not seeking the Lord God. In fact, Abram was not looking for God at all. He was a polytheist (believing in many gods) from Ur of the Chaldeans. In other words, he was a heathen who, like every man since the Fall, was dead in his transgressions and sin (Eph. 2:1). However, the Lord chose to reveal Himself to Abram by His grace and through no merit at all on Abram's part.

However, as we skip over to Genesis 15, we are given the specific account of Abram's salvation, where we read, "Then he believed in the LORD; and He reckoned it to him as righteousness" (Gen. 15:6). But why did Abram believe? Look at Genesis 15:1–5 for the answer. Bear in mind that what we have up to this point in Abram's life is a

promise from the Lord God. The promise or covenant that God is making with Abram will comprise three things, namely: land, descendants, and a seed.

Now, let's look at how the LORD God will begin to fulfill His covenant promise to Abram in Genesis 15. Keep in mind as you read, the fulfillment of God's promise to Abram will not look the way Abram thought; it never does! It's always much better!

Also remember, Abram will spend many years living in between the promise made and the promise fulfilled. Much like our life of faith, right?

1. Let's begin by recording what the word of the LORD revealed to Abram about Himself and Abram in Genesis 15:1?

What is Abram's state? ____ (1a)

What about God? 1) ____

2) ____

Note: The Hebrew word translated "shield" in this verse literally means protection, a refuge, and safety from one's enemies.[44]

So, what is the LORD God revealing to Abram? He is essentially saying, In your helpless state of fear, I am your protection and refuge. I am your safety, not just from your physical enemies but also your spiritual enemies because I AM your REWARD, Abram. In other words, rather than me giving you something from within yourself Abram, I am going to provide you with what you need most—Me!

2. How does Abram reply (v.2)? First, note how Abram addressed God in verse 2:

_____________________ _____________________

At first glance, you may not notice that a new name of God is being revealed for the first time in Scripture, the name, "Lord" (Gen. 15:2). Frequently, especially when we read our Bibles in a hurry, we miss these subtle, yet significant details.

For example, when you see the name "LORD" in all caps in Scripture (with the "L" as a larger cap), you are looking at the Hebrew name of God, *Yahweh*. Specifically, when writing this name, the Hebrews used the Tetragrammaton, the Hebrew name of God transliterated in four letters as *YHWH*, out of a deep reverence for His holiness and for fear of mispronouncing it. Yahweh, translated Jehovah, means, the Self-Existent One. In other words, He alone needs no one and nothing to exist. It is the name most frequently used of God in the Old Testament (6,823 times).[45]

However, the name "Lord," (capital "L," with lower case, "ord"), is the Hebrew name of God transliterated, *Adonai*. The name *Adonai* means, Master. This name of God indicates relationship. The particular use of this name of God implies Lordship, meaning, "His total possession of me and my total submission to Him as Lord and Master."[46]

Therefore, as we see the name "Lord GOD" used in Genesis 15:2 for the first time, specifically in relation to Abram and the Lord GOD, keep in mind, anytime man is discovering or able to acknowledge anything about God, you can be sure the Lord GOD is the one who has revealed Himself first. God is always the Initiator when it comes to man.

---

44. Warren Baker and Eugene Carpenter, eds., *The Complete Word Study Dictionary: Old Testament* (Chattanooga, TN: AMG Publishers, 2003), pp. 568-569.
45. Kay Arthur, *LORD, I Want To Know You* (Colorado Springs: WaterBrook Press, 1992), 55.
46. *Ibid.* 42.

Note: A careful study on the names of God throughout Scripture will reveal two things, accurately: **1)** God's name, which represents His character, nature, and attributes, and **2)** man's need. You will see a pattern, as God's name always coincides with what man needs.

3. Obviously, not understanding fully about his very great reward, whom does Abram offer to fulfill God's promise as his heir? ___________________________________

What is happening in verses 2–3? Could it be that Abram is feeling the weight and responsibility of God's promise? After all, God's promise for an offspring has proven void so far. Don't we all tend to want the Lord to give us something (someone) to help us out when what we really need most is Him?

As you read verses 2–3, do not miss the fact that Abram is offering to God an alternative plan. Do you see that humanity's bent is to try and help God out especially, when there has been a delay in the answer? Isn't the propensity within all people to strive to help God out in our flesh? A better question might be, "Did God need Abram's help?" Let's see how God answers Abram.

4. What does the LORD God say in response (v. 4)?

Then, we are told, the LORD took Abram outside and instructed him to "look toward the heavens, and count the stars, if you are able to count them" (Gen. 15:5), clearly a task for which Abram was unable to do.

5. What did the LORD say next to Abram in verse 5?

Note: The phrase, "So shall your descendants be," can be translated, "So shall your **seed** be."

6. Stop for a moment and look at Galatians 3:16 so that you can discover the identity of the seed Abram was just promised.

Who do you see? ___________________________________

*Above all, please do not miss who the LORD promises Abram in this verse. *

So, who is the LORD God promising Abram in verses 4–5? ____________________________

7. What is the LORD God doing in verses 4–5? To answer this question, look at Galatians 3:8. What is being preached to Abram at this moment?

Note: This is the same seed Adam and Eve were promised in the garden after they had sinned against the LORD God (Gen. 3:15). You see God's plan will not change, no matter how people try to alter it or how the enemy attempts to destroy it.

8. Now look at Genesis 15:6, which begins, "THEN..." following this obvious word of the gospel from the LORD, and because "Faith comes by hearing and hearing by the Word of God (Rom. 10:17).

What does Abram do in response to God's invitation of grace?

What, in turn, does the LORD do (v. 6)?

The word, "reckoned" in this verse is an accounting term that means, "to put to one's account." In other words, Abram believed the word of the LORD, and the LORD credited to Abram's account His righteousness. Even more specifically, Abram believed in the gospel of Jesus Christ (vv. 4–5). In essence, He was His reward!

Do you see man's only acceptable response to God's grace is faith? And by God's grace man is given the gift of faith, for Jesus Christ is the "author and perfecter of faith" (Heb. 12:12). In other words, He is the source of both!

There is only one way to be saved. Abram, and all of the Old Testament saints looked forward to the promised seed, Jesus Christ. And we, who live on the other side of the cross, are looking back at the fulfillment of God's promised seed, Jesus Christ.

All faith finds its foundation in the cross of Jesus Christ—alone!

9. Now, watch what the LORD says next to Abram in verse 7?

a. "__________ ___________ the LORD

b. who ____________________ you _____________ of Ur of the Chaldeans,

c. to ______________ you this _____________ to possess it."

As you look at verse 7, what do you see? By the way, the land is symbolic of the life!

Note: Isn't the LORD God essentially saying, *I am the one who brought you out of darkness and death in order to save you and give you life?*

What had Abram done to deserve this deliverance of God's grace? __________________

Do you see the definition of grace from man's perspective? God offers Himself (Life), and man has nothing to bring to grace except sin, darkness, and death.

10. How did Abram answer the LORD God in verse 8? (Note what he called Him).

________________________________, which means, "Master"!

Now, watch in Genesis 15:9–17 as the LORD God ratifies the covenant He has just made with Abram.

Note: The word, *berith*, is the Hebrew word for "covenant," which literally means to cut into pieces. A covenant was a solemn binding agreement made between two parties as they passed through the pieces of flesh.

The innocent animal(s) of sacrifice was cut into two halves while the parties making the covenant would pass between the pieces that had been cut. It was a bloody affair picturing the severity of the agreement. In essence,

the parties who were making the covenant were saying to one another, "May it be done to me as we have done to these animals if I break covenant with you." Therefore, the covenant the LORD God made that day with Abram was a matter of life and death.

It may interest you to know that the word "covenant" can be interchanged with the word "testament." Remarkably, the Bible is divided into two covenants or testaments. Everything promised in the Old Testament finds its fulfillment in the New Covenant through Christ. What an amazing God!

Watch closely in these verses as the LORD cuts a covenant with Abram. Pay careful attention to who walks between the pieces of flesh and who doesn't. Therein you will discover the picture of grace!

11. Answer the following questions from Genesis 15:9–17:

What does the LORD ask Abram to bring to Him (v. 9)?

What does Abram do with the sacrificial animals in verse 10?

What happens in verse 11?

As you consider the phrase, "birds of prey," what comes to mind? Think about the parable of the sower Jesus spoke of in Matthew 13:4 along with its interpretation in Matthew 13:19. What do you see?

Now, let's go back to Genesis 15:11.

d. Who is responsible to drive the birds away? ____________________

Note: When the Enemy shows up (and you can be assured he will), we are commanded to submit to God, resist the Enemy and he will flee (see James 4:7). If you look at the order in James 4:7, how, then, do we resist the devil? What will drive him away?

Isn't submission to God by obedience the result of faith? The answer is a resounding "Yes!"

Now, look at Genesis 15:12. As you read this verse, consider that it has symbolic meaning as well. What do you see about Abram? What state is he in, and what might that represent?

Note: The sun going down represents the darkness in which humanity finds itself without God. Furthermore, deep sleep is symbolic of spiritual death. In summation, humanity's state, apart from God, is a state of terror and great darkness! In reality, Abram has nothing to add to the covenant being ratified by God but darkness, sin, and death. Do you see grace?

In verses 13–15, what does the LORD predict about Abram and his descendants?

Note: Enslaved and oppressed. Doesn't that describe the state of all who are born in sin?

Now read Genesis 15:17. What, rather who, passed between the pieces of flesh that day?

Note: Isaiah 45:6 states, "I am the LORD, and there is no other." Because God is all the "other" one needs. He is often depicted in words that describe what He is like. For example, smoke and fire are often used to symbolize God's presence (Ex. 13:21; 19:18; Acts 2:3…).

Do you see that God alone passed between the pieces of flesh that day? In fact, on that day, while Abram slept, the LORD God inaugurated the covenant He had made with Himself from before the foundation of the world. On that day, God alone passed through the pieces of flesh in order to save and rescue the human race. Don't you see that humanity is merely the benefactor of the covenant made that day?

In reality, as noted earlier, Christ Jesus would ultimately fulfill the covenant made that day. Look at Hebrews 10:19–20. What do you see? Do you see the sacrificial lamb? Do you see His bloody flesh? Can you even begin to fathom the cost?

Ultimately, it would please the Father to offer His only begotten Son (Is. 53:10), to fulfill the covenant He made with Himself to rescue humanity as He slept (a metaphor for death) "in a state of terror and great darkness" (Gen. 15:12). The state of "terror and great darkness" represents the spiritual state of every man who is, "dead in his transgressions and sin" (Eph. 2:1).

Question for Thought: Scripture states, "For by grace you have been saved through faith; and that not of yourselves, it is the gift of God; not as a result of works, that no one should boast" (Eph. 2:8–9; emphasis added).

12. As you read Genesis 15, specifically concerning Abram's salvation and the inauguration of the covenant made, do you see Ephesians 2:8–9 in the life of Abram? If so, how?

Now, you may be thinking at this point in the lesson, *What does all this have to do with Galatians, and in particular, the issue of circumcision?* The answer to this question is of utmost importance because all of the Galatians, and Paul's argument, will hinge upon it. Ponder this question as we continue looking at the life of Abram in Genesis 17 (where circumcision is mentioned for the first time).

13. Let's begin by reading the entire account in Genesis 17:1–22.

14. As you read from verse 1 and then skip to verse 22, who is Abram's visitor?

Note: Theologians specifically refer to this heavenly visitor as a *Christophany*, which is an appearance of Christ in the Old Testament.

15. How old is Abram when the LORD appears to him in verse 1?

If you begin with Abram's age in Genesis 12 (75 years old) and consider his age in Genesis 17 (99 years old), when you do the math, you quickly discover that twenty-four years have passed since the promise was first given to Abram. Now that's a long time to wait.

16. How does the LORD identify Himself to Abram in verse 1?

Note: The Hebrew name, *sadday*, is transliterated, *El Shaddai*, which means, "God" or "All-Sufficient One." The word occurs only forty-eight times in the Old Testament with thirty-one of those times coming in the Book of Job. It is always used in conjunction with God's promise of fertility, land, and abundance with the idea that He can and will fulfill what He has promised.[47]

Note: Think about this particular name of God, and its meaning, especially in light of the Book of Job, which begins with great loss and suffering, yet God Almighty will ultimately provide Job with fertility, land, and abundance. Do you see fertility (descendants), land (life), and abundance (the Seed) at the end of the Book of Job?

As always, when God reveals Himself by a specific name, He is not only revealing who He is but also what humanity needs. Keep in mind, as we have already discovered, humanity is totally unable, within itself, to fulfill its own need making it utterly dependent on the LORD.

17. So, as we think back on Abram and Genesis 17, what is humanity's need in this chapter? Look at what the LORD says immediately after He identifies Himself as God Almighty. What does He command Abram (v. 1)?

Remember, one's walk is synonymous with one's life. The life God now requires of Abram is to be a blameless one before Him. You see, Genesis 15 is a picture of Abram's justification, but in Genesis 17, Abram's sanctification becomes the topic.

47. Warren Baker and Eugene Carpenter, *The Complete Word Study Dictionary: Old Testament* (Chattanooga, TN: AMG Publishers, 2003), 1105.

Note: The term "blameless" is, first and foremost, not sinless. The Hebrew adjective used here is the word *tamiym*, which, when used in a moral sense means, "linked with truth, virtue, uprightness, and righteousness." Think about it. Who is our link with truth, virtue, and righteousness? Our blamelessness is attached to a Person! Do you see it?[48]

Fundamentally, the term blameless is a relational term, whether in relationship with God and/or another person. In this instance, the LORD God requires Abram to walk before Him in this manner—something that left to himself, Abram is unable to do.

Do you see it? The LORD God knows that the requirement He has just made of Abram is an utter impossibility apart from Him. Therefore, He will preface His requirement by revealing who He is—God Almighty.

His name always precedes man's need at the time of revelation. After Abram's day of salvation (Gen. 15:6), Abram's life was not blameless. Neither is ours. God, Himself, will be the source of truth, virtue, uprightness, and righteousness, both initially (justification) and in the process (sanctification) of this life of faith—until we are glorified.

If you think about the revelation of who God is in this chapter, and what He requires of Abram (a blameless walk), you cannot help but think back one chapter, to Genesis 16, where Abram and Sarai take matters into their own hands. In an effort to do for God what they did not believe God was able to do for them, we have Hagar and the birth of Ishmael.

In other words, in between Abram's salvation (Gen. 15) and the revelation of God Almighty (Gen. 17), sits Genesis 16. Sadly, and even more telling, there is no recorded fellowship between God and Abram in Genesis 16. In fact, Genesis 16 is completely devoted to Abram and Sarai's alternative plan. Consequently, the result of their plan was the birth of Ishmael. He represents the product of the flesh, and the flesh can never please God (Rom. 8:8). Like Abram and Sarai, our flesh (alternative plans) will only produce Ishmaels.

However, Genesis 17 is a testimony of God's exceedingly great grace in spite of our failures. It is a glorious demonstration of His ability to carry out His eternal plan in spite of the "Ishmaels" we create in our flesh. Genesis 17 is proof that no one and nothing can thwart the hand of God Almighty. It also serves as confirmation that when we are faithless, He remains faithful (2 Tim. 2:13).

18. Now, look at what God said next to Abram in Genesis 17:2.

a. "___________ _________________ establish My covenant between Me and you,

and

b. ___________ _________________ multiply you exceedingly."

Notice who is both initiating and fulfilling the requirements of the covenant that had been made with Abram?

19. What is Abram's response in verse 3?

This is always the response when the created encounter the Creator.

Now let's focus on Genesis 17:4–14 in particular. You will notice that there is nothing new added to the covenant. You will also see as you read the verses together that the LORD God divides the covenant He made with Abram into two parts, namely: God's part and Abraham's part.

48. *Ibid.*, 1232.

Consider the phrases: 1) "As for Me..." (v. 4) BY GRACE

and

2) "Now as for you... (v. 9) THROUGH FAITH

Do you see it?

And although Abraham has a part, the faith necessary to do his part comes from God as well, for grace and faith are gifts of God (Eph. 2:8).

20. First, let's consider the covenant in the order God presents it: His part. Make a list of examples where you see the LORD *reminding* Abram He had taken both the initiative and the responsibility for in the covenant He had made with Abram.

a. _______________ covenant is with you (v. 4)

b. You shall be the ________________ of a _____________________ of __________________

Note: Notice the LORD is taking ownership of the covenant He made. Obviously, the promise for Abram to become a father is not something Abram could have done on his own, for he and Sarai had tried for many years to accomplish, but to no avail.

c. What does the LORD do to Abram in verse 5?

d. Why does the LORD God change his name, according to verse 5b?

"For I will ____

Note: In Hebrew, the name, Abram means, "exalted father," but the LORD changes his name to Abraham, which means, "father of a multitude."[49]

Indeed, Abram was and is still renowned as the exalted father. But do you see where the LORD changed his name to match his new identity as the father of a multitude of nations? Do you think the change of name denotes a change in physical identity, or could this be a change in his spiritual identity as well? Not only is Abraham identified in Scripture as the physical father of the Jewish nation, but he is also identified spiritually as the father of faith (Rom. 4:10–11).

Could the LORD God require Abraham to walk (live) before Him in faith? Keep in mind at all times that whatever the LORD requires He will be the supply!

Think also about this promise, which includes a multitude of nations. Look at Revelation 7:9–10. What do you see?

*Always keep in mind, when you see the word "throne," think, "Throne of Grace," for that is what the LORD God named it (Heb. 4:16).

e. Of what does the LORD remind Abraham again in verse 6?

49. *Ibid.*, 13.

1)

2)

3)

In other words, I will make you what you are not!

Again, is Abraham able to accomplish any of these promises on his own?

f. With whom will the LORD establish His covenant according to verse 7?

1)

2)

g. How long will the covenant last according to verse 7?

h. What does the LORD promise Abraham and his descendants in verse 8?

(Symbolically, the Christian life.)

i. Most importantly, He reminds Abraham at the end of verse 8,

"...and I will be ______________________ ____________________."

The ultimate promise of the Bible: "I will be your God."

As you read over God's part of the covenant He established with Abraham, do you see that it is clearly a covenant of grace? God is doing it all! Man is adding no merit on his own, and in fact, can only contribute weakness, failure, and sin. That, my friend, is the very definition of grace!

Notice, however, God's covenant of grace demands a response! Therefore, we must consider humanity's response, according to God, by looking at Abraham's part., "Now as for you . . ." (Gen. 17:9).

21. Read Genesis 17:9. What is Abraham's part of the covenant God made with him?

22. What is the purpose of circumcision, according to Genesis 17:11?

Do you see an outward sign of the inward grace of God?

23. Look at the symbolism of the sign of circumcision in verse 11. Where was it to occur specifically?

In the ________________________________ of the foreskin.

Note: The male reproductive organ.

24. Who is to be circumcised according to Genesis 17:12–13?

Do you see a multitude of nations in these verses?

25. What happens to the uncircumcised (v. 14)?

Why?

A refusal to surrender and obey God's Word is the definition of unbelief. In other words, it is the exact opposite of faith. Do you see that this warning is God's invitation of grace?

26. Next, God speaks to Abraham regarding Sarai. What does He do first (v. 15)?

Remember, a change of name represents a change in identity.

How will she be known according to verse 16? ______________________________

27. Notice Abraham's response to God's Word in verse 17.

a. What does he do? ______________________________

and

____

Note: Isaac's name means laughter. Notice who will get the final laugh (Ps. 2:4)?

b. What does Abraham say and note where he says it?

28. Who does Abraham want God to consider instead (v. 18)?

29. What does God say to Abraham's alternative (fleshly) plan (v. 19)?

"But Sarah, your wife shall bear you a son." Now, compare that statement with Genesis 15:4. What do you see?

Do you see that God sees Abraham and Sarah as one flesh? His promise to Abraham included Abraham's wife, Sarah. What a kind and gracious God we serve!

30. With whom was God establishing His everlasting covenant (v. 19)?

Do you also see that God's plan had not changed over twenty-four years (ultimately, twenty-five years pass before Isaac is born [Gen. 21:1]) despite Abram's futile effort to alter it and the Enemy's attempt to destroy it?

Why would the Enemy try to destroy this plan? Think about who was coming from this descendant?

Do you also see how the Enemy can deceive us into thinking we can help God with our plan through our flesh? Are we easy targets because deep within our flesh, we want to be god? We don't like His plan. We have a better plan in mind.

31. Now, skip down to Genesis 17:23. How did Abraham respond to God's gift of grace? What do you see?

Remember, the only acceptable response to grace is faith! Genuine saving faith responds in surrender and obedience. Did you notice his obedience occurred on the very day God spoke?

WHAT ABOUT YOU?

Has the Lord spoken to you through His Word? Did you sense a struggle in your will because you think you have a better plan than God? Has your obedience been immediate?

Remember, where there is no surrender and no obedience, there is no saving faith, in spite of what you may profess. Saving faith acts on God's Word!

32. So in conclusion, what are we to make of circumcision? Did it save Abraham? Is it a requirement for salvation? Any thoughts?

33. Now, look at the following cross-references regarding circumcision. What do you see?

a. Romans 2:28–29

Note: Who circumcises the heart? ____

b. Romans 4:9–10. When was faith reckoned to Abraham? Was it before or after circumcision?

c. Colossians 2:11

Note: The Greek verb in Colossians 2:11 translated, "circumcised," is in the passive voice, meaning the subject is being acted upon. The LORD God is the one who is circumcising the heart of man. He is in the process of removing our flesh and replacing it with His Spirit.

Circumcision did not save Abraham, nor can it save anyone else for that matter. Circumcision, in Scripture, is called a sign (Gen. 17:11). A sign is used to point to something else, and in this case, someone else—the Seed!

Therefore, circumcision represents the outward sign or mark of an inner spiritual reality. Like water baptism, it is an outward sign in the New Testament of an inward spiritual reality. Baptism does not save. Circumcision does not save. Christ alone saves! Circumcision, like baptism, is a response in faith to the grace we have been given.

CONCLUDING THOUGHTS TO CONSIDER IN REGARD TO HIS PERFECT PLAN AND TIMING:

As you consider the following things, keep in mind the reason we exist, which is for His glory. Rest assured, His glory will always result in our highest good.

First, consider the specific timing of circumcision, on the eighth day of life. You may not know this, but I learned from my nursing background that Vitamin K, which is necessary for the blood to clot, is at its highest peak in a human being on the eighth day of life.

In the United States, every newborn male is given an injection of Vitamin K before circumcision. This is done so that they can send baby boys home sooner than the eighth day. Who knew? Only the Amazing Creator and Life Sustainer!

Secondly, think about the timing of God's plan in regard to circumcision and the conception of Isaac. What had to physically (and literally) be removed before God Almighty fulfilled His promise of Isaac? In light of this, what does this act spiritually symbolize in the heart of man? Any thoughts?

And finally, consider the "delayed" timing in Isaac's birth. Why the delay? To help answer this question, look at the following cross-references for help.

a. Hebrews 11:11–12. (Note in particular what is said about Sarah and Abraham.)

b. Romans 4:19–21

Do you think any of these things are coincidental?

Do you see that for Abraham and Sarah to have conceived and had a son before the time God had planned, they would have been like every couple who has a child? Why did God wait until Sarah's womb was dead?

Consider the following equation:

Dead + Dead = Dead **BUT** Dead + God Almighty = Life (Isaac)

Who alone will receive all of the glory when you factor into the equation their dead situation? Every time Abraham (or anyone else for that matter) looked at Isaac all that could truthfully be said is, "Look what God did!"

In conclusion, as we think back to Galatians and consider the issue Paul is addressing, do you see why it is necessary to consider which came first: Abraham's salvation or his circumcision, and/or Abraham's salvation and the Law?

Remember, as we continue in Galatians that the Judaizers not only wanted to require circumcision, but also the entire Law for salvation. By taking a quick look at the life of Abraham, we have seen that his salvation preceded his circumcision.

As for the Law, Abraham's salvation preceded the Law by over four hundred years! With these facts in mind, can you add circumcision or any part of the works of the Law for salvation?

And, last of all, consider Paul's gospel message of grace afresh. Understand from the life of Abraham that like Abraham, you are not a candidate for the grace of God until you realize that you have no merit within yourself!

In fact, only when you and I are willing to cry out in total surrender, complete helplessness, utter weakness, sin, and failure, do we become a candidate for His grace. That's what makes it so amazing!

To God alone be the glory!

Lesson 9

A PRIVATE ENCOUNTER

GALATIANS 2:1–10

In our last lesson, we focused our attention on the issue that was disrupting the Galatians and distorting the gospel of Christ (Gal. 1:7) by examining the life of Abraham and in particular, the timing of his circumcision concerning his salvation.

With that background, we can now look at Paul's defense to the Galatians as he addresses the issue with them.

We will begin by dividing Galatians 2:1–21 into two segments, namely: **A Private Encounter (Gal. 2:1–10),** and **A Public Confrontation (Gal. 2:11–21)**. The Public Confrontation will be split into two parts due to the amount of information covered. Keep in mind that Paul is addressing the Galatian believers the entire time. Both of these encounters will prove to the Galatian church that the pure message of the gospel of Jesus Christ is by grace alone through faith alone and prove that any other message is a false gospel.

As you will see, Galatians 2:1, begins by stating, "Then after an interval of fourteen years . . ." Notice, that Paul is in the middle of his testimony, which started in Galatians 1:11, and over the next ten verses, Paul describes a private encounter he, Barnabas, and Titus had with Peter and "those who were of reputation" (Gal. 2:2, 6).

For the purpose of clarification, and in order to identify where to place the private encounter described in Galatians 2:1–10, we must consider that according to Scripture, Paul made only five visits to Jerusalem, specifically:

#1 He met with Peter and James for fifteen days (Gal. 1:18–20).

#2 He brought an offering to Jerusalem (Acts 11:25—12:25; Gal. 2:1–2).

#3 He met with the Jerusalem Council (Acts 15).

#4 He went up and greeted the church (Acts 18:22–23).

#5 He testified to James, all of the elders, and the Jerusalem church of "all the things God had done among the Gentiles" (Acts 21:17–20).

You also need to be aware that there are two primary schools of thought regarding the meeting described in Galatians 2:1–10. Some commentators place the events described in Galatians 2:1–10 with the Jerusalem Council (Acts 15). For contextual purposes, allow me to explain both views briefly.

As just mentioned, the first view places the incident described in these verses alongside the events recorded in Acts 15, which have come to be known as the Jerusalem Council. In other words, some biblical commentators believe that Paul is referencing Acts 15 in these verses.

Note: The Jerusalem Council, which is mentioned in Acts 15, was the first of seven councils, which proved necessary in order to confront heresy within the Church.

You see, when it comes to the Church, there are essentials and non-essentials within the body of Christ. The essentials comprise doctrines that are life and death matters, such as One Way to the Father—Jesus Christ, the deity, and humanity of Jesus Christ, the inherent, inspired, infallible and absolute authority of all Scripture (to name only a few).

Nonessentials, which can be very divisional, include topics such as: mode of baptism (i.e., immersion versus sprinkling), church polity (i.e., congregation-led versus elder-led), prophetic interpretation (i.e., pre/mid/post-tribulation views; premillennial and millennial versus amillennial view); charismatic gifts (cessation versus continuation view), again, to name only a few.

In other words, essential doctrines are hills to die upon, and nonessential doctrines are matters of interpretation that do not add to or subtract from our salvation. The issue Paul is addressing is an essential doctrine in which he will stake his reputation and very life.

The second view teaches the events in Galatians 2:1–10 are parallel to the "famine visit" recorded in Acts 11:25—12:25. This view places the timeline within the context of Galatians 1 in terms of Paul's testimony. For example, Galatians 2:1, begins by stating, "Then after an interval of fourteen years . . ." You may recall in Galatians 1 that Paul began his defense of the gospel from his conversion (Gal. 1:11–17). Therefore, we must assume that the fourteen years Paul is recounting in Galatians 2:1 is a reference to the fourteen years following his conversion.

You may also recall Paul's first visit (fifteen days) to Jerusalem (post-conversion, and three years from his Arabian desert time), referenced in Galatians 1:18, coinciding perfectly with Acts 9:26. His second visit to Jerusalem, which is recorded in Acts 11:29—12:25, seems to be more congruent with the details in Galatians 2:1–10. In fact, those who adhere to the Jerusalem Council theory have to bypass the visit Paul and Barnabas made in Acts 11:29—12:25 to establish the Jerusalem Council position in Acts 15.

Consider the following comments taken from church historian, Timothy George, in his commentary on Galatians, as he compares the two views, stating,

> *The differences between Acts 15 and Galatians 2 are more striking than the similarities. In Acts 15 Paul and Barnabas are sent as part of an official delegation from the church at Antioch to resolve a dispute introduced into their congregation by intruders from Judea. In Galatians 2, however, Paul himself, prompted by a divine revelation, takes the initiative for the meeting. The council of Acts 15 was clearly a public meeting involving lengthy discussions and presentations addressed to the whole assembly by Peter, Paul, Barnabas, and James. By contrast, the conference of Gal 2 was carried on in private conversation among the principal leaders.*
>
> *Most telling of all, however, is the fact that nowhere in Galatians does Paul refer to the outcome of the Jerusalem Council or to the apostolic decree which, according to Acts, he and Barnabas later distributed among the churches of Syria, Cilicia, and also Galatia (Acts 16:4).* [50]

Quoting in his commentary from the late biblical scholar, F. F. Bruce, George adds, "As Bruce has observed, 'After the publication of the apostolic decree of Acts 15:20–29, it would have been difficult for Judaizing preachers invoking the authority of the leaders of the Jerusalem church to impose circumcision on Gentile Christians.'"[51]

Furthermore, if you keep reading in Galatians 2:11–16 (which we will look at in the next lesson), you will see that Peter goes down to Antioch, where Paul records a very public confrontation. The events described in Acts 15 occur when Paul travels to Jerusalem. Now, if Galatians 2:1–10 were describing the events in Acts 15, there

50. Timothy George, *Galatians: Vol 30* (Nashville: Broadman & Holman Publishers, 1994), pp. 136-137.
51. *Ibid.*

would have been no need for a public confrontation in Antioch, because the matter would have been settled at the Jerusalem Council, right?

Therefore, for these stated reasons, I tend to lean toward the second position, and therefore, do not believe Galatians 2:1–10 is a reference to the events in Acts 15. I believe Paul is addressing the issue that eventually led to the necessity for the Council. And this is the position from which we will proceed. Do not let the two views on the timeline cause concern, because this would fall into the category of nonessentials. I just want you to be aware that there are at least two positions out there in case you were to encounter them.

Regardless of the timeline, which again is a nonessential matter, the issue itself is essential. Paul is defending the gospel of grace. For Paul, no price is too high. No sacrifice too great. The timing of Paul's private meeting (Gal. 2:1–10) and his public confrontation (Gal. 2:11–16) is critical because the early church is being established.

In essence, the gospel of grace is under attack. The Enemy had disguised himself as an angel of light (2 Cor 11:14), and the Galatians had become the Enemy's prey. The message of Christ + _________ was a distortion of epic proportion. Anything added to the saving grace of Christ alone changes the message entirely. In fact, the Judaizer's message is perpetrating the lie that Christ's work on the cross is not sufficient for salvation.

In reality, the Judaizers, in their deception, had become the instruments the Enemy was using to target the churches in Galatia. If Paul had not addressed the issue head-on and quickly, the early church would have had two messages of salvation, great confusion, and no liberty! Watch what Paul says and does to defend the truth. Let's get started.

A PRIVATE ENCOUNTER

Read Galatians 2:1–10 and answer the following questions.

1. Who goes up to Jerusalem with Paul fourteen years following his conversion (v. 1)?

a. ______________________________

b. ______________________________

2. Now, let's look at the two men Paul intentionally chooses to take along with him to Jerusalem. Look at the following cross-references to learn more about each man.

A. Let's start with Barnabas. Look at Acts 4:36, where he is first mentioned in Scripture, and answer the following questions:

1. What was Barnabas' birth name?

2. From what Jewish tribe did Barnabas come?

3. Where was he from?

4. Who calls him Barnabas?

5. What does his name (Barnabas) mean?

Notice the disciples rename him. Do you think they are matching his character and actions with his new name? His lineage and reputation has made him a "man of reputation."

6. Now, as a way of reminder, turn again to Acts 9:26–27 to see when and how Barnabas enters Paul's life? What do you see?

B. Now, let's look at Titus. (**Note:** Titus is not mentioned by name in the Book of Acts. However, Paul mentions him thirteen times in his letters in addition to an entire letter, which he explicitly addresses to him by name.)

1. What do you learn about Titus in Titus 1:4?

Note: Titus had a difficult assignment. He was the bishop (pastor) of Crete, which was infamously known as a place for liars, evil beasts, and lazy gluttons" (Titus 1:12).

2. Now, look at Galatians 2:3. What does Paul tell us about Titus regarding his heritage, and in particular, circumcision?

3. Do you see Paul's strategy in taking these two specific men with him to Jerusalem? Any thoughts?

Note: Think about it: Although very different, Barnabas and Titus both accompany Paul for the sake of the gospel. Barnabas is a circumcised Jew from the tribe of Levi who is highly respected among the disciples. Now, compare him with Titus, a Greek (Gentile) who is uncircumcised. Do you see the beauty of salvation, which would include both a circumcised Jew and an uncircumcised Gentile? Do you see the brilliance of the argument, which proves that circumcision is not necessary, or Titus would not have been included?

4. What reason does Paul give in verse 2a for going up to Jerusalem with these two men?

So basically, who sends Paul, Barnabas, and Titus to Jerusalem? ____________________________

5. With whom do they meet in Jerusalem, according to verse 2?

Note: Paul uses the phrase, "those who were of reputation," namely, Peter, James, and John (Gal. 2:9), not because that is how he viewed them, but because that is how the Judaizer's referred to the apostles. Remember, for the Judaizer; outward appearance is everything.

6. What does he submit to them?

7. What sort of meeting takes place (v. 2)? In other words, how does he approach "those who were of reputation?"

In ____________________________

Now, let's look at the end of verse 2. What do you make of the phrase, ". . . for fear that I might be running or had run in vain"? Is Paul expressing doubt, error, or fear in his message? Before you answer this question, look at the following information:

Note: Oftentimes, Paul uses figurative language, such as the metaphor of running, in comparison with the Christian life. According to Spiros Zodhiates, Paul uses it here as a means of expressing strenuous efforts in the Christian life and cause.[52]

Likewise, the word, "vain," specifically used here, means, "fruitless, without usefulness or success."[53] Interestingly, the same word is used in 1 Thessalonians 2:1 to describe Paul's arrival in Thessalonica, which had not proven to be in vain, meaning "unaccompanied with the demonstration of Spirit and power."[54]

Paul is not expressing doubt in his message. He knows that his efforts are not in vain because they are Spirit-led. Actually, the ones who are running in vain are the Judaizer's. You see, without the Spirit, our fleshly efforts are futile. The Judaizer's message of Christ + circumcision (or any other fleshly effort) is not the message of grace Paul is preaching.

8. Now, let's look at Galatians 2:3. Notice the verse begins with the contrasting word, "BUT..."

a. What does Paul say specifically about Titus in verse 3?

BUT, **<u>not even</u>** Titus

1) who was ________________ ________________

2) though he was a ______________________________

3) was ____

Note: The Greek word translated "compelled," needs to be addressed. First, it is in the passive voice, which means that the subject (Titus) is not choosing the action but is being acted upon. It is the Greek word, *anaginosko*, which, when defined means, "to know by reading."[55]

52. Spiros Zodhiates, *The Complete Word Study Dictionary New Testament* (Chattanooga, TN: AMG Publishers, 1993), 1394.
53. *Ibid.,* 856
54. *Ibid.*
55. *Ibid.*, 145.

b. With that stated, who is the outside source compelling Titus in the faith concerning circumcision?

c. What does God's Spirit use to compel and instruct?

Now, look at Romans 10:17. What does the Spirit of God always use as a foundation for faith?

d. So, what is Paul saying in verse 3 about Titus?

Note: Do you see Paul's point? If God's Spirit (using God's Word) is not compelling Titus to be circumcised, then why should he or anyone else make it essential in regard to salvation?

e. Now, re-read Galatians 2b–3. Does Paul fear that the gospel he had been preaching to the Gentiles was incorrect? For Paul, is the message of grace alone by faith alone inadequate? After all, Titus was an uncircumcised Greek. Paul is asking, "Is Titus required to be circumcised to be saved, or is Christ alone enough? What do you think?

9. Now, watch in Galatians 2:4, as Paul skillfully identifies the true source of the Galatian's disruption while exposing their agenda.

a. Who is the source?

b. What had they done?

c. Why have they crept in?

d. What is their **agenda**? ". . . in order to ________________________________."

Now, I think at this point, it would be helpful to look at a few definitions and verb tenses to get a better picture of what was happening within the churches of Galatia. Please be aware that the same thing continues to happen in the church today.

Let's begin with the term, false brethren, which is the Greek word *pseudadelphos*. In Galatians 2:4, it specifically means, "those who had become members of the Christian church **outwardly**, sharers in its fellowship of life and love, but in reality, were not so **inwardly**. Therefore, they had no right to be counted as brothers. They had the companionship of the brothers, but the real kinship of spiritual life was missing."[56]

Next, the word "sneaked," literally means to come in by stealth. The active voice is used here, meaning that the Judaizers are not there by accident; instead, they are on a mission. Whether they know it or not, who do you think is the commander of this mission, and why?

Doesn't the Enemy, who stands against Jesus Christ, do everything by stealth and in hiding?

And finally, let's look at the term, liberty, which is a key repeated word throughout Galatians. In fact, it is used eleven times in the letter, which is more than all of the other letters Paul wrote together.[57]

What does that tell you about the Book of Galatians and its primary message in comparison with the other letters Paul penned?

Note: The message of God's grace brings liberty! Tuck that away in your memory as a place in Scripture to turn when your liberty in Christ is being threatened.

Furthermore, the word "liberty" (*eleutheria*) is a noun; therefore, it is a state of being rather than an action being taken. Frequently, when we think of the word "liberty," we think of it in terms of a verb or something we are doing. By erroneously making it a verb, some have taken it to mean a license to sin or do whatever they want. Nothing could be further from the truth.

In reality, the definition, as it is used in this verse, represents the freedom presented as a signal or sign of blessing in the economy of *grace*. It is in direct contrast with the economy exhibited in the Old Testament of religious regulations and legal restrictions.[58] Likewise helpful, the antonym of liberty is bondage or yoke.

Notice from verse 4, in whom do we have liberty?

Do you see that liberty (as a state of being) is only available for those who are in Christ?

Consequently, those who are not in Christ are yoked with or in bondage to sin. It is their state of being, which is just another way of saying, "You were dead in your transgressions and sin" (Eph. 2:1).

So, what is Paul saying? How can a believer be subject again to bondage? You may be thinking, and rightly so, "If Christ has liberated a believer, how then can that person be subject to a state of bondage?" In other words, "Can a believer lose liberty in Christ as a state of being?" The answer is, "No!"

56. Spiros Zodhiates, *The Complete Word Study Dictionary New Testament* (Chattanooga, TN: AMG Publishers, 1993), 1491.
57. H. L. Willmington, *Willmington's Guide to the Bible* (Wheaton, IL: Tyndale House Publishers, Inc., 1984), 397.
58. Spiros Zodhiates, The Complete Word Study Dictionary New Testament (Chattanooga, TN: AMG Publishers, 1993), 565.

Therefore, in an effort to better understand Paul's warning in verse 4, let's look at the word "bondage," and more specifically, the part of speech he used. Interestingly, in this verse, the Greek word translated "bondage," is not a noun but a verb. In fact, it is an aorist subjunctive middle verb, meaning:

- Aorist tense – A punctiliar action, meaning at a point in time (as opposed to present tense, which is a continuous action).
- Subjunctive Mood – Indicates the mood of probability. The action is thought of as possible or potential.
- Middle voice – The subject is both initiating and participating in the action.

10. With all of the information provided above, let's look again at Galatians 2:4. This verse is pivotal for every believer to understand what the Enemy's agenda is for him or her. What is the Enemy's mission for those who are in Christ? Take your time in answering. The answer provides essential information every believer must know.

Note: Paul is speaking to the church here. He is warning the church that false brethren have crept in, while cautioning them that the Enemy has an agenda. Paul is not placing doubt on whether they belong to the Lord. In actuality, he affirms that their liberty is secure in Christ Jesus.

However, he is warning them of a hidden danger that we, as believers, can and will face. Although saved from the penalty of sin, a sin can still have power over a believer. In other words, the enemy knows he cannot have you. He knows you belong to Christ. However, if he can, his goal is to render you useless, bound in a sin that keeps you under his yoke in an area of your life. Whether he gains access inwardly (through the flesh) or outwardly (via the world) makes no difference to him.

So how serious is this danger? It's a matter of being rendered useless during your time of stay on earth (1 Peter 1:17). No true believer of Christ wants that—right?

11. If you look closely at Galatians 2:5a, you will discover how Paul combated the false brethren? What do you see?

12. What is Paul's purpose in not yielding under the lies of the enemy, according to verse 5b?

    ". . . so that ____."

13. So, what does Paul mean, "We did not yield in subjection to them . . . ?" To understand what he is saying, look at James 4:7, which says the same thing but in a slightly different way. Pay close attention to the order in James 4:7, for the order in Scripture always matters. How does James (and Paul) instruct the believer to combat the enemy or the lies of the false brethren who can creep into the fellowship of believers?

Do you see that through submission to God is how we resist the Enemy? In fact, when we surrender and obey God's Word, we not only resist the Enemy, but according to James 4:7, he must flee! Keep that in mind the next time the Enemy comes your way!

Note: Paul is saying in Galatians 2:5 that if he had yielded to the lies of the false brethren (adding circumcision to Christ), the gospel message he had brought to them would have been in jeopardy. Something Paul was not going to allow even if it cost him his reputation or worse, his life.

14. Now, as you continue reading Galatians 2:6, what are we to make of this? Is Paul going rogue? Is he boasting by saying that those "who were of high reputation" contributed nothing to him? Is he somehow demeaning them? What is he saying?

    a. First of all, to whom is Paul referring when he says, "those who were of high reputation?" Look further at Galatians 2:9 for help.

Do not be alarmed at how Paul describes the men (Peter, James, and John) and what he says about them afterward. Remember, he is merely repeating what the Judaizers were saying in their attempt to slight Paul. Keep in mind that the Judaizers had placed doubt on Paul's apostleship and his authority. Ironically, they were the ones concerned with things like reputation and position. For them, it was all about the outward presentation. They had no idea the real issue was their heart.

Could Paul be using the words of the false brethren here in an attempt to make a point? Is this just another way of Paul communicating that he has no doubt whatsoever about his apostleship or the gospel message he was teaching, because both had come directly from the Lord Jesus? Whatever the intent, we can know for sure that Paul was not boasting, nor was he slandering the disciples. For, in either case, the Lord would not be pleased.

    b. More importantly, what do we learn about God in verse 6?

    c. Since God is not like man, what is Paul implying the false brethren had done?

Note: Because God does not show partiality, the gospel is for the Jew and Gentile alike. Weren't the false teachers the ones who were guilty of showing partiality? Sadly, the innate tendency of all flesh is to show partiality.

15. Did you notice that when Paul was facing the lies of the false brethren, he did not confront them? Whom did he confront, and what can we learn from Paul when it happens to us? What do you see?

16. Why were the apostles not able to contribute anything to Paul or his message? What did they see and do? Look at verses 7–10 and list the four things Paul specifically mentions to answer this question. [**Hint:** Note the verbs used for help].

a. . . . *seeing* that I *had been* ______________________________ with the gospel (v. 7)

Note: The Greek verb translated "had been," is in the passive voice, meaning that the subject (Paul) had been acted upon. Furthermore, the perfect tense is used, indicating a completed action in the past with present and future results.

b. . . . *recognizing* the _________________________ that had been given to me (v. 9a)

Once again, the Greek verb translated "had been" is in the passive voice, meaning that the subject (Paul) had been acted upon. Do you recognize the grace that has been given to you?

c. . . . *gave* to me and Barnabas the ____ (v. 9b)

Note: When a person of high rank has extended the right hand of fellowship with another, he is extending equal honor with himself and recognizing him to be of equal dignity.[59]

Note: When you see the passive verbs translated "entrusted," "recognizing," and "gave," you are looking at grace defined. Since grace is God's invitation, and grace always precedes faith, what was Paul's response to be?

d. . . . *asked* us to ____ (v. 10)

Note: There are two Greek words for our one English word "poor," the first being *ptocheia*, which means completely helpless where begging is the only means of survival, and the second is *penes*, which means poor, but capable of providing for oneself. The word Paul uses here in Galatians 2:10 is *ptocheia*.

Due to the rapid growth of a social gospel today, this distinction is necessary. Often, we confuse the *ptocheia* with the *penes*.

Now, as you look at what James, Peter (Cephas), and John had witnessed and done, what could they possibly have added or contributed to Paul's message of grace?

17. What is Paul's strategy in this private encounter (v. 2) with Peter, now, in verse 7? What do you see?

Do you see that Peter and Paul had been entrusted with the same message (the gospel) and the same ministry (preaching), but a different audience?

18. Once again, with whom does Paul credit the work both he and Peter were entrusted (v. 8)?

Note: The phrase, "effectually worked," indicates the operative ability (power source) to produce an effect.

Pastor and author, John MacArthur, beautifully explains the effectual work of God, stating, "The same Spirit who energized (worked so as to produce results) and empowered Peter energized and empowered Paul, and the Spirit has but one gospel."[60]

---

59. *Ibid.*, 405.
60. John MacArthur, *The MacArthur New Testament Commentary Galatians* (Chicago: Moody Press, 1987), 41.

Think about it, the same Spirit who energized Peter and Paul for His work is still working in the lives of those He has called out today to bring the good news of the grace of Jesus Christ—an overwhelming thought, huh?

19. Look at Ephesians 4:4–6. What do you see? What is the one constant word?

"There is ___________ __________________

___________ __________________

just as also you were called in ___________ __________________ of your calling;

___________ __________________

___________ __________________

___________ __________________

(v. 6) ___________ __________________ and ______________

who is *over* all

and

through all

and

in all.

20. As you look at Ephesians 4:4–6, how does this silence the false brethren whose message is Christ + _________?

21. One last question. Where are we in Ephesians 4:4–6?

Are we not just the recipients of God's grace?

Of what then, is Ephesians 4:4–6 a picture? __________________

In closing, I ran across something Dr. Harold Willmington said in his comments on Galatians. He stated, "Grace is a way *to* life and a way *of* life" (emphasis added). Do you agree? Paul said it this way to the believers in Colossae, stating, "As you, therefore, have received Christ Jesus the Lord, so walk in Him" (Col. 2:6: emphasis added).

WHAT ABOUT YOU?

What have you been adding to Christ?

Has the Enemy of your soul deceived you into some form of bondage? Is there a specific sin that is having power over your life right now?

Maybe it is not your sin. Perhaps it is a sin of another, which has resulted in hurt, discouragement, and depression. Does the Enemy have you in the snare of self-pity, striving, or unforgiveness?

If so, cry out for the Savior to save you from the power of the sin that has so easily entangled you. Know that you are either submitting to the Enemy's lies or God's Spirit and Word. Ask Him to cause you to submit to Him and Him alone. He can empower you to do His will if you let Him. Your Savior is waiting to make the exchange (Is. 61:1–3).

Look at the exchange the Lord offers in the following outline of Isaiah 61:2–3:

What We Bring to Him:	**What He Gives in Exchange:**
ashes (dust spread over the head of someone grieving loss)	garland (victorious wreath worn around the head)
mourning	oil of gladness (Holy Spirit)
spirit of fainting	mantle of praise

Look over these columns closely, what do you see? I see GRACE!

Read Isaiah 30:18. Do you believe that He longs to be gracious to you?

Will you let Him?

Lesson 10

A Public Confrontation: Part One

GALATIANS 2:11–16

In the last lesson, we examined a private meeting in Jerusalem, which had been orchestrated by the Lord. Through a revelation, Paul, Barnabas, and Titus had been sent to James, Peter, and John in order to submit the gospel message that Paul had been preaching to the Gentiles (vv. 1–10). All were in complete agreement that the message of the gospel was by grace through faith in Jesus Christ—alone.

But as we keep reading in Galatians 2:11–16, Paul describes another encounter with Peter. However, this meeting is very different than the one described in the previous lesson. Instead of Paul going to Jerusalem, Peter came to Antioch. Rather than a private encounter, the matter of discussion had turned public. Rather than agreement, the issue at hand had divided them.

In this lesson, Paul finds himself in the uncomfortable place of confrontation with his brother in Christ. In fact, he finds himself face to face with Peter, who is playing the role of a hypocrite and leading others to do the same. Because the gospel is at stake, Paul will confront the matter straightforward and without compromise. But watch carefully, as he does so in a very gracious and loving manner. Let's get started.

Begin by reading Galatians 2:11–16 and answer the following questions using these verses.

1. Where does the meeting in Galatians 2:11–16 take place?

2. Who initiated the visit?

Note: Paul refers to Simon Peter as Cephas in this chapter. You will recall from a previous lesson that Simon was his name in the Hebrew language, Peter was his Greek name, but Cephas was his name in the Aramaic language. The Aramaic and Hebrew dialect were very similar. Remember there were two places called Antioch in Scripture. There was Antioch of Pisidia and Antioch in Syria. The language spoken in Syria was Aramaic, which is probably why Paul refers to Peter by that particular name.

3. What did Paul do and why (v. 11)?

4. What specifically had Peter done to deserve Paul's correction (v. 12)?

Note: The word "withdraw" (*hupostello*) describes a partial or gradual separation. However, the words "hold himself aloof" (*aphorizo*), denote a complete and final separation from the combined fellowship of the Jewish and Gentile meals, both the common meals eaten at the church (the Lord's supper/communion or love-feasts as they were referred to in the early church), and the meals eaten at the homes of the Gentiles.[61]

5. Why was Peter acting in such a manner according to verse 12b?

Doesn't this remind you of Peter's denial (Matt. 26:69–75)? Didn't Peter deny Christ three times because of the fear of man?

6. Now, look at Proverbs 29:25 and answer the following questions:

a. What do you learn about the fear of man (v. 25a)?

Note: The Enemy can use the flesh and the world as his lure. When a believer succumbs to the lies of the flesh or the world, the Enemy has gained access to your heart (your mind). His goal is to bind you in fear and render you useless (unfruitful).

b. What is the exact opposite of the fear of man (v. 25b)?

Would it surprise you to discover that "faith" is a synonym for trusting the Lord?

c. Think about it. What is actually behind the fear of man? Is it love for man or a love for self? Explain.

Now, before we go further into the lesson, we need to look back and see how the Lord had previously revealed Himself, and His will to Peter regarding, in particular, freedom from the Old Testament (Mosaic) food laws.

7. Read the account in Acts 10 and answer the following questions:

a. How is Cornelius described in verses 1–2?

Note: The setting takes place in Caesarea of Palestine (or Maritime), on the coast of the Mediterranean. Herod the Great rebuilt it with great majesty and strength and named it in honor of Caesar Augustus. Historian, Josephus, called it one of the largest cities in Palestine whose inhabitants were mostly Greeks.[62]

---

61. Kenneth S. Wuest, *Wuest's Word Studies From the Greek New Testament: Galatians, Volume One* (Grand Rapids, MI: Wm. B. Eerdmans Publishing Co., 1972), 72.
62. Spiros Zodhiates, *The Complete Word Study Dictionary New Testament* (Chattanooga, TN: AMG Publishers, 1993), 806.

The Italian army had been commissioned by Rome to keep order. An Italian cohort would comprise a group of approximately six hundred soldiers who understood rank and authority. A centurion was the commander of one hundred men.

In the description of Cornelius, did you notice something different? He was a religious man, without Christ, but things were about to change. Let's keep reading.

b. About the ninth hour (3 p.m., one of the hours designated for prayer), an angel of God came to Cornelius in a vision. What did he instruct Cornelius to do (vv. 5–6)?

c. As you look at the angelic encounter with Cornelius, what are some of the details that stand out most to you and why from verses 3–6?

Note: Did you notice that the angel knew Cornelius by name? Do you see that God works through human instruments and that His instructions are clear and specific?

d. What did Cornelius do after the angel departed (vv. 7–8)?

On the next day, while the servants of Cornelius were on their way, we find another in prayer about the sixth hour (noon, another hour designated for prayer).

e. Write who is praying and describe what happened to him (vv. 9–16)? Note in particular what the Lord said to Peter in verse 15.

While Peter was "greatly perplexed" at what had just happened, the men who had been sent by Cornelius appeared at the gate inquiring about Peter (vv. 17–18).

f. What did the Spirit say to Peter (vv. 19–20)?

Note: The Greek word translated "misgivings," means "to separate oneself from another." Interesting choice of words wouldn't you say? Isn't that exactly what Peter had been doing?[63]

g. What specifically did the men tell Peter about his mission in verse 22? In other words, what was Peter's mission from the Lord regarding Cornelius?

Note: Isn't this just an open invitation for Peter to preach the gospel of Jesus Christ?

h. Peter invited the men to lodge with him, and they left for Caesarea the next day (v. 23). Who was waiting on Peter and the men, and whom had he assembled together (v. 24)?

Note: What about your close relatives and friends? Have you invited them to hear the gospel of Jesus Christ?

i. What did Cornelius do when he met Peter (v. 25)?

j. How did Peter respond according to verse 26?

k. What does Peter tell Cornelius in verse 28?

l. What question does Peter ask Cornelius in verse 29?

As Cornelius reports what happened to him just four days prior, he then simply tells Peter, "Now then, we are all present before God to hear all that you have been commanded by the Lord" (v. 33).

m. Now, methodically record fact by fact what Peter said in response to Cornelius' request in the space provided (vv. 34–43).

Now, as you look over all that Peter said, who was his main topic?

63. *Ibid.*, 431.

What do you see in the facts presented?

Note: Do you see the life, death, burial, and witnessed resurrection of the Lord Jesus Christ? This, in a nutshell, is the gospel of grace (1 Cor 15).

What specifically is said about Jesus Christ in verse 43?

n. What happened when Peter finished presenting the gospel message of Jesus Christ in verse 44?

As you read verses 45–46, you will discover the same sequence of events occur when the Jews are filled with the Holy Spirit in Acts 2. In essence, Acts 10 represents the day of Pentecost for the Gentiles.

8. Now, let's continue reading in Acts 11:1–18 and answer the following questions:

a. What happens when Peter returns to Jerusalem after the Gentiles heard the gospel and had received the Holy Spirit (v. 2)?

Can you imagine? Sad response isn't it.

b. Now, record what the circumcised brethren specifically said to Peter (v. 3)?

Notice in verses 4–15, Peter retells the entire story in the sequence in which it had occurred.

c. What are we told Peter remembers in verse 16?

Note: It may interest you to know that the Greek word translated "baptized," is in the passive voice, which signifies that the subjects were acted upon by an outside source. In other words, God the Spirit baptized them in Christ!

Now, look at John 14:26. Jesus tells His disciples about the ministry of the Holy Spirit. How does John 14:26 compare with what happened to Peter in Acts 11:16?

d. What is Peter's conclusion, according to Acts 11:17?

e. How do the people respond to Peter in Acts 11:18?

Note: Look again at Acts 11:18. Who grants repentance?

Where does this repentance lead?

One final comment regarding the passages in Acts as compared to what we have seen so far in Galatians 2:11–12. Did you happen to notice the number of references to the fear of the Lord in Acts 10? Do you see that we either fear the Lord or man? Do you also see that the fear of man is actually deception rooted in a love for self? Remember this love of self is in all of us and will be until we are glorified.

Now, do you understand why Paul so adamantly opposed Peter, and Peter stood condemned (Gal. 2:11)? What Peter was doing was willful. The events detailed in Acts 10–11 precede Galatians. The Lord had clearly revealed to Peter His will concerning the Old Testament food laws, proving once again, that the deep-rooted love of self is strong, and in dire need of a Savior over its intrinsic power.

Now, leaving the Book of Acts, let's return to Galatians 2.

9. Read Galatians 2:13. How did Peter's fear of man (self-love) affect those around him? What happened?

Note: Both Greek verbs translated "joined," and "were carried away," are in the passive voice, which, as you recall, means that the subject is being acted upon. In other words, the willful decision to separate from the Gentiles, which the Lord had clearly denounced, has led to a joining with, and being carried away in the sin of hypocrisy. You may recall from the gospels that the Lord Jesus' harshest words are directed at the religious hypocrite (Matt. 23:23–33).

10. As you read Galatians 2:13, what warning and truth do you see?

Note: Leadership is very important. If you are a spiritual leader, Galatians 2:13 should cause concern, and serve as a warning. Even a significant leader like Peter, can get off track. Anytime a spiritual leader is saying something that God's Word is not saying—beware! Never veer from God's Word, no matter how influential the leader may be; and leaders, take heed that you are saying and doing what God's Word says—period! No one is above God's Word.

11. Peter's influence had affected others and was leading them astray. What exactly does Paul call Peter's error in verse 13?

Herein is where we must pause.

You see, every believer has the potential to be a hypocrite. Innate within human flesh is a deep-rooted love of self. It entered into the heart of man at the Fall. Sadly, it resides in all of us to some degree!

Similarly dangerous, a hypocrite is someone who knows the truth at least intellectually! Therefore, the sin of hypocrisy is willful in the sense that what a person says he believes, and what he does do not match. God hates hypocrisy, and because He hates it, we must look into it a little deeper.

Therefore, while researching the word, hypocrisy, I ran across a rather lengthy but extremely helpful bit of information from the late theologian, Spiros Zodhiates. Due to its significance, I am including his definition in its entirety in this lesson. I think you will find Dr. Zodhiates' insights most beneficial. I know I did.

He states,

> *The noun hupokrisis was generally used for flattery or evil deception. Hypocrisy is a thing God cannot tolerate (Job 22:16), and which He continually exposes (Job 5:13). Idolatry is a form of hypocrisy which keeps a man from being perfect, i.e., wholehearted, with the Lord his God (Deut. 18:13). . . . All false prophecy was hypocrisy—the saying of one thing that pleased, and not the thing that was true. The person most deceived was the hypocrite himself (Is. 33:14; Job 27:8), but he was also a danger to the society in which he lived (Job 15:34).*
>
> *In the New Testament and especially the synoptics (Matthew, Mark and Luke), few sins are so directly denounced as hypocrisy. In John's Gospel it is equated with pseudos, falsehood, lying, which is equally condemned. Our Lord presents this evil as something hidden that one day will be made manifest, a sin which glories in misleading another by smooth flatteries (Matt. 22:16). The religious hypocrites of Jesus' day went about in long robes seeking to be reverenced by public salutations, taking honor for granted and cloaking oppressive avarice with long prayers (Mark 12:38–40). Hypocrisy cleanses the outside of the cup and platter while leaving them full of extortion and wickedness. It makes men as hidden tombs, white and shining outwardly but foul from within (Luke 11:44).*
>
> *Hypocrisy is a sin that is exposed by our Lord as no other because it corrupts the conscience averting holiness of life. It substitutes the ceremonial and formal for the personal and practical (Matt. 15:6). It uses ecclesiastical rule as a substitute for judgment and the love of God (Luke 11:42). It cannot receive the truth, because its eye is on man and not on God (John 5:44). It makes inquiries not in order to hear the truth, but in order to refute it (John 9:27, 28). It is chained to its error by a confident assurance that it alone is right (John 9:41).*
>
> *Direct denunciation is the only way to confront hypocrisy, a foe of all truth. The hypocrite is in a special sense the child of the father of lies (John 8:44). Hypocrisy not being able to live with truth and can defend itself only through the persecution of others (John 8:37). The reason for the vehement denunciation by Christ of the Pharisees in Matthew 23 was that sitting in Moses' seat, they showed a spirit in which truth cannot dwell. The Pharisees neither entered the kingdom nor allowed others to enter (Matt. 16:3–4). Hypocrisy stands in opposition to faith as it worked to debase the whole man, just as faith works to regenerate him. It takes away the key of knowledge (Luke 11:52).*
>
> *In the Sermon on the Mount (Matt. 5:1) hypocrisy is set in contrast to the kingdom of heaven. To a hypocrite, what is outwardly performed is most important and not what is believed in the heart. The Lord teaches that deliberate care must be taken that one's righteousness be not done for the public eye. Hypocrisy is the opposite of that singleness of eye that fills the whole body with light; it turns the light that is in a man to darkness. Hypocrisy, though attempting to serve two masters, really serves none. It sees splinters in its brother's eye while ignoring beams in its own. It is sheep's clothing without, but a ravenous wolf within. As it corrupted Judaism, it was ready to corrupt Christianity, and indeed has made inroads. The Lord treated the publican and the harlot as the lost sheep He had come to seek. For*

them He opened wide the door of the kingdom. But He knew that the hypocrites could only pretend to enter.

The ultimate hypocrite presented in Scripture is the Antichrist, the one who stands in place of Christ. He will represent the new hypocrisy. He will come in Christ's name saying, "I am he" (Mark 13:6). He will try to deceive even the elect.

Hypocrisy can be equated with the blasphemy against the Holy Spirit (Matt. 12:22–37); Mark 3:20–30; Luke 12:1–12). Both hypocrisy and the resistance of the conviction of the Holy Spirit are the negation of faith.[64]

12. Now, as you review Dr. Zodhiates' explanation of hypocrisy, what stands out most, and why in regard to Galatians 2:11–13?

13. Now, let's pick up in Galatians 2:14–16 and survey Paul's argument with Peter. Answer the following questions using these verses.

    a. What exactly did Paul see in verse 14a?

    b. What was at stake, according to Paul, in verse 14a?

Notice, it was not Paul's opinion or preference that brought about the confrontation with Peter. It was a matter of truth regarding the gospel of Jesus Christ. In other words, it was an essential matter; therefore, it needed to be addressed. Peter's conduct had not been straightforward. His conduct did not align with the truth of the gospel.

    c. Where did this confrontation occur, according to verse 14b?

    d. Why do you think Paul confronted Peter in public? Any thoughts?

64. *Ibid*, 1422-1423.

Note: Early church theologian and philosopher, Augustine, when commenting on Galatians 2:14 said, "It is not advantageous to correct in secret an error which injured openly."[65]

I've also heard it said, "In the arena that you sin, you confess." In other words, if the sin was committed in privacy, then a private confession is necessary. However, if publicly, then a public confession is required. You see, we do not sin in private, nor do we obey in private. Others are watching and may be following.

14. Now, let's look closely at Paul's flow of argument (vv.14–16). If you examine how skillfully Paul changes from the subject of "you," to "we," and later to "I" (vv.17–21) you will see a kind but straightforward rebuke.

a. Let's get started by looking closely at the subject, "You" in an attempt to follow his flow of argument. Fill in the blanks as we begin.

"If you, being a Jew, ______________________ like the Gentiles and not like the Jews, how is it that you ___________________________ the Gentiles to _______________________ like Jews?

Note: Consider the following statements made by the late Greek New Testament Bible scholar, Kenneth S. Wuest, as he explains Paul's argument, stating,

> The word live here, from *zao*, does not refer to the moral living according to Gentile or Jewish fashion, but to the shaping of the life with reference to the external social observances in the Christian fellowship, such as Levitical restrictions on eating. The present tense of live must not be pressed to the point of teaching that Peter at the time of this rebuke, was living as the Gentiles do, for he was not. It describes a mental attitude or habit which had in times past shown itself in outward actions, and which was still in force, but which was being hypocritically covered up by Peter's action of withdrawing from fellowship with the Gentiles. It shows that Peter had not in principle abandoned it, but had trimmed his sails to the sudden change of wind that came from Jerusalem.[66]

Peter knew that what he was doing was not right. He knew what the Lord had shown him. Like all hypocrisy, the underlying conviction had not changed in his mind. Only the behavior had changed. In other words, the internal conviction remained the same, but the external behavior did not match, making him the picture of deception, which says one thing but does another.

b. Now watch in verses 15–16 as Paul changes the subject from "You," to "We." What does Paul argue?

15 "We are Jews by ________________________________,
and
not ________________________________
from among the ________________________;
16 nevertheless
knowing that a man is ____________ ________________________________
by ____
but
through ____
even

65. Kenneth Wuest, *Wuest Word Studies in the New Testament Galatians*, 74.
66. *Ibid.*, pp.74-75.

we have ____________________________ in Christ Jesus,

that

we may be ____________________________

by ____ in Christ,

and

not by ____

since by **the works of the Law** shall ______ flesh be __________________. (emphasis added)

Notice by using the word, "we," Paul was including himself. Anytime you are confronting someone in the matter of faith, be sure and include yourself, for we have all fallen short of the grace of God and in matters of faith. No one is excluded or above another.

Note also that Paul was not calling the Gentiles sinners because he believed the Jews were not. Rather, he was saying that the Jews had been entrusted with the Law of God unlike the Gentiles. In essence, this was not a moral rebuke but a legal one. The Gentiles were without the Law and had been excluded from the Abrahamic Covenant. In other words, Paul argues, "We know what it means to live by the Law and yet, we were not saved by it."[67]

c. Now let's look specifically at the contrast in verse 16, for in this verse you will find the key to the Book of Galatians. Notice that in his confrontation, Paul argues from what they both knew to be the truth. What is contrasted in verse 16?

Versus

Do you see why it is the key verse and phrase in the Book?

d. Now let's look at a few of the Greek words used in order to gain insight into verse 16. First, the preposition, "by," is the Greek word, *dia*, meaning "through," and it indicates the channel through which one secures salvation.[68]

Next, the word "justified" is from *dikaioo*, which means righteousness. Therefore, it is the act of God in justifying a believing sinner, which consists of taking away his guilt and his penalty, since Christ bore both on the cross. The imputation of Christ's righteousness, whereby the believer stands not only guiltless and uncondemned for time and eternity, but is also positively positioned righteous in the sight of the eternal laws of God.[69]

Interestingly, the Greek word for "justified," which is used twice in this verse, is in the passive voice both times, meaning that the subject is being acted upon by an outside source. In other words, no man can justify himself. In fact, Christ alone is the outside source who has justified the believer. It is His righteousness alone that has been imputed to our account for He alone is righteous.

Oftentimes, when we hear a discussion concerning the Law versus grace, we may be inclined to think we are saying one at the expense of the other. As if we are by grace commanded to neglect the Law. However, the phrase, "by the works of the Law," tends to bring great clarity, at least in my mind. For the phrase, "by the works of the Law," implies the flesh versus the Spirit.

67. John MacArthur, *The MacArthur New Testament Commentary Galatians* (Chicago, IL: Moody Press, 1987), 55-56.
68. Kenneth Wuest, *Wuest Word Studies in the Greek New Testament Galatians* (Grand Rapids, MI: William B. Eerdmans Publishing Co., 1980), 78.
69. *Ibid.*

e. What are we told about the works of the Law and our flesh in 16b?

As we bring this lesson to a close and consider Paul's need to confront Peter in Galatians 2:11–16, consider comments made by New Testament Bible scholar and teacher, Harold Willmington, who explains, "Peter had allowed the ever-present Judaizers to pressure him into withdrawing from all Gentile believers upon the arrival of some influential Jews from Jerusalem. Paul soundly rebukes Peter for this."[70]

Furthermore adding, "By doing what he did, Peter was denying five major doctrines:

- The unity of the church (2:14)
- Justification by faith alone (2:15–16)
- Freedom from the Law (2:17–18)
- The all-sufficiency of the indwelling Christ (2:19–20)
- The grace of God (2:21)."[71]

As you can see, in this lesson we have examined the first two doctrines Paul is addressing, and in the next lesson we will look closely at the final three (vv. 17–21).

But as we bring this lesson to a close, how are the first two doctrines specifically addressed by Paul in Galatians 2:11–16? Any closing thoughts?

WHAT ABOUT YOU?

Have you been playing the role of a hypocrite in an area of your life? You may be telling yourself it is for the sake of unity, but does the unity you are seeking to preserve include unity with Christ? In other words, can you stay unified with Christ and remain unified in the matter of compromise?

Are you adding anything to the gospel of grace? Ask the Holy Spirit to evaluate your heart. Allow the Spirit of God to use His Word to reprove and correct you. In other words, ask the Holy Spirit to apply 2 Timothy 3:16 to your life so that 2 Timothy 3:17 will be true!

Are you willing to "do" what He has instructed?

70. H. L. Willmington, *Willmington's Guide to the Bible* (Wheaton: Tyndale House Publishers, Inc., 1984), 399.
71. *Ibid.*

Notes

Lesson 11

A Public Confrontation: Part Two

GALATIANS 2:17–21

In the last lesson, we began our examination of Paul's public confrontation with Peter, who had been cowering to the Judaizer's influence. Once again, Peter, responding in fear and in his effort to please man, had compromised the message of grace by refusing to eat (fellowship) with the Gentiles.

Deep within his heart, Peter knew the truth. He was fully aware that man is justified by grace alone through faith in the finished work of Christ. The Lord had gone to great lengths to clearly relay the message of His grace, which included the Gentiles when He sent Peter to the house of Cornelius (Acts 10).

Peter had witnessed firsthand, and in fact, was the instrument God had chosen to preach the gospel of Jesus Christ to Cornelius and his household. He saw how the Spirit of God worked mightily through the message of grace as he witnessed the Spirit "fall" upon the house of Cornelius (Acts 10:44).

Later, Peter, testifying to the "circumcised" who had taken issue with him for eating with the uncircumcised (Acts 11:2–3), publicly declared, "If God, therefore, gave the same gift as He gave to us also after believing in the Lord Jesus Christ, who was I that I could stand in God's way?" (Acts 11:17).

But now, to appease the Judaizers, his message of grace seems to have changed, at least outwardly. Now, he was declaring by his actions, that man could be righteous by his own ability (through striving and works) to keep the Law. In other words, what he was saying and doing did not match. In fact, they were the exact opposite.

We have seen and witnessed, even in our own life that striving to keep the Law creates hypocrisy—the very sin for which Paul was publicly confronting Peter. Clearly, religion breeds hypocrites! And sadly, lurking within all flesh, there are hypocrites. For the unbeliever, it leads to death. In regard to the flesh of the believer, it renders him/her useless. The pull and bent of our flesh is drawn to the works of the Law, as we can find ourselves, at times, more concerned with "doing," instead of "being." God, on the other hand, focuses on the heart (being) that is in desperate need of transformation. Don't you sense the pull?

You may find yourself, as I did, asking, "What in the world was Peter thinking? How could he of all people be influenced by the Judaizer's message? Why does he keep falling into the trap of the fear of man?" If you and I are willing to be honest, the same questions could be asked of us today. The enemy of our soul continues to deceive the believer of God in an effort to render him or her useless. The temptation can be subtle.

As I thought about these things, the Lord reminded me of something Peter said in his final letter near the end of his life, as he encouraged fellow believers by warning them against false prophets. He said,

> *You, therefore, beloved, be on your guard lest, being carried away by the error of unprincipled men, you fall from your own steadfastness, but grow in the grace and knowledge of our Lord and Savior Jesus Christ. To Him be the glory, both now and to the day of eternity. Amen* (2 Peter 3:17–18).

Did you happen to notice that the fall is connected with one's **own** steadfastness? Only God remains steadfast. Peter knew firsthand what it was like to be carried away by the error of unprincipled men. And in the kindness of the Lord Jesus, Paul was the instrument God chose to reveal the sin of his hypocrisy.

Using the present tense verb here, Peter had learned that a disciple of Christ is one who continues throughout life to grow in the grace and knowledge of our Lord and Savior Jesus Christ. Think about it; we are all in the process of growing in the grace and knowledge, no matter who we are, or how long we have walked with Christ.

The definition of the Greek word translated "grow" is also telling. According to Zodhiates, "for someone or something to grow (*auxano*), he/it must be acted upon by an outward power or have the element of life within him or it.[72]

He uses, for example, the lilies that grow (Matt. 6:28), the seed that is produced (Matt. 13:32) and the fruit that comes from the seeds (Mk. 4:8). In all these instances, it was something living that could grow because of the element of life within it. This growth, however, was not because of any unique ability of the seeds, but because of the quality of life so implanted by God Himself.[73]

Contrastingly, the antonym for the verb used in 2 Peter 3:18 (*auxano*) is the verb, *prokopto*, which has in it the character of human achievement due to conscious effort.[74]

Marvel at the wisdom of God, as the Spirit chose the word "grow" (*auxano*) in 2 Peter 3:18, making it very clear that He alone is the outward source of power that causes the believer to grow in both the grace and knowledge of our Lord and Savior Jesus Christ, rather than by human achievement or effort. It should encourage every believer to know that even the apostle Peter continued to grow in this grace and knowledge while he was on earth.

WHAT ABOUT YOU?

Can you say that you are continuing to grow in the grace and knowledge of our Lord and Savior Jesus Christ? If not, stop and ask Him to be the Source. Allow His Spirit to show you the areas where you have been striving to grow by human achievement and performance. Confess this as sin. Ask Him to grant repentance in this area of your heart. The fact that you can pray this type of prayer is evidence of God at work, for no man is able to see or confess these things if left to himself.

If there is growth, praise and thank Him because He is both the initiator and provider of the grace and knowledge by which you are growing. You are merely responding to His grace in faith, which, by the way, is also a gift from Him.

Now let's get started as we continue looking at Paul's public confrontation with Peter.

A PUBLIC CONFRONTATION: PART TWO

As you recall from our previous lesson, with the help of Dr. Willmington, we began to examine the first two out of five essential doctrines that were being compromised by Peter's hypocrisy. In review, the five doctrines in danger include:

1. The unity of the church (2:14)
2. Justification by faith alone (2:15–16)
3. Freedom from the Law (2:17–18)

---

72. Spiros Zodhiates, *The Complete Word Study Dictionary New Testament* (Chattanooga, TN: AMG Publishers, 1993), 289.
73. *Ibid.*
74. *Ibid.*

4. The all-sufficiency of the indwelling Christ (2:19–20)

5. The grace of God (2:21)[75]

In part one of the confrontation, in Galatians 2:14, we saw how the early church was about to be split wide apart between Jew and Gentile as the Judaizer's message grew in influence. We saw how even Barnabas was carried away by their hypocrisy (v. 13).

Furthermore, the message of grace alone through faith alone is also addressed in Galatians 2:14–15. Due to the magnitude of the deception spread by the Judaizers, Paul could not stay quiet. The importance of grace alone through faith alone cannot be overstated or ignored. There is only one means of salvation—Christ alone. Anything added to the message of grace alone is not only a distortion of the gospel but a deadly lie with eternal repercussions.

As we begin part two, let's pick up in verses 17–18, where we find Paul in mid-argument, stating, "But if, while seeking to be justified in Christ, we ourselves have also been found sinners, is Christ then a minister of sin? May it never be! For if I rebuild what I have once destroyed, I prove myself to be a transgressor."

Due to the difficulty in wording, and in order to help with Paul's scholarly logical approach to the argument, read the following excerpt from Dr. Wuest for clarity. Wuest explains,

> The word if is from *ei*, referring to a fulfilled condition. The Christian Jews, in seeking to be justified in Christ, were shown to be sinners just like and in the same class as the Gentiles. When they sought justification in Christ and thus by grace, it was an admission on their part that there is no justification by works, that the seeker is not justified, and is, therefore, a sinner. The attempt to be justified in Christ awakens the consciousness of sin and compels the Jew to put himself on the plane of the Gentile. The Jew who calls the Gentile a sinner, in seeking to be justified by faith, is forced to admit that he is a sinner also. He has found that the law has failed him as a justifying agency.[76]

1. Now, as we attempt to trace the Judaizer's argument, what is their "logical" conclusion about Christ at the end of verse 17? What does Paul ask?

Read carefully as Dr. Wuest helps to explain how Paul unravels the "logic" behind the Judaizer's argument. He states, "The Judaizers argued in view of the fact that the violation of the law is sin; therefore, abandonment of the law in an effort to be justified in Christ is also sin. Thus, Christ is the promoter of sin."[77]

2. What is Paul's immediate conclusion (17b)?

3. What does Paul say to support his logical conclusion in verse 18?

---

75. H. L. Willmington, *Willmington's Guide to the Bible* (Wheaton: Tyndale House Publishers, Inc., 1984), 399.
76. Kenneth S. Wuest, *Word Studies in the Greek New Testament: Galatians, Vol. One* (Grand Rapids, MI: William. B. Eerdmans Publishing Co., 1972), 78.
77. *Ibid.*

In other words, Paul is arguing that any attempt to rebuild on the works of the Law, rather than rely on the grace of God, would make Paul a transgressor. In essence, Paul is arguing that any attempt to return to the Law as a means for justification is a sin.

Note: It may interest you to know that each time the word "justified" is used (vv. 16–17) it is in the passive voice, meaning that the subject is acted upon. With that in mind, what do you see about justification?

Do you see that justification is something that happens to you? You are not the one justifying yourself. It takes God to justify man.

4. What does Paul say about the Law in verse 19a?

5. What was the purpose of Paul's death to the Law according to verse 19b?

". . . so that ____."

Note: The Law showed Paul his sin because it not only exposed his sin; it also revealed his complete inability to keep it. Rather than freedom from the Law itself, we are free from the works of the Law to save us. Therefore, there is freedom from the Law as a means of salvation.

Think back to the Israelites when Moses read the Law to them, and they all said in unison and with all sincerity, "All the words which the LORD has spoken we will do!" (Ex. 24:3). Try as they did, they could not keep the Law. Think about it, if man could keep the Law, Jesus would not have had to come and die for man. Only one man kept the Law of God in its entirety—Jesus Christ.

And finally, as we come to Galatians 2:20, we find ourselves at the climax of Paul's experience. In fact, if ever there was a life verse to encapsulate Paul's salvation, Galatians 2:20 is it. If you examine it closely, you will see that it is a perfect depiction of what happened when Jesus Christ rescued you as well. As you will discover, spiritual life begins with death—Jesus' death.

6. Take your time as you answer the following questions from Galatians 2:20. Though tedious, your diligence to study will prove extremely beneficial in the end and is well worth your time and effort. What God's Word says is paramount. This is one place where we are encouraged to work (2 Tim. 2:15).

Do not be discouraged or become frustrated. I have provided a detailed examination of Galatians 2:20 on the following page for your consideration. Try to work through the verse yourself with the information provided first.

   a. Paul begins by making the statement, "I have been crucified with Christ . . ." The Greek verb Paul specifically used is perfect indicative passive.

Note: The perfect tense represents an action in the past with present and future results. The indicative mood specifies a statement of fact. The passive voice indicates that the subject was acted upon.

Considering the tense, mood, and voice, what does Paul mean when he declares, "I have been crucified with Christ"?

Look at the following diagram of the statement, "I have been crucified with Christ . . ." below:

Galatians 2:20

What Happened at Salvation?

I <u>have been</u> crucified with Christ...

↓

Perfect Tense	Past	Justification	I have been crucified...	New Life Entered and Began!
	Present	Sanctification	I am being crucified...	New Life in Process!
				How? Deny self
				Take up my cross
				Follow Him
	Future	Glorification	I will be crucified...	New Life Completed!

Indicative Mood Statement of Fact!

Passive Voice The subject is being acted upon.

God is doing it! → Initiator → By Grace →

So, what am I doing? → Responder → Through Faith

[When **<u>His work</u>** on the cross was completed, He cried out with a loud voice, "**IT IS FINISHED**!" (John 19:30)]

b. Next, Paul states, "... and it is no longer I who live, but Christ lives in me."

Note: The Greek verb translated "live(s)," is present indicative active. The present tense indicates continuous action. The indicative mood is a statement of fact. And the active voice means that the subject is performing the action. With that being stated, what is Paul saying?

c. In the next section of the verse, Paul states, "... and the life which I now live in the flesh, I live by faith in the Son of God ..."

Note: The Greek verb translated "live" once again, is present indicative active (see above). However, the word "flesh" as it is used here, is a reference to the physical "flesh and blood" body.

Furthermore, as you will recall from the first lesson, saving faith has three components:

- A firm conviction of God's Word
- Personal surrender of the will to the Word of God
- Obedience to the Word of God[78]

Note: The order is critical. God is always the Initiator! Notice that the first component begins with God. Salvation is from the Lord (Ps 3:8; Jon 2:9). It is the Spirit of God who convicts, and He uses the Word of God to do so (Rom 10:17).

Now, with all of the information provided, what is Paul saying here?

Now, examine the diagram on the next page as a visual for clarification:

78. W. E. Vine, *Vine's Expository Dictionary of Old and New Testament Words* (Vol 2: E-Li) (Grand Rapids, MI: Fleming H. Revell, 1981), 71.

... and it is no longer I who live,

but

(By Grace) (Through Faith)

↓ ↓

Christ lives in me; ↓

↓

... and the life which I now live

in the flesh(body)

Note: The word, flesh, here means, physical body.

... I live by faith

in the Son of God

who loved me

and

delivered Himself
up for me.

Live

Present Tense	Continuous (habit of life)
Indicative Mood	Statement of Fact
Active Voice	The subject (me/you) is performing the action by responding to the Spirit's leading through the Word

By Grace

What is grace?

God is the Initiator and Provision

Through Faith

What does it mean to respond in faith?

(Spirit + The Word)

↓ ↓

Firm conviction to God's Word

Our Response

Personal surrender to God's Word

Obedience to God's Word

*Do you see that the Christian life is a process of dying **so that** we can live?

d. And again, from verse 20, what is Paul telling us about the one in whom we place our faith?

1) ____________________

2) ____________________

Note: It may interest you to know that both of the Greek verbs used here are aorist active participles. The aorist tense represents a punctiliar action in the past (at a point in time). The active voice means that the subject is performing the action.

e. As you consider the verb tense and voice, what do you learn about Christ?

____

____

And finally, in regard to Galatians 2:20, consider the following comments from one of my favorite Bible teachers, pastor, and author, Alistair Begg. The following is taken from Begg's modernization of the late Charles Haddon Spurgeon's book entitled, *Morning and Evening*. In reference to Galatians 2:20 he states,

> **The Paradox of Christianity**
>
> I have been crucified with Christ.
>
> Galatians 2:20
>
> The Lord Jesus Christ acted in what He did as a great public representative person, and His dying upon the cross was the virtual dying of all His people. In Him all His people rendered justice its due and made an expiation to divine vengeance for all their sins. The apostle of the Gentiles delighted to think that as one of Christ's chosen people, he died upon the cross in Christ. He did more than believe this doctrinally—he accepted it confidently, resting his hope upon it. He believed that by virtue of Christ's death, he had satisfied divine justice and found reconciliation with God.
>
> Beloved, what a blessed thing it is when the soul can, as it were, stretch itself upon the cross of Christ and feel, "I am dead; the law has killed me, and I am therefore free from its power, because in Christ I have borne the curse, and in the person of my Substitute all that the law could do by way of condemnation has been executed upon me, for I am crucified with Christ."
>
> But Paul meant even more than this. He not only believed in Christ's death and trusted in it, but he actually felt its power in himself, causing the crucifixion of his old corrupt nature. When he saw the pleasures of sin, he said, "I cannot enjoy these: I am dead to them." Such is the experience of every true Christian. Having received Christ, he is to this world as one who is utterly dead. Yet, while conscious of death to the world, he can at the same time exclaim with the apostle, "I live." He is fully alive to God. The Christian's life is a matchless riddle. The unconverted cannot comprehend it; even the believer himself cannot understand it. Dead, yet alive! Crucified with Christ, and yet at the same time risen with Christ in newness of life! Union with the suffering, bleeding Savior and death to the world and sin are soul-cheering things. May we learn to live evermore in the enjoyment of them![79]

79. Alistair Begg, *Truth for Life*, online, https://www.truthforlife.org/resources/daily-devotionals/12/14/0/ accessed December, 14, 2018.

7. And lastly, let's look at Galatians 2:21 to see Paul's alarming conclusion for those who believe that righteousness is achieved through the Law. Answer the following questions from verse 21:

   a. What is the person who believes that righteousness is attained through the (works of) Law in danger of saying/doing in regard to:

The grace of God- ____

The death of Christ - ____

Note: The word "nullify" is the Greek word *atheteo*, which means to make void.

Can you see the degree of insanity by making these assertions? Can you see how religion/works are a deceptive attempt by the enemy to nullify the grace of God and render His work on the cross, needless?

Can you even begin to imagine standing before a Holy God some day and saying, "Your grace was null and void and the death of your Son, Jesus, was needless"? That is exactly what the person who is relying on his works/religion is saying. Overwhelmingly frightening thought isn't it?

Now, do you see why it was necessary for Paul to confront Peter and why Peter stood condemned (Gal. 2:11)? True love confronts heresy that leads to hypocrisy. Do you see how the doctrines of the sufficiency of the indwelling Christ and the grace of God were in danger of being compromised?

Before we bring this lesson to a close, let's retrace **how** Paul confronted Peter. This exercise will prove helpful if you are ever prompted by the Holy Spirit to confront a brother or sister in Christ who is in error of compromising an essential doctrine of the faith. (**Notice** I emphasized the term prompted by the Spirit. Confronting another person is not a place in which you put yourself without the Spirit leading.)

8. Beginning with verse 14, record how Paul proceeds? [**Hint:** Start with the subjects. Look at the order and flow: You, We, and I.] What do you see?

Note: Did you notice how Paul moves seamlessly from Peter, to both Peter and Paul, and then ends with himself? By placing himself as the subject instead of Peter, Paul's technique serves as a great equalizer and takes the focus off of Peter.

A FEW FINAL THOUGHTS

As I meditated on the flow of Paul's argument, I saw the following truths:

First, Paul begins by calling Peter out with a question, which basically asks, "Peter, do you realize that you are saying one thing and doing another" (v. 14)?

Next, Paul immediately begins to diffuse the situation by placing himself alongside Peter. In verse 15, Paul states, "We are Jews by nature and not sinners from among the Gentiles (emphasis added)."

At first glance, it appears as if Paul is calling the Gentiles sinners while excluding the Jews from sin. However, a closer look will prove the opposite. Paul is actually saying that they (Jew and Gentile) are each in the same state of

sin and need of justification. The fact that the word translated "justified" is in the passive voice is a clear indication that the subject is being acted upon by an outside source and is unable to justify himself.

Furthermore, the lie that Jews and Gentiles were different could not have been further from the truth; for the true spiritual issue of all mankind is the heart. In actuality, they were more unified than either of them knew. Both were sinners in need of a Savior.

You will recall from the previous lesson, prior to his conversion, Paul described himself as being *in Judaism* (Gal. 1:13–14). After his conversion, Paul described himself and his new identity as being *in Christ*. In fact, Paul's favorite self-description in all thirteen of his letters (which comprise a large portion of the New Testament) is the phrase, *in Christ*.

To aid in our understanding of the phrase, in Christ, I will gladly defer to Dr. Wuest, who explains, "The new life is a Person within a person, living out His life in that person."[80]

Beautiful thought, isn't it?

Like Saul (pre-conversion Paul), the Jews (including the Judaizers) prided themselves with the identity that they were in Judaism. Therefore, they believed they could be justified before God by the works of the Law, something a Gentile could never do unless he converted to Judaism and came under the works of the Law.

Do you see that whether in Judaism or a complete rebel (Gentiles) neither group was in Christ? In fact, each group just displayed different manifestations of the same issue, the flesh. In other words, justification by the works of the Law (in Judaism) was every bit as ineffective to justify man as being an outright rebel to the Law. Whether rebel or religious, both were in the snare of the Enemy, these thoughts made me think of the two faces of pride.

In 1 Peter 5:8, he is called a roaring lion, which represents the outright rebellious man. However, in 2 Corinthians 11:14, we are told that Satan masquerades as an angel of light, a fitting description for the religious.

As I thought about the word, masquerade, it made me think of the word hypocrite, and the sin by which Peter had fallen prey. Religion, or the works of the Law, could never save anyone. Man, try as he did (and still does), could not keep the Law. Only the Man—Jesus perfectly kept the Law of God. Our dependence is upon His work, not our own.

Note: The word "masquerade" is the Greek word, *metaschematizo*, which means to change the outward form or appearance of something. *Metaschematizo* stands in direct contrast to the Greek word, *metamorphoo*, which, when translated, means to transform from within.[81]

It is possible for Satan to *metaschematizo*, outwardly transform himself into an angel of light, but it is altogether beyond his power to *metamorphoo* or a change inwardly. Similarly, man may change his outward appearance but finds himself utterly helpless to change from within.[82]

Furthermore, as I continued to meditate on the contrast between the phrases, "by the works of the Law" versus "faith in Christ Jesus," I saw the following flow of thought, which I have entitled, "The Flesh Versus the Spirit." It is located at the end of this lesson. Take time to study the diagram provided. I think you will find it helpful.

As I pondered the key-repeated word, liberty, the following thought crossed my mind, and I think it's from Him.

---

80. Kenneth S. Wuest, *Wuest's Word Studies from the Greek New Testament: Galatians, Volume One* (Grand Rapids, MI: William B. Eerdmans Publishing Co., 1972), 82.
81. Spiros Zodhiates, *The Complete Word Study Dictionary New Testament* (Chattanooga, TN: AMG Publishers, 1993), 972-973.
82. *Ibid.*

Liberty in Christ is not the freedom to do as I please. The liberty Christ is offering and provides is the freedom not to be okay. In essence, it's the freedom to be human and in need of a Savior. It gives man the freedom **not** to have all the answers, to cease striving to live the perfect life, to control everyone and everything around you as you see fit—all while playing the role of a hypocrite yourself. It's the freedom to be weak, helpless, vulnerable, lonely, have all the answers, to cease striving to live the perfect life, to control everyone and everything around you as you see fit—all while playing the role of a hypocrite yourself. It's the freedom to be weak, helpless, vulnerable, lonely, and angry. (Feel free to add whatever state you may find yourself). Ask Him to make the exchange (Is. 61:2–3).

For example, when my heart is hurt, instead of trying to get over it myself, ignore the hurt, or justify myself in the pain, I am learning to bring my hurt to Him. I come to Him as I am, and I ask Him to make the exchange in my heart. In other words, I bring to Him the ashes, the mourning, and the spirit of fainting that the hurt has caused. I ask Him to save me by making the exchange for His garland (the sign of victory), oil of gladness, and garment of praise. Only He can save my heart from the hurt that has had power over it.

In reality, He gives you the freedom to not be the Savior and the liberty to need One! And praise be to God; we have One—the Lord Jesus Christ!

Remember: We are never to strive to be like God as He is God. We were created to be a man/woman who needs God. Therefore, we are to live as Christ did <u>as Man</u>—always surrendering His will in obedience to the Father because He loved His Father.

The late pastor and author, Wayne Barber said, "Our flesh is a magnet to the works of the Law." So true, isn't it? Do you not sense the pull of your flesh to try to please God? Do you ever feel the need to "do" in order to "get"? As if we can put God in our debt? Impossible. Are you willfully refusing to obey a clear Word He has revealed to you? Christ did not come to renew or rehab our flesh. He came to replace it! Our flesh must be put to death. Only the Spirit of God knows what, how, and when to accomplish His work in us. Will you let Him?

On the next page, consider a brief summary of the contrast between the unbeliever's flesh as it manifests itself in either religion or rebellion versus the believer the Spirit in light of our stick figures:

Unbeliever

In the Flesh

Manifests himself in two ways:

↙ ↘

In Religion	In Rebellion
Strives to keep the Law	Rebels against the Law
Loves the works of the Law	Hates the Law
Breeds Hypocrites/Lies	Breeds anarchy
Relies on self-works to "please God" but is actually pleasing self	Works to please self
Is deceived	Is willful

↘ ↙

Both want to be the authority!

Both serve self!

Both love self!

Both want the glory!

Results in Bondage

Believer

In Christ

Manifests himself in two ways:

↙ ↘

In the Flesh	In the Spirit
Religious or Rebellious	Lets God perform His Word by surrender and obedience to His Word
	Breeds transparency/truth
	Relies on Christ's finished work

Bows before the Authority!

Serves God!

Loves God!

Gives God the glory!

Results in Unbelief/Bondage **Results in Faith/Liberty**

A brief summary of Galatians 2, in light of our stick figure, which will represent the danger of adding to Christ:

The Spirit	versus	**The Flesh**
Drawn to God and the things of God		Drawn to the works of the Law
	For the Galatians –	Circumcision
		Dietary restrictions
		Observation of holy days
	For us today -	Church attendance
		Bible study/prayer
		Baptism

Even "spiritual" things can be done with the heart motive to get (as if we can place God in our debt).

Behavior modifications

Worldly counsel/help

Anything external added to Christ and His finished work on the cross can be placed in the blank.

These are things my flesh/the world loves because when you peel off the layers of religion, it is really just all about me!

The Spirit	The Flesh
Is true worship	Is disguised in the face of religion
↓	↓
Is drawn to the Spirit/God's Word	Is a magnet for works
Loves and seeks the approval of God	Loves and seeks the approval of man
Loves and seeks God's face	Loves and seeks my face (to be seen by man)
Is more concerned with the internal (heart)	Is more concerned with the outward appearance

In regard to <u>Circumcision</u>:

Circumcises the heart (inwardly)	Circumcises the flesh (outwardly)
↓	↓
Spirit of God + Word of God – Sword (scalpel)	Strives to keep the list of dos and don'ts
↓ ↓	↓
Causes us to surrender and obey	When unable to keep, we hide, cover, and blame
↓	↓
Leads to transparency	Leads to hypocrisy
↓	↓
Leads to freedom, joy, and gratitude	Leads to bondage, depression, and complaining
Renders us useful to the Master	Renders us useless

The Spirit	The Flesh
Is true worship	Is disguised in the face of religion

In regard to <u>the works of the Law</u>:

Responds, "All that You have said, only You can do!"	Responds, "All that You have said, I can and will do!"
Spirit of God + Word of God	Strives to keep the list of dos and don'ts
↓ ↓	↓
Causes us to surrender and obey	When unable to keep, we hide, cover, and blame
↓	↓
Leads to transparency	Leads to hypocrisy
↓	↓
Leads to freedom, joy, and gratitude	Leads to bondage, depression, and complaining

Do you see that no matter what you add in the blank (Christ + ________), you are adding yourself to the equation?

Anything added to Christ is nothing more than subtraction!

Consider the following illustration of Galatians 2:20:

BORN IN SIN: **Unbeliever**

Under sin's penalty
Under sin's power
Under sin's presence

Inwardly – Dominated by the flesh
Outwardly- Dominated by the world
↓
Both under the dominion of Satan

RE-BORN IN CHRIST:

"I have been crucified with Christ . . ."

God's Gracious Invitation	**Our Response:**		
By Grace	**Through Faith**	OR	**Through Unbelief**
God's Spirit using God's Word draws			
God's Spirit opens eyes/ ears to hear the gospel			
The Spirit + The Word			
↓ ↓			
A firm conviction of God's Word	Personal surrender of our will		Refusal to surrender our will
	Obedience to the Word of God		Disobedience to God's Word

OR

"... and it is no longer I who live, but Christ lives in me;"

Christ in me via the Spirit

I have been saved from the **penalty of sin (justification).

"... and the life which I now <u>live</u> in the flesh (physical body) I live by faith in the Son of God..."

<u>The Spirit</u> versus **Our Residual Flesh** will respond either:

By Grace	**Through Faith** <u>OR</u>	**Through Unbelief**
The Spirit + The Word	Personal surrender of the will	Refusal to surrender the will
↓ ↓	Obedience to the Word of God	Disobedience
A firm conviction of God's Word		

As I surrender and obey, I am being saved from the **power of sin (sanctification). Christ living His life through you and me!

Do you see that as a believer, when you and I surrender our will and obey God's Word as the Spirit leads, our flesh is put to death? But when we refuse to surrender and obey, we grieve and quench God's indwelling Spirit and, in turn, feed our flesh.

When we choose the latter, sin has been given power over us in an area of our heart. When we respond to God's invitation of grace by faith (surrender and obedience), we find ourselves in the process of being sanctified by grace through faith and thereby, saved from the power of sin.

So just as we were saved from the penalty of sin (justification) by grace through faith, we are being saved from the **power** of sin (sanctification) by grace through faith. Is that what Paul means in Colossians when he states, "Just as you therefore have received Christ Jesus the Lord, so walk in Him" (Col. 2:6)? I think so.

Do you also see that Christ, living in you by His Spirit, **causes** you to respond in faith (Ezek. 36:26–27)?

Made in the USA
Columbia, SC
03 October 2021

46492482R00098

↗ Frieze from Persepolis, fifth century BCE

PERSIAN PERIOD: CHRONOLOGY

Edict of Cyrus: Return to Zion	536 BCE
Second Temple completed	c. 516 BCE
Ezra comes to Jerusalem	c. 458 BCE
Nehemiah appointed governor of Judea	c. 445 BCE
Nehemiah's second visit	c. 432 BCE
Alexander the Great conquers Judea	332 BCE

Chapter One
Persian Period
(536–332 BCE)

BROAD OUTLINE OF THE PERIOD

- Ezra and Nehemiah introduced the concept of the exclusivity of the Jewish people.
- Ezra and Nehemiah implemented a widespread program of universal Jewish education.
- The Jews in Judea developed a form of self-government and were ruled by a theocracy of priests.
- The Diaspora expanded considerably.
- Jerusalem and the Temple became the focus of Jewish life for the expanded Jewish communities.

ESSENTIAL QUESTIONS AND SUGGESTED ANSWERS

1. In your opinion, was the large community that remained in Persian-occupied Babylonia of their own free will still considered as living in exile? Should all Jews live in Israel?

In my opinion, they were living in exile much the same way as Jews are living outside of Israel today. Ideally, in the opinion of the Sages, all Jews should make aliya. Practically, for many reasons, this did not happen in the Second Temple period nor today.

2. Why did the majority of Jews voluntarily stay in Babylonia, rather than return to the Jewish homeland? Are there any modern-day parallels?

The majority of Jews stayed in Babylonia because they had heeded Jeremiah's advice (Jeremiah 29:4–7) and made themselves comfortable socially, linguistically, and financially. This has a parallel to the position of many Jews in the western world today.

3. Why is the old adage, "no news is good news" particularly applicable to Jewish history in this period?

Generally speaking, the "dates to remember" in Jewish history are when something catastrophic happened to the Jewish people. The fact that there are no "dates to remember" in the Persian period is a good indication that this was largely a peaceful period in Jewish history.

4. What would cause you, like Nehemiah, to risk position and wealth to help your people?

I hope I would act in a similar way to Nehemiah if I felt that the Jewish people or the Jewish state were at risk, or in peril. There comes a time when one has to think beyond oneself and selflessly ask the questions: "What is good for my people?" "What is good for my religion?" "What is good for my country?" An example of this are the Israeli youth and lone soldiers who serve in the IDF or national service and put their lives on hold for years as they act to protect our people, land, and traditions.

5. Why were Ezra and Nehemiah so opposed to intermarriage?

They both felt that Judaism as a monotheistic faith would cease to be if it were diluted with the polytheistic practices of the surrounding peoples.

6. How do you feel about intermarriage or about dating outside the religion? Is it a threat to Judaism?

Currently more than seven out of ten American Jews marry out of the faith. In Italy it is a staggering nine out of ten. Judaism is the only monotheistic faith in numerical decline. We cannot blame our enemies for this. It is self-inflicted. The philosopher Emil Ludwig Fackenheim taught that we should follow the 614th commandment and not grant Hitler a posthumous victory by intermarriage. The issue of intermarriage was a major concern during both Ezra and Nehemiah's tenures. Intermarriage, which had reached grave proportions, was one of the most serious problems facing the emerging second commonwealth, as it still is today.

7. What new institutions and developments in the Jewish community did Ezra and Nehemiah introduce?

They introduced the idea of public Torah readings on Mondays and Thursdays. They also set the precedent of leadership not being hereditary; rather, it is to be based on the ability of the individual to teach and lead. This concept led to the position of Scribe and later Rabbi.

8. Why is it necessary to have a program of universal, widespread, religious education?

The central prayer of the Jewish faith, the *Shema*, clearly states, "You shall teach it to your children." Without a program of widespread religious education Judaism will die out. It is vital to transmit the knowledge and passion to the next generation.

Commentary on the Chapter Illustrations

Page 4

Iraqi Jews arriving in Israel during "Operation Ezra and Nehemiah," 1951

This photograph is meant to draw parallels between our ancient history and the modern era. To understand who we are today, we must begin by searching in our past. "Know where you came from, and where you are going" (Ethics of the Fathers 3:1). In addition, the naming of a modern Israeli rescue operation after the two characters featured in this chapter is a connection between past and present. Most of the Jews in Babylonia did not heed Ezra and Nehemiah's plea to return home and help with the project of nation building, as they had made themselves comfortable in their new Diaspora home. Sadly, almost 2,500 years later the remaining 125,000 Jews of this area, now known as Iraq, were forced to flee in fear of their lives with almost no material possessions or property. At least we had a Jewish state that successfully organized a massive airlift that finally brought these Jews back to their ancestral homeland.

The Law of Return providing a safe haven for Jewish communities under threat is what many consider to be Israel's most important piece of legislation. Over a four year period, starting in May 1948, more than 680, 000 Jews arrived in Israel, doubling the population. Of these, 120,000 were Holocaust survivors, yet an equally large migration came from Iraq. The Iraqi Jews threatened by anti-Jewish violence made their way to the newly formed Jewish state. They relinquished their nationality and their property and positions in society, which dated back thousands of years. As former Knesset speaker Shlomo Hillel (1923–2021), an Iraqi Jew who helped organize the Iraqi Jewish aliya, recalled:

> **They left their homes in the morning. They traveled three or four hours, and in the evening they found themselves in tents with no electricity or running water. They were relieved to leave Iraq, but for no one is it easy to leave their comfortable home and find themselves living in tents in winter-time. However, most of them realized that this was the only way to do it.[9]**

Page 5

Tel Lakhish with the remains of the Persian governor's palace

This photograph shows one of the very few archaeological remains from the Persian period in Israel. The Persian period is also known as the silent period, as archaeological remains are very rare. Generally speaking, the "dates to remember" in Jewish history are when something catastrophic happened to the Jewish people. The fact that there are no "dates to remember" in the Persian period in the Land of Israel is a good indication that this was largely a peaceful period in Jewish history.

Page 6

Illustration of Persian stone lotus flower

This symbolizes the Persian Empire, crumbling because of "Alpha," symbolizing Alexander the Great, destroying it to its roots. ▼

Plaque with horned lion-griffins:

This gold Persian amulet (and the gold cup on the cover) illustrate the illustriousness and opulence of Persian culture. ▼

Page 7

Map of the Persian Empire

This shows the Persian Empire at its largest extent and illustrates just how much territory Alexander the Great conquered. After the Persian Empire fell, the Jews lived in the Roman, Ptolemaic, Seleucid, and Parthian Empires. ▶

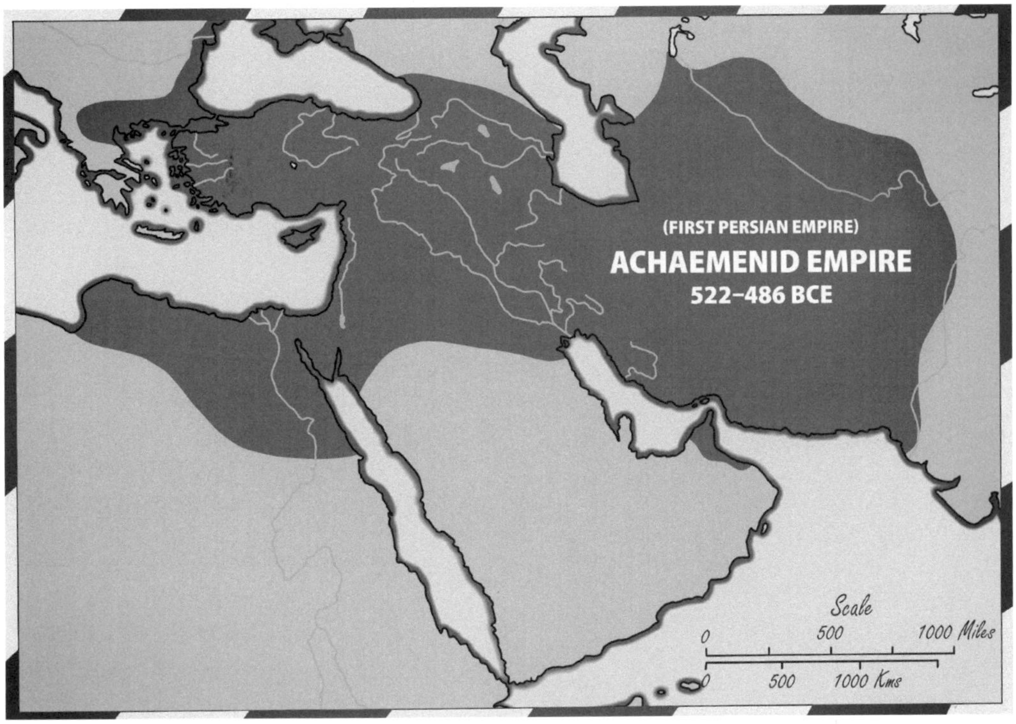

Page 8

Cyrus Cylinder, 539 BCE

This is one of the most dramatic confirmations of the biblical narrative. The baked-clay cuneiform cylinder on which the Edict is recorded is on display in the British Museum. The Edict is a dramatic record of Cyrus's proclamation, which applied to all the subjected people of the former Babylonian Empire, including the Jews. ▼

Tomb of Cyrus the Great, c. 600–530 BCE

Cyrus the Great, who was the founder of the Persian Empire, was buried in Pasargadae, which is located in modern-day Iran, following his death in 530 BCE. According to literary sources, Alexander the Great ordered the restoration of the tomb in the fourth century BCE. It is fascinating to be able to see an image of the tomb of a king mentioned in the Bible. ▼

Page 11

Contemporary one shekel coin

This is based on the original Persian coin, and has the name of the Persian satrapy (province) "Yahud" (Judea) inscribed on it. It is important to note that for the entire duration of the period covered in this book (536 BCE–136 CE) the Jewish homeland was known as Judea. The name "Syria-Palestina" was only introduced by the Emperor Hadrian in 136 CE after the Bar Kokhba Revolt in an attempt to "dejudify" the troublesome Jewish province. ▼

Page 14

Alexander the Great defeating Darius III of Persia at the Battle of Issus in 333 BCE

This mosaic, located in Pompeii, Italy, is believed to depict the Battle of Issus where Alexander's forces defeated the Persian army of Darius III. Alexander appears on the left side of the mosaic, riding his horse Bucephalus into battle. Darius is depicted fleeing on his chariot as his forces are routed.

Measuring 18.7 x 8.9 feet (5.7 x 2.7 meters), the mosaic was created from approximately one and a half million tiles. ▼

Page 17

Woman playing harp

In 586 BCE, the Jews of Judea were exiled by Nebuchadnezzar II, king of Babylon. "By the rivers of Babylon, there we sat down, yea, we wept, when we remembered Zion. We hung our harps upon the willows in its midst" (Psalms 137:1–2). In 536 BCE, the Persian king, Cyrus, allowed the Jews to return to the Land of Israel, where once again they could play their harps in Jerusalem.

Film Clip Links to Enhance the Chapter

"Like the Springs in the Negev" (2:00 min.)
Filmed by the author at a spring in the Negev to illustrate one of the key features that kept the Jews Jewish wherever they lived, "yearning for Zion."

https://www.youtube.com/watch?v=wgqubkg6bZE

Menora decoration at the Golan Archaeological Museum, Katzrin

HELLENISTIC AND HASMONEAN PERIODS: CHRONOLOGY

Alexander the Great annexes Judea	332 BCE
Death of Alexander the Great; empire split between his successors	323 BCE
Ptolemaic control of Judea	301–200 BCE
Seleucid control of Judea	200–142 BCE
Hasmonean revolt	167–164 BCE
Independent Hasmonean dynasty	142–63 BCE
Rome conquers Judea	63 BCE

Chapter Two From the Advent of Hellenism to Hanukkah (332–164 BCE)

BROAD OUTLINE OF THE PERIOD

- **Alexander the Great conquered the entire Persian Empire in eleven years.**
- **These territories, which included almost the entire Jewish Diaspora, became strongly marked by Greek culture.**
- **Upon Alexander's death, his empire was divided among his generals. The Jews therefore fell under two different jurisdictions: the Seleucid dynasty in the east, which included the Jews of the Babylonian community, and the Ptolemaic dynasty in the west, which included the Jews of Egypt. The province of Judea, between these two areas, was an object of contention.**
- **Jews in Judea lived peacefully under Ptolemaic rule for more than a century.**
- **The Seleucids defeated the Ptolemids and began to enforce Hellenism.**
- **Some Jews responded with acceptance, others by active revolt.**
- **In 142 BCE, the Jews in Judea gained independence. Their independence lasted for almost a century, until the Roman conquest in 63 BCE.**

ESSENTIAL QUESTIONS AND SUGGESTED ANSWERS

1. What were the two factors that contributed to the defeat of the Seleucid Greeks? In what way was this defeat "miraculous"?

The Seleucid Greeks were weakened by internal strife within the Seleucid Empire and the guerilla techniques of the Jewish defenders of Judea. It was "miraculous" because one of the world's greatest military forces, with a huge numerical superiority was outmaneuvered, outfought, and ultimately defeated by a much smaller, lesser trained guerilla army.

2. In what way does the modern State of Israel empower Jews worldwide?

Even if Jews choose not to live in Israel, its very existence empowers Jews for two reasons. They know that they always have a place to go to if things are bad where they live, and if they get in trouble the State has a powerful military that can rescue them and come to their aid, as in the case of Entebbe. In addition, the achievements of the Jewish state are a source of pride to most Jews worldwide.

3. Why are we Jews sometimes our own worst enemies? Why is it so difficult for us to realize what we have in common as opposed to focusing on what divides us?

Unfortunately, human nature seems to make it easier to see what divides or separates us from other groups and focus on the negative, as opposed to recognizing the positive and commonalities.

4. Why is Alexander the Great remembered so favorably in Jewish history?

Simply because he did not destroy the Temple or lay Judea to waste.

5. Is there a way to synthesize Judaism and Hellenism, or are they mutually exclusive?

It would be extremely difficult, as the core values of these two lifestyles are inherently contradictory.

6. Is Hellenism similar to any current lifestyle? If so, how does Judaism relate to this similarity?

Hellenism is very similar to the modern western materialistic lifestyle. Judaism always emphasizes the spiritual over the material.

7. What are some of the reasons for the success of the first phase of the Hasmonean revolt?

The Hasmoneans used their superior knowledge of the terrain for guerilla warfare to harass and ambush the numerically superior Seleucid forces. They did not allow them to form the phalanx.

8. Why does Judah continue to be such an inspirational figure for contemporary Jews?

Judah fought for what he believed in despite seemingly impossible odds. He was a selfless leader, who ultimately died for his beliefs. He believed that it was better to die free than live as a slave. His beliefs and heroism inspired his brothers and contemporary followers as much as they continue to inspire contemporary Jews. He did not just "talk the talk" but he "walked the walk" and always led his forces from the front by personal example.

Commentary on the Chapter Illustrations

Page 18

Menora decoration at the Golan Archaeological Museum, Katzrin

The Menora was the most featured Jewish symbol on ancient Jewish synagogues. It is depicted on capitals, as seen here, on lintels, and on mosaic floors. It symbolized the yearning for the rebuilt Temple by depicting the ritual object most associated with the Temple and its predecessor the Tabernacle, created by the biblical Betzalel. This is an example of "adaptation without assimilation," the Jewish ability to use the creative arts of the surrounding culture and synthesize, juxtapose, adapt, and incorporate Jewish symbols within. ▼

Page 20

Tetradrachma coin of Alexander the Great

Alexander is portrayed as Hercules on this coin. In addition to commercial use, coins were used as propaganda tools. This is the way Alexander wanted to appear to his subjects. The use of images of coins throughout this book enables students to see a visual image of ancient leaders, thus enhancing the learning experience, while at the same time conveying the message that the minters of the coin desired to convey to its users. ▶

Page 21

Map of Alexander the Great's empire, fourth century BCE

The map of Alexander the Great's empire illustrates just how much territory Alexander the Great conquered. After Alexander's untimely death, his empire was split up among his generals, known as the *Diadochi*. Two generals, Ptolemy and Seleucus, lay claim to Judea, with its strategic location and coastline. For more than a century Judea was part of the Ptolemaic Empire (301–200 BCE), until the Seleucid army, under Antiochus III, defeated the Ptolemaic army at modern-day Banias. The Seleucids annexed Judea to their empire, where it remained until gaining quasi-independence in 142 BCE, after the Hasmonean revolt. ▼

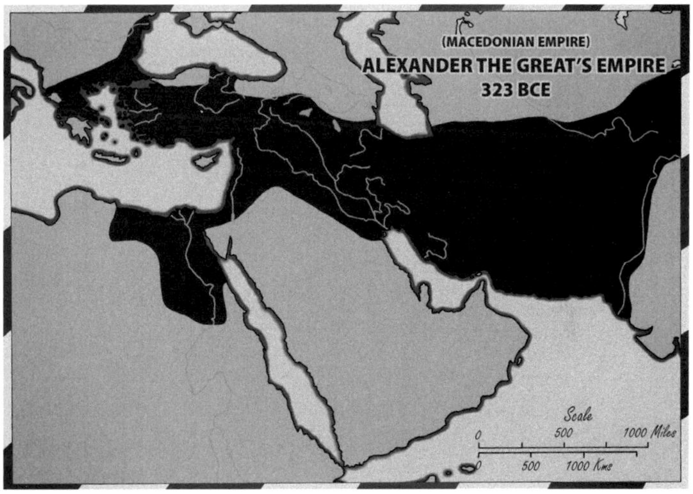

Page 22

Terracotta amphora depicting a footrace, c. 530 BCE

The philosophy of the Hellenists, who placed materialism above spirituality, could be summarized as: "Regard mainly the container." In other words, external beauty is of paramount importance. ▼

Marble head of Greek general, first-century CE Roman copy of a fourth-century BCE Greek bronze original

The Corinthian helmet that the Greek general is wearing is decorated with rams' heads and griffins, and is similar to a type that appears in depictions of the Greek goddess Athena.

Statues portraying powerful men were very popular in Roman times. While made from marble, the eyes would have been made from inlays of another material. ▼

Page 25

Seleucid silver tetradrachma coin of Antiochus IV, 168–164 BCE

It adds another dimension when we have a visual of a famous historical figure. In this coin we see the Seleucid ruler, Antiochus IV, the protagonist of the Hanukkah story, as he wanted to be seen. He was the first Seleucid king to use divine epithets on coins. The reverse of the coin is stamped with "King Antiochus, God Manifest, Bearer of Victory." Antiochus IV is traditionally portrayed in Jewish sources as a crazed, megalomaniac despot whose subjects changed his epithet "Epiphanes," meaning "god-manifest," to "Epimanes," meaning "the mad one." ▶

Page 26

Judah the Maccabee

This depiction of Judah the Maccabee by the French biblical illustrator Gustav Dore depicts Judah as the archetypal selfless Jewish hero who fearlessly fought against seemingly impossible odds for the greater glory of God and the Jewish people. Judah's deeds have continued to inspire generations of Jews. ▶

Page 28

Greek hoplite soldier

◀ Hoplite soldiers were the ancient Greek infantry, who fought in close formation. As can be seen in this image, the soldier wore a metal helmet, breastplate, and greaves. He carried a shield on one arm, and his weapons were a sword and a six-foot-long (two meters) thrusting spear. The hoplite soldiers fought in compact formation, usually eight lines deep, so that the combination of their weight and tight formation meant that they were able to break through enemy lines and win battles. These were the type of soldiers that the Hasmoneans fought against in their revolt against the Seleucids.

Greek helmet

◀ This helmet, known as the Corinthian helmet, covered the entire head of the wearer, with only slits for the eyes and mouth. Constructed out of a single sheet of bronze, it provided excellent protection for the soldier who wore it.

Page 30

Early menora graffiti

Early menora graffiti from the first century CE, uncovered in the Jewish Quarter excavations after the Six-Day War, is the earliest depiction of a menora yet discovered. It was carved into the wall when the Second Temple was still standing. It clearly depicts the Menora with a triangular base, as mentioned in the traditional Jewish sources, not the base we are more familiar with from the Arch of Titus and the symbol of the State of Israel. ▶

Page 31

Menora on the Arch of Titus

The Menora, as depicted on the Arch of Titus in Rome, is shown being carried into exile, "taking the light out of Zion." The same Menora was chosen to be the symbol of the State of Israel, symbolizing returning the light to Zion. ◀

Page 32

The symbol of the State of Israel

The official emblem of the State of Israel is a menora. The artists took as their model the depiction of the menora in relief on the Arch of Titus in Rome. The menora on the arch symbolizes taking the light out of Zion and the menora on the state symbol symbolizes restoring the light to Zion. The olive branches on either side represent Israel's yearning for peace. The combination of a menora and olive branches can be traced to a specific text, one of the mystical visions of the prophet Zechariah.

> **Now the angel who talked with me came back and wakened me, as a man who is wakened out of his sleep. And he said to me, "What do you see?" So I said, "I am looking, and there is a menora of solid gold with a bowl on top of it, and on the menora seven lamps with seven pipes to the seven lamps. Two olive trees are by it, one at the right and the other at its left.**
>
> (Zechariah 4:1–3) ▼

Page 33

IDF, the "Modern Maccabees"

Photograph taken by the author of the soldiers in his IDF unit at a briefing. The setting sun diffracted through the soldiers and appears to be a *Magen David* (Star of David). ▶

Page 34

Hellenistic period olive oil press being excavated at Marissa

This olive oil press is from the second century BCE, the period of the struggle between the Hasmoneans and the Hellenized Jews and the Hellenists. Olives were a main source of income in the Hellenistic period, used for both ritual and practical purposes. ▼

Page 36

Hanukkiot constructed with IDF cartridges, with Hellenistic period oil lamp, in the Hasmonean Synagogue in Modiin

Only after we arrived at the massive base "somewhere in the Negev" for our *milluim* (IDF reserve duty) were we told that we would be going to a small, isolated group of tents in the middle of nowhere. Upon arrival at our million star accommodation the folks in our unit started asking if anyone had brought a *Ḥanukkiah* (aka menora). One guy strangely had brought candles, but no one had a *Ḥanukkiah*. ▼

One of my lasting memories of the combat medics course I took during my regular service was the phrase, "a good medic knows how to improvise." That day we had "live fire" exercises with a lot of different ordinance. I collected nine cartridge cases and the links from the sand and reconnected them.

I vividly remember that night lighting that *Ḥanukkiah* for my combat unit in the middle of the desert and singing together with my fellow IDF brothers-in-arms from all different ethnic and religious backgrounds the *Al Hanisim* ("for the miracles") prayer of Hanukkah and thinking of the significance of the words, "The few against the many...in those days and at this time."

(Tuvia Book)[10]

Film Clip Links to Enhance the Chapter

"In those Days and these Days" (*Al Hanisim*)
(6:00 min.)
In those days, Jews rose up to defend Judaism and the Jewish homeland and, in these days, we have the IDF, the "Modern Maccabees," who defend the Jewish people and homeland. Filmed by the author in the ancient Hasmonean synagogue in Modiin with a very special *Ḥanukkiah*.

https://www.youtube.com/watch?v=N-GAfNjFjVA

Hellenistic Sarcophagus depicting Greeks battling barbarians, Ashkelon, 2nd century BCE ↗

↗ Menora from the ancient Ein Gedi Synagogue mosaic floor, fifth century CE

HASMONEAN DYNASTY: CHRONOLOGY

	Hasmonean revolt renewed; Seleucid Empire in decline, with ongoing battles for succession	161–152 BCE
Jonathan	Jonathan appointed High Priest and governor of Judea by Alexander Balas	152–142 BCE
Simeon	Jonathan murdered by Tryphon but succeeded by Simeon, who declares independence	142–134 BCE
John Hyrcanus	Simeon and two sons murdered by his son-in-law Ptolemy. Simeon succeeded by son John Hyrcanus	134–104 BCE
Judah Aristobulus	John Hyrcanus dies a natural death and is succeeded by son Judah Aristobulus	104–103 BCE
Alexander Janneus	Judah Aristobulus kills one of his brothers but is succeeded by another, Alexander Janneus	103–76 BCE
Salome Alexandra	Alexander Janneus marries Judah Aristobulus's widow Salome Alexandra, who succeeds him	76–67 BCE
	Salome Alexandra rules effectively, but her two sons battle for succession	67–63 BCE
Aristobulus II (Pompey)	Salome Alexandra's younger son, Aristobulus II, wrests control from his brother Hyrcanus II; both ask Rome to mediate; Pompey invades, marking end of Jewish independence	63 BCE
Hyrcanus II	Hyrcanus II is ethnarch of Judea under Roman rule; Antipater and his two sons Phasael and Herod, descendants of Idumean converts, are powerful advisors	63–40 BCE
Mattathias Antigonus	Herod named king of Judea by Roman Senate; Mattathias Antigonus, son of Aristobulus II, allies with Parthians and wrests control of Judea	40–37 BCE
Herod	Herod, aided by Rome, defeats Mattathias Antigonus and rules Judea until his death	37–4 BCE

Chapter Three
The Hasmoneans
(164–63 BCE)

BROAD OUTLINE OF THE PERIOD

- In 142 BCE, Judea, under Simeon, became fully independent from Seleucid rule.
- John Hyrcanus (134–104 BCE) expanded Judea's borders to almost the size of David's kingdom.
- The Hasmonean kings pursued a policy of forced conversion to newly annexed territories.
- Hasmonean kings became gradually more Hellenized, but never denied the basic Jewish and theocratic character of their kingdom.
- Two sects became dominant in this period: the Sadducees, representing the conservative political establishment (including the high priesthood and the aristocracy), and the Pharisees, representing the wider general populace but lacking political power.
- In 63 BCE, as a result of the civil war between Hyrcanus II and Aristobulus II, the Roman general Pompey invaded Judea and effectively ended almost a century of Jewish independent rule.

ESSENTIAL QUESTIONS AND SUGGESTED ANSWERS

1. Why are the Hasmoneans so venerated, despite all of their flaws?

People are always nostalgic about the past and tend to talk about the "good old days" and forget all the bad. Jews remember that for a brief century during the Second Temple period Jews were ruled by Jews in the Jewish homeland. Myopically they forget the excesses of the Hasmonean dynasty such as fratricide and forced conversion, as well as the descent into becoming what they had sought to replace.

2. What would cause you to risk your life to fight for your religion like Judah and his brothers did? What, in your opinion, is worth fighting for?

Personally, I would risk my life to defend my country, my people, my religion, and my family. Judah and his brothers fought the world's first battle for religious freedom. They fought for the right to practice Judaism freely in the Jewish homeland and for the honor and dignity of Jews worldwide. These are causes I would also have fought for. Judah's deeds have continued to inspire generations of Jews. He was the archetypal selfless Jewish hero who fearlessly fought against seemingly impossible odds for the greater glory of God and the Jewish people.

3. What was the initial aim of the Hasmonean revolt? What was the ultimate result of the revolt?

The aim was to fight against both Hellenized Jews and the Hellenistic authorities and bring back pure monotheism to Judea. The result was the driving out of the Seleucids and the establishment of an independent Jewish state ruled by the Hasmoneans.

4. Why does Judah continue to be an inspirational figure in Jewish history?

Judah fought for what he believed in despite seemingly impossible odds. He was a selfless leader, who ultimately died for his beliefs. He believed that it is better to die free than live as a slave. His beliefs and heroism inspired his brothers and contemporary followers as much as it continues to inspire contemporary Jews. He didn't just "talk the talk" but he "walked the walk" and always led his forces from the front by personal example.

5. What do the names and coins of succeeding Hasmonean rulers reveal about their regime?

The names became increasingly Hellenized and the use of the titles the rulers gave themselves eventually went from the relatively benign to ethnarch (governor of the people) "King and High Priest." This reveals that the Hasmonean rulers ultimately morphed into what they had intended to replace. They in essence ignored the "checks and balances" of Judaism and held both spiritual and temporal titles. In addition, the king was only supposed to be from the House of David and the High Priest was supposed to be a descendant of Tzadok.

6. From the onset of their rule, what did the Hasmoneans do that alienated segments of the Jewish population?

They adopted Hellenistic names and practices and favored the priestly sect known as the Sadducees.

7. What were the results of the Hasmonean policies of forced conversion and territorial expansion?

Judea grew to the largest it had ever been territorially. However, the forced converts had an ambivalent attitude to Judaism at best.

8. Why is Salome Alexandra so lionized in traditional Jewish history? What were some of her achievements?

She was seen as a peacemaker between the Jewish sects. She elevated the status of the Pharisees that her husband Alexander Janneus had persecuted, and she did not go to war, but rather consolidated the Hasmonean territories. She is remembered as a moderate and wise ruler.

9. What led to the formation of different Jewish sects in Hasmonean Judea? Why do Jews always seem to belong to different "sects"? Discuss.

The formation of sects in Judea was caused by a polarization of the Jewish population. On the one hand there were the wealthy urban cosmopolitan Jews who lived in upper Jerusalem and were sympathetic to Hellenistic culture and led by the priestly sect, and on the other there were the poorer provincial Jews who lived largely in the countryside or lower Jerusalem, were more traditional, and were led by the rabbis. Jews always seem to belong to different sects or groups throughout our history for varying factors, whether the sects of the Second Temple period, or the Hasidim or Mitnagdim, Jewish Pre-State underground movements, or the different factions of Judaism today. It is never a good thing, as we tend to be our own worst enemies sometimes. We Jews need to respect what we have in common, not what divides us. United we stand and divided we fall.

10. Was the Hasmonean dynasty inherently doomed to failure? Why did the Hasmonean state ultimately collapse?

The Hasmonean dynasty was doomed to collapse due to a number of factors. These included:

a. Rome had recently annexed Syria to its empire, Judea was now on its land border. It was just a matter of time before the mighty Roman Empire sought to expand its territories.
b. The Hasmonean kingdom was embroiled in ever-increasing dynastic strife that culminated with the civil war between Salome Alexandra's two sons. The Hasmoneans suffered from the same evils as other dynasties, including the loss of group cohesiveness.
c. The Hasmoneans alienated vast chunks of the Jewish population with their inability to resolve the inherent tensions of syncretism. They were unable to function as Hellenistic-style warrior-kings and simultaneously represent the Jewish hopes for a more spiritual leadership.

There were tremendous internal tensions between the various sects of Jews that had developed during the Hasmonean regime. The Jews did not present a united front against foreign invasion.

Commentary on the Chapter Illustrations

Page 40

Hyrcania Hasmonean fortress, Judean Desert

This is one of a line of strategic palace fortresses on the eastern border with the Parthian Empire. Many of these fortresses, such as Masada, which were initially constructed by the Hasmonean rulers, were subsequently enlarged and beautified by Herod the Great (37–4 BCE). ▶

Page 44 ▲

Bronze prutah coin issued by King John Hyrcanus, 130 BCE

Obverse: Paleo-Hebrew inscription in wreath: "Yehohanan the High Priest and Council of the Jews." Reverse: Double cornucopia adorned with ribbons with a pomegranate between horns, borders of dots. Minted in Jerusalem.

Bronze prutah coin issued by Judah Aristobulus, 104 BCE

Judah Aristobulus was the first ruler of the Hasmonean dynasty to declare himself "king," and was the eldest of the five sons of John Hyrcanus, the previous leader. Obverse: Hebrew inscription in wreath: "Yehuda the High Priest and the Council of the Jews." Reverse: Double cornucopia adorned with ribbons with a pomegranate between horns. ▼

Page 45

Ruins of the Alexandrium (Sartaba) Hasmonean fortress, built by Alexander Janneus, in the Jordan Valley

This palace was named after his wife Salome Alexandria. This strategic fortress, like many Hasmonean palace-fortresses, was later enlarged by Herod the Great (37–4 BCE). ▼

Page 47

Bronze prutah coin issued by Alexander Janneus, 103 BCE

The reverse side inscription reads "Yehonatan the king" in Paleo-Hebrew between the rays of a star within a diadem. ▼

Bronze prutah coin issued by Alexander Janneus, 103 BCE

The obverse side inscription reads, ΑΛΕΞΑΝΔΡΟΥ ΒΑΣΙΛΕΩΣ (King Alexander) in Greek around an anchor. These coins caused huge controversy among the more traditional Pharisee Jews who believed that a king could only be appointed by a divinely inspired prophet. ▼

Page 50

Phylacteries (tefillin) from Qumran

These tefillin for the head were found by Yigal Yadin in the early 1960s in the caves near Qumran. They are from the time of the Bar Kokhba Revolt (132–136 CE). They illustrate the continuity of Judaism, where to this day similar head tefillin are donned. ▼

Page 51

Mikve at the Essene community in Qumran

Qumran, which is situated on the northwestern shore of the Dead Sea, was an ideal habitat for the separatist and ascetic community of Essene Jews who resided here in the first century BCE and the first century CE. As the sect practiced strict purity standards, mikvaot [ritual baths] were built, and remains of a number of mikvaot have been discovered at Qumran. The mikve was used for various purification rituals as prescribed in the Torah, especially in the book of Leviticus. Menstruation, sex, childbirth, contact with a corpse, skin disease, and performing animal sacrifice were all considered to be sources of impurity which would require immersion in a mikve to become ritually pure. Fresh water from nearby rivers was channeled into the mikve via aqueducts. ▶

Page 52

Qumran caves, where the Dead Sea Scrolls were hidden by the Essenes

This photograph is of Cave 4. It was in this cave that the most significant finds of the Dead Sea Scrolls were discovered. These include more than 15,000 scroll fragments from over 200 books. Of the eleven caves discovered at Qumran, there are sections from every book of the Tanakh (Hebrew Bible) apart from the book of Esther. In contrast, no New Testament books or fragments have been found. ◀

Page 53

Part of the Isaiah Scroll, written by the Essenes in the first century BCE in Qumran

Part of the Dead Sea Scrolls collection housed in the Shrine of the Book in Jerusalem. As no other Hebrew manuscripts of such antiquity exist, including all sixty-six chapters of the book of Isaiah, and because of both the known and hitherto unknown material they contain, the Dead Sea Scrolls have proved of immense importance for our understanding of the Judaism in the late Second Temple period.

▶

Page 54

Queen Salome Alexandra (76–67 BCE)

Illustration of Queen Salome Alexandra. Shulamit or Shlomzion was the archetypal good ruler. She was much loved by the later rabbinical authorities because, according to rabbinic tradition, she restored the supremacy of the Sages and placated the Pharisee sect. During her tenure upon the throne, Salome Alexandra presided over the nation's greatest period of peace and prosperity. She campaigned to interpret the Jewish religious laws and civil codes to give women greater rights. History is generally dominated by males. It is rare and significant to find inspirational female role models.

◀

Page 56

Contemporary bust of Gnaeus Pompeius Magnus - Pompey (106–48 BCE)

Gnaeus Pompeius Magnus was a military commander and political leader who served Rome up until the time he was assassinated in 48 BCE. He is known in history as Pompey. In the year 63 BCE, while still fighting, both Aristobulus II and Hyrcanus II went to the Roman General Pompey asking for aid. This proved to be a monumental error of judgment. Pompey backed Hyrcanus and ordered Aristobulus to give up his fortresses and arms, which he refused to do. Even though the supporters of Hyrcanus (the Pharisees) opened the gates of Jerusalem to the Romans, the Romans met determined resistance from Aristobulus's army, which was ensconced on the Temple Mount. Only after a bitter three-month battle did Pompey finally manage to subdue the defenders.

This marked the end of Judean independence and Judea became a Roman province. To add insult to injury, Pompey also callously, and with complete disregard to Jewish sensibilities, entered the Holy of Holies in the Temple, an act which shocked, upset, and outraged the Jews as only the High Priest could enter this space, and then only on Yom Kippur. ▼

Contemporary bust of Gaius Julius Caesar (100–44 BCE)

Caesar was positively disposed to the Jews, especially after Hyrcanus switched allegiance from Pompey and aided Caesar in the Roman civil war. Caesar showed the Jews his gratitude for their help. He revoked the harsh decrees and burdensome taxation imposed by Pompey. He also allowed the walls and fortifications of Jerusalem to be rebuilt and restored Jaffa, as well as a number of other coastal cities, to Jewish rule.
▼

Page 57

Menora from the ancient Ein Gedi Synagogue mosaic floor, fifth century CE

The synagogue at Ein Gedi stood from the third to the sixth century, during the period of Roman and Byzantine rule. For 1,500 years, until its accidental discovery in the 1970s, this synagogue floor was buried in the desert waiting to tell the story of the little village. The design is exquisite: a carpet of geometrically precise intersecting circles surrounds a lovely central mosaic square of exotic birds. At the northern end of the synagogue (facing Jerusalem) is a *bima* and a semicircular niche for storing the Torah scroll. Among the many archaeological finds discovered here was a scroll from the book of Leviticus and a bronze seven-branched menora. The northern end of the mosaic also features menora decorations symbolizing the yearning for redemption and a rebuilt Temple. ▼

Page 59 ▲

Hasmonean period oil lamp with coins of Alexander Janneus and John Hyrcanus

It adds a third tangible dimension when one can see the type of oil lamps used in the Hasmonean period and one can see the coins. It makes history more real when one has a visual reference.

Page 61

Hellenistic period columbarium, Beit Guvrin

Beit Guvrin national park is replete with eighty-five columbarium caves, once used for raising doves and still inhabited by many pigeons. The main columbarium is the most impressive of the Tel Maresha caves, dug in the third century BCE. Some two thousand nesting niches are carved into the columbarium, reflecting the ancient premium put on their meat, eggs, dung, and value as sacrificial offerings. It was abandoned together with the city, when most of the inhabitants fled as a result of the Hasmonean monarchs trying to force the population to convert to Judaism.
▼

Film Clip Links to Enhance the Chapter

Explore three desert fortresses of the Maccabees that can still be seen in Israel today:

Alexandrium/Sartaba
https://www.youtube.com/watch?v=QCeLg_nC4ek (1:31 min.)

Hyrcania
https://www.youtube.com/watch?v=7v9qR_EEE-AU&t=4s (1:08 min.)

Kypros
https://www.youtube.com/watch?v=LxOxBpRY29A (1:21 min.)

Mosaic from a Roman villa, comprised of twenty-eight different colors, Tzippori, 3rd century CE ↗

↗ Scythopolis, Beit She'an

ROMAN RULE OVER JUDEA: CHRONOLOGY

Roman Ruler	Roman Governor / Procurator of Judea	Jewish Ruler
Pompey and Triumvirate 63–49 BCE	57–55 BCE Gabinius	Hyrcanus II 63–40 BCE (Antipater 63–43 BCE)
Julius Caesar 49–44 BCE		
Mark Anthony 44–27 BCE		Mattathias Antigonus 40–37 BCE Herod the Great 37–4 BCE
Augustus 27 BCE–14 CE	6–10 CE Coponius 10–13 CE M. Ambivius 13–15 CE Annius Rufus	Herod Antipas, Tetrarch of Galilee and Perea 4 BCE–39 CE Herod Archelaus Ethnarch of Samaria, Judea, and Idumea 4 BCE–6 CE Herod Philip, Tetrarch of Iturea and Trachonitis 4 BCE–39 CE
Tiberius 14–37 CE	15–26 CE Valerius Gratus 26–36 CE Pontius Pilate 36–38 CE Marcellus	
Caligula 37–41 CE	38–41 CE Marullus	Herod Agrippa I 37–44 CE
Claudius 41–54 CE	44–46 CE Cuspius Fadus 46–48 CE Tiberius Alexander 48–52 CE Ventidius Cumanus 52–59 CE M. Antonius Felix	Herod Agrippa II Tetrarch of Iturea and Trachonitis; c. 56 CE also parts of Galilee and Perea 53–93 CE
Nero 54–68 CE	59–62 CE Porcius Festus 62–65 CE Albinus 65–66 CE Gessius Florus	
Galba 68–69 CE Otho 69 CE Vitellius 69 CE Vespasian 69–79 CE		

Chapter Four
Roman Rule: Herod and the Procurators (63 BCE–66 CE)

BROAD OUTLINE OF THE PERIOD

- **During the early period of Roman rule Jerusalem remained the focus for Jews in the Diaspora.**
- **Initially the Romans treated the Jews well and granted Jewish religious autonomy.**
- **Jews represented eight percent of the Roman Empire.**
- **In 37 BCE the Romans executed the last Hasmonean king, Antigonus II, and Herod was crowned king of Judea.**
- **After Herod's death in 4 BCE his kingdom was divided up between his sons. After 6 CE these lands came under direct Roman rule as the new province of Judea.**
- **In the decade leading up to the Great Revolt the Roman procurators seem to have deliberately trampled on Jewish religious feelings and imposed heavy taxes.**
- **In 66 CE the Jews rose up in revolt against Rome.**

ESSENTIAL QUESTIONS AND SUGGESTED ANSWERS

1. Describe Herod's achievements during his reign and describe Herod's personal life and the motivating factors behind his murderous actions.

Herod built many cities in Judea for the aggrandizement of Rome including Sebaste and Caesarea with its wondrous harbor. To ingratiate himself to the Jews, Herod rebuilt the Temple Mount and the Second Temple, the Jewish people's holiest and central institution, thereby creating one of the wonders of the ancient world. His personal life was chaotic. He divorced his first wife and married a Hasmonean princess to attempt to add an air of legitimacy to his reign. However, he was deeply paranoid and suspicious and ultimately murdered many of his own family members. Thus began a long spiral of murder and purging that would increase with Herod's own descent into the abyss of madness. The outward grandeur and prosperity of Herod's reign concealed the increasing turbulence of his private life.

2. Was a revolt inevitable once Judea came under direct Roman rule?

Revolt was inevitable once Judea came under direct Roman rule for several factors. These include the treatment by the inept and cruel Roman procurators, the increasingly polarized Jewish population, economic oppression, and religious humiliation.

3. Why were Mattathias Antigonus and Agrippa I so loved by the Jews?

Both Mattathias and Agrippa I were decedents of the much-loved Hasmonean dynasty. Both were charismatic and represented a halcyon period of Jewish self-rule and a freedom from the tyrannical Roman overlords.

4. Why was the Second Temple so important to the Jews throughout the world and in Judea?

The Second Temple was the physical and spiritual epicenter of the Jewish world. It was the location of the Divine Presence. Every Jew, wherever they lived, tried to "go up" to the Temple in their lifetime, especially during the three "Foot Festivals" of Passover, Shavuot, and Sukkot.

5. Who were the procurators, and what were their aims? What were the factors that made the Jewish masses antagonistic toward them?

The Procurator was a Roman official primarily responsible for law and order as well as financial matters of the province and was directly answerable to the emperor. His position was lucrative and sought after. The procurators became increasingly avaricious until the Jewish masses eventually broke and declared war on Rome and its procurators.

6. In your opinion, was war the only solution for the Jews?

There were various factors that led to the outbreak of war, such as economic oppression and religious humiliation. At that time, the Jews decided that they had to fight to remain free. While there are always other options, the Jews felt they had exhausted all of them and there was no other choice.

7. How does archaeology contribute to a clear picture of the rebuilt Second Temple and Herod's other major building projects? Provide examples.

Archaeology provides a clear picture of the rebuilt Second Temple. After the Six-Day War archaeologists uncovered much more than the small, exposed section of the western supporting wall. They uncovered the entire western, southern, and eastern walls of the Temple Mount as well as the street and Hulda Gates stairs and the blocked gates. In addition, the top section of the Western Wall had been thrown down on the street two millennia earlier by the soldiers of the Roman Tenth Legion. This too was uncovered.

Commentary on the Chapter Illustrations

Page 62

Scythopolis, Beit She'an ►

In the course of the excavations of Tel Beit She'an, remains of twenty strata/settlements were exposed, which date from the Neolithic/Chalcolithic periods (fifth to fourth millennium BCE) to the Byzantine period (seventh century CE). In the Bible it is mentioned as the place where the inhabitants displayed the bodies of King Saul and his sons until they were redeemed and buried by the men of Jabesh-Gilead:

> **When the men of Jabesh-Gilead heard about it, what the Philistines had done to Saul, all their stalwart men set out and marched all night. They removed the bodies of Saul and his sons from the wall of Beit She'an and came to Jabesh and burned them there. Then they took the bones and buried them under the tamarisk tree in Jabesh, and they fasted for seven days.**
>
> (I Samuel 31:8–13)

In the Hellenistic period, Beit She'an was renamed Scythopolis (city of the Scythians) and grew, extending southeast to Tel Itztaba. The city reached its maximum size and prosperity during the Roman-Byzantine period, when a new civic center was built in the valley southwest of the tel, surrounded by residential quarters; in the Byzantine period it was also fortified with a city wall. In the Early Arab period, Beit She'an-Scythopolis declined; it was destroyed by earthquake in 749 CE.

Page 64

Sardonyx cameo portrait of Augustus Caesar, c. 41–54 CE

Formally known as Octavian, Augustus Caesar was Julius Caesar's adopted great-nephew and nominated heir. Following the Battle of Actium in 31 BCE, where he defeated Mark Anthony, he consolidated his power. In 27 BCE he became Augustus Caesar, and is considered by many to have been the most successful of all the Roman emperors. He succeeded in expanding the Roman Empire and maintaining peace and prosperity. He died in 14 CE at the age of 75.

Following the Battle of Actium, Herod the Great switched his allegiance from Mark Anthony to Augustus. Herod constructed the large port city of Caesarea in honor of Augustus. ▼

Page 65

Bronze prutah coin issued by Mattathias Antigonus, 40–37 BCE

This coin was minted during the reign of the last Hasmonean ruler, Mattathias Antigonus. It has the quintessential Jewish motif of the Menora (with a triangular base) juxtaposed with a Greek text. It is symbolic of the attempts of the Hasmonean dynasty to try and harmonize (with different levels of success) these two very contradictory world views. ▼

Page 67

Marble bust of Augustus Caesar c. 14–37 CE

Augustus Caesar famously said of the murderous Herod, "I'd rather be Herod's pig than his son." Being a pig in Herod's household in Judea would have been much safer than being a family member. ▼

High Priest Aristobulus

In 35 BCE the handsome eighteen-year-old brother-in-law of Herod, the young High Priest Aristobulus III, "accidentally" drowned in the pool of Herod's palace in Jericho while "playing" with some of Herod's bodyguards. His death marked the end of potential Hasmonean takeover of Herod's throne.

At first they were only spectators of Herod's servants and acquaintances as they were swimming; but after a while, the young man, at the instigation of Herod, went into the water among them, while such of Herod's acquaintances as he had appointed to do it, dipped him as he was swimming, and plunged him under water, in the dark of the evening, as if it had been done in sport only; nor did they desist till he was entirely suffocated. And thus was Aristobulus murdered, having lived no more in all than eighteen years, and kept the high priesthood one year only; which high priesthood Ananelus now recovered again.

(Josephus)[11] ▼

Page 68

Decorated capital, Herodium

Upper Herodium was constructed over a small pre-existing hill; Herodium was a fortress for Herod to quickly flee to from Jerusalem and a luxurious palace for his enjoyment. This capital is one of the luxurious details, which also included colorful frescoes and mosaics, as well as a Roman style bathhouse. This is an example of "adaptation without assimilation" – the ability of the Jewish people to use the creative arts of the surrounding culture and synthesize, juxtapose, adapt, and incorporate Jewish symbols. ▼

Page 69

Herod's sarcophagus from Herodium

This sarcophagus was reconstructed from fragments by Israeli archaeologists after it was deliberately and systematically destroyed in antiquity, probably by Jewish rebels opposing the Romans. ▶

Page 70

The Second Temple, Holyland Hotel model at the Israel Museum, Jerusalem

This model is built on a 1:50 scale using the original building materials and topography of Jerusalem. It depicts Jerusalem in all its glory in the year 66 CE on the eve of the outbreak of the Great Revolt. The model is based on both contemporary written sources and archaeology. ▼

Page 71

Royal Stoa ceiling fragment

This is one of the few ceiling fragments found from the Royal Stoa that was on the top of the Temple Mount. Its design is comprised of geometric swastikas juxtaposed with flowers. It was found on the Herodian street near the Western Wall by Israeli archaeologists. ▼

Page 71

Second Temple facade, Holyland Hotel model

This recreation of the facade of the Second Temple is based on a Bar Kokhba tetradrachma coin which might have been designed by someone who saw the actual building. ▼

Page 72

Street from the Second Temple period adjacent to southern wall of the Temple

It is meaningful to walk on the same street our ancestors walked on two millennia ago on their way to the Temple. We are literally walking in their footsteps – links in the chain of Jewish continuity. ▼

Post-1967 archaeological excavations of the southern section of the Western Wall

It is one thing to say, "The Temple was destroyed on Tisha BeAv in the year 70 CE." It is quite another to see the physical remains of that destruction. To see the massive ashlar stones weighing many tons that were pushed down on the street by the Roman soldiers. What we see is Tisha BeAv in the year 70 CE frozen in time. ▶

Page 73 ▲

Southern steps of the Temple Mount leading to the Hulda Gates

The steps were designed to slow down the pilgrims and promote a sense of awe before entering the Temple compound itself. Every detail was thought of, both physically and religiously. The fact that mourners circulated clockwise allowed them to be recognized and comforted.

"Beit Hatkiyah" inscription

This inscription is from the southwest corner of the Temple Mount. It marks the place where a Levite would stand and blow the shofar to proclaim the imminent arrival of the Sabbath or a holiday. This tradition continues in Jerusalem to this day, where a siren sounds before the start of the Sabbath or a holiday to give Jerusalemites notice of the imminent arrival of the holy day and to finish their preparations. ▼

Page 74

"Ennion" glass jug

Ennion was a prominent glass artist in the ancient Near East, whose glassware was a luxury commodity that commanded high prices. The fact that a similar jug to this one was uncovered in post-1967 digs in the Jewish Quarter in the ruins of the "Priestly Mansion" attests to an opulent lifestyle enjoyed by the inhabitants of the mainly Sadducee Upper City of Jerusalem. ▼

Elegant tableware uncovered in excavations of the Upper City

This tableware was uncovered in post-1967 digs in the Jewish Quarter in the ruins of the Priestly Mansion. It attests to an opulent lifestyle enjoyed by the inhabitants of the mainly Sadducee Upper City of Jerusalem. ▼

Page 75

Pontius Pilate inscription, Caesarea

This is the only monumental inscription mentioning Pontius Pilate found in situ in Israel. It was found in secondary use in the Roman Theater in Caesarea. ▼

Page 76
Bronze prutah coin minted by Pilate in Jerusalem

This bronze prutah coin, minted during the rule of Pontius Pilate (30–32 CE), features the Pagan symbol of the *lituus* (augurs' wand used in pagan rituals). Pilate was the only Roman procurator who incorporated a pagan symbol on his coins. This lack of sensitivity to his Jewish subjects in Judea is symbolic of his deeply divisive rule. ▼

Bronze prutah coin minted by Herod Agrippa I in Jerusalem

Herod Agrippa was deeply loved by both the Jews and the Romans. If he had lived longer, the Great Revolt might not have occurred. This coin features wheat of the Land of Israel as a symbol of the prosperity of the land during his rule. ▼

Page 78

Ancient capital from Jericho

There are extensive archaeological remains of Herod's palace at Jericho, which is located in the Judean Desert, on the bank of Wadi Qelt, near the northern tip of the Dead Sea. He likely chose it because it is in the Judean Desert, so it is warm in the winter time, and because the Hasmonean kings had already built palaces and an infrastructure of water channels for bathhouses and spas. Herod constructed a royal villa complete with royal gardens and an Olympic-sized swimming pool. ▼

Page 79

Caesarea National Park

The construction of the glorious port city of Caesarea was the brainchild of Herod the Great. Built on the site of a dilapidated town, the new city was constructed between 22 and 10/9 BCE. In addition to building the largest artificial harbor in the Eastern Mediterranean, there was a temple, theaters, bathhouses, and a sewer system. The city was named Caesarea after the Augustus Caesar who was the Roman emperor. ▼

Page 81

"He who never saw the building of Herod never saw a beautiful building" (Bava Batra 4a)

They said: He who never saw the Building of Herod never saw a beautiful building. With what did he build it? With stones of alabaster and marble. Some say with stones of alabaster, stibnite, and marble. One row went in and one went out so that it could be plastered. He [Herod] thought of covering it with gold. The Sages said to him, "Leave it alone, as it is more beautiful thus, as it looks like the waves of water."

(Bava Batra 4a)

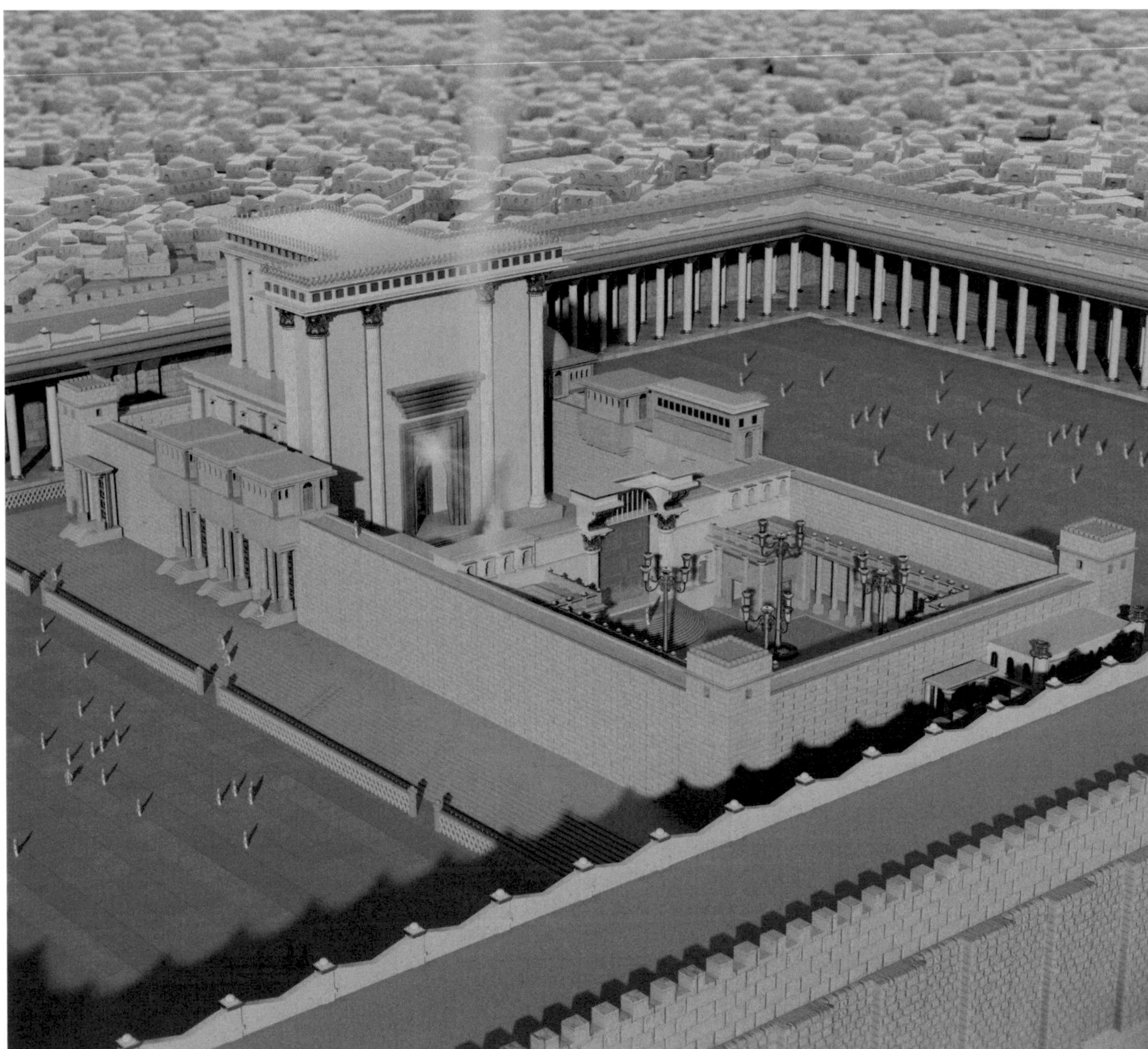

Page 83

Herodium from the air

The Herodium, a mountain fortress palace built by King Herod, was also the king's burial site. Herod's tomb was discovered in 2007 by the Israeli archaeologist Ehud Netzer. Herod built the fortress by first erecting a double-walled cylinder, which had an outer diameter of 200 feet (60 meters). He then created a massive landfill of earth and gravel surrounding the cylinder. The archaeological remains indicate that the cylinder was seven stories high, although the top two or three stories cannot be seen today. In addition, Herod constructed four towers at the corresponding points of the compass.

Film Clip Links to Enhance the Chapter

The Temple from Destruction to Rebirth – 70–1967 CE (4:36 min.)
Filmed by the author on the location of the archaeological remains of Herod's Second Temple. Understand what remains and how significant this site is to Jews both then and now.

https://www.youtube.com/watch?v=HQN5_Khhb10

↗ Gamla Synagogue ruins, first century CE

THE GREAT REVOLT: CHRONOLOGY

Jews of Judea rise up in revolt against Rome	66 CE
Fall of Jotapata, Gamla, and the Galilee	67 CE
Rome in turmoil after Nero's suicide – Year of the Four Emperors	68–69 CE
Vespasian elected Emperor	69 CE
Vespasian's son Titus destroys Jerusalem and the Second Temple	70 CE
Final rebel outpost of Masada falls	73 CE

Chapter Five The Great Revolt (66–73 CE)

BROAD OUTLINE OF THE PERIOD

- In 66 CE, after decades of Roman misrule, the Jews rose in revolt against Rome. While there were both spiritual and mundane reasons for the revolt, the direct sparks that led to it were the excesses of the last procurator, Florus, and Nero's anti-Jewish decrees.
- Within a year, despite initial Jewish successes, Nero's Roman legions commanded by Vespasian had overrun most of the country north of Jerusalem.
- A hiatus in the fighting followed, due to a succession crisis in Rome. During this time the Jewish factions battled among themselves.
- In 69 CE the attack on Jerusalem resumed under Titus, the son of Vespasian, and culminated with the destruction of Jerusalem and the Temple in 70 CE.
- In 73 CE the final rebel outpost of Masada fell, effectively ending Jewish independence in the land until 1948, with the brief exception of the period of the Bar Kokhba Revolt (132–135/6 CE).

ESSENTIAL QUESTIONS AND SUGGESTED ANSWERS

1. What were the goals of the Pharisees, Sadducees, Essenes, and Zealots?

Although the goals of the four sects were the same, that is, the establishment of a just Jewish regime in Judea, they differed sharply on the tactics for fighting the Romans.

2. What tactics did they promote to achieve these goals?

The Sadducees would have probably been prepared to cooperate with the Romans and work out a compromise solution; the Pharisees promoted non-violent protest; the Essenes preferred to isolate themselves; and the Fourth Philosophy/Zealots advocated military overthrow of the evil Roman regime.

3. Why was the lack of a unified approach fatal in the Jewish struggle against the Roman regime in Judea?

The various sects and leaders who held the different parts of Jerusalem had a two-year lull in fighting against the Romans which they failed to take advantage of between 68–70 CE. Rather than unite against a common enemy, they used that time to kill each other and burn each other's surplus food stocks. By the time the Roman army resumed its offensive they faced a severely depleted Jewish force. United we stand, divided we fall.

4. What was the Fourth Philosophy?

The Zealots were the militant activist wing of the Pharisee faction. These Zealots are sometimes referred to as the Fourth Philosophy, after Josephus's description, and comprised disparate groups, including the notorious Sicarii.

5. Why did Masada become a powerful symbol for the early Zionists?

According to Yael Zerubavel, Masada became such a powerful symbol for early Zionists because it represents Zion and it symbolizes the broken link between the people and the land, which exile introduced.

6. Based on the evidence, do you think the mass suicide happened the way Josephus describes it?

Based on the archaeological evidence of the remains of the family group found in the lower palace, the bodies found in the cave under the southern wall, and the ostracon with the name of Ben Yair, together with parts of the Western Palace that had been clearly burned and the remains of food found in the store houses, it appears that there is overwhelming archaeological evidence to support Josephus's narrative of the mass suicide.

7. In your opinion, were the Jews justified in revolting against Rome? Did they really think that they could win?

The Jews at the time were fighting for an idea. It is better to die as free men than to live as slaves. In Judaism it is not just the way that one lives, but also how one dies that speaks volumes about the person.

8. What is your opinion of Josephus?

There is an opinion that Josephus as a person was clearly a despicable self-serving turncoat. However, as a historian he was a master of his genre. His narrative is incredibly accurate and insightful, as long as it was not about him personally.

9. Why was the Roman military campaign delayed for two years? What were the Jewish defenders of Jerusalem doing during this period?

In 68 CE Nero committed suicide, and in the next year, known as the Year of the Four Emperors, Rome was plunged into civil strife. In quick succession, three rulers (Galba 68–69 CE, Otho 69 CE, and Vitellius 69 CE) succeeded Nero. Each was assassinated after a few months in office. Vespasian's soldiers and supporters made a case that Vespasian, himself a highly decorated, popular, and honored general, had more right to take up the leadership of the Roman Empire than did Vitellius. Vespasian realized that he would have to suspend the final siege on Jerusalem, leave Judea, and personally travel to fight for his position. By the time Titus resumed the offensive on Jerusalem, in the spring of 70 CE, two years had elapsed since it had been suspended.

10. Why did the defenders of Masada carry on fighting when the Romans seemed invincible?

To paraphrase the fighters of a similarly seemingly hopeless revolt against a far larger enemy, the fighters of the Warsaw Ghetto Revolt in 1943 said that they were fighting for "three lines in a history book." Both groups of Jews know that their actions would ultimately lead to military defeat, but they were fighting for an idea. It is better to die as free men than to live as slaves.

Commentary on the Chapter Illustrations

Page 84

Gamla Synagogue ruins, first century CE

Gamla Synagogue is one of the earliest synagogues uncovered in the Land of Israel. It was built while the Second Temple was still standing. It features stone benches around the walls and beautifully finished masonry carved out of the local basalt stone. There is a mikve adjacent to the structure and a small room that apparently housed the Torah. The many Ballista stones found in the synagogue, which was built next to the city's wall, attest to the ferocity of the fighting.

Page 86

Bronze sestertius Vespasian coin, 71 CE

This coin was minted in 71 CE. On the obverse side is the head of Vespasian, the Roman ruler during this period, together with a Latin inscription of his titles. The reverse side depicts a Jewish woman mourning under a palm tree, with a Roman solider standing on the other side, and the inscription *Judaea Capta.*

This bronze sestertius coin is part of the *Judaea Capta* series that was minted to commemorate the Roman Empire's victory over the Jewish rebels and the destruction of the Temple in Jerusalem. While there are a number of different images depicted on the reverse side of these coins, the image here is the one most frequently found. It depicts a woman in mourning, seated on the right-hand side of a palm tree. The woman is believed to represent Jerusalem, and the palm tree is said to represent Judea. On the left-hand side of the palm tree is the image of a Roman soldier standing in a victorious pose. The legend *Judaea Capta* ["captured Judea"] is inscribed around the image and is said to indicate that the "barbarian" province has been subdued by Rome's civilizing forces and that the Jewish population is now subjected to *Pax Romana.*

▼

Page 88

Roof tile with the stamp of the Tenth Legion (LEG X FR) and the symbols of a wild boar and a ship

The symbols of the Roman Tenth Legion that fought in Judea were a wild boar and a ship. The first of these symbols was deeply offensive to the majority of the Jewish population of Judea. ▼

Page 89

Roman legionary

This well armed and disciplined legionary is illustrative of the forces that were arrayed against the Jews.

▼

Page 90

Gamla with defense wall and synagogue in the foreground

It is possible to see the heavily fortified and thick wall built on the Achilles heel of Gamla, the eastern approach. The rest of the city has the natural defenses provided by the steep ravines on the other sides. Despite the best attempts by the defenders to hold their city, after a ferocious siege and battle lasting weeks, the sheer weight of forces and engineering superiority of the Romans ensured that they ultimately prevailed. ▶

Page 93

Silver tetradrachma Revolt coin

The Revolt coins were minted form the silver of the Temple treasury and remind the Jews of what they were fighting for – the holy city of Jerusalem. These coins were intrinsically a form of propaganda proclaiming that the Jews of Judea wanted the independence to practice their religion in their land. The pomegranates were symbols of the Land of Israel, and the chalice was a symbol of the Temple service. These Revolt coins were minted for each year of the revolt. There are even a few examples of the rare "year five" coins from the last year of the revolt. ▼

Page 95

The Roman destruction of Jerusalem, Painting by David Roberts, 1850

This artist's depiction of the siege of Jerusalem in 70 CE was painted by the British artist David Roberts in 1850. Roberts, who was a member of the Royal Academy, used Josephus's account of the Roman siege and destruction of Jerusalem as his guide in creating this work.

The original oil-on-canvas painting, measuring 12 x 7 feet (3.66 x 2.13 meters), won great critical acclaim, with many critics and collectors considering it to be Roberts's finest work. Unfortunately, the original painting was lost, and we are only able to view it from lithographs copied before it went missing. ▼

Page 97

Mosaic floor and stone table

The beautiful mosaics on Masada were designed by Jewish artisans and only contain geometric and floral images. They are illustrative of the concept of "adaptation without assimilation." This is the idea that the Jews incorporated the good features of the outside world but did not fully assimilate. ▼

Page 98

Northern end of Masada showing Herod's hanging palace

Herod's engineers carved three "steps" out of the northern end of the mountain and built a retaining wall under the lowest tier, which, in addition to a palace, also contains a private bathhouse. ▼

"The Three Paratroopers of 1967"

The illustration is based on the famous David Rubinger photograph of three paratroopers standing in silent awe in front of the recaptured Western Wall after the battle for Jerusalem in 1967. The photograph has become the defining image of one of the most significant moments in Israel's history. The picture encapsulated the moment shared by Israelis and Jews across the world who had for over two millennia dreamed of one day reuniting Jerusalem and restoring Jewish sovereignty. ▶

Page 100

Fresco and columns at Lower Northern Hanging Palace, Masada

The frescoes on Masada were made by applying paint onto wet plaster. As the plaster dried it absorbed the paint. This explains why the colors are almost as fresh today as when they were applied over two millennia ago. ▶

Page 101

Mosaic floor, Western Palace, Masada

This multicolored geometric designed floor is a typical example of Herod's construction. Many scholars believe that Herod chose not to use images of animals, people, or gods in his mosaics, out of respect for the Jewish population who believed that doing so would violate the commandment against making images. Mosaic work is an example of "adaptation without assimilation," in that the Jewish population adapted artistic techniques of the surrounding cultures, but made sure to incorporate their own Jewish symbols and not violate the Torah laws. ▶

The mosaic is located in the private bathhouse in the Western Palace of Masada. The structures on the corners, just visible in the photograph, were built over the mosaic by Jewish rebels during the Great Revolt. Concern about damaging something of such beauty was not at the forefront of the rebels' minds when building these structures.

Page 102

Masada defenders' remains are reburied with full IDF honors

During archaeological excavations of Masada, the remains of twenty-seven warriors who were believed to have defended the fortress were uncovered. In 1969, they were buried in a ceremony, with full military honors, in a small grotto at the foot of Masada. The service was conducted by the Chief Rabbi of the IDF, General Shlomo Goren, and attended by Israeli cabinet ministers and senior members of the armed forces. ▶

Page 103

Young woman's braided hair found in situ in the lower level of the "Hanging Palace," Masada

This beautifully braided hair, belonging to a woman in her early twenties, was found in situ in the private bathhouse of Herod's lowest hanging palace on Masada. It was found together with the skeleton of the woman, a young man, also in his twenties, and a child. The man's armor and arrows, with their wooden shafts still attached, and leather sandals belonging to the woman and child were all found together in a family group. These remains would seem to attest to the accuracy of the suicide narrative of Josephus. ▼

Youth group ascending the Roman siege ramp at Masada

Climbing to the summit of Masada has been a rite of passage for many Jewish youth both in the pre-independence era and even more since the establishment of the State of Israel. Whatever the time period, it provides a connection to the first century CE Jews who fought against the Roman occupation of their country. Today there are two walking routes to the fortress. The photograph shows visitors climbing the steep Rampart Path, which is on the western side of the site. This path can be climbed in approximately 15 minutes. ▼

Page 104

Yigal Yadin – archaeologist, soldier, and politician

▼ Between 1963 and 1965 Yigal Yadin led an excavation of Masada, overcoming the many difficulties in the excavation of such a site. His book *Masada: Herod's Fortress and the Zealots' Last Stand*, published in 1966, appeared in a variety of languages. His ability to impart his knowledge and theories to such a wide and varied readership is a talent that many educators would like to emulate in communicating with their students.

Page 105

Judaea Capta coin minted in 80 CE

This coin, minted after the suppression of the Great Revolt, depicts a palm tree symbolizing Judea. On one side of the tree is a triumphant Roman soldier, on the other, a weeping Jewish woman representing the fate of the defeated Jews. ▼

Israel Liberata coin

This coin, minted in 1958, also depicts a palm tree. The Roman soldier, like the empire he fought for, has vanished. In his place the Jewish woman now stands triumphant holding a baby in the air, representing the rebirth of the Jewish people. Her husband is planting a new sapling symbolizing the rebirth of a once barren land. ▼

Page 106

Gamla

Gamla is located in the Golan Heights, and is bordered on all sides by deep wadis with only one approachable footpath. During the Great Revolt of 66 CE, Gamla was famous for its spirited defense against the Roman forces.

The earliest settlement of the site is said to date from the Early Bronze Age. The site was reinhabited by exiles returning from Babylon, and later Herod the Great settled Jews here as part of his policy of populating his border cities.

Gamla is often known as "Masada of the North." ▼

Page 107

Gamla: Defense wall, tower, and synagogue

Gamla's natural defenses meant that only the eastern side needed to be protected against invading forces. In 66 CE this wall was fortified by the Jewish rebels defending Gamla against the Roman forces who were advancing across the Galilee. Led by the Roman general, Vespasian, three Roman legions attacked the city and a month later they succeeded in penetrating the city's defenses. The Jewish fighters managed to repel the Romans, who subsequently withdrew. However, a second Roman attack, a few days later, led to the Romans capturing the city. According to Josephus, nine thousand Jewish lives were lost in the fighting.

The synagogue, dated to the first century CE, is one of the earliest known in Israel. It was built near the entrance to the city in the "Galilean style" that featured three rows of columns, tiers of side benches, and heart-shaped corner pillars. There was also an alcove for Torah scrolls in the northwestern corner. Remains of a mikve [ritual bath] have been found near the synagogue. ▼

Page 109

Masada from the south, as seen from Mount Elazar ▶

In this view of Masada, seen from the Roman camp on the adjacent Mount Elazar, opposite the southern side of the fortress, it is possible to see the caves under the southern defensive walls. In one of these caves, archaeologists found the remains of over twenty bodies, with clothing fragments, from the Second Temple period. These could possibly be the remains of some of Masada's last defenders. These remains were buried with full IDF honors.

Page 111

IDF soldiers in modern-day Israel learning about Israel's past in front of the ruins of old Jerusalem

◀ Andrea Bronfman founded a program for combat soldiers called *Tarbut Yom Aleph* (Sunday Culture). The idea of this program is that IDF soldiers visit a site of historical, religious, or natural beauty before returning to their base after weekend leave. The aim is to instill in the soldiers a love of their heritage and what they are fighting to preserve. In this photograph a group of soldiers from the Givati Brigade are participating in a *Tarbut Yom Aleph* session in front of remains from the First Temple period in area G, in the City of David, Jerusalem.

Page 114

Masada from the air

Masada's summit is 190 feet (58 meters) above sea level, and approximately 1,500 feet (460 meters) above the level of the Dead Sea. The mountain is 1,950 feet (600 meters) long, 650 feet (200 meters) wide, and its circumference is 4,250 feet (1,330 meters). ▶

Page 115

Capital from synagogue at Kfar Nahum (Capernaum) depicting ritual objects used in the Temple, third century CE

This capital is from the synagogue at Kfar Nahum and depicts three Jewish motifs: a seven-branch Menora, an incense shovel, and a shofar. Also depicted on the capital are Corinthian acanthus leaves.

The Menora was a common motif decorating ancient synagogues, and was depicted on capitals, lintels, and mosaic floors. As a ritual object associated with both the Temple and the earlier Tabernacle, it is believed to have symbolized the yearning of the Jewish community for the Temple, and is an example of "adaptation without assimilation." ▼

Film Clip Links to Enhance the Chapter

The Qumran Revolt Coin (4:36 min.)
Presenting a very special "For the Freedom of Zion" coin from the second year of the Great Revolt against Rome (68 CE) at the site of Qumran in the Judean Desert.
https://www.youtube.com/watch?v=EofNOwhnDIM

Masada and the Secrets of Jewish Survival (1:38 min.)
The three secrets of Jewish survival are discussed on location on Masada with eleventh grade students from Australia.
https://www.youtube.com/watch?v=BNom6bke9wU

The Tale of Two Coins (3:13 min.)
Standing on top of Mount Elazar next to the ruins of the Roman camp overlooking Masada from the south, the author looks at a very special coin which conveys the message of Masada.

https://www.youtube.com/watch?v=F-6SJPZaQvw

↗ Mount Meron Synagogue, third century CE

THE YAVNEH REVOLUTION: CHRONOLOGY

Second Temple destroyed	70 CE
Rabban Yohanan ben Zakkai establishes Yavneh	c. 80 CE
Rabban Gamliel II *nasi* at Yavneh	c. 80–120 CE
Outbreak of the Bar Kokhba Revolt	132 CE

Chapter Six
The Yavneh Revolution
(70–132 CE)

BROAD OUTLINE OF THE PERIOD

- In 70 CE, after a protracted siege, the Second Temple fell to the Romans.
- During the siege of Jerusalem, a leader of the Pharisees, Rabban Yohanan ben Zakkai, obtained permission from the Romans to establish a non-political academy in the southern coastal town of Yavneh.
- The academy replaced the Sanhedrin as the body responsible for administering Jewish law and as the center of Jewish life over the next two generations. It produced some of the most famous rabbis in Jewish history.
- The main preoccupation of the leadership was to keep Judaism alive without the political entity of the state and without control of Jerusalem or a Temple, and to consolidate their national life on new foundations.
- The belief in the return to Jerusalem, the future renewal of the Temple, and a return to independent Jewish life in the Land of Israel, coupled with a belief and yearning for the imminent coming of the Messiah, became central features in the lives of Jews.

ESSENTIAL QUESTIONS AND SUGGESTED ANSWERS

1. Has Judaism ever been in a crisis similar to that which it faced after the destruction of the Second Temple, and if so, how was it overcome?

After the destruction of the First Temple, Judaism was in a similar crisis, having lost its institutions in one fell swoop. However, the Jews exiled in Babylon heeded the advice of Jeremiah to "Build houses and settle down; plant gardens and eat what they produce. Marry and have sons and daughters; find wives for your sons and give your daughters in marriage, so that they too may have sons and daughters. Increase in number there; do not decrease. Also, seek the peace and prosperity of the city to which I have carried you into exile. Pray to the Lord for it, because if it prospers, you too will prosper" (Jeremiah 29:4–7).

2. What were the major institutions lost with the destruction, and how did Judaism replace them?

The Temple and its rituals were replaced with the synagogue and prayer. The priesthood was replaced by the Sages. The Sanhedrin was replaced by the *beit din*. The loss of national self-determination in Judea and Jerusalem was replaced by the Jewish authorities creating conditions for a continued national life without Jerusalem and the Temple. Jews would continue to "remember the Temple" and pray and hope for their eventual redemption and return to the land.

3. What was the significance of the synagogue in the new reality facing the Jews?

The synagogue became the main public religious institution that fulfilled certain functions of the Temple in each Jewish community. Synagogues began to acquire an increased centrality in Jewish life. As they served as a center of meeting and of prayer, they became the spiritual, social, and educational focal point for the community.

4. What methods did the Sanhedrin at Yavneh use to continue the hegemony of the Land of Israel?

By establishing a central *beit din* in Yavneh, Rabban Yohanan ben Zakkai maintained the Land of Israel as the center of the Jewish people and preserved ultimate authority in matters of halakha (Jewish law) there.

5. How effective were the *takkanot* of Rabban Yohanan ben Zakkai in helping the Jews adapt to the new reality?

The rulings of Rabban Yohanan ben Zakkai recognized the new reality of a post-Temple Jewish world. These rulings can be divided into two categories: those that were designed to keep the memory of the Temple alive, and those that were instituted to adjust to the lack of a Temple.

6. In your opinion, was Rabban Gamliel's autocratic rule a necessity for Jewish survival?

Rabban Gamliel's autocratic rule was necessary as he was trying to establish the authority of the *nasi* and bring order to the calendar, which would lead to unity in the Jewish world regarding observance and customs. In such circumstances it is possible to accept why Rabban Gamliel's autocratic rule was necessary for that time and that place.

7. What does the talmudic text from Ketubot 110b teach us about our connection to the Land of Israel? In light of this text, some assert that it is hypocritical for observant Jews to live outside of Israel; do you agree or disagree with this idea?

Jews were commanded by their spiritual leaders to yearn and hope for a return to a rebuilt Zion. The Sanhedrin continued to ardently stress the religious importance of the Land of Israel and the importance of settling it. Jews were constantly reminded of this ideal in the customs, liturgy, and legal codes developed in Yavneh. Today, Diaspora Jews who are Jewishly affiliated, and especially those who are religiously observant, usually prefer to live in largely Jewish neighborhoods. They continue to "yearn for Zion" even though the State of Israel has been a reality for over seven decades. Rabbi Kook referred to the times we live in as "the beginning of the messianic redemption." I believe that only when we Jews practice what we preach and fully return to Zion will there ever be a full redemption.

Commentary on the Chapter Illustrations

Page 116

Mount Meron Synagogue, third century CE

Only the partially reconstructed facade of this synagogue from the third century CE remains. It is near the traditional burial site of Rabbi Shimon Bar Yohai, who is attributed to being the composer of the mystical Zohar. The door of early synagogues faced Jerusalem as the Torah ark was not a permanent feature and only rolled in for the services. ▼

Page 118

Bronze batillum (incense shovel), late first to early second century CE

This is a Roman incense shovel from the first century CE, found in the Bar Kokhba caves. It is similar in appearance to those used in the Second Temple and is often depicted on early synagogue mosaic floors because of its association with Temple ritual. ▼

Page 119

"Shir Hama'alot"

A graphic depicting the Second Temple facade with modern buildings of Jerusalem and quotes from Psalm 128.

Psalm 128

A Song of Ascents.

1 Blessed is everyone who fears the Lord,
who walks in His ways.
2 For you shall eat the fruit of the labor
of your hands;
you will be happy,
and it shall be well with you.
3 Your wife shall be as a fruitful vine
in your house,
your children like olive shoots
around your table.
4 Behold, this man shall be blessed
who fears the Lord.
5 The Lord shall bless you from Zion,
and may you see the welfare of Jerusalem
all the days of your life.
6 Indeed, may you see your children's children.
Peace upon Israel! ▼

Page 121

Mosaic floor from the Ein Gedi synagogue

This third century CE synagogue floor contains a carpet mosaic, depictions of birds, and menoras. The inscriptions mention a curse on anyone who gives away the secret of the community (the ingredients of its world-famous perfume). ▼

Page 123

Tel Yavneh

The Bible and other historic sources contain numerous references to ancient Yavneh, which is considered one of the most important cities in the plains of the Sharon. It is located where the Via Maris crosses the Sorek Stream. It was named Yamnia by the ancient Greeks.

Following the destruction of Jerusalem, Yavneh became a religious and administrative center for the Jewish population, under the leadership of Rabban Yohanan ben Zakkai and Rabban Gamliel. The center of the old city was located at Tel Yavneh.

After Israel's independence in 1948, the modern city of Yavneh was constructed on the western side of Tel Yavneh. ▼

Page 124

Bowl fragments

This fourth-century CE Jewish glassware depicts two menoras, similar to the Menora of the Temple, flanking an ark with Torah scrolls inside. ▶

Page 125

Mosaic floor from the Hammat Tiberias Synagogue

The mosaic floor from the fourth century CE Hammat Tiberias Synagogue depicts a curtained ark in the center that is flanked on either side by a menora, a shofar, an incense shovel, and a lulav and etrog. The central panel of this synagogue floor contains a zodiac circle complete with a representation of the sun god Helios. ▼

Page 127

Limestone decorative fragment, Kfar Nahum Synagogue

Decorative fragment depicting a Star of David. This is part of the facade of the third century CE synagogue at Capernaum/Kfar Nahum on the northern shore of the Sea of Galilee. While there are numerous Jewish symbols on the facade, this is not one of them. It was simply a pleasing geometric symbol with no Jewish connotation until the sixteenth century, when it was used by the Jewish community of Prague on its communal flag. ▼

Page 128

Facade of Kfar Baram Synagogue, third century CE

Built in c. 220 CE, probably in honor of Rabbi Shimon bar Yohai, the architecture of the Kfar Baram synagogue is very similar to other synagogues constructed in the Galilee during this period. The synagogue is constructed from basalt stone, which was a common material for building in this area. The front entrance of the synagogue incorporates three doorways that face Jerusalem. In addition, there are eight columns with Attic bases that probably supported a porch. A winged Victory and images of animals are depicted on a carved frieze above the center of the entrance to the synagogue. ▼

Page 130

Limestone decorative fragment, Kfar Nahum

This is part of the facade of the third century CE synagogue at Capernaum/Kfar Nahum on the northern shore of the Sea of Galilee. It depicts a portable Torah ark on wheels. Until the fourth century CE the ark was not a permanent feature and was only rolled in for use in prayer services. This mosaic is illustrative of the concept of "adaptation without assimilation," whereby the Jews incorporated concepts of the outside world into their Judaism and even into synagogue design, but they did not fully assimilate. ▼

Film Clip Links to Enhance the Chapter

"Teach Your Children Well" (4:04 min.)
Tour Tel Gezer with an emphasis on the importance of Jewish education and literacy. It was these concepts that the Sages of the Yavneh Revolution were so devoted to preserving and championing in order to ensure Jewish continuity.
https://www.youtube.com/watch?v=3RkWUU_sYDk

↗ Remains of Bar Kokhba's warriors receiving a full state military burial at Nahal Hever

THE BAR KOKHBA REVOLT: CHRONOLOGY

Diaspora Revolt	**115–117 CE**
Hadrian's reign	**117–138 CE**
Hadrian proposes building a temple to Jupiter on the Temple Mount and bans circumcision	**130 CE**
Outbreak of the Bar Kokhba Revolt	**132 CE**
Fall of Beitar and the end of the revolt	**135–136 CE**

Chapter Seven
The Bar Kokhba Revolt
(132–135/36 CE)

BROAD OUTLINE OF THE PERIOD

- In 117 CE the two-year Diaspora Revolt was brutally crushed by Trajan.
- In 117 CE Hadrian succeeded Trajan and initiated extensive building throughout the Roman Empire.
- In 130 CE he proposed building a temple to Jupiter on the Temple Mount and banned circumcision. These actions, among others, provoked the Jews to take up arms against the Romans in 132 CE.
- Rabbi Akiva, a leading figure of the day, is said to have had a role in the rebellion and to have anointed the Jewish general of the uprising, Simeon Bar Kokhba, as the people's messianic hope.
- By 135 or 136 CE this third and last revolt, known as the Bar Kokhba Revolt, had been crushed in a brutal manner, with great devastation and loss of life.
- After the revolt, the Romans took steps to prevent another uprising by the Jews. Hadrian introduced a set of restrictions on the practice of Judaism, imposed a heavy tax, and renamed Judea "Syria-Palestina."
- The Galilee now became the center of the Jewish people in the Land of Israel, a fact that was to prove crucial to the survival of the Jewish people and of Judaism.

ESSENTIAL QUESTIONS AND SUGGESTED ANSWERS

1. What were the reasons for the revolt?

Hadrian's plan to rebuild Jerusalem as a pagan city complete with a temple to Jupiter on the Temple Mount together with his plan to ban circumcision were reasons for the revolt.

2. With the knowledge gained through hindsight and in view of the disastrous consequences, do you feel Bar Kokhba was justified in revolting against the seemingly invincible Roman army?

Personally, I do. There comes a time when one must stand up and fight. The story of the Bar Kokhba Revolt was deeply symbolic. It came to symbolize the hope that as the Jews returned to their homeland, they would be able to regain their honor by reclaiming their land, their language, and their ability to defend themselves. It inspired future generations in the long, dark night of exile and continues to inspire our Zionist youth to this day. It is not just how one lives but also how one dies that is a mark of our eternity.

3. Why were the Sages after the revolt so intent on "demilitarizing" Judaism, and what effect did this have on the collective Jewish memory of the revolt?

The Sages believed that if the Jews continued to revolt against overwhelmingly superior military forces, then the Jewish people would be annihilated. One way to do this was to suppress mention of the revolt except in texts that were critical of the revolt, leading to an extremely biased and distorted one-sided collective Jewish memory.

4. Why did Rabbi Akiva and other eminent Sages continue teaching the Torah after the unsuccessful conclusion of the war, despite being under the threat of death if caught?

They felt that Jews could not abandon the thing that gave Judaism life, the Torah itself.

5. Was Rabbi Akiva, in his position of the preeminent Judean Sage, acting irresponsibly in declaring Bar Kokhba to be the Messiah?

In my opinion, he wasn't. He generally believed that Bar Kokhba had the potential to be the Messiah and threw his whole weight behind what he believed in.

6. Why did the Romans react with such force to the revolt?

The Roman response to the Bar Kokhba Revolt was swift and brutally efficient, with disastrous consequences for the Jewish defenders. Hadrian knew that if one Roman province fell it would cause a domino effect and would motivate other provinces to rise in revolt.

7. How do you think the Jews managed to circumvent Hadrian's decrees?

The Jews managed to circumvent Hadrian's decrees by creatively having alternative options, such as reading the *haftara* instead of the Torah reading, and saying the second line of the *Shema* in silence.

8. Why were the early Zionists so intent on embracing the Bar Kokhba story?

In contrast to the tendency of the rabbinic tradition to gloss over the revolt, early Zionists eagerly seized on the story as proof that Jews, when faced with persecution, were capable of fighting for their dignity and self-respect.

9. How has archaeology enriched our knowledge of this period?

Fortunately for archaeologists, the dry air of the Judean Desert preserved perishable organic materials such as leather sandals and papyrus documents. Yigal Yadin and his team uncovered a wide range of artifacts that shed light on everyday Jewish life during the Roman period. The most outstanding finds were papyrus and wooden documents written or dictated by Bar Kokhba himself.

Commentary on the Chapter Illustrations

Page 132

Remains of Bar Kokhba's warriors receiving a full state military burial at Nahal Hever

Reburying remains of Bar Kokhba's warriors. The symbolic significance of the last warriors of a free independent Jewish state in the Land of Israel being buried by the new defenders of the Jewish homeland, the IDF, almost two millennia later is palpable. ▶

Page 134

Weight from the Bar Kokhba administration

The inscription reads," Simeon son of Kosba Prince of Israel and his administrator half," showing the attempt to set up a civil administration after the initial military triumph over the Roman military forces in the region. ▼

Page 135

Map of the Roman Empire in 117 CE

This map of the Roman Empire in 117 CE, in addition to showing how the Roman Empire stretched from Britannia in the north, the Iberian Peninsula in the east, northern Africa in the south, to Mesopotamia in its east, also clearly illustrates the strategic importance of maintaining the province of Judea as a land bridge to its African possessions, most significantly Egypt. ▼

Page 137

Silver tetradrachma Revolt coin

This illustration of a silver tetradrachma or selah coin was minted between 134 and 135 CE. On the obverse side the façade of the Jerusalem Temple is depicted. There is also the Hebrew inscription "Shimon," which refers to Shimon bar Kosiba (also known as Bar Kokhba), who was the Jewish rebel leader. The reverse side of the coin has an image of the four species, including the lulav and etrog, together with the Hebrew inscription, "For the freedom of Jerusalem." This refers to the rebels' short-lived freedom from Roman rule. ▼

Page 138

Doar Ivri postage stamp

Once again, the symbolism of the new Jewish state using a symbol of the last independent Jewish state on its first issued postage stamps is significant. ▼

Page 139

Roman amphitheater at Beit Guvrin

This amphitheater was built in the second century CE and is one of four known from the time that were located in the problematic and rebellious province of Judea. The others were in Shekhem, Caesarea, and Beit She'an. The gladiator contests that were featured here were a major source of income for the Roman troops stationed here, and they most likely used captured Jews as gladiators. ▼

Page 141

Gold Aureus coin of Hadrian

This coin depicts the emperor at the height of his powers as he would have appeared at the time of the suppression of the Bar Kokhba Revolt. ▼

Page 142 ▶

Limestone decorative fragment, Sythopolis/Beit She'an, c. first century CE

This is an illustration of a decorative fragment from a Roman period monumental building that was situated in the center of the city of Beit She'an. During the Hellenistic period, Beit She'an was renamed Scythopolis (city of the Scythians). During this period, the city grew and extended southeast to Tel Itztaba. The city reached its maximum size and prosperity during the Roman-Byzantine period, when a new civic center was built in the valley southwest of the tel, surrounded by residential quarters.

Page 143

Leather sandal from the Bar Kokhba period

Leather sandal from the second century CE, found in the Nahal Hever cave. Like all other organic objects found in the cave, it was preserved due to the dry desert air. ▼

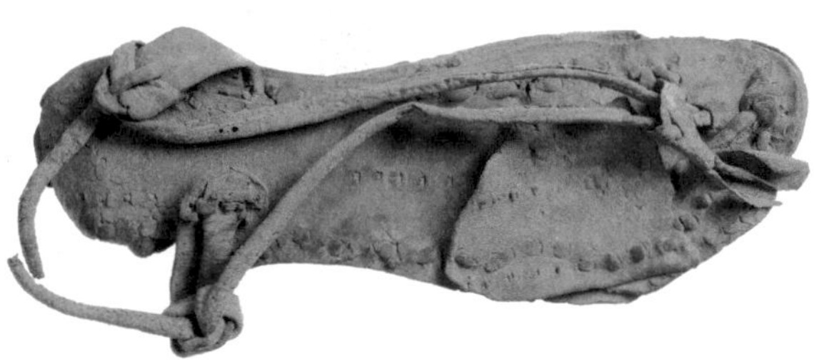

Page 145

Cave of Letters women's effects

These were taken while fleeing the Roman army and remained there for almost two millennia until they were uncovered by Israeli archaeologists in the 1960s. This woman took her mirror, jewelry box, eating utensils, house keys, and baskets. What would you take if you were fleeing in times of war? ▶

Bar Kokhba period legal deed

As a result of Babata taking her cache of legal documents with her when she fled to her cave refuge in the second century CE, our knowledge of this era has become so much richer. This is because the dry desert air, where the cave was located, helped in the preservation of these documents. ▼

Page 146

House key from Nahal Hever Bar Kokhba cave

This key was taken in the forlorn hope that its owner would one day be able to return and reclaim their property. Alas, this was not to be the case. ▼

Glass plates and wrapping from Cave of Letters

These remarkably preserved plates were wrapped with palm fronds and therefore not exposed to the air and have no traces of patina. Indeed, they look like they were just created. ▼

Child's linen shirt from Nahal Hever Bar Kokhba cave

This is the only example of a linen shirt from the Roman Empire that has been preserved. ▼

↗ Silver tetradrachma coin with Temple facade – inscription, "Shimon"

↗ Bronze Revolt coin with a date palm tree echoing a menora and symbolizing Judea and immortality – inscription, "Shimon"

Page 148

Pre-WWII Berlin Bar Kokhba sports club

This picture from the Yad Vashem archives depicting young Jewish athletes before the Holocaust reminds us of how the Bar Kokhba story served as an inspiration to the Zionist movements of the twentieth century. ▶

Page 149

Crawling in a Bar Kokhba period tunnel

It is still possible to crawl in some Bar Kokhba era "fighting fortresses" and to imagine what it must have been like at the time. Avoiding Roman forces above the ground, living like moles, and emerging from disguised entrances at night to ambush the enemy and then withdraw back underground. To enter these caves is experiential education at its best. ▶

Page 153

Cave of Horrors Dead Sea Scroll rescue dig

The last photograph in the book illustrates how treasures are still being uncovered in the Judean Desert, and how archaeology continues to enhance our knowledge of days of yore. This, of course, is not "his" story or "her" story, but rather, "our" Jewish story throughout the generations. ▼

Film Clip Links to Enhance the Chapter

The Oldest Pair of Tefillin in the World (6:28 min.)
In the early 1960s famed Israeli archaeologist, Yigal Yadin and his team, discovered many artifacts in the caves of the Judean Desert where they had been taken by Bar Kokhba fighters almost two millennia earlier. One of the artifacts found was a pair of tefillin - the oldest tefillin in the world. This is the story.
https://www.youtube.com/watch?v=bENxfDZ-rYVw&t=222s

Endnotes

1. Mark Twain, "Concerning the Jews," Harper's Magazine, volume 99, June–November 1899, p.535.
2. Jonathan Sacks, *Covenant & Conversation: A Weekly Reading of the Jewish Bible*, volume 1, (Jerusalem: Maggid, 2009), p. 119.
3. Grant Wiggins and Jay Mc Tighe, *Understanding by Design* (Alexandria, Virginia: Association for Supervision & Curriculum Development, 2005), p.14.
4. Gil Troy, *Why I Am a Zionist: Israel Jewish Identity and the Challenges of Today* (Montreal: BJEC, 2006).
5. Joseph Telushkin, *Jewish Literacy: The Most Important Things to Know About the Jewish Religion, Its People, and Its History*, (New York: William Morrow and Company, Inc, 2008), p.260.
6. Natan Sharansky, Interview with the *Jerusalem Post*, July 2010.
7. Mark Twain, "Concerning the Jews," Harper's Magazine, volume 99, June–November 1899, p.535.
8. Jonathan Netanyahu, *The Letters of Jonathan Netanyahu* (Jerusalem: Gefen, 2013), p.261.
9. Oral testimony by Shlomo Hillel from the film "In Search of Peace, Part One: 1948–1967," Moriah Films (2001).
10. Tuvia Book, "An IDF Heavy Metal Menorah," Times of Israel, December 2014.
11. Flavius Josephus, *Antiquities of the Jews* 15:53–56.

Image Credits

All images are copyright © Koren Publishers Jerusalem Ltd., except:

Introduction

Page xiii, Mark Twain, © A.F. Bradley, New York; page xiv, Yonatan Netanyahu, © Government Press Office; page xv, illustration of Entebbe rescue, © Tuvia Book; page xvii, "Cave of Horrors" Dead Sea Scroll rescue dig, © Israel Antiquities Authority / Eitan Klein.

Chapter 1

Title page, frieze from Persepolis,© Shutterstock / Borna_Mirahmadian; page 1, Persian minted coin, Photo © The Israel Museum, Jerusalem; page 3, Iraqi Jews arriving in Israel, © Government Press Office / Teddy Brauner; page 5, Tel Lakhish, © Tuvia Book; page 4, left image, illustration of Persian stone lotus flower, © Ayelet Book; page 4, right image, plaque with horned lion-griffins, © Metropolitan Museum of Art / Metalright Metalwork-Ornaments; page 4, map of Persian Empire, © Shutterstock / Keith Tarrier; page 5, top image, Cyrus Cylinder, © www.BibleLandPictures.com / Alamy Stock Photo; page 5, bottom image, Tomb of Cyrus, © Shutterstock / AlexelA; page 5, contemporary one shekel coin, © Shutterstock / Mordechai Meiri; page 6, Battle of Issus, © Berthold Werner; page 7, harp player, © Tuvia Book.

Chapter 2

Page 8, Menora decoration, © Government Press Office / Moshe Milner; page 9, Tetradrachma coin of Alexander the Great, © Plank; page 11, Menora decoration, © Government Press Office / Moshe Milner; page 11, Tetradrachma coin of Alexander the Great, © Plank; page 11, map of the Empire of Alexander the Great, © Shutterstock / Keith Tarrier; page 12, terracotta amphora, © Metropolitan Museum of Art / Rogers Fund, 1914; page 12, marble head, © Metropolitan Museum of Art / Fletcher Fund, 1924; page 12, Seleucid coin of Antiochus IV, Photo © The Israel Museum, Jerusalem; page 13, Judah the Maccabee, © Shutterstock / Nicku; page 13, Greek soldier, © Shutterstock / tsuneomp; page 13, Greek helmet, © Metropolitan / Rogers Fund, 1921; page 14, Menora graffiti, © Government Press Office / Cohen Fritz; page 14, Menora on Arch of Titus, © Tuvia Book; page 15, symbol of State of Israel, © Government Press Office / Amos Ben Gershom; page 15, IDF soldiers, the "Modern Maccabees", © Tuvia Book; page 15, olive oil press, © Tuvia Book; page 16, Hanukkiah, © Tuvia Book.

Chapter 3

Page 17, Hellenistic Sarcophagus, Ashkelon, © Tuvia Book; page 18, Ein Gedi Synagogue, mosaic floor, © Tuvia Book; page 19, bronze coin, © Israel Antiquities Authority / Clara Amit; page 22, Hyrcania Hasmonean fortress, © Tuvia Book; page 22, bronze coin of John Hycranus, © Israel Antiquities Authority / Clara Amit; page 22, bronze coin of Judah Aristobulus, © Israel Antiquities Authority / Clara Amit; page 23, Alexandrium (Sartaba) Hasmonean fortress, © Tuvia Book; page 23, bronze coin of Alexander Janneus, © Tuvia Book; page 23, bronze coin of Alexander Janneus, © Israel Antiquities Authority / Clara Amit; page 23, phylacteries from Qumran, © Israel Antiquities Authority / Clara Amit; page 24, Essene Mikve, Qumran © Tuvia Book; page 24, Qumran caves, © Tuvia Book; page 25, Isaiah Scroll, Shrine of the Book Photo © Israel Museum Jerusalem, by David Harris; page 25, Illustration of Queen Salome Alexandra, © Tuvia Book; page 26, left image, bust of Gnaeus Pompeius Magnus, © Carole Raddato from FRANKFURT, Germany; page 26, right image, bust of Gaius Julius Caesar, © FDRMRZUSA; page 27, Ein Gedi Synagogue mosaic floor, © Tuvia Book; page 27, Hasmonean period oil lamp, © Tuvia Book; page 28, Hellenistic columbarium from Beit Guvrin, © Tuvia Book.

Chapter 4

Page 29, Tzippori "Mona Lisa" Roman mosaic, © Tuvia Book; page 30, Beit She'an, © Tuvia Book; page 31, bronze Pontius Pilate coin, © Tuvia Book; page 33, Beit She'an, © Tuvia Book; page 33, Augustus Caesar sardonyx cameo, © Metropolitan Museum of Art / Purchase, Joseph Pulitzer Bequest, 1942; page 34, bronze Mattathias Antigonus coin, © www.BibleLand- Pictures. com / Alamy Stock Photo; page 34, marble bust of Augustus Caesar, © Metropolitan Museum of Art/ Rogers Fund, 1908; page 34, illustration of High Priest Aristoblus © Ayelet Book; page 35, decorated capital, © Tuvia Book; page 35, sarcophagus, Staff Archaeological Officer in the Civil Administration of Judea and Samaria, Photo © Israel Museum, Jerusalem by Meidad Suchowolski; page 35, Holyland Model at Israel Museum, © Tuvia Book; page 36, Royal Stoa ceiling fragment, © Tuvia Book; page 36, Second Temple, Holyland Model, Israel Museum, © Tuvia Book; page 36, top image, street from the Second Temple, © Tuvia Book; page 37, archaeological excavations, © Tuvia Book; page 37, southern steps, © Tuvia Book; page 37, bottom image, "Beit Hatikyah" inscription, Collection of the Israel Antiquities Authority, Photo © The Israel Museum, Jerusalem by David Harris; page 38, "Ennion" glass jug, © Metropolitan Museum of Art / Gift of J. Pierpont Morgan, 1917; page 38, elegant tableware, Collection of the Israel Antiquities Authority, Photo © The Israel Museum, Jerusalem; page 38, Pontius Pilate inscription, Collection of the Israel Antiquities Authority, Photo © The Israel Museum, Jerusalem by Avraham Hay; page 38, Pontius Pilate bronze prutah, © Tuvia Book; page 39, Herod Agrippa I bronze prutah, © CNG; page 39, illustration of ancient capital, Jericho, © Tuvia Book; page 39, Caesarea National Park from the air, Asaf T.; page 40, Second Temple, © HaRav Menachem Makover, courtesy of Harenu Bevinyans; page 41 Herodion from the air, © Asaf T.

Chapter 5

Page 42, Ancient Gamla Synagogue, © Government Press Office / Moshe Milner; page 43, silver tetra-drachma Revolt coin, © Israel Antiquities Authority / Clara Amit; page 45, Ancient Gamla Synagogue, © Government Press Office / Moshe Milner page 46, Vespasian coin, © CNG; page 46, LEG X FR tile, Collection of the Israel Antiquities Authority, Photo © The Israel Museum, Jerusalem; page 46, Roman legionary, © Shutterstock / Algol; page 47, Gamla with defense wall, © EdoM; page 47, silver tetra-drachma Revolt coin, © Israel Antiquities Authority / Clara Amit; page 47, painting by David Roberts, © Misa123a; page 48, Second Temple period mosaic floor, © Dror Avi; page 48, The Three Paratroopers, illustration © Tuvia Book; page 48, northern "Hanging Palace," Masada © Tuvia Book; page 49, fresco and columns at Lower Northern Hanging Palace, Masada © Tuvia Book; page 49, mosaic floor, Western Palace, Masada, © Tuvia Book; page 49, Yigal Yadin at reburial of Masada defenders' remains at Masada, © Government Press Office / Milner Moshe; page 50, braided hair from Masada, Collection of the Israel Antiquities Authority, Photo © The Israel Museum, Jerusalem, by Vladimir Naikhin; page 50, Yigal Yadin, © Government Press Office / Pridan Moshe; page 50, youth group ascending Roman ramp at Masada, © Tuvia Book; page 50, Judea Capta coin, Photo © The Israel Museum, Jerusalem; page 51, Israel Liberata coin, © Tuvia Book; page 51, Gamla, © Tuvia Book; page 51, Gamla defense wall, © Tuvia Book; page 52, Masada from the south, © Tuvia Book; page 52, IDF soldiers being guided by Tuvia Book, © Shmuel Shantall; page 53, Masada from the air, © Government Press Office / Moshe Milner; page 53, Capital from Kfar Nahum Synagogue, © Tuvia Book.

Chapter 6

Page 54, Mount Meron synagogue, © Tuvia Book; page 55, glass fragment, © Metropolitan Museum of Art / Rogers Fund, 1918; page 57, Mount Meron synagogue, © Tuvia Book page 57, bronze shovel, © Metropolitan Museum of Art / Purchase, 1900; page 58, Shir Hama'alot, Illustration © Tuvia Book; page 58, Ein Gedi synagogue mosaic floor, © Tuvia Book; page 59, Tel Yavneh, © Government Press Office / Sa'ar Ya'acov; page 59, Jewish glass bowl fragment, © Metropolitan Museum of Art / Rogers Fund, 1918; page 59, Hammat Tiberias Synagogue mosaic, © Tuvia Book; page 60, Kfar Nahum Synagogue, Star of David, © Tuvia Book; page 60, Kfar Baram synagogue facade, Illustration © Tuvia Book; page 61, Kfar Nahum Synagogue, Torah ark, © Tuvia Book.

Chapter 7

Page 62, reburial of remains of Bar Kokhba's warriors, © Government Press Office / Beno Rutenberg; page 63, Silver Tetradrachma Bar Kokhba Revolt coin, © CNG;

page 65, weight from Bar Kokhba, Collection of the Israel Antiquities Authority, Photo © The Israel Museum, Jerusalem; page 65, reburial of remains of Bar Kokhba's warriors, © Government Press Office / Beno Rutenberg; page 65, map of the Roman Empire in 117 CE, © Shutterstock / Peter Hermes Furian; page 66, silver Bar Kokhba tetradrachma Revolt coin, Illustration © Tuvia Book; page 66, Doar Ivri postage stamp, © Tuvia Book; page 66, Roman amphitheater, Beit Guvrin © Tuvia Book; page 66, gold aureus coin of Hadrian, © Metropolitan Museum of Art / Gift of Joseph H. Durkee, 1899; page 67, limestone fragment, Beit Shean, Illustration ©Tuvia Book ; page 67, leather sandal from the Bar Kokhba period, © Israel Antiquities Authority / Clara Amit; page 67, Cave of Letters women's effects, Collection of the Israel Antiquities Authority, Photo © Israel Museum, Jerusalem, by Moshe Caine; page 67, Bar Kokhba legal deed, © robertharding / Alamy Stock Photo; page 68, house key,© Israel Antiquities Authority / Clara Amit; page 68, glass plates and wrapping from the Cave of Letters, Collection of the Israel Antiquities Authority, Photo © The Israel Museum, Jerusalem by David Harris; page 68, linen shirt, © Israel Antiquities Authority / Miki Koren; page 68, silver Bar Kokhba Revolt Temple coin, © CNG; page 68, bronze Bar Kokhba Revolt palm tree coin, © Israel Antiquities Authority / Clara Amit; page 69, pre-WWII Berlin Bar Kokhba sports club, © Yad Vashem, Photo Archive, Jerusalem; page 69, Tuvia Book crawling in Bar Kokhba tunnel, © Marli Kohl.

About the Author

Dr. Tuvia Book was born in London and raised in both the UK and South Africa. After making aliyah at the age of seventeen, and studying in yeshiva, he volunteered for the IDF where he served in an elite combat unit. Upon his discharge, he completed his BA at Bar-Ilan University, as well as certification in graphic design. He then served as the information officer at the Israeli Consulate of Philadelphia, while earning a graduate degree in Jewish Studies. Upon his return to Israel, Dr. Book graduated from a course of study with the Israeli Ministry of Tourism and is a licensed tour guide. He has also obtained a doctorate in education. In addition, his artwork has been commissioned on every continent (except Antarctica).

Dr. Book has been working in the field of Jewish education, both formal and informal, for many years. He has guided and taught Jewish students and educators from around the world for some of Israel's premier educational institutions and programs. He has lectured in Israel, North America, Australia, New Zealand, Europe, and South Africa.

Dr. Book served as a *shaliaḥ* (emissary) for the Jewish Agency for Israel as the director of Israel and Zionist Education at the Board of Jewish Education of Greater New York (JEP). He was a lecturer and educational guide at the Alexander Muss Institute for Israel Education (AMIIE) in Israel for a decade. He has lectured at both Bar-Ilan University and Hebrew University.

Dr. Book is the author (and illustrator) of the internationally acclaimed Israel education curriculum, *For the Sake of Zion: A Curriculum of Israel Studies and Moral Dilemmas of the Modern Israeli Soldier.* His current book, a history of the Jewish people during the Second Temple period, will be part of a series on Jewish history to be published by Koren.